JavaScript Step by Step, Third Edition

Steve Suehring

Published with the authorization of Microsoft Corporation by:
O'Reilly Media, Inc.
1005 Gravenstein Highway North
Sebastopol, California 95472

ISBN: 978-0-7356-6593-4

3 4 5 6 7 8 9 10 11 LSI 8 7 6 5 4 3

Printed and bound in the United States of America.

Microsoft Press books are available through booksellers and distributors worldwide. If you need support related to this book, email Microsoft Press Book Support at mspinput@microsoft.com. Please tell us what you think of this book at *http://www.microsoft.com/learning/booksurvey*.

Acquisitions and Developmental Editor: Russell Jones

Production Editor: Melanie Yarbrough

Editorial Production: nSight, Inc.

Technical Reviewer: John Grieb

Copyeditor: nSight, Inc.

Indexer: nSight, Inc.

Cover Design: Twist Creative • Seattle

Cover Composition: Karen Montgomery

Illustrator: nSight, Inc.

I would like to dedicate this book to Mom and Dad.

—Steve Suehring

Contents at a Glance

Contents

PART I   JAVAWHAT? THE WHERE, WHY,
         AND HOW OF JAVASCRIPT

Chapter 1   **JavaScript is more than you might think**   **3**

What do you think of this book? We want to hear from you!

Microsoft is interested in hearing your feedback so we can continually improve our books and learning resources for you. To participate in a brief online survey, please visit:

microsoft.com/learning/booksurvey

Chapter 8   Objects in JavaScript   147

Chapter 9   The Browser Object Model   165

Chapter 10 An introduction to JavaScript libraries
and frameworks 183

Chapter 11 An introduction to jQuery 187

PART II INTEGRATING JAVASCRIPT INTO DESIGN

Chapter 12 The Document Object Model   207

Chapter 13 JavaScript events and the browser   229

Chapter 16   JavaScript and CSS   291

Chapter 17   jQuery effects and plug-ins   303

Chapter 21 Developing for Windows 8   367

Chapter 22 Using Visual Studio for Windows 8 development   377

Introduction

Much has changed since the first edition of JavaScript Step by Step was written in 2007: the underlying JavaScript specification received a major update; Microsoft released new versions of Internet Explorer and Windows; the Chrome browser came of age, as did mobile web usage; and JavaScript development frameworks have matured and are now ubiquitous.

This third edition of *JavaScript Step by Step* builds on the foundation laid down by the first two editions. While the underlying architecture of the JavaScript language has remained largely the same, use of JavaScript has become pervasive, with huge year-over-year increases and an expanded importance to developers. With that in mind, the layout and coverage of the book have also remained largely the same, with some notable exceptions. The book now places extra emphasis on JavaScript event handling and the use of jQuery to speed development. The book also includes a final section on Windows 8 development using JavaScript. However, this book is most definitely not Microsoft-centric.

One of the first things I asked prior to accepting the offer to write *JavaScript Step by Step* was whether it had to focus on Microsoft products. The answer was a firm "no." The book was and is intended to be a general tutorial on using JavaScript, including best practices for using JavaScript on the web.

The biggest influence Microsoft has had on the book was to make sure that I used the term "Internet Explorer" when referring to IE. You'll see this absence of bias reflected throughout the book, which contains exercises showing plain text editors rather than heavy development tools. While it's true that most of the screen shots show Internet Explorer (I almost said IE), the code was tested across several browsers (Chrome and Firefox to name two), but it proved difficult to obtain the proper legal clearances required to show many screen shots of other browsers. In fact, most of the book's code was written in Vim, accessed on a Debian Linux system running Apache, and run from Firefox first before being cross-browser tested and then set up for screen shots.

Throughout the book, you'll find highlights and additions for the new features in the latest version of JavaScript. Also, the examples used in the book received greater scrutiny in multiple browsers to reflect the reality of today's web landscape. Reader feedback from the earlier editions is reflected in the content of this edition and was the impetus for adding jQuery and emphasizing event handling.

Housekeeping aside, this book provides an introductory look at JavaScript, including some of its core functions as well as features and paradigms such as Asynchronous JavaScript and XML (AJAX).

The first part of the book examines JavaScript and helps you get started developing JavaScript applications. You don't need any specific tools for JavaScript development, so you'll see how to create JavaScript files in Microsoft Visual Studio, in Eclipse, and in Notepad (or any other text editor). The book examines JavaScript functions and the use of JavaScript in the browser, along with the aforementioned jQuery. Finally, the book provides coverage of Windows 8 app development using HTML, CSS, and JavaScript.

Who should read this book

This book is for beginning JavaScript programmers or people who are interested in learning the basics of modern JavaScript programming: the language syntax, how it works in browsers, what the common cross-browser problems are, and how to take advantage of AJAX and third-party libraries such as jQuery to add interactivity to your webpages.

Assumptions

This book expects that you have at least a minimal understanding of concepts surrounding web development. You should be at least somewhat familiar with HTML. CSS is also helpful to know, but neither HTML nor CSS are required prerequisite knowledge for completing this book. The examples shown provide all the HTML and CSS whenever necessary.

Who should not read this book

This book isn't meant for experienced JavaScript programmers.

Organization of this book

This book is divided into four sections, each of which focuses on a different aspect of JavaScript programming. Part I, "Javawhat? The where, why, and how of JavaScript," provides the foundation upon which JavaScript is programmed. Included in this part are chapters to get you up to speed creating JavaScript programs as well as chapters discussing the syntax of JavaScript. Part II, "Integrating JavaScript into design," looks closely at the interactions between JavaScript and its primary role of web programming. Part III, "AJAX and server-side integration," shows the use of JavaScript to retrieve and parse information from web services. Finally, Part IV, "JavaScript and Windows 8," shows how to create a Windows 8 app with HTML, CSS, and JavaScript.

Conventions and features in this book

This book takes you step by step through the process of learning the JavaScript programming language. Starting at the beginning of the book and following each of the examples and exercises will provide the maximum benefit to help you gain knowledge about the JavaScript programming language.

If you already have some familiarity with JavaScript, you might be tempted to skip the first chapter of this book. However, Chapter 1, "JavaScript is more than you might think," details some of the background history of JavaScript as well as some of the underlying premise for this book, both of which might be helpful in framing the discussion for the remainder of the book. Chapter 2, "Developing in JavaScript," shows you how to get started with programming in JavaScript. If you're already familiar with web development, you might already have a web development program, and therefore you might be tempted to skip Chapter 2 as well. Nevertheless, you should become familiar with the pattern used in Chapter 2 to create JavaScript programs.

The book contains a Table of Contents that will help you to locate a specific section quickly. Each chapter contains a detailed list of the material that it covers.

The coverage of Windows 8 app development is limited to the final section of the book, so if you're not interested in making a Windows 8 app (it's really easy) then you can safely skip that last section without missing any of the valuable information necessary to program in JavaScript for the web. If you're looking for a more comprehensive book on Windows 8 development with HTML5 and JavaScript, a beginner's book, *Start Here! Build Windows 8 Apps with HTML5 and JavaScript* will be available from Microsoft Press in May (pre-order here: *http://oreil.ly/build-w8-apps-HTML5-JS*).

In addition, you can download the source code for many of the examples shown throughout the book.

System Requirements

You will need the following hardware and software to complete the practice exercises in this book:

- An operating system capable of running a web server. For the section on Windows 8 development, you'll need Windows 8, but none of the other examples require Windows.

- A text editor such as Notepad, Vim, or an Integrated Development Environment (IDE) such as Visual Studio or Eclipse. For Windows 8 development, you'll specifically need Visual Studio 2012 for Windows.

- An Internet connection so you can download software and chapter examples.

Code Samples

Most of the chapters in this book include exercises that let you interactively try out new material learned in the main text. The code for those exercises and many other examples can be downloaded from:

http://aka.ms/JavaScriptSbS/files

Follow the instructions to download the 9780735665934_files file.

Installing the Code Samples

Follow these steps to install the code samples on your computer so that you can use them with the exercises in this book.

1. Unzip the 9780735665934_files.zip file that you downloaded from the book's website to a location that is accessible by your web server.

2. If prompted, review the displayed end user license agreement. If you accept the terms, select the accept option, and then click Next.

 Note If the license agreement doesn't appear, you can access it from the same webpage from which you downloaded the 9780735665934_files.zip file.

Using the Code Samples

Unzipping the sample code creates several subfolders, one for each chapter of the book. These subfolders may contain additional subfolders, based on the layout necessary for a given chapter.

Acknowledgments

There are so many people that help in the book writing process. I'd like to first thank Russell Jones at Microsoft Press. He has provided excellent guidance and is always a pleasure to work with. Thanks to John Grieb for providing excellent technical feedback for this edition. I should also thank Jim Oliva and John Eckendorf, if for no other reason than I do so in every other book I write.

I'd also like to thank Terry Rapp for being understanding about my scheduling conflicts. Thanks to Chris Tuescher for years of friendship and support. Many people have helped me through the years, and it all led to me sitting here, writing this sentence. Duff Damos, Kent Laabs, Pat Dunn, and the entire Nightmare Productions Ltd and Capitol Entertainment crews are just as responsible for getting me here as anyone. Thanks to Dave, Sandy, Joel, and the gang at Ski's. Thanks also to Mrs. Mehlberg and Mrs. Jurgella for extra attention and just being great.

Finally, thank you, dear reader. This book has been highly successful (at least by my standards) and your feedback and contact over the years has been helpful. Please follow me on Twitter @stevesuehring or drop me a line by going to my website at *http://www.braingia.org*.

Errata & Book Support

We've made every effort to ensure the accuracy of this book and its companion content. Any errors that have been reported since this book was published are listed on our Microsoft Press site at Oreilly.com:

> *http://aka.ms/JavaScriptSbS/errata*

If you find an error that is not already listed, you can report it to us through the same page.

If you need additional support, email Microsoft Press Book Support at mspinput@microsoft.com.

Please note that product support for Microsoft software is not offered through the addresses above.

We Want to Hear from You

At Microsoft Press, your satisfaction is our top priority, and your feedback our most valuable asset. Please tell us what you think of this book at:

http://www.microsoft.com/learning/booksurvey

The survey is short, and we read every one of your comments and ideas. Thanks in advance for your input!

Stay in Touch

Let's keep the conversation going! We're on Twitter: *http://twitter.com/MicrosoftPress*

Javawhat? The where, why, and how of JavaScript

The first section of the book, by far the largest, includes just about everything you need to know about basic JavaScript syntax. You'll start things off by learning some of the background and history of JavaScript. It may sound boring, but Chapter 1 will help to frame the discussion and tone of the remainder of the book.

Chapter 2 gets you started with JavaScript development by showing how to create a page with JavaScript using several different tools such as Visual Studio, Eclipse, and a plain old text editor.

The discussion of JavaScript syntax begins in Chapter 3 and continues for the remainder of the first part of the book. You'll learn about conditionals, operators, functions, loops, and even get an introduction to jQuery.

CHAPTER 1

JavaScript is more than you might think

After completing this chapter, you will be able to

- Understand the history of JavaScript.

- Recognize the parts of a JavaScript program.

- Use the *javascript* pseudo-protocol.

- Understand where JavaScript fits within a webpage.

- Understand what JavaScript can and cannot do.

- Understand how JavaScript is used in Windows 8.

A brief history of JavaScript

JavaScript isn't Java. There! With that clarification out of the way, you can move on to bigger, more important learning, like how to make cool sliders. In all seriousness, JavaScript is one implementation of a specification known as ECMAScript. You'll learn more about ECMAScript later in this chapter.

Where did JavaScript come from? You might not know the rich and storied history of JavaScript— and you might not really care much about it, either. If that's the case, you might be tempted to jump ahead to the next chapter and begin coding JavaScript. Doing so, of course, would be a mistake— you'd miss all the wonderful information that follows in this chapter. And understanding a bit about the history of JavaScript is important to understanding how the language is implemented in various environments today.

JavaScript was originally developed by Brendan Eich at Netscape sometime in 1995–1996. Back then, the language was called LiveScript. That was a great name for a new language—and the story could have ended there. However, in an unfortunate decision, the folks in marketing had their way, and the language was renamed to JavaScript. Confusion soon ensued. You see, Java was the exciting new language at the time, and someone decided to try to capitalize on Java's popularity by using its name. As a result, JavaScript found itself associated with the Java language. This was a disadvantage for JavaScript, because Java, although popular in the sense that it was frequently used, was also unpopular because it had earned a fairly bad reputation—developers used Java in websites to present data or to add useless enhancements (such as annoying scrolling text). The user experience suffered because Java required a plug-in to load into the web browser, slowing down the browsing process and causing grief for visitors and accessibility problems. Only in recent years has JavaScript begun to separate from this negative Java association, but, almost weekly, I still hear people confuse Java and JavaScript. You'll hopefully no longer do that!

JavaScript is not a compiled language, which makes it look and feel like a language that lacks power. But programmers new to JavaScript soon came to realize its strengths and usefulness for both simulating and creating interactivity on the World Wide Web. Up until that realization, programmers developed many websites using only simple Hypertext Markup Language (HTML) and graphics that often lacked both visual appeal and the ability to interact with the site's content. With Microsoft Windows 8, JavaScript now has an avenue for creating full-fledged applications that don't rely on the web browser.

Early JavaScript concentrated on client-side form validation and working with images on webpages to provide rudimentary, although helpful, interactivity and feedback to the visitor. When a visitor to a website filled in a form, JavaScript instantly validated the contents of the web form rather than making a round-trip to the server. Especially in the days before broadband was pervasive, preventing the round-trip to the server was a great way to help applications seem a little quicker and more responsive—and it still is.

Enter Internet Explorer 3.0

With the release of Microsoft Internet Explorer 3.0 in 1996, Microsoft included support for core JavaScript, known in Internet Explorer as JScript, and support for another scripting language called Microsoft Visual Basic, Scripting Edition, or VBScript. Although JavaScript and JScript were similar, their implementations weren't exactly the same. Therefore, methods were developed to detect which browser the website visitor was using and respond with appropriate scripting. This process is known as *browser detection*, and is discussed in Chapter 11, "An introduction to jQuery." Although it is considered undesirable for most applications, you'll still see browser detection used, especially with the advent of mobile devices that have their own special look and feel.

And then came ECMAScript

In mid-1997, Microsoft and Netscape worked with the European Computer Manufacturers Association (ECMA) to release the first version of a language specification known as ECMAScript, more formally known as ECMA-262. Since that time, all browsers from Microsoft have implemented versions of the ECMAScript standard. Other popular browsers, such as Firefox, Safari, and Opera, have also implemented the ECMAScript standard.

ECMA-262 edition 3 was released in 1999. The good news is that browsers such as Microsoft Internet Explorer 5.5 and Netscape 6 supported the edition 3 standard, and every major browser since then has supported the version of JavaScript formalized in the ECMA-262 edition 3 standard. The bad news is that each browser applies this standard in a slightly different way, so incompatibilities still plague developers who use JavaScript.

The latest version of ECMAScript, as formalized in the standard known as ECMA-262, was released in late 2009 and is known as ECMA-262 edition 5. Version 4 of the specification was skipped for a variety of reasons and to avoid confusion among competing proposals for the standard. ECMA-262 edition 5.1 is becoming more widely supported as of this writing and will likely (I'm hopeful) be in versions of popular browsers such as Internet Explorer, Chrome, Firefox, Opera, and Safari by the time you read this book.

It's important to note that as a developer who is incorporating JavaScript into web applications, you need to account for the differences among the versions of ECMA-262, and among the many implementations of JavaScript. Accounting for these differences might mean implementing a script in slightly different ways, and testing, testing, and testing again in various browsers and on various platforms. On today's Internet, users have little tolerance for poorly designed applications that work in only one browser.

Accounting for those differences has become much easier in the last few years, and there are two primary reasons. First, web browsers have consolidated around the specifications for HTML, CSS, and JavaScript, and the vendors have worked to bring their interpretation of the specifications closer to one another. The second reason that accounting for differences has become easier is that JavaScript libraries have become more popular. Throughout the book, I'll show the use of the jQuery library to make JavaScript easier.

Important It is imperative that you test your websites in multiple browsers—including web applications that you don't think will be used in a browser other than Internet Explorer. Even if you're sure that your application will be used only in Internet Explorer or if that's all you officially support, you still should test in other browsers. This is important both for security and because it shows that you're a thorough developer who understands today's Internet technologies.

So many standards...

If you think the standards of JavaScript programming are loosely defined, you're right. Each browser supports JavaScript slightly differently, making your job—and my job—that much more difficult. Trying to write about all these nuances is more challenging than writing about a language that is implemented by a single, specific entity, like a certain version of Microsoft Visual Basic or Perl. Your job (and mine) is to keep track of these differences and account for them as necessary, and to try to find common ground among them as much as possible.

The DOM

Another evolving standard relevant to the JavaScript programmer is the *Document Object Model (DOM)* standard developed by the World Wide Web Consortium (W3C). The W3C defines the DOM as "a platform- and language-neutral interface that allows programs and scripts to dynamically access and update the content, structure, and style of documents." What this means for you is that you can work with a specification to which web browsers adhere to develop a webpage in a dynamic manner. The DOM creates a tree structure of objects for HTML and Extensible Markup Language (XML) documents and enables scripting of those objects. JavaScript interacts heavily with the DOM for many important functions.

Like JavaScript, the DOM is interpreted differently by every browser, making life for a JavaScript programmer more interesting. Internet Explorer 4.0 and earlier versions of Netscape included support for an early DOM, known as Level 0. If you use the Level 0 DOM, you can be pretty sure that you'll find support for the DOM in those browsers and in all the browsers that came after.

Microsoft Internet Explorer 5.0 and Internet Explorer 5.5 included some support for the Level 1 DOM, whereas Windows Internet Explorer 6.0 and later versions include some support for the Level 2 DOM. The latest versions of Internet Explorer, Chrome, Firefox, Safari, and Opera support the Level 3 DOM in some form. Safari provides a representation of the WebKit rendering engine. The WebKit rendering engine is also used as the basis for the browser on devices such as the iPhone and iPad and on Android-based devices.

If there's one lesson that you should take away while learning about JavaScript standards and the related DOM standards, it's that you need to pay particular attention to the code that you write (no surprise there) and the syntax used to implement that code. If you don't, JavaScript can fail miserably and prevent your page from rendering in a given browser. Chapter 12, "The Document Object Model," covers the DOM in much greater detail.

> **Tip** The W3C has an application that can test the modules specified by the various DOM levels that your web browser claims to support. This application can be found at *http://www.w3.org/2003/02/06-dom-support.html*.

What's in a JavaScript program?

A JavaScript program consists of *statements* and *expressions* formed from *tokens* of various categories, including keywords, literals, separators, *operators*, and *identifiers* placed together in an order that is meaningful to a JavaScript interpreter, which is contained in most web browsers. That sentence is a mouthful, but these statements are really not all that complicated to anyone who has programmed in just about any other language. An expression might be:

```
var smallNumber = 4;
```

In that expression, a token, or reserved word—*var*—is followed by other tokens, such as an identifier (*smallNumber*), an operator (=), and a literal (*4*). (You learn more about these elements throughout the rest of the book.) The purpose of this expression is to set the variable named *smallNumber* equal to the integer *4*.

Like in any programming language, statements get put together in an order that makes a program perform one or more functions. JavaScript defines functions in its own way, which you read much more about in Chapter 7, "Working with functions." JavaScript defines several built-in functions that you can use in your programs.

Using the *javascript* pseudo-protocol and a function

1. Open a web browser.

2. In the address bar, type the following code and press Enter:

   ```
   javascript:alert("Hello World");
   ```

   After you press Enter, you see a dialog box similar to this one:

Congratulations! You just programmed your first (albeit not very useful) bit of JavaScript code. However, in just this little bit of code, are two important items that you are likely to use in your JavaScript programming endeavors: the *javascript* pseudo-protocol identifier in a browser and, more importantly, the *alert* function. You'll examine these items in more detail in later chapters; for now, it suffices that you learned something that you'll use in the future!

> **Note** Internet Explorer 10 in Windows 8 sometimes doesn't display or use the *javascript* pseudo-protocol correctly. If you find that is the case, try using a different browser, such as Firefox or Chrome.

JavaScript is also *event-driven*, meaning that it can respond to certain events or "things that happen," such as a mouse click or text change within a form field. Connecting JavaScript to an event is central to many common uses of JavaScript. In Chapter 11, you see how to respond to events by using JavaScript.

JavaScript placement on your webpage

If you're new to HTML, all you need to know about it for now is that it delineates elements in a webpage using a pair of matching tags enclosed in brackets. The closing tag begins with a slash character (/). Elements can be nested within one another. JavaScript fits within *<SCRIPT>* tags inside the *<HEAD> </HEAD>* and/or *<BODY> </BODY>* tags of a webpage, as in the following example:

```
<!doctype html>
<html>
```

```
<head>
<title>A Web Page Title</title>
<script type="text/javascript">
// JavaScript Goes Here
</script>
</head>
<body>
<script type="text/javascript">
// JavaScript can go here too
</script>
</body>
</html>
```

JavaScript placed within the *<BODY>* tags executes as it is encountered by the browser, which is helpful when you need to write to the document by using a JavaScript function, as follows (the function calls are shown in boldface type):

```
<!doctype html>
<html>
<head>
<title>A Web Page Title</title>
<script type="text/javascript">
// JavaScript Goes Here
</script>
</head>
<body>
<script type="text/javascript">
document.write("hello");
document.write(" world");
</script>
</body>
</html>
```

Because of the way browsers load JavaScript, the current best practice for placing JavaScript in your HTML is to position the *<SCRIPT>* tags at the end of the *<BODY>* element rather than in the *<HEAD>* element. Doing so helps to ensure that the content of the page is rendered if the browser blocks input while the JavaScript files are being loaded.

When you're using JavaScript on an Extensible Hypertext Markup Language (XHTML) page, the less-than sign (<) and the ampersand character (&) are interpreted as XML, which can cause problems for JavaScript. To get around this, use the following syntax in an XHTML page:

```
<script type="text/javascript">
<![CDATA[
    // JavaScript Goes Here
]]>
</script>
```

Browsers that aren't XHTML-compliant don't interpret the CDATA section correctly. You can work around that problem by placing the CDATA section inside a JavaScript comment—a line or set of lines prefaced by two forward slashes (//), as shown here:

```
<script type="text/javascript">
//<![CDATA[
    // JavaScript Goes Here
//]]>
</script>
```

Yes, the code really is that ugly. However, there's an easy fix for this: use external JavaScript files. In Chapter 2, "Developing in JavaScript," you learn exactly how to accomplish this simple task.

Document types

If you've been programming for the web for any length of time, you're probably familiar with Document Type declarations, or DOCTYPE declarations, as they're sometimes called. One of the most important tasks you can do when designing your webpages is to include an accurate and syntactically correct DOCTYPE declaration section at the top of the page. The DOCTYPE declaration, frequently abbreviated as DTD, lets the browser (or other parsing program) know the rules that will be followed when parsing the elements of the document.

An example of a DOCTYPE declaration for HTML 4.01 looks like this:

```
<!DOCTYPE html PUBLIC "-//W3C//DTD HTML 4.01//EN"
    "http://www.w3.org/TR/html4/strict.dtd">
```

If you're using a Microsoft Visual Studio version earlier than version 2012 to create a web project, each page is automatically given a DOCTYPE declaration for the XHTML 1.0 standard, like this:

```
<!DOCTYPE html PUBLIC "-//W3C//DTD XHTML 1.0 Transitional//EN" "http://www.w3.org/TR
/xhtml1/DTD/xhtml1-transitional.dtd">
```

HTML version 5 uses a much simpler DOCTYPE:

```
<!DOCTYPE html>
```

If you fail to declare a DOCTYPE, the browser interprets the page by using a mode known as *Quirks Mode*. Falling back to Quirks Mode means that the document might end up looking different from your intention, especially when viewed through several browsers.

If you do declare a DOCTYPE, making sure that the resulting HTML, cascading style sheet (also known as CSS), and JavaScript also adhere to web standards is important so that the document can be viewed as intended by the widest possible audience, no matter which interface or browser is used. The W3C makes available an online validator at *http://validator.w3.org/*, which you can use to validate any publicly available webpage.

Tip Use the Markup Validator regularly until you're comfortable with coding to standards, and always check for validity before releasing your web project to the public.

What JavaScript can do

JavaScript is largely a complementary language, meaning that it's uncommon for an entire application to be written solely in JavaScript without the aid of other languages like HTML and without presentation in a web browser. Some Adobe products support JavaScript, and Windows 8 begins to change this, but JavaScript's main use is in a browser.

JavaScript is also the J in the acronym AJAX (Asynchronous JavaScript and XML), the darling of the Web 2.0 phenomenon. However, beyond that, JavaScript is an everyday language providing the interactivity expected, maybe even demanded, by today's web visitors.

JavaScript can perform many tasks on the client side of the application. For example, it can add the needed interactivity to a website by creating drop-down menus, transforming the text on a page, adding dynamic elements to a page, and helping with form entry.

Before learning about what JavaScript can do—the focus of this book—you need to understand what JavaScript can't do, but note that neither discussion is comprehensive.

What JavaScript can't do

Many of the operations JavaScript can't perform are the result of JavaScript's usage being somewhat limited to a web browser environment. This section examines some of the tasks JavaScript can't perform and some that JavaScript shouldn't perform.

JavaScript can't be forced on a client

JavaScript relies on another interface or host program for its functionality. This host program is usually the client's web browser, also known as a *user agent*. Because JavaScript is a client-side language, it can do only what the client allows it to do.

Some people are still using older browsers that don't support JavaScript at all. Others won't be able to take advantage of many of JavaScript's fancy features because of accessibility programs, text readers, and other add-on software that assists the browsing experience. And some people might just choose to disable JavaScript because they can, because of security concerns (whether perceived or real), or because of the poor reputation JavaScript received as a result of certain annoyances like pop-up ads.

Regardless of the reason, you need to perform some extra work to ensure that the website you're designing is available to those individuals who don't have JavaScript. I can hear your protests already: "But this feature is really [insert your own superlative here: cool, sweet, essential, nice, fantastic]." Regardless of how nice your feature might be, the chances are you will benefit from better interoperability and more site visitors. In the "Tips for using JavaScript" section later in this chapter, I offer some pointers that you can follow for using JavaScript appropriately on your website.

It might be helpful to think of this issue another way. When you build a web application that gets served from Microsoft Internet Information Services (IIS) 6.0, you can assume that the application will usually work when served from an IIS 6.0 server anywhere. Likewise, when you build an application for Apache 2, you can be pretty sure that it will work on other Apache 2 installations. However, the same assumption cannot be made for JavaScript. When you write an application that works fine on your desktop, you can't guarantee that it will work on somebody else's. You can't control how your application will work after it gets sent to the client.

JavaScript can't guarantee data security

Because JavaScript is run wholly on the client, the developer must learn to let go. As you might expect, letting go of control over your program has serious implications. After the program is on the client's computer, the client can do many undesirable things to the data before sending it back to the server. As with any other web programming, you should never trust any data coming back from the client. Even if you've used JavaScript functions to validate the contents of forms, you still must validate this input again when it gets to the server. A client with JavaScript disabled might send back garbage data through a web form. If you believe, innocently enough, that your client-side JavaScript function has already checked the data to ensure that it is valid, you might find that invalid data gets back to the server, causing unforeseen and possibly dangerous consequences.

 Important Remember that JavaScript can be disabled on your visitor's computer. You cannot rely on cute tricks to be successful, such as using JavaScript to disable right-clicks or to prevent visitors from viewing the page source, and you shouldn't use them as security measures.

JavaScript can't cross domains

The JavaScript developer also must be aware of the *Same-Origin Policy*, which dictates that scripts running from within one domain neither have access to the resources from another Internet domain, nor can they affect the scripts and data from another domain. For example, JavaScript can be used to open a new browser window, but the contents of that window are somewhat restricted to the calling script. When a page from my website (*braingia.org*) contains JavaScript, that page can't access any JavaScript executed from a different domain, such as *microsoft.com*. This is the essence of the Same-Origin Policy: JavaScript has to be executed in or originate from the same location.

The Same-Origin Policy is frequently a restriction to contend with in the context of frames and AJAX's *XMLHttpRequest* object, where multiple JavaScript requests might be sent to different web servers. With the introduction of Windows Internet Explorer 8, Microsoft introduced support for the *XDomainRequest* object, which allows limited access to data from other domains.

JavaScript doesn't do servers

When developing server-side code such as Visual Basic .NET or PHP (a recursive acronym that stands for *PHP: Hypertext Preprocessor*), you can be fairly sure that the server will implement certain functions, such as talking to a database or giving access to modules necessary for the web application. JavaScript doesn't have access to server-side variables. For example, JavaScript cannot access databases that are located on the server. JavaScript code is limited to what can be done inside the platform on which the script is running, which is typically the browser.

Another shift you need to make in your thinking, if you're familiar with server-side programming, is that with JavaScript, you have to test the code on many different clients to know what a particular client is capable of. When you're programming server-side, if the server doesn't implement a given function, you know it right away because the server-side script fails when you test it. Naughty administrators aside, the back-end server code implementation shouldn't change on a whim, and thus, you more easily know what you can and cannot code. But you can't anticipate JavaScript code that is intended to run on clients, because these clients are completely out of your control.

Note There are server-side implementations of JavaScript, but they are beyond the scope of this book.

Tips for using JavaScript

Several factors go into good web design, and really, who arbitrates what is and is not considered good anyway? One visitor to a site might call the site an ugly hodgepodge of colors and text created as if those elements were put in a sack and shaken until they fell out onto the page; the next visitor might love the design and color scheme.

Because you're reading this book, I assume that you're looking for some help with using JavaScript to enhance your website. I also assume that you want to use this programming language to help people use your site and to make your site look, feel, and work better.

The design of a website is not and will never be an entirely objective process. The goal of one website might be informational, which would dictate one design approach, whereas the goal of another website might be to connect to an application, thus requiring specialized design and functionality. That said, many popular and seemingly well-designed sites have certain aspects in common. I try to break down those aspects here, although I ask you to remember that I didn't create a comprehensive list and that the items reflect only one person's opinions.

A well-designed website does the following:

- **Emphasizes function over form** When a user visits a website, she usually wants to obtain information or perform a task. The more difficult your site is to browse, the more likely the user is to move to another site with better browsing.

Animations and blinking bits come and go, but what remain are sites that have basic information presented in a professional, easily accessible manner. Using the latest cool animation software or web technology makes me think of the days of the HTML *<BLINK>* tag. The *<BLINK>* tag, for those who never saw it in action, caused the text within it to disappear and reappear on the screen. Nearly all web developers seem to hate the *<BLINK>* tag and what it does to a webpage. Those same developers would be wise to keep in mind that today's exciting feature or special effect on a webpage will be tomorrow's *<BLINK>* tag. Successful websites stick to the basics and use these types of bits only when the content requires them.

Use elements like a site map, alt tags, and simple navigation tools, and don't require special software or plug-ins for viewing the site's main content. Too often, I visit a website only to be stopped because I need a plug-in or the latest version of this or that player (which I don't have) to browse it.

Although site maps, alt tags, and simple navigation might seem quaint, they are indispensable items for accessibility. Text readers and other such technologies that enable sites to be read aloud or browsed by individuals with disabilities use these assistive features and frequently have problems with complex JavaScript.

- **Follows standards**   Web standards exist to be followed, so ignore them at your own peril. Using a correct DOCTYPE declaration and well-formed HTML helps ensure that your site will display correctly to your visitors. Validation using the W3C's Markup Validator tool is highly recommended. If your site is broken, fix it!

- **Renders correctly in multiple browsers**   Even when Internet Explorer had 90 percent market share, it was never a good idea for programmers to ignore other browsers. Doing so usually meant that accessibility was also ignored, so people with text readers or other add-ons couldn't use the site. People using operating systems other than Microsoft Windows might also be out of luck visiting those sites.

Although Internet Explorer is still the leader among web visitors, there's a great chance that at least 3 or 4 of every 10 visitors might be using a different browser. Of course, this variance depends largely on the subject matter. The more technical the audience, the more you need to accommodate browsers other than Internet Explorer. Therefore, if your site appeals to a technical audience, you might need your site to work in Firefox, Safari, or even Lynx.

Regardless of the website's subject matter, you never want to turn away visitors because of their browser choice. Imagine the shopkeeper who turned away 3 of every 10 potential customers just because of their shoes. That shop wouldn't be in business too long—or at the very least, it wouldn't be as successful.

If you strive to follow web standards, chances are that you're already doing most of what you need to do to support multiple browsers. Avoiding the use of proprietary plug-ins for your website is another way to ensure that your site renders correctly. You need to look only as far as the iPad to see a device that is popular but whose use is restricted because it doesn't natively support Flash. For this reason, creating sites that follow standards and avoid proprietary plug-ins ensures that your site is viewable by the widest possible audience.

- **Uses appropriate technologies at appropriate times**   Speaking of plug-ins, a well-designed website doesn't overuse or misuse technology. On a video site, playing videos is appropriate. Likewise, on a music site, playing background music is appropriate. On other sites, these features might not be so appropriate. If you feel that your site needs to play background music, go back to the drawing board and examine why you want a website in the first place! I still shudder when I think of an attorney's website that I once visited. The site started playing the firm's jingle in the background, without my intervention. Friends don't let friends use background music on their sites, unless your friend is from the band Rush and you are working on the band's website.

Where JavaScript fits

Today's web is still evolving. One of the more popular movements is known as *unobtrusive scripting*. The unobtrusive scripting paradigm contains two components, progressive enhancement and behavioral separation. *Behavioral separation* calls for structure to be separated from style, and for both of these elements to be separated from behavior. In this model, HTML or XHTML provides the structure, whereas the CSS provides the style and JavaScript provides the behavior. Progressive enhancement means adding more features to the page as the browser's capabilities are tested; enhancing the user experience when possible but not expecting that JavaScript or a certain JavaScript function will always be available. In this way, the JavaScript is unobtrusive; it doesn't get in the way of the user experience. If JavaScript isn't available in the browser, the website still works because the visitor can use the website in some other way.

When applied properly, unobtrusive scripting means that JavaScript is not assumed to be available and that JavaScript will fail in a graceful manner. Graceful degradation helps the page function without JavaScript or uses proper approaches to make JavaScript available when it's required for the site.

I'm a proponent of unobtrusive scripting because it means that standards are followed and the resulting site adheres to the four recommendations shared in the previous section. Unfortunately, this isn't always the case. You could separate the HTML, CSS, and JavaScript and still end up using proprietary tags, but when you program in an unobtrusive manner, you tend to pay closer attention to detail and care much more about the end result being compliant with standards.

Throughout this book, I strive to show you not only the basics of JavaScript but also the best way to use JavaScript effectively and, as much as possible, unobtrusively.

A note on JScript and JavaScript and this book

This book covers JavaScript as defined by the ECMA standard, in versions all the way through the latest edition 5. This is distinct from Microsoft's implementation of JScript, which is not covered in this book. For an additional reference on only JScript, I recommend the following site: JScript (Windows Script Technologies) at *http://msdn.microsoft.com/en-us/library/hbxc2t98.aspx*.

Which browsers should the site support?

Downward compatibility has been an issue for the web developer for a long time. Choosing which browser versions to support becomes a trade-off between using the latest functionality available in the newest browsers and the compatible functionality required for older browsers. There is no hard and fast rule for which browsers you should support on your website, so the answer is: it depends.

Your decision depends on what you'd like to do with your site and whether you value visits by people using older hardware and software more than you value the added functionality available in later browser versions. Some browsers are just too old to support because they can't render CSS correctly, much less JavaScript. A key to supporting multiple browser versions is to test within them.

Internet Explorer used to be the king of web browsers, in usage at least, certainly not as rated by developers. Today, Internet Explorer, in some version, is still ranked among the highest in usage numbers on sites of general interest. However, specialty or technology-related sites have much lower usage of Internet Explorer. On those sites, you'll see much more usage of Firefox, Chrome, Safari, Opera, and other browsers. Even on sites of general interest, browsers like Chrome and Firefox are quite popular, too. All of this means that you need to develop for and test in various browsers before releasing a website for public consumption.

> **Note** While the screen shots in this book show Internet Explorer, the code for this book was written for and tested in Firefox first, along with several other browsers. Screen shots in Internet Explorer are shown strictly for legal reasons—more specifically, due to difficulty in obtaining enough legal clearances to show numerous screen shots from other browsers.

Obtaining an MSDN account from Microsoft will give you access to legacy products, including older versions of Internet Explorer. Additional resources are the Application Compatibility Virtual PC Images, available for free from Microsoft. These allow you to use a time-limited version of Microsoft Windows containing older versions of Internet Explorer, too. For more information, see *http://www.microsoft.com/downloads/details.aspx?FamilyId=21EABB90-958F-4B64-B5F1-73D0A413C8EF&displaylang=en*.

Many web designs and JavaScript functions don't require newer versions of web browsers. However, as already explained, verifying that your site renders correctly in various browsers is always a good idea. See *http://browsers.evolt.org/* for links to archives of many historical versions of web browsers. Even if you can't conduct extensive testing in multiple browsers, you can design the site so that it fails in a graceful manner. You want the site to render appropriately regardless of the browser being used.

And then came Windows 8

Microsoft Windows 8 represents a paradigm shift for JavaScript programmers. In Windows 8, Microsoft has elevated JavaScript to the same level as other client-side languages, such as Visual Basic and C#, for developing Windows 8 applications. Before Windows 8, if you wanted to create an application that ran on the desktop, you'd need to use Visual Basic, C#, or a similar language. With Windows 8, you need only use HTML and JavaScript to create a full-fledged Windows 8–style app.

Windows 8 exposes an Application Programming Interface (API), providing a set of functions that enable the JavaScript programmer to natively access behind-the-scenes areas of the operating system. This means that programming for Windows 8 is slightly different from programming JavaScript for a web browser.

Of course, your web applications will still work in Internet Explorer, which comes with Windows 8. These web applications are distinct and separate from the Windows 8 native applications.

This book will show how to develop for Windows 8 using JavaScript. Before you get there, you'll see how to create JavaScript programs that run in web browsers.

Exercises

1. True or False: JavaScript is defined by a standards body and is supported on all web browsers.

2. True or False: When a visitor whose machine has JavaScript disabled comes to your website, you should block his access to the site because there's no valid reason to have JavaScript disabled.

3. Create a JavaScript definition block that would typically appear on an HTML page within the *<HEAD>* or *<BODY>* block.

4. True or False: It's important to declare the version of JavaScript being used within the DOCTYPE definition block.

5. True or False: JavaScript can appear in the *<HEAD>* block and within the *<BODY>* text of an HTML page.

CHAPTER 2

Developing in JavaScript

After completing this chapter, you will be able to

- Understand the options available for developing in JavaScript.

- Configure your computer for JavaScript development.

- Use Microsoft Visual Studio 2012 to create and deploy a JavaScript application.

- Use Eclipse to create and deploy a JavaScript application.

- Use Notepad (or another editor) to create a JavaScript application.

- Understand options for debugging JavaScript.

JavaScript development options

Because JavaScript isn't a compiled language, you don't need any special tools or development environments to write and deploy JavaScript applications. Likewise, you don't need special server software to run the applications. Therefore, your options for creating JavaScript programs are virtually limitless.

You can write JavaScript code in any text editor; in whatever program you use to write your Hypertext Markup Language (HTML) and cascading style sheet (CSS) files; or in powerful integrated development environments (IDEs) such as Visual Studio. You might even use all three approaches. You might initially develop a web application with Visual Studio but then find it convenient to use a simple text editor such as Notepad to touch up a bit of JavaScript. Ultimately, you should use whatever tool you're most comfortable with.

This book doesn't really discuss or give much specific direction on JavaScript editors; you can use whatever you want. With that said, when you get into developing for Windows 8, which is covered in this book, you'll find that Visual Studio makes your life much easier by providing templates and helper applications for creating Windows 8 apps. In any event, this chapter shows three different ways to program with JavaScript: using Visual Studio, Eclipse, and Notepad.

My own development environment

In case you think that this is a Microsoft-only (or even Microsoft-centric) book, you might be surprised to learn that most of the examples that you see in this book were written in Vim and tested first in Firefox before being run in Internet Explorer so that I could take a screen shot.

For me personally, I have Vim readily available from just about anywhere—it's lightweight and gets out of the way. And Firefox provides excellent feedback through its Firebug add-on (which you'll see later). This combination has worked for me for years. However, I wouldn't really consider using Vim for any of the .Net work that I do. Visual Studio works well for Microsoft-centric development and websites that will run solely on Microsoft technologies. The Windows 8 examples shown in the book are completely done in Visual Studio to take advantage of the Windows 8 JavaScript libraries.

After you've been developing JavaScript for a while, you'll notice that you do some of the same things on every webpage. In such cases, you can just copy and paste the repeated code into the webpage that you're developing. Better still, you can create an external file containing common functions that you can then use throughout the sites you develop. Chapter 7, "Working with functions," has more information about functions, although you'll see functions used throughout the book.

Configuring your environment

This section looks at JavaScript development using a few different tools. You should be able to use whatever tool you feel most comfortable with for your JavaScript and website development, so don't consider this to be an exhaustive or prejudicial list of tools.

One useful JavaScript development tool is Visual Studio 2012. A simple web server—the ASP.NET Development Server—comes with the installation of Visual Studio 2012, which makes deploying and testing the applications in this book a little easier. However, this does not mean that you should go out and purchase Visual Studio 2012 just for JavaScript development. If you choose to use Eclipse, the second tool discussed in this chapter, you can still test the JavaScript code that you write. Likewise, you can test the JavaScript code even if you don't use an IDE at all.

Another option for web development is Visual Studio 2012 Express for Web. This tool, available at *http://www.microsoft.com/express*, provides the Visual Studio interface and several tools and add-ons in a free package made just for web development. There is also an Express version for Windows 8 development available from that same URL.

You don't absolutely need a web server for most JavaScript development. The notable exception to this is when you're developing using Asynchronous JavaScript and XML (AJAX). AJAX cannot use the *file://* protocol, which, in addition to the Same-Origin Policy covered in Chapter 1, "JavaScript is more than you might think," prevents AJAX from working unless you use a web server. The bottom line: if AJAX development is in your future, you need a web server.

AJAX notwithstanding, development does become a little easier if you have a web server handy. Any web server will work because all you really want to do is serve HTML and JavaScript, and maybe a little CSS for fun. I've had great luck with Apache, available from *http://httpd.apache.org*. Apache runs on many platforms, including the Microsoft Windows platform, and continues to be the most popular web server on the Internet.

Configuring Apache or any web server is beyond the scope of this book, and again, having a web server is not required. The Apache website has some good tutorials for installing Apache on Windows, and if you're using just about any version of Linux, Apache will likely be installed already or is easily installed. Many of the examples used in the book will work whether you're using a web server or just viewing the example locally. However, a web server is necessary to take advantage of examples that use AJAX.

Writing JavaScript with Visual Studio 2012

Visual Studio 2012 lets developers quickly deploy web applications with JavaScript enhancements. Visual Studio 2012 Express Edition is available as a free download at *http://www.microsoft.com/ express*, along with other tools related to development. Installation is typically a matter of executing the downloaded file from Microsoft, possibly installing a Web Platform installer first, but you should refer to the documentation for the latest information at the time of installation.

 Note The first portion of this book will use Visual Studio 2012 Express for Web, which includes the necessary templates for web-based JavaScript development. Windows 8 development uses a different set of templates, and those will be shown in the Windows 8 section of the book.

Your first web (and JavaScript) project with Visual Studio 2012

It's time to create a web project and write a little JavaScript. If you're not using Visual Studio, skip ahead in this chapter to the section "Writing JavaScript with Eclipse" or the section "Writing JavaScript without an IDE" for information about working in other development environments. I won't forget about you, I promise!

 Note You can download the code found in these examples and throughout the book. See this book's Introduction for directions about downloading the companion content.

Creating a web project with JavaScript in Visual Studio 2012

1. Within Visual Studio, select New Web Site from the File menu. This opens the New Web Site dialog box.

2. Select ASP.NET Empty Web Site (the language selection—Visual Basic or Visual C#—is not important), as shown here. Change the name to **jsbs**, with a path appropriate to your configuration. When the information is correct, click OK. Visual Studio creates a new project.

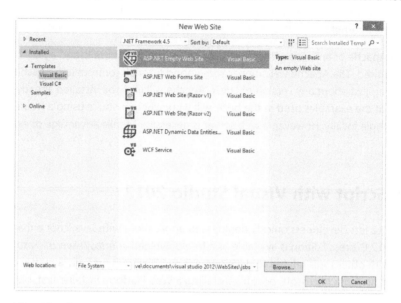

3. Visual Studio 2012 creates an empty project for you... really empty, with not even so much as a default page. Create a new file by selecting New File from the File menu. The Add New Item dialog box opens, as shown in the following graphic. Select HTML Page, change the name to **index.html**, and then click Add. Visual Studio opens the new file and automatically enters the DOCTYPE and other starting pieces of an HTML page for you.

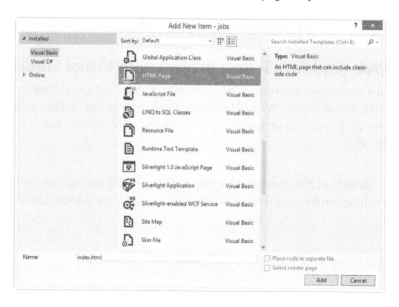

4. In the index.html page, place your cursor between the *<TITLE>* and *</TITLE>* tags, and change the title to **My First Page**. Your environment should look like the one shown here:

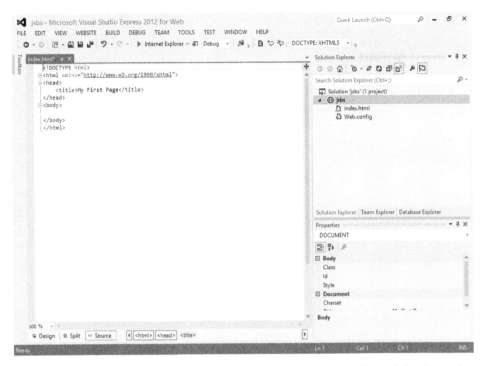

5. Between the opening *<BODY>* tag and the closing *</BODY>* tag, add the following code:

```
<script type="text/javascript">
    function yetAnotherAlert(textToAlert) {
        alert(textToAlert);
    }
    yetAnotherAlert("This is Chapter 2");
</script>
```

6. Select Save All from the File menu. The finished script and page should resemble the screen shown here:

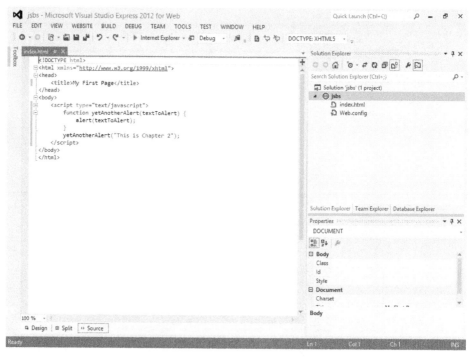

7. To view the page, select Start Debugging from the Debug menu. This starts the ASP.NET Development Server (if it's not already started) and takes you to the page in your default browser. You might see a dialog, like the following, indicating that the debugging isn't enabled in your web.config. Click OK to dismiss this dialog (and enable debugging).

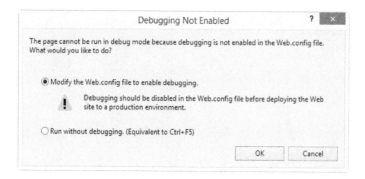

Now you should receive a page with an alert, similar to the alert shown here:

8. Click OK, and then close the browser.

The script works as follows. First, the script tag is opened and declared to be JavaScript, as shown by this code:

```
<script type="text/javascript">
```

> **Note** You can declare your script is JavaScript in other ways, but the approach you see here is the most widely supported.

Next, the script declares a function, *yetAnotherAlert,* which accepts one argument, *textToAlert,* as follows:

```
function yetAnotherAlert(textToAlert) {
```

The function has one task: to pop an alert into the browser window with whatever text has been supplied as the function argument, which the next line accomplishes:

```
alert(textToAlert);
```

The end of the function is delineated by a closing brace (*}*). The next line of the script calls the function you just declared with a quoted string argument:

```
yetAnotherAlert("This is Chapter 2");
```

With this script, you're ready to develop JavaScript in Visual Studio 2012. But before you celebrate, consider sticking with me and learning about how to use external files to store your JavaScript code.

Using external JavaScript files with Visual Studio 2012

JavaScript doesn't need to be contained wholly within the HTML files of your website. Instead, you can take advantage of the *src* attribute of the *<SCRIPT>* tag. Attributes within tags help to further define or provide more specifics about the element. For example, a *<FORM>* element might have an *action* attribute that defines what action should happen when the form is submitted. Using the *src* attribute of the *<SCRIPT>* tag, you can define the location of an external JavaScript file. The web browser then reads the JavaScript contained within the specified file when it loads the webpage. Using external

JavaScript files means that you can maintain common JavaScript code in one place, as opposed to maintaining it within each individual page—which will save you a lot of work.

At this point, you should have a working webpage (built using Visual Studio) that displays an alert, thanks to some nifty JavaScript. The webpage you developed in the previous section contains the JavaScript code within the *<BODY>* portion of the page. In the following section, I show you how to place JavaScript into an external file and then reference that code from within your HTML page.

Creating an external file for JavaScript using Visual Studio 2012

1. If the index.html file isn't open, open it by going into Visual Studio and selecting Open Project from the File menu. Select the project in which you saved the index.html file (available in the companion content as firstindex.html), and open the file. Your environment should look something like the environment in step 6 in the previous example.

2. Create a new file to hold the JavaScript code by selecting New File from the File menu. The Add New Item dialog box appears. In the list of templates, select JavaScript File and change the name to **myscript.js**, as shown in the following screen, and then click Add. Note that your list might differ depending on your Visual Studio installation. You can find this source file, titled myscript.js, in the Chapter 2 sample code.

> **Note** If you see only JScript file instead of JavaScript file, you might not have the Express Edition for Web of Visual Studio 2012. However, a JScript file type will work just fine.

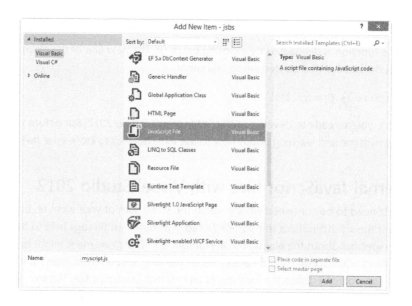

3. A new empty JavaScript file opens and is added to your web project. You should see a tab for the new myscript.js file and another for the index.html file, as shown in the next screen. If the index.html file isn't opened in a tab, open it by double-clicking it in the Solution Explorer.

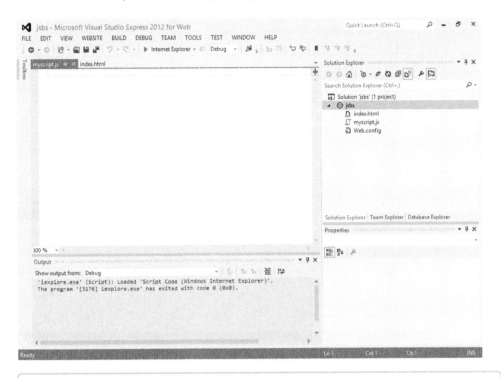

Note The colloquial extension for JavaScript and JScript is .js, but you are not required to use it. I chose to use a JavaScript type of file in the preceding step 2 because this file type automatically selects the correct file extension. You could just as easily have selected Text Document from the Add New Item dialog box and then named the file with a .js extension.

4. Click the index.html tab to make it active, and highlight the JavaScript code in between the opening and closing *<SCRIPT>* tags. Don't copy the *<SCRIPT>* tags themselves.

5. Copy the highlighted code to the Clipboard by selecting Copy from the Edit menu.

6. Click the myscript.js tab, move the cursor below the first line, and select Paste from the Edit menu. The copied code is pasted at the cursor's location. Change the text of the *yetAnotherAlert* function call parameter so that it reads as follows: "This is the Second Example." The code is shown here:

```
function yetAnotherAlert(textToAlert) {
    alert(textToAlert);
}
yetAnotherAlert("This is the Second Example.");
```

7. Save the myscript.js file by selecting Save from the File menu. The file should look like the following:

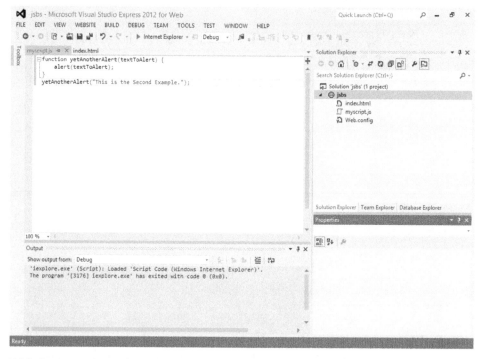

8. With the JavaScript code contained in its own file named myscript.js (you did save that file, right?), you can just delete the code from the index.html file, including the opening and closing *<SCRIPT>* tags.

9. Inside the *<HEAD>* section, after the closing *</TITLE>* tag, place the following:

```
<script type="text/javascript" src="myscript.js"></script>
```

The entire contents of index.html should now be the following:

```
<!DOCTYPE html>
<html>
<head>
    <title>My First Page</title>
    <script type="text/javascript" src="myscript.js"></script>
</head>
<body>
</body>
</html>
```

10. Save index.html.

11. View the page in a web browser by selecting Start Debugging from the Debug menu. The page will be served through the web server, and your browser window, if not already open, will open to the page. The result should be an alert with the text "This is the Second Example." An example of this is shown here:

12. Click OK to close the alert dialog box.

You've developed JavaScript with Visual Studio 2012. From here, you can skip ahead to the section on debugging or keep reading to learn about JavaScript development using other tools.

Writing JavaScript with Eclipse

Another popular IDE among web developers (and developers who use other languages) is Eclipse. Developers using Eclipse can install different frameworks to assist in specific development tasks. For example, web developers might use the Web Tools Platform or PHP (PHP Hypertext Preprocessor) development tools to create an environment that simplifies many common tasks for them. Discussion of the many potential Eclipse projects is beyond the scope of this book, but I discuss how to use the base Eclipse installation to develop JavaScript.

If you want to develop JavaScript with Eclipse, take a moment to download the software and, if necessary, the Java runtime environment. Details and download locations are available from the Eclipse website (*http://www.eclipse.org*). In this section of the book, I assume that you've never used Eclipse and are learning it for the first time. However, this section does not include a tutorial on installing Eclipse. I recommend you read the documentation included with Eclipse and available on the Eclipse website for the most up-to-date information.

Your first web (and JavaScript) project with Eclipse

It's now time to create a webpage with JavaScript using Eclipse. If you're not using Eclipse, this section isn't for you, and you can skip it. Later in the chapter, I show you how to develop without using any IDE, and give you some tips for debugging JavaScript.

 Note This section reviews how to use the version of Eclipse known as Eclipse Classic. Your Eclipse environment might look a little different from the screen shots included in this section. The first time you open Eclipse, you are asked to select a workspace. Choose the default.

Creating a web project with JavaScript in Eclipse

1. Create a new project by selecting File | New | Project. The New Project dialog box appears.

2. Select Project from within the General Wizards area, and click Next.

3. Enter **Chapter2** in the Project Name text box, and click Finish, as shown here:

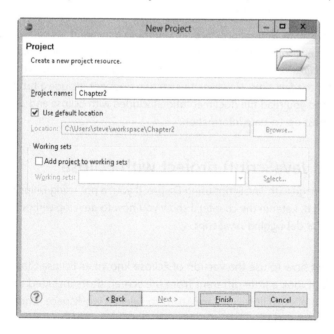

4. The Chapter2 project folder opens in Package Explorer without files listed, as depicted here:

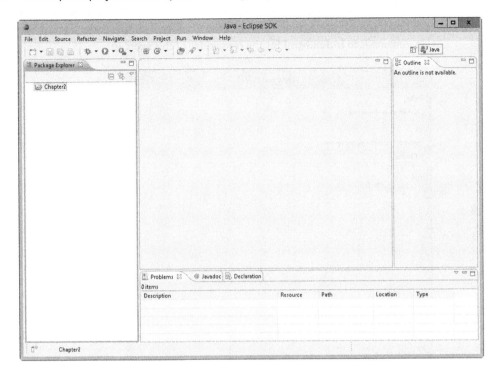

5. Right-click the Chapter2 folder, click New, and then click File. The New File dialog box opens. In the File Name text box, type **index.html**, as shown in the next screen, and click Finish. You can find this file, titled firstindex.html, in the Chapter 2 sample code. If you'd like to use this file, rename it to **index.html** for the remainder of this exercise.

6. After you click Finish, Eclipse opens the page in its own web browser. However, you want to edit the page, not view it, so right-click index.html in Package Explorer, select Open With, and click Text Editor. The page opens in an editor directly in Eclipse, as shown here:

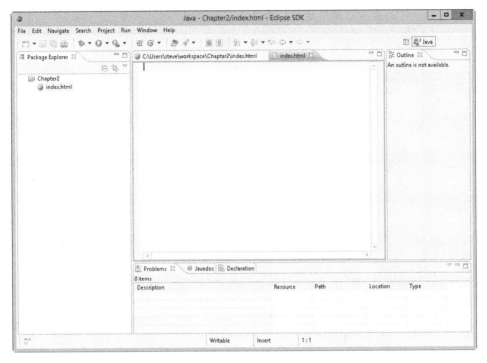

7. At last it's time to write some code! In the editor, type the following:

```
<!DOCTYPE html>
<html>
<head>
    <title>My First Page</title>
</head>
<body>
    <script type="text/javascript">
        function yetAnotherAlert(textToAlert) {
            alert(textToAlert);
         }
        yetAnotherAlert("This is Chapter 2");
    </script>
</body>
</html>
```

8. Select Save from the File menu. If you receive an error about character encoding, select "Save as UTF-8." The finished script and page should resemble the one shown in the following graphic:

```
C:\Users\steve\workspace\Chapter2\index.html        index.html
<!DOCTYPE html>
<html xmlns="http://www.w3.org/1999/xhtml">
<head>
    <title>My First Page</title>
</head>
<body>
    <script type="text/javascript">
        function yetAnotherAlert(textToAlert) {
            alert(textToAlert);
        }
        yetAnotherAlert("This is Chapter 2");
    </script>
</body>
</html>
```

9. To view the page, right-click the file in Project Explorer, select Open With, and then click Web Browser. You will see the file locally through the Eclipse browser, and you should receive a page with an alert, similar to the following:

Alternatively, you can view the file through a different web browser on your computer, such as your system's default web browser. To do this, browse to the file (for example, my copy of the file is located in the C:\Users\Steve\workspace\Chapter2\ folder), and then double-click the file.

In this example, you created a basic webpage with some embedded JavaScript. The JavaScript portion of the page contains just a few elements. First, the script tag is opened and declared to be JavaScript, as shown in this code:

```
<script type="text/javascript">
```

Next, the script declares a function, *yetAnotherAlert*, which accepts one argument, *textToAlert*:

```
function yetAnotherAlert(textToAlert) {
```

The function has one task: to pop up an alert into the browser window with whatever text has been supplied as the function argument, which the next line accomplishes:

```
alert(textToAlert);
```

The function is delineated by a closing brace:

```
}
```

The script then calls the function you just declared with a quoted string argument, as follows:

```
yetAnotherAlert("This is Chapter 2");
```

In this brief example, you saw how to code JavaScript using Eclipse. The next section shows how to place the JavaScript in an external file, a common approach to using JavaScript.

Using external JavaScript files with Eclipse

By the time you read this, you should have a working webpage (created with Eclipse) that displays an alert. The webpage you developed in the previous section contains the JavaScript code within the *<BODY>* tag portion of the page. In this section, I describe how to place JavaScript into an external file and then refer to that code from within your HTML page.

Creating an external file for JavaScript using Eclipse

1. If the index.html code isn't already open in Eclipse, open it. (You can find this file in the companion content as firstindex.html.) Select the project in which you saved the index.html file, and open the file in an editor by right-clicking the file, selecting Open With, and then clicking Text Editor.

2. Create a new file to hold the JavaScript code by selecting New and then File from the File menu. The New File dialog box opens. Type **myscript.js** in the File Name text box, as shown here, and click Finish:

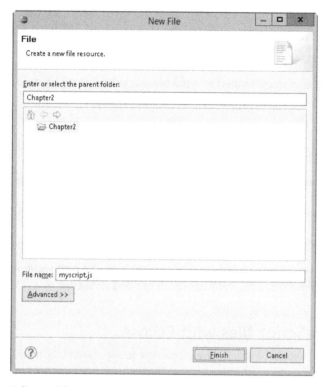

3. Eclipse adds a new empty JavaScript file to your project. If this file doesn't open automatically, right-click the myscript.js file in Project Explorer, select Open With, and then click Text Editor. You should now see tabs for both the new myscript.js file and the index.html file. You might also see the My First Page webpage.

Note Although you are not required to use the colloquial extension for JavaScript, which is .js, doing so might help you more easily identify files later.

4. Click the index.html tab to make it active, and highlight the JavaScript code you wrote earlier, highlighting just the code between the opening <SCRIPT> and closing </SCRIPT> tags, not the tags themselves. (You don't need those right now, but you'll revisit the topic shortly.)

5. Copy the highlighted code to the Clipboard by selecting Copy from the Edit menu.

6. Click the myscript.js tab, and paste the code by selecting Paste from the Edit menu. Change the text of the function call to "This is the Second Example." The code looks like this:

```
function yetAnotherAlert(textToAlert) {
    alert(textToAlert);
}
yetAnotherAlert("This is the Second Example.");
```

7. Save the myscript.js file by selecting Save from the File menu. The file should look similar to the screen shown here:

8. With the JavaScript code contained in its own file named myscript.js (you did save that file, right?), you can just delete the code from the index.html file, including the opening and closing *<SCRIPT>* tags.

9. Inside the *<HEAD>* section, after the closing *</TITLE>* tag, place the following:

```
<script type="text/javascript" src="myscript.js"></script>
```

The entire contents of index.html should now be the following:

```
<!DOCTYPE html>
<html xmlns="http://www.w3.org/1999/xhtml">
<head>
    <title>My First Page</title>
    <script type="text/javascript" src="myscript.js"></script>
</head>
<body>
</body>
</html>
```

10. Save index.html.

11. View the page in a web browser by right-clicking index.html in Package Explorer, pointing to Open With, and then clicking Web Browser. The page is served locally, and a browser window opens to the page. The result should be an alert with the text "This is the Second Example," as shown here:

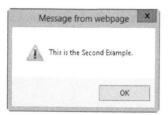

This basic primer about JavaScript development with Eclipse is complete. However, there's much more to it, and I recommend visiting the Eclipse website for more information about development with the Eclipse platform.

Writing JavaScript without an IDE

You can just as easily forgo the IDEs in favor of a simpler approach to JavaScript development. Any text editor like Notepad or Vim will work fine for JavaScript development. However, I recommend against using word processors such as Microsoft Office Word for JavaScript development because they can leave artifacts within the resulting file, which in turn can wreak havoc on the resulting website.

Your first web (and JavaScript) project with Notepad

This section shows an example of JavaScript development with Notepad.

Creating a webpage with JavaScript in Notepad

1. In Microsoft Windows 8, you can open Notepad by using Search and typing **Notepad**, and then clicking Notepad to open it.

2. Enter the following HTML into Notepad; this can be found in the companion content as firstindex.html:

```
<!DOCTYPE html>
<html xmlns="http://www.w3.org/1999/xhtml">
<head>
    <title>My First Page</title>
</head>
<body>
    <script type="text/javascript">
        function yetAnotherAlert(textToAlert) {
```

```
        alert(textToAlert);
    }
    yetAnotherAlert("This is Chapter 2");
</script>
</body>
</html>
```

3. Select Save from the File menu. You are presented with a Save As dialog box. By default, Notepad adds a .txt extension to the document name unless you use double quotation marks. Therefore, be sure to place double quotation marks around the file name—for example, *"index.html"*. If you omit the quotation marks, Notepad will add the .txt extension and save the file as "index.html.txt" instead. The following image shows an example of using double quotation marks around the file name. Be sure to note where you save this document.

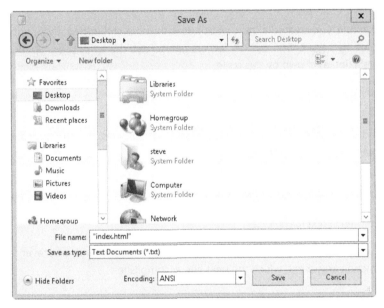

4. To view the page, use the web browser of your choice to browse to the location where you saved the file. (If, as in the screen shown in the previous step, you saved the file to the desktop, browse there.)

 Note If you are using Internet Explorer, you might receive an alert about viewing blocked content. To view the page, click Allow Blocked Content.

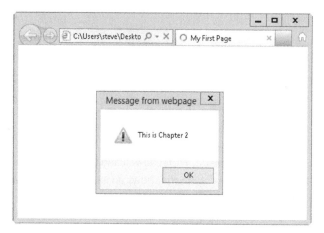

So far in this example, you created a basic webpage with some embedded JavaScript. The JavaScript portion of the page contains just a few elements. First, the script tag is opened and declared to be JavaScript, as shown by this code:

```
<script type="text/javascript">
```

> **Note** You can declare that your script is JavaScript in other ways, but the approach you see here is the most widely supported.

Next, the script declares a function, *yetAnotherAlert*, which accepts one argument, *textToAlert*:

```
function yetAnotherAlert(textToAlert) {
```

The function has one task: to pop up an alert in the browser window with whatever text has been supplied as the function argument, which the next line accomplishes:

```
alert(textToAlert);
```

The function is delineated by a closing brace (*}*). The script then calls the function you just declared with a quoted string argument:

```
yetAnotherAlert("This is Chapter 2");
```

In this brief example, you've seen how to code JavaScript without an IDE. The next section shows how to place the JavaScript in an external file, a quite common approach to JavaScript usage.

Using external JavaScript files without an IDE

By the time you read this, you should have a working webpage (created in Notepad) that displays an *alert()* dialog box. The webpage you developed in the previous section contains the JavaScript code within the *<BODY>* tag portion of the page. This section shows how to place JavaScript into an external file and then refer to that code from within your HTML page.

Creating an external file for JavaScript using Notepad

1. If the index.html file isn't open, open it. If you're using Notepad, you might need to right-click the file and select Open With, and then select Notepad.

2. Highlight the JavaScript code you wrote earlier, highlighting just the code between the opening *<SCRIPT>* and closing *</SCRIPT>* tags, not the tags themselves. (You don't need those right now, but you'll revisit the topic shortly.)

3. Copy the highlighted code to the Clipboard by selecting Copy from the Edit menu.

4. Create a new file to hold the JavaScript code by selecting New from the File menu. The new file opens. Paste the JavaScript code into the file by selecting Paste from the Edit menu. Change the text of the parameter to the function call so that it reads "This is the Second Example." This code is shown here:

```
function yetAnotherAlert(textToAlert) {
    alert(textToAlert);
}
yetAnotherAlert("This is the Second Example.");
```

5. Save the file by selecting Save from the File menu. Type **myscript.js** in the File Name text box, and be sure to include double quotation marks because the extension needs to be .js and not .txt.

 Note The colloquial extension for JavaScript files is .js, but you don't have to use it. However, doing so might help you identify files more easily later.

6. With the JavaScript code contained in its own file named myscript.js (you did save that file, right?), you can just delete the code from the index.html file, including the opening and closing *<SCRIPT>* tags.

7. Inside the *<HEAD>* section, after the closing *</TITLE>* tag, place the following:

```
<script type="text/javascript" src="myscript.js"></script>
```

The entire contents of index.html should now be the following:

```
<!DOCTYPE html>
<html xmlns="http://www.w3.org/1999/xhtml">
<head>
    <title>My First Page</title>
    <script type="text/javascript" src="myscript.js"></script>
</head>
<body>
</body>
</html>
```

8. Save index.html.

9. View the page in a web browser. The result, shown in the following screen, should be an alert with the text "This is the Second Example.":

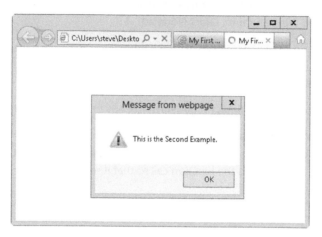

This primer on JavaScript development without an IDE is complete. Although this example used Notepad, several other editors might be more suited to basic development, including the afore-mentioned Vim and Textpad from Helio Software Solutions, both of which are more powerful than Notepad.

Debugging JavaScript

Debugging JavaScript can be an alarming experience, especially in more complex applications. Some tools, such as Venkman (*http://www.mozilla.org/projects/venkman/*), can assist in JavaScript debugging, but the primary tool for debugging JavaScript is the web browser. Major web browsers include some JavaScript debugging capabilities. Among the programs you should consider using is Firebug, a notable add-on to Firefox. Firebug is available at *http://www.getfirebug.com/*.

I find Firebug to be virtually indispensable for web development, especially web development with JavaScript and AJAX. This software enables you to inspect all the elements of a webpage and to see the results of AJAX calls and CSS, all in real time, which makes debugging much easier. Later in the book, you'll see more on Firebug.

I recommend using Firebug for developing JavaScript and debugging it. When debugging JavaScript, I find that the *alert()* function is quite useful. A few well-placed *alert()* functions can show you the values contained within variables and what your script is currently doing. Of course, because *alert()* causes a dialog box to open, if you place an *alert()* within a loop and then mistakenly cause that loop to repeat endlessly without exiting, you'll find that you need to exit the web browser uncleanly, perhaps using Task Manager.

Exercises

1. Create a new webpage, and call it mysecondpage.htm. Create a script in JavaScript within the *<BODY>* portion of the page and have that script display an *alert()* dialog box with your name. Try this script in at least two different web browsers.

2. Edit the webpage that you created in Exercise 1, create a function within the *<HEAD>* portion of the page, and move the *alert()* dialog box that you currently have in the *<BODY>* script into your new function. Call the new function from the existing *<BODY>* script.

3. Move the function created in Exercise 2 to an external JavaScript file, and link or call this file from within your webpage.

CHAPTER 3

JavaScript syntax and statements

After completing this chapter, you will be able to

■ Understand the basic rules of using the JavaScript programming language.

■ Place JavaScript correctly within a webpage.

■ Recognize a JavaScript statement.

■ Recognize a reserved word in JavaScript.

A bit of housekeeping

The rest of the book looks more closely at specific aspects of JavaScript and how they relate to specific tasks. However, you must walk before you can run, so before examining JavaScript in more depth, you should learn some of its *lexical structure*—that is, the rules of the language, also known as *syntax rules*.

Case sensitivity

JavaScript is case sensitive. You must be aware of this when naming variables and using the language keywords. A variable named *remote* is not the same as a variable named *Remote* or one named *REMOTE*. Similarly, the loop control keyword *while* is perfectly valid, but naming it *WHILE* or *While* will result in an error.

Keywords are lowercase, but variables can be any mix of case that you'd like. As long you are consistent with the case, you can create any combination you want. For example, all the following examples are perfectly legal variable names in JavaScript:

```
buttonOne
txt1
a
C
```

Tip You'll typically see JavaScript coded in lowercase except where necessary—for example, with function calls such as *isNaN()*, which determines whether a value is Not a Number (the *NaN* in the function name). You learn about this in Chapter 4, "Working with variables and data types."

Chapter 4 provides much more information about variables and their naming conventions. For now, remember that you must pay attention to the case when you write a variable name in JavaScript.

White space

For the most part, JavaScript ignores *white space*, which is the space between statements in JavaScript. You can use spaces, indenting, or whatever coding standards you prefer to make the JavaScript more readable. However, there are some exceptions to this rule. Some keywords, such as *return*, can be misinterpreted by the JavaScript interpreter when they're included on a line by themselves. You'll see an example of this problem a little later in this chapter.

Making programs more readable is a good enough reason to include white space. Consider the following code sample. It includes minimal white space and indenting.

```
function cubeme(incomingNum) {
if (incomingNum == 1) {
return "What are you doing?";
} else {
return Math.pow(incomingNum,3);
}
}
var theNum = 2;
var finalNum = cubeme(theNum);
if (isNaN(finalNum)) {
alert("You should know that 1 to any power is 1.");
} else {
alert("When cubed, " + theNum + " is " + finalNum);
}
```

Now consider the same code with indenting.

```
function cubeme(incomingNum) {
    if (incomingNum == 1) {
        return "What are you doing?";
    } else {
        return Math.pow(incomingNum,3);
    }
}

var theNum = 2;
var finalNum = cubeme(theNum);

if (isNaN(finalNum)) {
    alert("You should know that 1 to any power is 1.");
```

```
} else {
    alert("When cubed, " + theNum + " is " + finalNum);
}
```

The second code sample performs just like the first, but it's easier to read and follow—at least it appears so to me! I find that it takes a short amount of time to actually write code but several years to work with it. When I visit the code a year later, I'm much happier when I've made the code more readable and easier to follow.

Comments

Speaking of creating more readable code and maintaining that code over the long term: Comments are your friends. Code that seems blatantly obvious now won't be nearly so obvious the next time you look at it, especially if a lot of time has passed since you wrote it. Comments can be placed into JavaScript code in two ways: multiline and single-line.

A multiline comment in JavaScript will look familiar to you if you've coded in the C programming language. A *multiline* comment begins and ends with /* and */, respectively, as the following code example shows:

```
/*  This is a multiline comment in JavaScript
It is just like a C-style comment insofar as it can
span multiple lines before being closed.   */
```

A *single-line* comment begins with two front slashes (//) and has no end requirement because it spans only a single line. An example is shown here:

```
// Here is a single-line comment.
```

Using multiple single-line comments is perfectly valid, and I use them for short comment blocks rather than using the multiline comment style previously shown. For example, look at this block of code:

```
// Here is another comment block.
// This one uses multiple lines.
// Each line must be preceded with two slashes.
```

Tip You might find it quicker to use the two-slash method for small comments that span one line or a few lines. For larger comments, such as those at the beginning of a program or script, the multiline comment style is a better choice because it makes adding or deleting information easier.

Semicolons

Semicolons are used to delineate expressions in JavaScript. Technically, semicolons are not required for most statements and expressions. However, the subtle problems that you can encounter when you don't use semicolons add unnecessary errors and hence unnecessary debugging time. In some instances, the JavaScript interpreter inserts a semicolon when you might not have wanted one at all. For example, consider this statement:

```
return
(varName);
```

In all likelihood, you wanted to write:

```
return(varName);
```

But JavaScript, acting on its own, inserts a semicolon after the *return* statement, making the code appear like this to the JavaScript interpreter:

```
return;
(varName);
```

This code won't work; the interpreter will misunderstand your intentions. If you used this code in a function, it would return *undefined* to the caller, which is unlikely to be what you want. This is an example where free use of white space is not allowed—you can't successfully use line breaks (explained in the next section) to separate the *return* keyword from the value that it's supposed to return.

> **Tip** You'll find programming in JavaScript much easier if you use semicolons as a rule rather than trying to remember where you might not have to use them.

But you definitely shouldn't use semicolons in one instance: when using loops and conditionals. Consider this bit of code:

```
if (a == 4)
{
    // code goes here
}
```

In this case, you wouldn't use a semicolon at the end of the *if* statement. The reason is that the statement or block of statements in opening and closing braces that follows a conditional is part of the conditional statement—in this case, the *if* statement. A semicolon marks the end of the *if* statement, and if improperly placed, dissociates the first part of the *if* statement from the rest of it. For example, the following code is wrong (the code within the braces will execute regardless of whether *a* equals 4):

```
if (a == 4);
{
    // code goes here
}
```

Tip When opening a loop or function, skip the semicolons.

Line breaks

Related closely to white space and even to semicolons in JavaScript are line breaks, sometimes called *carriage returns*. Known in the official ECMA-262 standard as "Line Terminators," these characters separate one line of code from the next. Like semicolons, the placement of line breaks matters. As you saw from the example in the previous section, placing a line break in the wrong position can result in unforeseen behavior or errors.

Not surprisingly, the most common use of line breaks is to separate individual lines of code for readability. You can also improve readability of particularly long lines of code by separating them with line breaks. However, when doing so, be aware of issues like the one illustrated by the *return* statement cited earlier, in which an extra line break can have unwanted effects on the meaning of the code.

Placing JavaScript correctly

JavaScript can be placed in a couple of locations within a Hypertext Markup Language (HTML) page: in the *<HEAD> </HEAD>* section or between the *<BODY>* and *</BODY>* tags. The most common location for JavaScript has traditionally been between the *<HEAD>* and *</HEAD>* tags near the top of the page. However, placing the *<SCRIPT>* stanza within the *<BODY>* section is becoming more common. Be sure to declare what type of script you're using. Although other script types can be used, because this is a JavaScript book, I'll declare the following within the opening *<SCRIPT>* tag:

```
<script type="text/javascript">
```

One important issue to note when you use JavaScript relates to pages declared as Extensible Hypertext Markup Language (XHTML). Therefore, JavaScript used within strict XHTML should be declared as follows:

```
<script type="text/javascript">
<![CDATA[
    //JavaScript goes here
]]>
</script>
```

Older browsers might not parse the CDATA section correctly. This problem can be worked around by placing the CDATA opening and closing lines within JavaScript comments, like this:

```
<script type="text/javascript">
//<![CDATA[
    //JavaScript goes here
//]]>
</script>
```

When you place the actual JavaScript code in a separate file (as you learn how to do in Chapter 2, "Developing in JavaScript"), you don't need to use this ugly CDATA section at all. You'll probably discover that for anything but the smallest scripts, defining your JavaScript in separate files—usually with the file extension .js—and then linking to those scripts within the page, is desirable. Chapter 2 shows this in full detail, but here's a reminder of how you link to a file using the *src* attribute of the *<SCRIPT>* tag:

```
<script type="text/javascript" src="myscript.js"></script>
```

Placing JavaScript in an external file has several advantages, including the following:

- **Separation of code from markup**   Keeping the JavaScript code in a separate file makes maintaining the HTML easier, and it preserves the structure of the HTML without you having to use a CDATA section for XHTML.

- **Easier maintenance**   Using JavaScript in a separate file, you can make changes to the JavaScript code in that separate file without touching the HTML on the site.

- **Caching**   Using a separate file for JavaScript enables web browsers to cache the file, thus speeding up the webpage load for the user.

JavaScript statements

Like programs written in other languages, JavaScript programs consist of statements put together that cause the JavaScript interpreter to perform one or more actions. And like statements in other languages, JavaScript statements can be simple or compound. This section briefly examines JavaScript statements, with the assumption that you've already seen several examples in the previous chapters and that you'll see others throughout the book.

What's in a statement?

As covered in Chapter 1, "JavaScript is more than you might think," a JavaScript statement, or expression, is a collection of tokens of various categories including keywords, literals, separators, operators, and identifiers that are put together to create something that makes sense to the JavaScript interpreter. A statement usually ends with a semicolon, except in special cases like loop constructors such as *if*, *while*, and *for*, which are covered in Chapter 5, "Using operators and expressions."

Here are some examples of basic statements in JavaScript:

```
var x = 4;
var y = x * 4;

alert("Hello");
```

The two types of JavaScript statements

JavaScript statements come in two basic forms, simple and compound. I won't spend a lot of time discussing statements because you don't really need to know much about them. However, you should know the difference between simple and compound statements. A *simple statement* is just what you'd expect—it's simple, like so:

```
x = 4;
```

A *compound statement* combines multiple levels of logic. An *if/then/else* conditional such as the one given here provides a good example of this:

```
if (something == 1) {
    // some code here
} else {
    // some other code here
}
```

Reserved words in JavaScript

Certain words in JavaScript are *reserved*, which means you can't use them as variables, identifiers, or constant names within your program because doing so will cause the code to have unexpected results, such as errors. For example, you've already seen the reserved word *var* in previous examples. Using the word *var* to do anything but declare a variable can cause an error or other unexpected behavior, depending on the browser. Consider this statement:

```
// Don't do this!

var var = 4;
```

The code example won't result in a direct error to a browser, but it also won't work as you intended, possibly causing confusion when a variable's value isn't what you expect.

The following table includes the words that are currently reserved by the ECMA-262 edition 5.1 specification:

break	delete	if	this	while
case	do	in	throw	with
catch	else	instanceof	try	
continue	finally	new	typeof	
debugger	for	return	var	
default	function	switch	void	

Several other words (shown in the following table) are reserved for future use and therefore shouldn't be used in your programs:

class	enum	extends	super
const	export	import	

The following table shows the words that are reserved for the future when in strict mode:

implements	let	private	public	yield
interface	package	protected	static	

A quick look at functions

You've already seen examples of functions in previous chapters. JavaScript has several *built-in functions*, which are functions that are defined by the language itself. I discussed the *alert()* function already, but there are several others. Which built-in functions are available depends on the language version you're using. Some functions are available only in later versions of JavaScript, which might not be supported by all browsers. Detecting a browser's available functions (and objects) is an important way to determine whether a visitor's browser is capable of using the JavaScript that you created for your webpage. This topic is covered in Chapter 11, "An introduction to jQuery."

> **Tip** You can find an excellent resource for compatibility on the QuirksMode website *(http://www.quirksmode.org/compatibility.html)*.

JavaScript is similar to other programming languages in allowing user-defined functions. An earlier example in this chapter defined a function called *cubeme()*, which raised a given number to the power of 3. That code provides a good opportunity to show the use of JavaScript in both the *<HEAD>* and *<BODY>* portions of a webpage.

Placing JavaScript with a user-defined function

1. Using Microsoft Visual Studio, Eclipse, or another editor, edit the file example1.html in the Chapter 3 sample code.

2. Within the webpage, add the code in bold type:

```
<!doctype html>
<html>
<head>
<script type="text/javascript">
function cubeme(incomingNum) {
    if (incomingNum == 1) {
        return "What are you doing?";
    } else {
```

```
            return Math.pow(incomingNum,3);
        }
    }
    </script>
        <title>A Chapter 3 Example</title>
    </head>

    <body>
    <script type="text/javascript">
    var theNum = 2;
    var finalNum = cubeme(theNum);
    if (isNaN(finalNum)) {
        alert("You should know that 1 to any power is 1.");
    } else {
        alert("When cubed, " + theNum + " is " + finalNum);
    }
    </script>

    </body>
    </html>
```

3. Save the page, and then run the code or view the webpage in a browser. You'll receive an alert like the following:

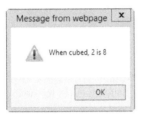

The code in this example incorporates the code from the earlier example into a full HTML page, including a DOCTYPE declaration. The code declares a function, *cubeme()*, within the *<HEAD>* section of the document, like this:

```
function cubeme(incomingNum) {
    if (incomingNum == 1) {
        return "What are you doing?";
    } else {
        return Math.pow(incomingNum,3);
    }
}
```

This code accepts an argument called *incomingNum* within the function. An *if/then* decisional statement is the heart of the function. When the incoming number equals *1*, the function returns the text string, "What are you doing?" When the incoming number is not equal to *1*, the *Math.pow* method is called, passing the *incomingNum* variable and the integer *3* as arguments. The call to *Math.pow* raises the incoming number to the power of 3, and this value is then returned to the calling function. This call is shown again in Chapter 4.

All the previous code was placed within the *<HEAD>* portion of the document so that it can be called by other code, which is just what we're going to do. The browser then renders the *<BODY>* section of the document, which includes another bit of JavaScript code. This next bit of code sets a variable, *theNum*, equal to the integer *2*:

```
var theNum = 2;
```

The code then calls the previously defined *cubeme()* function using the *theNum* variable as an argument. You'll notice that the variable *finalNum* is set to receive the output from the call to the *cubeme()* function, as follows:

```
var finalNum = cubeme(theNum);
```

The final bit of JavaScript on the page is another *if/then* decisional set. This code checks to determine whether the returned value, now contained in the *finalNum* variable, is a number. It does this by using the *isNaN()* function. If the value is not a number, an alert is displayed reflecting the fact that *1* was used as the argument. (Of course, there could be other reasons this isn't a number, but bear with me here and follow along with my example.) If the return value is indeed a number, the number is displayed, as you saw in the *alert()* dialog box shown in the preceding step 3.

JavaScript's strict mode

ECMA-262 edition 5 introduced a strict variant, commonly referred to as *strict mode*, which adds enhanced error checking and security. For example, to help fight against mistyped variable names, variable declarations require the use of the *var* keyword. Additionally, changes to the *eval()* function and other areas help JavaScript programmers to improve their code.

Strict mode is enabled with the following syntax, which is very similar to syntax used in Perl:

```
"use strict";
```

Strict mode is locally scoped, meaning that it can be enabled globally by placing the *use strict* line at the beginning of the script; or it can be enabled only within a function by placing the line within the function itself, like so:

```
function doSomething() {
    "use strict";
    // function's code goes here.
}
```

One strict mode enhancement that will help catch typographical errors is the prevention of undeclared variables. All variables in strict mode need to be instantiated prior to use. For example, consider this code:

```
"use strict";
x = 4;  // Produces a syntax error
```

When used in strict mode, the preceding code would create an error condition because the variable *x* hasn't been declared with the *var* keyword, as in the following example:

```
"use strict";
var x = 4;  // This syntax is ok
```

One of the notable security enhancements that strict mode provides is the change to how the *eval()* function is handled. The *eval()* function executes a string as if it were regular JavaScript code and can lead to security issues in certain cases. In strict mode, *eval()* cannot instantiate a new variable or function that will be used outside the *eval()* statement. For example, consider the following code:

```
"use strict";
eval("var testVar = 2;");
alert(testVar);  // Produces a syntax error.
```

In the preceding code example, a syntax error would be produced because strict mode is enabled and the *testVar* variable isn't available outside the *eval()* statement.

Strict mode also prevents the duplication of variable names within an object or function call:

```
"use strict";
var myObject = {
    testVar: 1,
    testVar: 2
};
```

The preceding code would produce a syntax error in strict mode because *testVar* is set twice within the object's definition. It's worth noting that Internet Explorer 10 might not actually catch this code as an error, depending on the view and mode in which the page is viewed. When viewed in IE10 Standards mode, the code does indeed produce an error. However, the code does produce an error condition in other browsers like Firefox and Chrome.

Like other aspects of ECMA-262 edition 5, strict mode might not be available in all browsers and likely won't be available for older browsers.

Exercises

1. Which of the following are valid JavaScript statements? (Choose all that apply.)

    a. if (var == 4) { // Do something }

    b. var testVar = 10;

    c. if (a == b) { // Do something }

    d. testVar = 10;

    e. var case = "Yes";

2. True or False: Semicolons are required to terminate every JavaScript statement.

3. Examine the following bit of JavaScript. What is the likely result? (Assume that the JavaScript declaration has already taken place and that this code resides properly within the *<HEAD>* section of the page.)

```
var orderTotal = 0;
function collectOrder(numOrdered) {
    if (numOrdered > 0) {
        alert("You ordered " + orderTotal);
        orderTotal = numOrdered * 5;
    }
return orderTotal;
}
```

Working with variables and data types

After completing this chapter, you will be able to

- Understand the primitive data types used in JavaScript.

- Use functions associated with the data types.

- Create variables.

- Define objects and arrays.

- Understand the scope of variables.

- Debug JavaScript using Firebug.

Data types in JavaScript

The *data types* of a language describe the basic elements that can be used within that language. You're probably already familiar with data types, such as strings or integers, from other languages. Depending on who you ask, JavaScript defines anywhere from three to six data types. (The answer depends largely on the definition of a data type.) You work with all these data types regularly, some more than others.

The six data types in JavaScript discussed in this chapter are as follows:

- Numbers

- Strings

- Booleans

- Null

- Undefined

- Objects

The first three data types—numbers, strings, and Booleans—should be fairly familiar to programmers in any language. The latter three—null, undefined, and objects—require some additional explanation. I examine each of the data types in turn and explain objects further in Chapter 8, "Objects in JavaScript."

Additionally, JavaScript has several reference data types, including the *Array*, *Date*, and *RegExp* types. The *Date* and *RegExp* types are discussed in this chapter, and the *Array* type is discussed in Chapter 8.

Working with numbers

Numbers in JavaScript are just what you might expect them to be: numbers. However, what might be a surprise for programmers who are familiar with data types in other languages like C is that integers and floating point numbers do not have special or separate types. All these are perfectly valid numbers in JavaScript:

```
4
51.50
-14
0xd
```

The last example, *0xd*, is a hexadecimal number. Hexadecimal numbers are valid in JavaScript, and you won't be surprised to learn that JavaScript allows math to be performed using all of the listed number formats. Try the following exercise.

Performing hexadecimal math with JavaScript

1. Using Microsoft Visual Studio, Eclipse, or another editor, edit the file example1.html in the Chapter04 sample files folder in the companion content.

2. Within the webpage, replace the TODO comment with the boldface code shown here:

```
<!doctype html>
<html>
<head>
<title>Hexadecimal Numbers</title>
<script type="text/javascript">
var h = 0xe;
var i = 0x2;
var j = h * i;
alert(j);
</script>
</head>
<body>
</body>
</html>
```

3. View the webpage in a browser. You should see a dialog box similar to this one:

The preceding script first defines two variables (you learn about defining variables later in this chapter) and sets them equal to two hexadecimal numbers, *0xe* (14 in base 10 notation) and *0x2*, respectively:

```
var h = 0xe;
var i = 0x2;
```

Then a new variable is created and set to the product of the previous two variables, as follows:

```
var j = h * i;
```

The resulting variable is then passed to the *alert()* function, which displays the dialog box in the preceding step 3. It's interesting to note that even though you multiplied two hexadecimal numbers, the output in the alert dialog box is in base 10 format.

Numeric functions

JavaScript has some built-in functions (and objects, too, which you learn about soon) for working with numeric values. The European Computer Manufacturers Association (ECMA) standard defines several of them. One more common numeric function is the *isNaN()* function. By *common*, I mean that *isNaN()* is a function that I use frequently in JavaScript programming. Your usage might vary, but an explanation follows nonetheless.

NaN is an abbreviation for *Not a Number,* and it represents an illegal number. You use the *isNaN()* function to determine whether a number is legal or valid according to the ECMA-262 specification. For example, a number divided by zero would be an illegal number in JavaScript. The string value "This is not a number" is obviously also not a number. Although people might have a different interpretation of what is and isn't a number, the string "four" is not a number to the *isNaN()* function, whereas the string "4" is. The *isNaN()* function requires some mental yoga at times because it attempts to prove a negative—that the value in a variable *is not* a number. Here are a couple of examples that you can try to test whether a number is illegal.

Testing the *isNaN()* function (test 1)

1. In Microsoft Visual Studio, Eclipse, or another editor, create a new HTML file or edit the isnan.html file in the companion content.

2. In the file, place the following markup. If you've created a new file with Vision Studio, delete any existing contents first.

```html
<!doctype html>
<html>
<head>
<title>isNaN</title>
</head>
<body>
<script type="text/javascript">
document.write("Is Not a Number: " + isNaN("4"));
</script>
</body>
</html>
```

3. View this page in a browser. In Visual Studio, press F5. You'll see a page like this one:

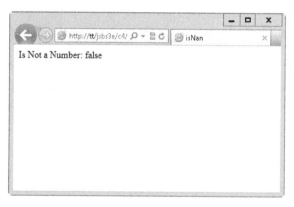

The function *isNaN()* returns *false* from this expression because the integer value 4 *is* a number. Remember that the meaning of this function is, "Is 4 Not a Number?" Well, 4 *is* a number, so the result is *false*.

Now consider the next example.

Testing the *isNaN()* function (test 2)

1. If you're running through Microsoft Visual Studio, stop the project. For those not running Visual Studio, close the web browser.

2. Edit isnan.html.

3. Change the *isNaN()* function line to read:

```javascript
document.write("Is Not a Number: " + isNaN("four"));
```

View the page in a browser, or rerun the project in Visual Studio. You'll now see a page like this:

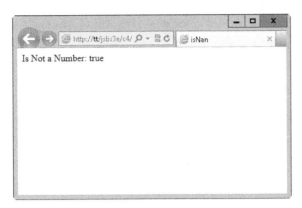

In second test case, because the numeral 4 is represented as a string of nonnumeric characters (*four*), the function returns *true*: the string *four* is not a number. I purposefully used double quotation marks in each code example (that is, *"4"* and *"four"*) to show that the quotation marks don't matter for this function. Because JavaScript is smart enough to realize that *"4"* is a number, JavaScript does the type conversion for you. However, this conversion can sometimes be a disadvantage, such as when you're counting on a variable or value to be a certain type.

The *isNaN()* function is used frequently when validating input to determine whether something— maybe a form variable—was entered as a number or as text.

Numeric constants

Other numeric constants are available in JavaScript, some of which are described in Table 4-1. These constants might or might not be useful to you in your JavaScript programming, but they exist if you need them.

TABLE 4-1 Selected numeric constants

Constant	Description
Infinity	Represents positive infinity
Number.MAX_VALUE	The largest number able to be represented in JavaScript
Number.MIN_VALUE	The smallest or most negative number able to be represented in JavaScript
Number.NEGATIVE_INFINITY	A value representing negative infinity
Number.POSITIVE_INFINITY	A value representing positive infinity

The *Math* object

The *Math* object is a special built-in object used for working with numbers in JavaScript, and it has several properties that are helpful to the JavaScript programmer, including properties that return the value of pi, the square root of a number, a pseudo-random number, and an absolute value.

Some properties are value properties, meaning they return a value, whereas others act like functions and return values based on the arguments sent into them. Consider this example of the *Math.PI* value property. Place this code between the opening *<SCRIPT TYPE="text/javascript">* and closing *</SCRIPT>* tags in your sample page:

```
document.write(Math.PI);
```

The result is shown in Figure 4-1.

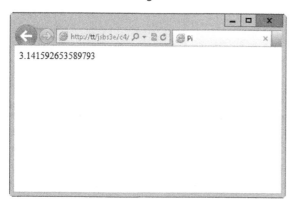

FIGURE 4-1 Viewing the value of the *Math.PI* property.

Dot notation

Dot notation is so named because a single period, or *dot*, is used to access the members of an object. The single dot (.) creates an easy visual delineator between elements. For example, to access a property that you might call the "length of a variable *room*," you would write *room.length*. The *dot* operator is used similarly in many programming languages.

Several other properties of the *Math* object can be helpful to your program. Some of them act as functions or methods on the object, several of which are listed in Table 4-2. You can obtain a complete list of properties for the *Math* object in the ECMA-262 specification at *http://www.ecma-international.org/publications/files/ECMA-ST/Ecma-262.pdf*.

TABLE 4-2 Select function properties of the *Math* object

Property	Definition
Math.random()	Returns a pseudo-random number
Math.abs(x)	Returns the absolute value of x
Math.pow(x,y)	Returns x to the power of y
Math.round(x)	Returns x rounded to the nearest integer value

Working with strings

Strings are another basic data type available in JavaScript. They consist of one (technically zero) or more characters surrounded by quotation marks. The following examples are strings:

- *"Hello world"*

- *"B"*

- *"This is 'another string'"*

The last example in the preceding list requires some explanation. Strings are surrounded by either single or double quotation marks. Strings enclosed in single quotation marks can contain double quotation marks. Likewise, a string enclosed in double quotation marks, like the ones you see in the preceding example, can contain single quotation marks. So basically, if the string is surrounded by one type of quotation mark, you can use the other type within it. Here are some more examples:

- *'The cow says "moo".'*

- *'The talking clock says the time is "Twelve Noon".'*

- *"'Everyone had a good time' was the official slogan."*

Escaping quotation marks

If you use the same style of quotation mark both within the string and to enclose the string, the quotation marks must be *escaped* so that they won't be interpreted by the JavaScript engine. A single backslash character (\) escapes the quotation mark, as in these examples:

- *'I\'m using single quotation marks both outside and within this example. They\'re neat.'*

- *"This is a \"great\" example of using \"double quotes\" within a string that's enclosed with \"double quotes\" too."*

Other escape characters

JavaScript enables other characters to be represented with specific escape sequences that can appear within a string. Table 4-3 shows those escape sequences.

TABLE 4-3 Escape sequences in JavaScript

Escape character	Sequence value
\b	Backspace
\t	Tab
\n	Newline
\v	Vertical tab
\f	Form feed
\r	Carriage return
\\	Literal backslash

Here's an example of some escape sequences in action.

Using escape sequences

1. In Visual Studio, Eclipse, or another editor, open your sample page.

2. Within the *<SCRIPT>* section, place the following line of JavaScript:

    ```
    document.write("hello\t\t\"hello\"goodbye");
    ```

3. View the page in a browser. You'll see a page like the following. Notice that the tab characters don't show through because the browser interprets HTML and not tab characters.

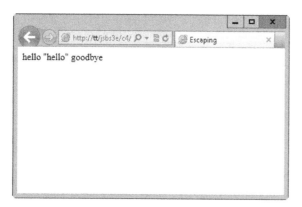

This rather contrived example shows escape sequences in action. In the code, the word *hello* is followed by two tabs, represented by their escape sequence of \t, followed by an escaped double-quote \" and then the word *hello* followed by another escaped double-quote \", finally followed by the word *goodbye*.

String methods and properties

JavaScript defines several properties and methods for working with strings. These properties and methods are accessed using dot notation ("."), explained earlier in this chapter and familiar to many programmers.

> **Note** In the same way I describe only some of the elements of JavaScript in this book, I cover only a subset of the string properties and methods available in the ECMA-262 specification. Refer to the ECMA specification for more information.

The *length* property on a *string* object gives the length of a string, not including the enclosing quotation marks. The *length* property can be called directly on a string literal, as in this example:

```
alert("This is a string.".length);
```

However, it's much more common to call the *length* property on a variable, like this:

```
var x = "This is a string.";
alert(x.length);
```

Both examples give the same result.

Some commonly used *string* methods, besides *substring*, include *slice, substr, concat, toUpperCase, toLowerCase,* and the pattern matching methods of *match, search,* and *replace.* I discuss each of these briefly.

Methods that change strings include *slice, substring, substr,* and *concat.* The *slice* and *substring* methods return string values based on another string. They accept two arguments: the beginning position and an optional end position. Here are some examples:

```
var myString = "This is a string.";
alert(myString.substring(3));  //Returns "s is a string."
alert(myString.substring(3,9));  //Returns "s is a"
alert(myString.slice(3));  //Returns "s is a string."
alert(myString.slice(3,9));  //Returns "s is a"
```

A subtle difference between *slice* and *substring* is how they handle arguments with negative values. The *substring* method will convert any negative values to 0, while *slice* will treat negative arguments as the starting point from the end of the string (counting backwards from the end, essentially).

The *substr* method also accepts two arguments: the first is the beginning position to return, and, in contrast to *substring/slice,* the second argument is the number of characters to return, not the stopping position. Therefore, the code examples for *substring/slice* work a little differently with *substr*:

```
var myString = "This is a string.";
alert(myString.substr(3));  //Returns "s is a string." (The same as substring/slice)
alert(myString.substr(3,9));  //Returns "s is a st" (Different from substring/slice)
```

The *concat* method concatenates two strings together:

```
var firstString = "Hello ";
var finalString = firstString.concat("World");
alert(finalString);  //Outputs "Hello World"
```

It's somewhat more common to use the plus sign (+) for concatenation, so the same output could be accomplished with this:

```
var finalString = firstString + "World";
```

The *toUpperCase* and *toLowerCase* methods, and their brethren *toLocaleUpperCase* and *toLocaleLowerCase,* convert a string to all uppercase or all lowercase, respectively:

```
var myString = "this is a String";
alert(myString.toUpperCase());  // "THIS IS A STRING"
alert(myString.toLowerCase());  // "this is a string"
```

Note The *toLocale* methods perform conversions in a locale-specific manner.

As I stated, numerous string properties and methods exist. The remainder of the book features other string properties and methods, and you can always find a complete list within the ECMA specification at *http://www.ecma-international.org/publications/files/ECMA-ST/Ecma-262.pdf*.

Booleans

Booleans are kind of a hidden, or passive, data type in JavaScript. By *hidden,* or *passive*, I mean that you don't work with Booleans in the same way that you work with strings and numbers; you can define and use a Boolean variable, but typically you just use an expression that evaluates to a Boolean value. Booleans have only two values, *true* and *false*, and in practice, you rarely set variables as such. Rather, you use Boolean expressions within tests, such as an *if/then/else* statement.

Consider this statement:

```
If (myNumber > 18) {
    //do something
}
```

A Boolean expression is used within the *if* statement's condition to determine whether the code within the braces will be executed. If the content of the variable *myNumber* is greater than the integer 18, the Boolean expression evaluates to *true*; otherwise, the Boolean evaluates to *false*.

Null

Null is another special data type in JavaScript (as it is in most languages). *Null* is, simply, nothing. It represents and evaluates to *false*. When a value is *null*, it is nothing and contains nothing. However, don't confuse this nothingness with being empty. An empty value or variable is still full; it's just full of emptiness. Emptiness is different from *null*, which is just plain nothing. For example, defining a variable and setting its value to an empty string looks like this:

```
var myVariable = '';
```

The variable *myVariable* is empty, but it is not null.

Undefined

Undefined is a state, sometimes used like a value, to represent a variable that hasn't yet contained a value. This state is different from *null*, although both *null* and *undefined* can evaluate the same way. You'll learn how to distinguish between a null value and an undefined value in Chapter 5, "Using operators and expressions."

Objects

Like functions, objects are special enough to get their own chapter (Chapter 8, to be exact). But I still discuss objects here briefly. JavaScript is an object-based language, as opposed to a full-blown object-oriented language. JavaScript implements some functionality similar to object-oriented functionality, and for most basic usages of JavaScript, you won't notice the difference.

Objects in JavaScript are a collection of properties, each of which can contain a value. These properties—think of them as *keys*—enable access to values. Each value stored in the properties can be a value, another object, or even a function. You can define your own objects with JavaScript, or you can use the several built-in objects.

Objects are created with curly braces, so the following code creates an empty object called *myObject*:

```
var myObject = {};
```

Here's an object with several properties:

```
var dvdCatalog = {
    "identifier": "1",
    "name": "Coho Vineyard"
};
```

The preceding code example creates an object called *dvdCatalog*, which holds two properties: one called *identifier* and the other called *name*. The values contained in each property are *1* and *"Coho Vineyard"*, respectively. You could access the *name* property of the *dvdCatalog* object like this:

```
alert(dvdCatalog.name);
```

Here's a more complete example of an object, which can also be found in the sample code in the file object.txt:

```
// Create four new objects
var star = {};
// Create properties  for each of four stars.
star["Polaris"] = new Object;
star["Deneb"] = new Object;
star["Vega"] = new Object;
star["Altair"] = new Object;
```

Examples later in the book show how to add properties to these objects and how to access properties. There's much more to objects, and Chapter 8 gives that additional detail.

Arrays

You've seen in the previous example how to create an object with a name. You can also use array elements that are accessed by a numbered index value. These are the traditional arrays, familiar to programmers in many languages. You just saw several objects, each named for a star. The following code creates an array with four elements.

```
var star = new Array();
star[0] = "Polaris";
star[1] = "Deneb";
star[2] = "Vega";
star[3] = "Altair";
```

The same code can also be written like this, using literal notation, represented by square brackets:

```
var star = ["Polaris", "Deneb", "Vega", "Altair"];
```

Arrays can contain nested values, creating an array of arrays, as in this example that combines the star name with the constellation in which it appears:

```
var star = [["Polaris", "Ursa Minor"],["Deneb","Cygnus"],["Vega","Lyra"],
["Altair","Aquila"]];
```

Finally, although less common, you can call the *Array()* constructor with arguments:

```
var star = new Array("Polaris", "Deneb", "Vega", "Altair");
```

 Note Calling the *Array()* constructor with a single numeric argument sets the length of the array rather than the value of the first element, which is what you might expect.

The new ECMA-262 edition 5 specification added several new methods for iterating and working with arrays. Arrays, including methods that iterate through them and work with them, are covered in more detail in Chapter 8.

Defining and using variables

Variables should be familiar to programmers in just about any language. Variables store data that might change during the program's execution lifetime. You've seen several examples of declaring variables throughout the previous chapters of this book. This section formalizes the use of variables in JavaScript.

Declaring variables

Variables are declared in JavaScript with the *var* keyword. The following are all valid variable declarations:

```
var x;
var myVar;
var counter1;
```

Variable names can contain uppercase and lowercase letters as well as numbers, but they cannot start with a number. Variables cannot contain spaces or other punctuation, with the exception of the underscore character (_). The following variable names are invalid:

```
var 1stCounter;
var new variable;
var new.variable;
var var;
```

Take a look at the preceding example. Whereas the first three variable names are invalid because characters are used that aren't valid at all (or aren't valid in that position, as is the case with the first example), the last variable name, *var*, is invalid because it uses a keyword. For more information about keywords or reserved words in JavaScript, refer to Chapter 3, "JavaScript syntax and statements."

You can declare multiple variables on the same line of code, as follows:

```
var x, y, zeta;
```

These can be initialized on the same line, too:

```
var x = 1, y = "hello", zeta = 14;
```

Variable types

Variables in JavaScript are not strongly typed. It's not necessary to declare whether a given variable will hold an integer, a floating point number, or a string. You can also change the type of data being held within a variable through simple reassignment. Consider this example, where the variable x first holds an integer but then, through another assignment, it changes to hold a string:

```
var x = 4;
x = "Now it's a string.";
```

Variable scope

A variable's *scope* refers to the locations from which its value can be accessed. Variables are *globally scoped* when they are used outside a function. A globally scoped variable can be accessed throughout your JavaScript program. In the context of a webpage—or a document, as you might think of it—you can access and use a global variable throughout.

Variables defined within a function are scoped solely within that function. This effectively means that the values of those variables cannot be accessed outside the function. Function parameters are scoped locally to the function as well.

Here are some practical examples of scoping, which you can also find in the companion code in the scope1.html file:

```
<script type="text/javascript">
var aNewVariable = "I'm Global.";
function doSomething(incomingBits) {
    alert(aNewVariable);
    alert(incomingBits);
}
doSomething("An argument");
</script>
```

The code defines two variables: a global variable called *aNewVariable* and a variable called *incomingBits,* which is local to the *doSomething()* function. Both variables are passed to respective *alert()* functions within the *doSomething()* function. When the *doSomething()* function is called, the contents of both variables are sent successfully and displayed on the screen, as depicted in Figures 4-2 and 4-3.

FIGURE 4-2 The variable *aNewVariable* is globally scoped.

FIGURE 4-3 The variable *incomingBits* is locally scoped to the function.

Here's a more complex example for you to try.

Examining variable scope

1. Using Visual Studio, Eclipse, or another editor, edit the file scoping.html in the Chapter04 sample files folder, which you can find in the companion content.

2. Within the page, replace the TODO comment with the boldface code shown here (the new code can be found in the scoping.txt file in the companion content):

```
<!doctype html>
<html>
<head>
    <title>Scoping Example</title>
    <script type="text/javascript">
    var aNewVariable = "is global.";
    function doSomething(incomingBits) {
        alert("Global variable within the function: " + aNewVariable);
        alert("Local variable within the function: " + incomingBits);
    }
    </script>

</head>
<body>
<script type="text/javascript">
```

```
    doSomething("is a local variable");
    alert("Global var outside the function: " + aNewVariable);
    alert("Local var outside the function: " + incomingBits);

</script>
</body>
</html>
```

3. Save the file.

4. View the file in a web browser. The result is three alerts on the screen.

   The first alert is this:

   The second alert is this:

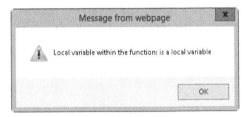

   The third alert looks like this:

But wait a minute—examine the code. How many calls to the *alert()* function do you see? Hint: two are in the *<HEAD>* portion, and another two are within the *<BODY>* portion, for a total of four calls to the *alert()* function. So why are there only three alerts on the screen when four calls are made to the *alert()* function in the script?

Because this is a section on variable scoping (and I already explained the answer), you might already have figured it out. But this example demonstrates well how to troubleshoot JavaScript problems when the result isn't what you expect.

The next procedure requires the use of the Firebug add-on to the Mozilla Firefox web browser. As a web developer, I'm going to assume that you have Firefox installed. (See Chapter 1, "JavaScript is more than you might think," for reasons why you should.) If you don't yet have Firefox, download it from *http://www.mozilla.com/firefox/*.

Installing Firebug

This first procedure walks you through installing Firebug in Firefox. Although Internet Explorer has a script debugger, and you could also use F12 Developer Tools, Firebug is very powerful and flexible.

1. With Firefox installed, it's time to get the Firebug add-on. Accomplish this task by going to *http://www.getfirebug.com/*. On that site, click the Install Firebug link. When you do so, you'll be asked to choose the version of Firebug to install. Install the version that corresponds to your version of Firefox (or is as close as possible to the version of Firefox that you have).

2. When you click the install link, you'll be sent to Mozilla's site, where you get to click another button, this one labeled "Add To Firefox." A Software Installation dialog box opens, as shown in the following screen. Click Install Now.

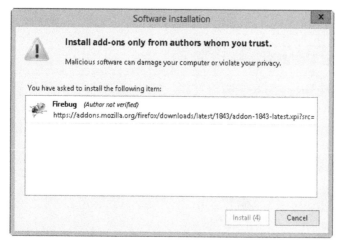

3. The installation completes when you restart Firefox, so click Restart Firefox after the add-on finishes downloading.

4. Firefox closes and opens again, showing the installed add-on. Congratulations! Firebug is installed. Notice a small icon in the upper-right corner of the Firefox browser window. (The Firefox development team keeps moving buttons around, so the Firebug button might not be in the upper right when you read this.) Click the icon to open the Firebug console, shown here:

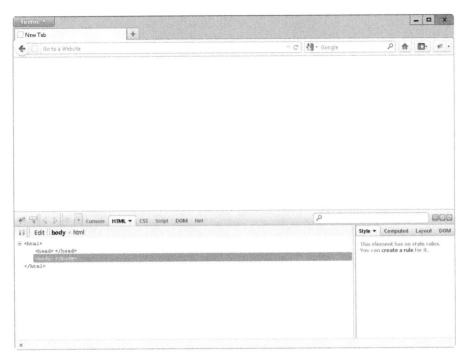

5. Firebug's JavaScript console is disabled, but don't worry—the next procedure walks you through enabling and using it. Feel free to experiment with Firebug by enabling it.

With Firebug installed, you can troubleshoot the earlier problem you encountered in the scoping example of only three of the four expected alerts being displayed.

Troubleshooting with Firebug

1. Open Firefox and open the scoping.html example that was created earlier in this chapter. The JavaScript code again executes as before, showing the three alerts. Close all three alerts. You end up with a blank page loaded in Firefox.

2. Click the Firebug icon in Firefox browser window so that Firebug opens.

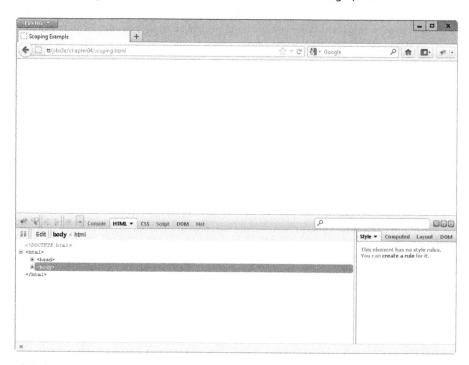

3. Click the Script tab to open the Script pane, and notice that it is disabled. Click the arrow/triangle next to the word *Script*, and click Enabled.

4. Click the Console tab, click the arrow/triangle next to the word *Console*, and click Enabled. You can see here that the Console is now activated:

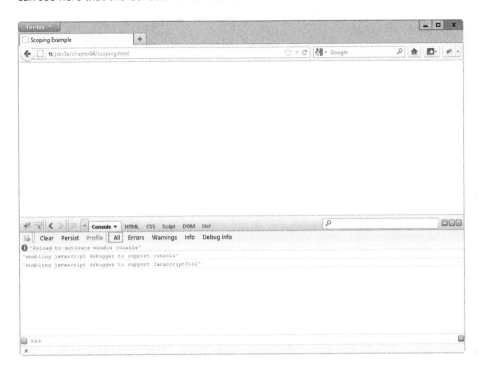

5. With both the Console and Script panes enabled, click the Reload button on the main Firefox toolbar. The page reloads, and the JavaScript executes again. All three alerts are displayed again, but notice now that Firebug has discovered an error, denoted by the red X indication in the Firebug Console:

6. The error, as you can see, is that the variable *incomingBits* isn't defined. This window also shows the line number at which the problem occurred. However, notice that because of the way the document is parsed, the line number in your original source code might not always be accurate. Regardless, you can see that *incomingBits* is not defined within the *<BODY>* section of the webpage because its scope is limited to the *doSomething()* function.

This procedure demonstrated not only the use of Firebug but also the effect of local versus global scoping of variables. Firebug is an integral part of JavaScript (and webpage) debugging. I invite you to spend some time with Firebug on just about any site to see how JavaScript, CSS, and HTML all interact.

In this procedure, the fix would be to define the variable *incomingBits* so that it gets instantiated outside the function call. (This new line of code follows and is in the file scoping-fixed.html in the Chapter04 folder in the companion content.) Because this variable was defined only as part of the function definition, the variable didn't exist outside the function's scope.

```
<!doctype html>
<html>
<head>
    <title>Scoping Example</title>
    <script type="text/javascript">
```

```
        var aNewVariable = "is global.";
        function doSomething(incomingBits) {
            alert("Global variable within the function: " + aNewVariable);
            alert("Local variable within the function: " + incomingBits);
        }

    </script>

</head>
<body>
<script type="text/javascript">
    var incomingBits = " must be defined if necessary.";
    doSomething("is a local variable");
    alert("Global var outside the function: " + aNewVariable);
    alert("Local var outside the function: " + incomingBits);

</script>
</body>
</html>
```

You can find more information about functions in Chapter 7, "Working with functions."

The *Date* object

The *Date* object includes many methods that are helpful when working with dates in JavaScript—too many, in fact, to examine in any depth in a broad-based book such as this—but I do show you some examples that you might incorporate in your projects.

One of the unfortunate aspects of the *Date* object in JavaScript is that the implementation of its methods varies greatly depending on the browser and the operating system. For example, consider this code to return a date for the current time, adjusted for the local time zone and formatted automatically by the *toLocaleDateString()* method:

```
var myDate = new Date();
alert(myDate.toLocaleDateString());
```

When run in Internet Explorer 10 on a computer running Windows 8, the code results in a date like that shown in Figure 4-4.

FIGURE 4-4 The *toLocaleString()* method of the *Date* object in Internet Explorer 8.

Figure 4-5 shows what happens when that same code is executed in Firefox 12 on a Mac.

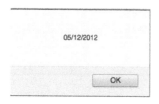

FIGURE 4-5 The *toLocaleString()* method of the *Date* object displays the message differently in Firefox on Mac.

The difference between these two dialog boxes might seem trivial, but if you were expecting to use the day of the week in your code (Monday, in the examples), you'd be in for a surprise. And don't be fooled into thinking that the implementation issues are merely cross-operating system problems. Differences in the implementation of the *Date* object and its methods exist in browsers on products running Microsoft Windows as well.

The only way to resolve these and other implementation differences in your JavaScript application is to perform both cross-browser and cross-platform tests. Doing so adds time to the application development cycle, but finding and fixing a problem during development is probably less costly than finding and fixing the problem after users discover it in a production environment.

The *Date* object can be handed a number of arguments, ranging from zero arguments to up to seven arguments. When the *Date* object constructor is passed a single string argument, the string is assumed to contain the date. When it is passed a number type of argument, the argument is assumed to be the date in milliseconds since January 1, 1970, and when it is passed seven arguments, they're assumed to be the following:

```
new Date(year, month, day, hours, minutes, seconds, milliseconds)
```

Note Only *year* and *month* are required arguments; the others are optional.

Remember the following points when using a *Date* object:

- The year should be given with four digits unless you want to specify a year between the year 1900 and the year 2000, in which case you'd just send in the two-digit year, 0 through 99, which is then added to 1900. So, 2008 equals the year 2008, but 98 is turned into 1998.

- The month is represented by an integer 0 through 11, with 0 being January and 11 being December.

- The day is an integer from 1 to 31.

- Hours are represented by 0 through 23, where 23 represents 11 P.M.

- Minutes and seconds are both integers ranging from 0 to 59.

- Milliseconds are an integer from 0 to 999.

Although the following procedure uses some items that won't be covered until later chapters, you're looking at the *Date* object now, so it's a good time learn how to write the date and time to a webpage—a popular operation.

Writing the date and time to a webpage

1. Using Visual Studio, Eclipse, or another editor, edit the file writingthedate.html in the Chapter04 sample files folder in the companion content.

2. Within the page, add the code in boldface type shown here:

```
<!doctype html>
<html>
<head>
    <title>the date</title>
</head>
<body>
    <p id="dateField"> </p>
    <script type = "text/javascript">
    var myDate = new Date();
    var dateString = myDate.toLocaleDateString() + " " + myDate.toLocaleTimeString();
    var dateLoc = document.getElementById("dateField");
    dateLoc.innerHTML = "Hello - Page Rendered on " + dateString;
    </script>
</body>
</html>
```

3. When saved and viewed in a web browser, you should receive a page like this (although the date you see will be different from what's shown here):

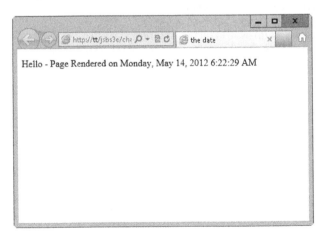

The relevant JavaScript from the preceding steps is repeated here:

```
var myDate = new Date();
var dateString = myDate.toLocaleDateString() + " " + myDate.toLocaleTimeString();
var dateLoc = document.getElementById("dateField");
dateLoc.innerHTML = "Hello - Page Rendered on " + dateString;
```

The JavaScript related to the *Date* object is rather simple. It takes advantage of the *toLocaleDateString()* method, which you've already seen, and its cousin, *toLocaleTimeString()*, which returns the local time. These two methods are concatenated together with a single space and placed into the *dateString* variable, like this:

```
var dateString = myDate.toLocaleDateString() + " " + myDate.toLocaleTimeString();
```

The remainder of the code writes the contents of the *dateString* variable to the webpage, which is covered in more detail in Part 2.

Counting down to a certain date in the future

1. Using Visual Studio, Eclipse, or another editor, edit the file countdown.html in the Chapter04 sample files folder, which you can find in the companion content.

2. Add the following code shown in boldface type to the page:

```
<!doctype html>
<html>
<head>
    <title>the date</title>
</head>
<body>
    <p id="dateField"> </p>
    <script type = "text/javascript">
    var today = new Date();
    var then = new Date();
    // January 1, 2014
    then.setFullYear(2014,0,1);
    var diff = then.getTime() - today.getTime();
    diff = Math.floor(diff / (1000 * 60 * 60 * 24));
    var dateLoc = document.getElementById("dateField");
    dateLoc.innerHTML = "There are " + diff + " days until 1/1/2014";
    </script>

</body>
</html>
```

3. Save the page, and view it in a web browser. Depending on the date on your computer, the number of days represented will be different, but the general appearance of the page should look like this:

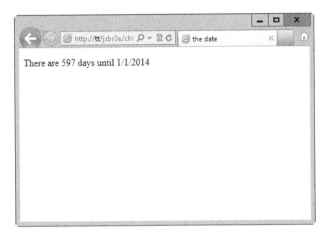

Tip Be careful when using JavaScript dates for anything other than displaying them. Because the dates are dependent on the visitor's time, don't rely on them when an accurate time might be important—for example, in an ordering process.

The exercise you just completed used some additional functions of both the *Math* and *Date* objects, namely *floor()* and *getTime()*. While this book covers a lot of ground, it's not a complete JavaScript language reference. For that and even more information, refer to the ECMA-262 standard at *http://www.ecma-international.org/publications/standards/Ecma-262.htm*.

The next procedure shows how to calculate (or better yet, roughly estimate) the time it takes for a webpage to load in a person's browser.

Note The next procedure isn't accurate because it doesn't take into consideration the time required for the loading and rendering of images (or other multimedia items), which are external to the text of the webpage. A few more bits load after the script is finished running.

1. Using Visual Studio, Eclipse, or another editor, edit the file render.html in the Chapter04 sample files folder, which you can find in the companion content.

2. Add the following code shown in boldface type to the page:

```
<!doctype html>
<html>
<head>
    <title>the date</title>
    <script type = "text/javascript">
    var started = new Date();
    var now = started.getTime();
    </script>
</head>
<body>
    <p id="dateField"> </p>
    <script type = "text/javascript">
    var bottom = new Date();
    var diff = (bottom.getTime() - now)/1000;
    var finaltime = diff.toPrecision(5);
    var dateLoc = document.getElementById("dateField");
    dateLoc.innerHTML = "Page rendered in " + finaltime + " seconds.";
    </script>

</body>
</html>
```

3. Save the page, and view it in a web browser. Depending on the speed of your computer, web server, and network connection, you might receive a page that indicates only 0 seconds for the page load time, like this:

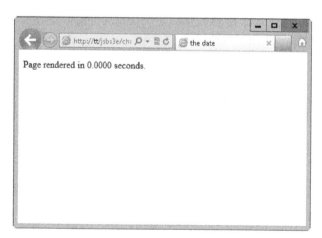

4. If your page takes 0.0000 seconds, as mine did, you can introduce a delay into the page so that you can test it. (I'd never recommend doing this on a live site because I can't think of a reason you'd want to slow down the rendering of your page! But introducing a delay can come in handy for testing purposes.) Using a *for* loop is a cheap and easy way to slow down the JavaScript execution:

```
for (var i = 0; i < 1000000; i++) {
   //delay

}
```

The value I chose, 1000000, is arbitrary. You might need to choose a larger or smaller number to cause the desired delay. The final code looks like this:

```
<!doctype html>
<html>
<head>
    <title>the date</title>
    <script type = "text/javascript">
    var started = new Date();
    var now = started.getTime();
    for (var i = 0; i < 1000000; i++) {
        //delay
    }
    </script>
</head>
<body>
    <p id="dateField"> </p>
    <script type = "text/javascript">
    var bottom = new Date();
    var diff = (bottom.getTime() - now)/1000;
    var finaltime = diff.toPrecision(5);
    var dateLoc = document.getElementById("dateField");
    dateLoc.innerHTML = "Page rendered in " + finaltime + " seconds.";
    </script>

</body>
</html>
```

5. Save the page, and view it again in a web browser. You should see some delay in the page load, which causes the value to be a positive number:

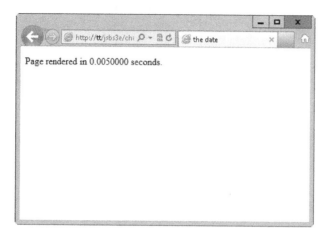

When using this or similar functions to determine the page load times, to calculate the most accurate value, place the initial variable near the top of the page or script, and then place another one near the bottom of the page.

Note The *now()* method of the *Date()* object can also be used as a substitute for *getTime()*.

You just learned about a few of the more than 40 methods of the *Date* object. Many of these methods have UTC (Coordinated Universal Time) counterparts, meaning that they can get or set the date and time in UTC rather than local time. Table 4-4 lists the methods that return dates. With the exception of *getTime()* and *getTimezoneOffset()*, all these methods have UTC counterparts that are called using the format *getUTCDate()*, *getUTCDay()*, and so on.

TABLE 4-4 The *get* methods of the *Date* object

Method	Description
getDate()	Returns the day of the month
getDay()	Returns the day of the week
getFullYear()	Returns the four-digit year and is recommended in most circumstances over the *getYear()* method
getHours()	Returns the hours of a date
getMilliseconds()	Returns the milliseconds of a date
getMinutes()	Returns the minutes of a date
getMonth()	Returns the month of a date
getSeconds()	Returns the seconds of a date
getTime()	Returns the milliseconds since January 1, 1970
getTimezoneOffset()	Returns the number of minutes calculated as the difference between UTC and local time

Many of the *get...()* methods have siblings prefixed with *set*, as shown in Table 4-5. And like their *get* brethren, most of the *set...()* methods have UTC counterparts, except for *setTime()*.

TABLE 4-5 The *set* methods of the *Date* object

Method	Description
setDate()	Sets the day of the month of a date
setFullYear()	Sets the four-digit year of a date; also accepts the month and day-of-month integers
setHours()	Sets the hour of a date
setMilliseconds()	Sets the milliseconds of a date
setMinutes()	Sets the minutes of a date
setMonth()	Sets the month as an integer of a date
setSeconds()	Sets the seconds of a date
setTime()	Sets the time using milliseconds since January 1, 1970

The *Date* object also has several methods for converting the date to a string in a different format. You already reviewed some of these methods, such as *toLocaleDateString()*. Other similar methods include *toLocaleString()*, *toLocaleTimeString()*, *toString()*, *toISOString()*, *toDateString()*, *toUTCString()*, and *toTimeString()*. Feel free to experiment with these, noting that *toISOString()* is a new method in the ECMA-262 version 5 specification and support for it might not be available in all browsers. (It's notably missing from most versions of Internet Explorer.) The following simple one-line code examples will get you started experimenting. Try typing them in the address bar of your browser:

```
javascript:var myDate = new Date(); alert(myDate.toLocaleDateString());

javascript:var myDate = new Date(); alert(myDate.toLocaleString());

javascript:var myDate = new Date(); alert(myDate.toGMTString());

javascript:var myDate = new Date(); alert(myDate.toLocaleTimeString());

javascript:var myDate = new Date(); alert(myDate.toString());

javascript:var myDate = new Date(); alert(myDate.toISOString());

javascript:var myDate = new Date(); alert(myDate.toDateString());

javascript:var myDate = new Date(); alert(myDate.toUTCString());

javascript:var myDate = new Date(); alert(myDate.toTimeString());
```

You can also write these code samples without creating the *myDate* variable, like so:

```
javascript: alert(new Date().toUTCString());
```

Using the *RegExp* object

Regular expressions are the syntax you use to match and manipulate strings. If you've heard of or worked with regular expressions before, don't be alarmed. Regular expressions have an unnecessarily bad reputation solely because of their looks. And, lucky for me, we shouldn't judge things solely on looks alone. With that said, if you've had a bad experience with regular expressions, I'd ask that you read through this section with an open mind and see whether my explanation helps clear up some confusion.

The primary reason that I have confidence in your ability to understand regular expressions is that you're a programmer, and programmers use logic to reduce problems to small and simple pieces. When writing or reading a regular expression, the key is to reduce the problem to small pieces and work through each.

Another reason to have confidence is that you've probably worked with something close to regular expressions before, so all you need to do is extend what you already know. If you've worked with a command prompt in Microsoft Windows or with the shell in Linux/Unix, you might have looked for files by trying to match all files using an asterisk, or star (*) character, as in:

```
dir *.*
```

or:

```
dir *.txt
```

If you've used a wildcard character such as the asterisk, you've used an element akin to a regular expression. In fact, the asterisk is also a character used in regular expressions.

In JavaScript, regular expressions are used with the *RegExp* object and some syntax called *regular expression literals*. These elements provide a powerful way to work with strings of text or alphanumerics. The ECMA-262 implementation of regular expressions is largely borrowed from the Perl 5 regular expression parser. Here's a regular expression to match the word *JavaScript*:

```
var myRegex = /JavaScript/;
```

The regular expression shown would match the string "JavaScript" anywhere that it appeared within another string. For example, the regular expression would match in the sentence "This is a book about JavaScript," and it would match in the string "ThisIsAJavaScriptBook," but it would not match "This is a book about javascript," because regular expressions are case sensitive. (You can change this, as you'll see later in this chapter.)

With that short introduction you're now prepared to look at regular expressions in more detail. The knowledge you gain here will prepare you for the remainder of the book, helping you not only understand how to work with strings in JavaScript but also understand how to use regular expressions in other languages. This section provides a reference for regular expression syntax and shows a couple simple examples.

The syntax of regular expressions

Regular expressions have a terse—and some would argue cryptic—syntax. But don't let terse syntax scare you away from regular expressions, because in that syntax is power. This is a brief introduction to regular expressions. It's not meant to be exhaustive. (There are entire books on regular expressions.) However, you'll find that this gentle introduction will serve you well for the remainder of the book. Don't worry if this material doesn't sink in on the first read through. There are multiple tables that make it easy to use as a reference later.

The syntax of regular expressions includes several characters that have special meaning, including characters that anchor the match to the beginning or end of a string, a wildcard, and groups of characters, among others.

Table 4-6 shows several of the special characters.

TABLE 4-6 Common special characters in JavaScript regular expressions

Character	Description
^	Sets an anchor to the beginning of the input.
$	Sets an anchor to the end of the input.
.	Matches any character.
*	Matches the previous character zero or more times. Think of this as a wildcard.
+	Matches the previous character one or more times.
?	Matches the previous character zero or one time.
()	Places any matching characters inside the parentheses into a group. This group can then be referenced later, such as in a replace operation.
{n, }	Matches the previous character at least n times.
{n,m}	Matches the previous character at least n but no more than m times.
[ ]	Defines a character class to match any of the characters contained in the brackets. This character can use a range like 0–9 to match any number or like a–z to match any letter.
[^]	The use of a caret within a character class negates that character class, meaning that the characters in that class cannot appear in the match.
\	Typically used as an escape character, and meaning that whatever follows the backslash is treated as a literal character instead of as having its special meaning. Can also be used to define special character sets, which are shown in Table 4-7.

In addition to the special characters, several sequences exist to match groups of characters or nonalphanumeric characters. Some of these sequences are shown in Table 4-7.

TABLE 4-7 Common character sequences in JavaScript regular expressions

Character	Match
\b	Word boundary.
\B	Nonword boundary.
\c	Control character when used in conjunction with another character. For example, \cA is the escape sequence for Control-A.
\d	Digit.

Character	Match
\D	Nondigit.
\n	Newline.
\r	Carriage return.
\s	Single whitespace character such as a space or tab.
\S	Single nonwhitespace character.
\t	Tab.
\w	Any alphanumeric character, whether number or letter.
\W	Any nonalphanumeric character.

And finally, in addition to the characters in Table 4-7, you can use the modifiers *i*, *g*, and *m*. The *i* modifier specifies that the regular expression should be parsed in a case-insensitive manner, while the *g* modifier indicates that the parsing should continue after the first match, sometimes called *global* or *greedy* (thus the *g*). The *m* modifier is used for multiline matching. You'll see an example of modifier use in an upcoming example.

The *RegExp* object has its own methods, including *exec* and *test*, the latter of which tests a regular expression against a string and returns *true* or *false* based on whether the regular expression matches that string. However, when working with regular expressions, using methods native to the *String* type, such as *match*, *search*, *split*, and *replace*, is just as common.

The *exec()* method of the *RegExp* object is used to parse the regular expression against a string and return the result. For example, parsing a simple URL and extracting the domain might look like this:

```
var myString = "http://www.braingia.org";
var myRegex = /http:\/\/\w+\.(.*)/i;
var results = myRegex.exec(myString);
alert(results[1]);
```

The output from this code is an alert showing the domain portion of the address, as shown in Figure 4-6.

FIGURE 4-6 Parsing a typical web URL using a regular expression.

A breakdown of this code is helpful. First you have the string declaration:

```
var myString = "http://www.braingia.org";
```

This is followed by the regular expression declaration and then a call to the *exec()* method, which parses the regular expression against the string found in *myString* and places the results into a variable called *results*.

```
var myRegex = /http:\/\/\w+\.(.*)/i;
var results = myRegex.exec(myString);
```

The regular expression contains several important elements. It begins by looking for the literal string *http:*. The two forward slashes follow, but because forward slashes (/) are special characters in regular expressions, you must escape them by using backslashes (\),making the regular expression *http:\/\/* to this point.

The next part of the regular expression, *\w*, looks for any single alphanumeric character. Web addresses are typically *www*, so don't be confused into thinking that the expression is looking for three literal *ws*—the host in this example could be called *web*, *host1*, *myhost*, or *www*, as shown in the code you're examining. Because *\w* matches any single character, and web hosts typically have three characters (*www*), the regular expression adds a special character + to indicate that the regular expression must find an alphanumeric character at least once and possibly more than once. So now the code has *http:\/\/\w+*, which matches the address *http://www* right up to the *.braingia.org* portion.

You need to account for the dot character between the host name (*www*) and the domain name (*braingia.org*). You accomplish this by adding a dot character (.), but because the dot is also a special character, you need to escape it with \.. You now have *http:\/\/\w+\.*, which matches all the elements of a typical address right up to the domain name.

Finally, you need to capture the domain and use it later, so place the domain inside parentheses. Because you don't care what the domain is or what follows it, you can use two special characters: the dot, to match any character; and the asterisk, to match any and all of the previous characters, which is any character in this example. You're left with the final regular expression, which is used by the *exec()* method. The result is placed into the *results* variable. Also note the use of the *i* modifier, to indicate that the regular expression will be parsed in a case-insensitive manner.

If a match is found, the output from the *exec()* method is an array containing the last characters matched as the first element of the array and an index for each captured portion of the expression.

In the example shown, the second element of the array (*1*) is sent to an alert, which produces the output shown in Figure 4-6.

```
alert(results[1]);
```

That's a lot to digest, and I admit this regular expression could be vastly improved with the addition of other characters to anchor the match and to account for characters after the domain as well as non-alphanumerics in the host name portion. However, in the interest of keeping the example somewhat simpler, the less-strict match is shown.

The *String* object type contains three methods for both matching and working with strings and uses regular expressions to do so. The *match*, *replace*, and *search* methods all use regular expression pattern matching. Because you've learned about regular expressions, it's time to introduce these methods.

The *match* method returns an array with the same information as the *Regexp* data type's *exec()* method. Here's an example:

```
var emailAddr = "suehring@braingia.com";
var myRegex = /\.com/;
var checkMatch = emailAddr.match(myRegex);
alert(checkMatch[0]); //Returns .com
```

This can be used in a conditional to determine whether a given email address contains the string *.com*:

```
var emailAddr = "suehring@braingia.com";
var myRegex = /\.com/;
var checkMatch = emailAddr.match(myRegex);
if (checkMatch !== null) {
    alert(checkMatch[0]); //Returns .com
}
```

The *search* method works in much the same way as the *match* method but sends back only the index (position) of the first match, as shown here:

```
var emailAddr = "suehring@braingia.com";
var myRegex = /\.com/;
var searchResult = emailAddr.search(myRegex);
alert(searchResult); //Returns 17
```

If no match is found, the *search* method returns *-1*.

The *replace* method does just what its name implies—it replaces one string with another when a match is found. Assume in the email address example that I want to change any .com email address to a .net email address. You can accomplish this by using the *replace* method, like so:

```
var emailAddr = "suehring@braingia.com";
var myRegex = /\.com$/;
var replaceWith = ".net";
var result = emailAddr.replace(myRegex,replaceWith);
alert(result); //Returns suehring@braingia.net
```

If the pattern doesn't match, the original string is placed into the *result* variable; if it does, the new value is returned.

> **Note** You can use several special characters to help with substitutions. Please see the ECMA-262 specification for more information about these methods.

Later chapters show more examples of *string* methods related to regular expressions. Feel free to use this chapter as a reference for the special characters used in regular expressions.

References and garbage collection

Some types of variables or the values they contain are primitive, whereas others are reference types. The implications of this might not mean much to you at first glance—you might not even think you'll ever care about this. But you'll change your mind the first time you encounter odd behavior with a variable that you just copied.

First, some explanation: objects, arrays, and functions operate as *reference types*, whereas numbers, Booleans, *null*, and *undefined* are known as *primitive types*. According to the ECMA-262 specification, other primitive types exist, such as *Numbers* and *Strings*, but *Strings* aren't relevant to this discussion.

When a number is copied, the behavior is what you'd expect: The original and the copy both get the same value. However, if you change the original, the copy is unaffected. Here's an example:

```
// Set the value of myNum to 20.
var myNum = 20;
// Create a new variable, anotherNum, and copy the contents of myNum to it.
// Both anotherNum and myNum are now 20.
var anotherNum = myNum;
// Change the value of myNum to 1000.
myNum = 1000;
// Display the contents of both variables.
// Note that the contents of anotherNum haven't changed.
alert(myNum);
alert(anotherNum);
```

The alerts display *1000* and *20*, respectively. When the variable *anotherNum* gets a copy of *myNum*'s contents, it holds on to the contents no matter what happens to the variable *myNum* after that. The variable does this because numbers are primitive types in JavaScript.

Contrast that example with a variable type that's a reference type, as in this example:

```
// Create an array of three numbers in a variable named myNumbers.
var myNumbers = [20, 21, 22];
// Make a copy of myNumbers in a newly created variable named copyNumbers.
var copyNumbers = myNumbers;
// Change the first index value of myNumbers to the integer 1000.
myNumbers[0] = 1000;
// Alert both.
alert(myNumbers);
alert(copyNumbers);
```

In this case, because arrays are reference types, both alerts display *1000,21,22*, even though only *myNumbers* was directly changed in the code. The moral of this story is to be aware that object, array, and function variable types are reference types, so any change to the original changes all copies.

Loosely related to this discussion of differences between primitive types and reference types is the subject of garbage collection. *Garbage collection* refers to the destruction of unused variables by the JavaScript interpreter to save memory. When a variable is no longer used within a program, the interpreter frees up the memory for reuse. It also does this for you if you're using Java Virtual machine or .NET Common Language Runtime.

This automatic freeing of memory in JavaScript is different from the way in which other languages, such as C++, deal with unused variables. In those languages, the programmer must perform the garbage collection task manually. This is all you really need to know about garbage collection.

Learning about type conversions

Before finishing the discussion on data types and variables, you should know a bit about *type conversions*, or converting between data types. JavaScript usually performs implicit type conversion for you, but in many cases, you can explicitly cast, or convert, a variable from one type to another.

Number conversions

You've already seen a conversion between two number formats, hexadecimal to base 10, in the example discussed in the section "Data types in JavaScript" earlier in this chapter. However, you can convert numbers to strings as well. JavaScript implicitly converts a number to a string when the number is used in a string context.

To explicitly convert a number to a string, cast the number as a string, as in this example:

```
// Convert myNumString as a string with value of 100
var myNumString = String(100);
```

String conversions

In the same way that you can convert numbers to strings, you can convert strings to numbers. You do this by casting the string as a number.

```
var myNumString = "100";
var myNum = Number(myNumString);
```

 Tip JavaScript converts strings to numbers automatically when those strings are used in a numeric context. However, in practice, I've had hit-or-miss luck with this implicit conversion, so I usually just convert to a number whenever I want to use a number. The downside of doing this is that you have to execute some extra code, but doing that is better than the uncertainty inherent in leaving it up to a JavaScript interpreter.

Boolean conversions

Booleans are converted to numbers automatically when used in a numeric context. The value of *true* becomes *1*, and the value of *false* becomes *0*. When used in a string context, *true* becomes "true", and *false* becomes "false". The *Boolean()* function exists if you need to explicitly convert a number or string to a Boolean value.

Exercises

1. Declare three variables—one number and two strings. The number should be *120*, and the strings should be "5150" and "Two Hundred Thirty".

2. Create a new array with three numbers and two strings or words.

3. Use the *alert()* function to display the following string, properly escaped: Steve's response was "Cool!"

4. Use Firebug to examine three of your favorite websites. Look closely for any JavaScript errors that Firebug reports. Bonus: Use Internet Explorer to view those same three websites, and debug the errors using Internet Explorer tools and other related tools.

CHAPTER 5

Using operators and expressions

After completing this chapter, you will be able to

- Understand the operators available in JavaScript.

- Use JavaScript operators to perform math, equality tests, relational tests, and assignments.

- Use the *void* operator to open a new window by using a link.

Meet the operators

The ECMA-262 specification defines assorted operators of various forms. These include the following:

- Additive operators

- Multiplicative operators

- Bitwise operators

- Equality operators

- Relational operators

- Unary operators

- Assignment operators

- The comma operator

Operators can be used both on literal values, such as the numeral 10, and on variables and other objects in JavaScript.

Additive operators

The term *additive operators* includes both addition and subtraction operators, which makes the term seem like a misnomer. But as my fifth grade math teacher would remind me, subtraction is just addition with a negative number. As you might guess, the operators for addition and subtraction are + and –, respectively. Here are some examples of how they are used:

```
4 + 5;   // This would be 9.
x + y;   // Adds x and y together.
5 - 1;   // Results in 4.
```

The addition operator operates in different ways, depending on the types of the values being added. When adding two strings, the addition operator concatenates the left and right arguments. You can get odd results when the types being added differ because JavaScript must convert one of the types before performing the addition (or any math operation). For example, you won't get the expected results when you think you have a numeric variable but the JavaScript interpreter thinks you have a string. Here are some specific examples:

```
var aNum = 947;
var aStr= "Rush";
var anotherNum = 53;
var aStrNum = "43";
var result1 = aNum + aStr;   // result1 will be the string "947Rush";
var result2 = aNum + anotherNum;   // result2 will be the number 1000;
var result3 = aNum + aStrNum;   // result3 will be 94743;
```

In many cases, as discussed in Chapter 4, "Working with variables and data types," you can explicitly change or convert one type to another in JavaScript. Take a look at the *result3* variable in the previous example. You probably want *result3* to hold the result of the mathematical expression 947 + 43. But because the second value, represented by *aStrNum*, is a string, the expression concatenates the two values rather than adding them mathematically as numbers. However, using *Number()* converts *aStrNum* to a number so that you can use it as expected in a mathematical expression, such as addition. Here's the relevant code, corrected to do what you might think it would:

```
var aNum = 947;
var aStrNum = Number("43");
var result3 = aNum + aStrNum;   // result3 will be 990;
```

Multiplicative operators

Like additive operators, multiplicative operators behave just as you might expect; they perform multiplication and division. The multiplication operator (*) multiplies two numbers, whereas the division operator (/) divides numbers. Here's a multiplication example:

```
var mult = 2 * 2;
```

And division:

```
var divisi = 4 / 2;
```

The multiplicative operators include the modulo operator, which is indicated by the percent sign (%). The modulo operator yields the remainder of the division of two numbers. For example, the modulo of 4 divided by 3 is 1, as shown in the following bit of code:

```
var mod = (4 % 3);
```

Bitwise operators

Bitwise operators include AND, OR, XOR, NOT, *Shift Left*, *Shift Right With Sign*, and *Shift Right With Zero Fill*. Each operator is represented by one or more characters, as shown in Table 5-1.

TABLE 5-1 Bitwise operators

Operator	Meaning
&	AND
|	OR
^	XOR
~	NOT
<<	Shift Left
>>	Shift Right With Sign
>>>	Shift Right With Zero Fill

In-depth coverage of the bitwise operators is beyond the scope of this book, although I mention them in later chapters. You can find more information about bitwise operators in the ECMA-262 specification.

Equality operators

You use equality operators to test whether two expressions are the same or different. These operators always return Boolean types: either *true* or *false*. Table 5-2 lists JavaScript's equality operators.

TABLE 5-2 Equality operators

Operator	Meaning
==	Equal
!=	Not equal
===	Equal using stricter methods
!==	Not equal using stricter methods

As you can see from Table 5-2, you can test for equality and inequality in two different ways. These approaches differ in their strictness—that is, in the degree of equality they require to determine whether two values are truly equal. The stricter of the two, represented by a triple equals sign (===), requires not only that the values of a given expression are equal but also that the types are identical. The strict test would determine that a string with the value *"42"* is not equal to a number with the value of *42*, whereas the less strict equality test would find them to be equal. The example that follows is helpful for understanding this.

Testing the equality operators

1. Using Microsoft Visual Studio, Eclipse, or another editor, edit the file equality.html in the chapter05 sample files folder in the companion content.

2. In the webpage, replace the TODO comment with the boldface code shown here. (This code can be found in equality.txt.)

```
<!doctype html>
<html>
<head>
    <title>Equality</title>
    <script type = "text/javascript">
    var x = 42;
    var y = "42";
    if (x == y) {
        alert("x is equal to y with a simple test.");
    } else {
        alert("x is not equal to y");
    }
    </script>
</head>
<body>

</body>
</html>
```

3. Point your web browser to the newly created page. The code is fairly straightforward; it defines two variables, *x* and *y*. The variable *x* is set to the number value *42*, and *y* is set to the string value of *"42"* (notice the double quotation marks). The simple test for equality is next, using ==. This type of equality test measures only the values and ignores whether the variable types are the same. The *if* block calls the appropriate *alert()* function based on the result. You should receive an alert like this:

4. Change the equality test so that it uses the strict test. To do this, first change the equality test to use the stricter of the two equality tests (that is, ===), and then change the alert to read *strict* instead of *simple*. The full code should look like the following example. (The changed lines are shown in boldface type and are in the equality2.txt file in the companion content.)

```
<!doctype html>
<html>
<head>
    <title>Equality</title>
    <script type = "text/javascript">
    var x = 42;
    var y = "42";
    if (x === y) {
        alert("x is equal to y with a strict test.");
    } else {
        alert("x is not equal to y");
    }
    </script>
</head>
<body>

</body>
</html>
```

5. Point your web browser to the page again. The test for equality now uses the stricter test, ===. The stricter test is like the simpler equality test in that it examines the values, but it is different in that it also tests variable types. Because variable *x* is a number and variable *y* is a string, the preceding equality test fails. The appropriate *alert()* function is called based on the result. This time the alert looks like this:

Relational operators

Relational operators test expressions to find out whether they are greater than or less than each other, or whether a given value is in a list or is an instance of a certain type. Table 5-3 lists the relational operators in JavaScript.

TABLE 5-3 Relational operators

Operator	Meaning
>	Greater than
<	Less than
>=	Greater than or equal to
<=	Less than or equal to
in	Contained within an expression or object
instanceof	Is an instance of an object

You are probably familiar with the first four relational operators in Table 5-3, but here are some quick examples nonetheless. Take a look at the following code:

```
if (3 > 4) {
    // do something
}
```

The integer 3 is never greater than the integer 4, so this code will never evaluate to *true*, and the code inside the *if* block will never be executed. In a similar way, the following code tests whether the variable *x* is less than *y*:

```
if (x < y) {
    // do something
}
```

The *in* operator

The *in* operator is most commonly used to evaluate whether a given property is contained within an object. Be aware that the *in* operator searches for the existence of a property and not the value of that property. Therefore, the following code will work because a property called *star* is in the *myObj* object:

```
var myObj = {
    star: "Algol",
    constellation: "Perseus"
};

if ("star" in myObj) {
        alert("There is a property called star in this object");
}
```

The *in* operator is commonly used to iterate through an object. You see an example of this usage in Chapter 8, "Objects in JavaScript."

The *instanceof* operator

The *instanceof* operator tests whether a given expression, usually a variable, is an instance of the object or a particular data type. Yes, that's awkward. Rather than fumble around some more trying to explain it, I'll just skip ahead to an example, and then it will all make sense:

```
var myDate = new Date();
if (myDate instanceof Date) {
        //do something
}
```

Because the variable *myDate* is an instance of the built-in *Date* object, the *instanceof* evaluation returns *true*. The *instanceof* operator affects user-defined objects and on built-in objects, as shown in the preceding example.

Unary operators

Unary operators have a single operand or work with a single expression in JavaScript. Table 5-4 lists the JavaScript unary operators.

TABLE 5-4 Unary operators

Operator	Meaning
delete	Removes a property
void	Returns undefined
typeof	Returns a string representing the data type
++	Increments a number
--	Decrements a number
+	Converts the operand to a number
-	Negates the operand
~	Bitwise NOT
!	Logical NOT

Because the way you use unary operators isn't obvious, I explain them a little more in this chapter.

Incrementing and decrementing

You use the ++ and -- operators to increment and decrement a number, respectively, as shown in the following code:

```
var aNum = 4;
aNum++;
++aNum;
```

The placement of the operator in relation to the operand to which it is applied determines the value returned by the code. When appended to the variable (referred to as *postfixed*), as in the second line of code in the preceding example, the operator returns the value *before* it is incremented (or decremented, as the case may be). When prefixed, as in the last line of code from the preceding example, the operator returns the value *after* it is incremented (or decremented).

Here are a couple of examples showing the difference between prefixing and postfixing in code. The following is an example of postfixing:

```
var aNum = 4;
var y = aNum++;  // y now has the value 4, but aNum then has the value 5
```

The second example is prefixing:

```
var aNum = 4;
var y = ++aNum;  // y now has the value 5, as does aNum
```

In practice, you use the postfix increment operator more often than the prefix increment operator or the decrement operator because it is a convenient counter within a loop structure. You learn about looping in JavaScript in Chapter 6, "Controlling flow with conditionals and loops."

Converting to a number with the plus sign

The plus sign (+) is supposed to convert a value to a number. In practice, I find it to be somewhat unreliable—or at least not reliable enough to use in production code. When I need to convert something to a number, I use the *Number()* function explicitly. However, you can use the plus sign as a unary operator to attempt conversion, as follows:

```
var x = +"43";
```

This code results in the string *"43"* being converted to a number by JavaScript and the numeric value 43 being stored in the variable *x*.

Creating a negative number with the minus sign

It might come as no surprise that when you use a minus sign (-) in front of a number, the number is converted to its negative counterpart, as in this code:

```
var y = "754";
var negat = -y;
alert(negat);
```

Negating with *bitwise not* and *logical not*

The tilde (~) character is a *bitwise not*, and the exclamation point (!) is a *logical not*. These operators negate their counterparts. In the case of a *bitwise not*, its bit complement is given, so a *0* changes to a *-1* and a *-1* to a *0*. A *logical not*, which is the negation you use most frequently in JavaScript programming, negates the expression. If the expression is *true*, the *logical not* operator makes it *false*.

For more information about bitwise operations, see *http://en.wikipedia.org/wiki/Bitwise_operation*.

Using the *delete* operator

The *delete* operator takes a property of an object or the index of an array and removes it or causes it to become undefined. Here's a simple example using an array:

```
var myArray = ["The RCMP", "The Police", "State Patrol"];
delete myArray[0];  // myArray now contains only "The Police" and "State Patrol"
```

The preceding code creates an array called *myArray* and then promptly deletes the value at the first index, making it "undefined." The *delete* operator works with objects, too, as you can see in this next example.

Using the *delete* operator with objects

1. Using Visual Studio, Eclipse, or another editor, edit the file deleteop1.html in the chapter05 sample files folder in the companion content.

2. Create the contents for a base page from which you use the *delete* operator in a later step. In the page, replace the TODO comments with the following code shown in boldface. (The code can also be found in deleteop1.txt file in the companion content.)

```
<!doctype html>
<html>
<head>
    <title>The Delete Operator</title>
</head>
<body id="mainbody">
<script type="text/javascript">
    var polaris = new Object;
    polaris.constellation = "Ursa Minor";

    alert(polaris.constellation);
    delete(polaris.constellation);
    alert(polaris.constellation);
</script>

</body>
</html>
```

3. Save the file, and view it in your web browser. The first part of the output is this:

4. Click OK, and then the following alert will be shown:

This example's code defined a new object (which you'll learn more about in Chapter 8) called *polaris* and then added a property of Polaris's constellation named *constellation* that was set to the value *"Ursa Minor"*. Next, an alert was generated to show that the property did indeed exist. After that, the delete operator was used to delete that property. Finally, another alert was generated to show that the delete operator did its job. Don't worry much about the object and object property parts of this example; they'll make more sense in Chapter 8.

Returning variable types with the *typeof* operator

As you might expect, the *typeof* operator returns the variable type of the given operand. For example, using *typeof*, you can determine whether a given variable was created and is being used as a string, a number, or a Boolean; or whether that variable is a certain type of object or function. Consider this code:

```
var star= {};
if (typeof(star) == "object") {
        alert("star is an object");
}
```

The *typeof* operator returns *"number"* if a number is evaluated, *"string"* if a string type is evaluated, and (as you saw from the example), *"object"* if an object is evaluated. When you use properties, JavaScript smartly assumes that you want to know the type of variable that the property is, rather than the type of object, so it returns that property's *value* type. Here's an example that borrows a little code from earlier in the chapter.

Using the *typeof* operator

1. Using Visual Studio, Eclipse, or another editor, edit the file typeof.html in the chapter05 sample files folder in the companion content.

2. Within the webpage, add the following code shown in boldface (available in the file typeof.txt in the companion content):

```
<!doctype html>
<html>
<head>
    <title>The Typeof Example</title>

    <script type="text/javascript">
        var polaris = new Object;
        polaris.constellation = "Ursa Minor";

        alert(typeof polaris.constellation);
    </script>

</head>
<body>

</body>
</html>
```

3. The code within the *<SCRIPT>* tags creates a new object for the star Polaris and sets its *constellation* property to the string *"Ursa Minor"*. It then calls an alert dialog box using the *typeof* operator to show that the type of the *polaris.constellation* property is a string.

4. Save the file, and view it in a web browser. You get an alert like this:

Using the *typeof* operator, you can also see the difference between *null* and *undefined*.

Assignment operators

You already reviewed assignments in this chapter, and you've seen them throughout the book. The primary (or most frequently used) assignment operator is the equals sign (=). This type of operator is known as a *simple assignment*. JavaScript has many more assignment operators, including those listed in Table 5-5.

TABLE 5-5 Compound assignment operators

Operator	Meaning
*=	Multiplies the left operand by the right operand
/=	Divides the left operand by the right operand
%=	Provides the division remainder (modulus) of the left and right operand
+=	Adds the right operand to the left operand
-=	Subtracts the right operand from the left operand
<<=	Bitwise left shift
>>=	Bitwise right shift
>>>=	Bitwise unsigned right shift
&=	Bitwise AND
^=	Bitwise XOR
|=	Bitwise OR

Compound assignment operators provide shortcuts that save a few keystrokes and bytes. For example, you can add or subtract from a number using += and -=, respectively, as in this example:

```
var myNum = 10;
alert(myNum);
myNum += 30;
alert(myNum);
```

The first alert, just after the variable has been defined and set equal to 10, is shown in the following illustration:

The next alert, after using a compound addition assignment, is as follows:

The importance of byte conservation (a.k.a. minification)

Conserving bytes is an important topic for every JavaScript programmer. Byte conservation refers to programming with shortcuts so that the resulting program in JavaScript (or any other language, for that matter) consumes less memory and bandwidth. Each time you can take advantage of features to save bytes, such as compound assignment statements, the better off the program will be.

Fewer bytes means smaller scripts for users to download. Quantifying how many bytes you can save or how much that can assist you is difficult. Some programmers might argue that the effect is negligible—and for smaller scripts, that's probably true, especially because users increasingly have broadband or faster connections. But the positive effect smart shortcuts can have is very real for larger scripts, especially when those scripts have to be downloaded using a dial-up or other slow type of connection.

One common approach to saving bytes during downloads is through minification of JavaScript. *Minification* refers to the removal of all nonessential elements from a JavaScript file on a live or production website. The nonessential elements include not only comments but also spaces and carriage returns. The resulting minified files are fairly unreadable unless you reintroduce some spaces and carriage returns.

The comma operator

The comma operator separates expressions and executes them in order. Commonly, the comma is used to separate variable declarations, which enables multiple variables to be declared on one line:

```
var num1, num2, num3;
```

Alternatively, you can also set values:

```
var num1=3, num2=7, num3=10;
```

Exercises

1. Use the addition operator (+) to send three *alert()* dialog boxes to the screen. (You can use three separate programs.) The first alert should add two numbers. The second should add a number and a string. The third should add two strings. All should be represented by variables.

2. Use the postfix increment operator (++) to increment a number stored in a variable. Display the value of the variable before, while, and after incrementing. Use the prefix increment operator to increment the number and display its results before, while, and after incrementing by using an alert.

3. Use the *typeof* operator to check the type of variables you created in Exercise 1.

4. True or False: Unary operators don't appear in JavaScript very often.

5. True or False: It's always best to save bytes (using JavaScript shortcuts whenever possible) rather than use returns and indenting, which can slow down page loading.

CHAPTER 6

Controlling flow with conditionals and loops

After completing this chapter, you will be able to

- Understand the different types of conditional statements in JavaScript.

- Use the *if else* conditional statement to control code execution.

- Use the *switch* statement.

- Understand the different types of loop control structures in JavaScript.

- Use a *while* loop and a *do...while* loop to execute code repeatedly.

- Use different types of *for* loops to iterate through ranges of values.

If (and how)

The *if* statement evaluates an expression and, based on the results, determines which code, if any, executes within a program. More complex *if* statements can control which code executes based on multiple conditions. If you've booked a flight on the Internet, you know about making decisions. For example, you might want to go on a quick weekend getaway, so when pricing the ticket, you would say, "If the ticket costs less than $350, I'll book the flight; otherwise, I'll find a different getaway spot." Or suppose I want to take out the trash. Should I take the garbage to the curb tonight or wait until the morning? If the weather forecast is windy overnight, the trash might get blown all over the neighbor's lawn, but if I wait until morning, I might miss the garbage truck. (A third option would be to tell my wife that it's her turn to take out the garbage, but that's never worked in the past.)

Although JavaScript won't help you make these real-life decisions, it can be a great help by making programmatic decisions like these—that is, it can control how a program acts depending on whether a variable contains a certain value or a form field is filled in correctly. This section reviews the syntax of the *if* statement in JavaScript.

Syntax for *if* statements

The syntax for the *if* statement might be familiar to you if you've programmed in other languages, including Perl or PHP. The basic structure of an *if* statement is this:

```
if (some condition) {
    // do something here
}
```

> **Note** The *if* statement is sometimes called the *if* conditional. I use these terms interchangeably within this and other chapters to get you comfortable with both terms. But don't confuse the *if* conditional (the entire *if* statement) with the *if* condition, which is the Boolean expression that the *if* statement evaluates.

The *if* statement examines the validity, or truthfulness, of a condition to determine whether the code within the conditional (inside the braces) is to be executed. The condition is a Boolean expression that, when evaluated to *true*, causes the *if* statement to execute the code in the conditional. (You can negate an expression in the condition to cause the code to run if the expression evaluates to *false*.) Recall the use of Boolean and unary operators from Chapter 5, "Using operators and expressions." Here's an example:

```
if (! some condition) {
    // do something here
}
```

In this case, the condition starts with the negation operator, which means that the condition would need to evaluate to *false* for the code inside the conditional to execute.

The real-world airline cost example from earlier in the chapter might look like this in pseudo-code:

```
if (flightCost < 350) {
    bookFlight();
}
```

If the flight costs less than $350, the code within the conditional executes. The garbage example might look like this:

```
if (forecast != "windy") {
    takeGarbageOut();
}
```

Later in this chapter, I show you how to use an *else* statement to cause other code to execute when the condition is *false*.

You use *if* statement with many of the operators you learned about in Chapter 5, especially relational operators that test whether one value is greater than or less than another value and equality operators that test whether two values are equal to each other. Take a look at these examples:

```
var x = 4;
var y = 3;
// Equality test
if (x == y) {
    // do something
}
```

Because the value in variable *x* (4) does not equal the value in variable *y* (3), the code within the *if* conditional (inside the braces) doesn't execute. Here's an example with a relational operator:

```
var x = 4;
var y = 3;
// Relational test
if (x > y) {
    // do something
}
```

In this case, because the value in variable *x* (4) is greater than the value in variable *y* (3), the code within the braces executes.

The next section shows an example that you can perform yourself. This example takes advantage of the *prompt()* function to get input from a visitor through a simple interface.

The *prompt()* function in Internet Explorer

With the introduction of Windows Internet Explorer 7, the *prompt()* function is no longer enabled by default. If you attempt to use the *prompt()* function with Internet Explorer, you receive a security warning or possibly a page with the word *null*.

You can reliably get around this feature either by clicking the information bar and selecting an option to allow scripts or changing the security settings. For example, you can change security settings in Internet Explorer by selecting Internet Options from the Tools menu, clicking the Security tab, clicking Custom Level, and enabling the Allow Websites To Prompt For Information Using Scripted Windows option within the Scripting section, shown in Figure 6-1.

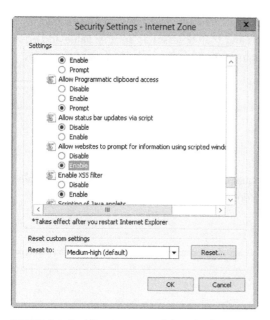

FIGURE 6-1 Enabling the *prompt()* function in Internet Explorer.

However, you can't rely on your visitors doing the same with their Internet Explorer settings. Therefore, the *prompt()* function is no longer as useful as it was before Internet Explorer 7 was introduced. Some programmers might argue that the *prompt()* function was annoying (and I agree that it created problems sometimes), but it did have its advantages, and disabling it does very little to enhance security. But sometimes it's useful for test purposes, such as in the following exercise.

Using *if* to make decisions about program flow

1. Using Microsoft Visual Studio, Eclipse, or another editor, edit the ifexample.html file in the Chapter06 sample files folder, which you can find in the companion content.

2. In the page, replace the TODO comment with the following code shown in boldface type.

```
<!doctype html>
<html>
<head>
    <title>An If Example</title>
</head>
<body>

<script type="text/javascript">
var inputNum = prompt("Please enter a number below 100:");
if (inputNum > 99) {
    alert("That number, " + inputNum + ", is not below 100.");
}
</script>
```

```
<p>This is an example from Chapter 6.</p>

</body>
</html>
```

3. Save the page, and view it in a web browser. If you attempt to view the page in Internet Explorer and receive a security warning, you need to change your security settings as described previously. You can also use Firefox or another browser instead.

4. When you view the page, you see a prompt asking for a number below 100. Internet Explorer typically fills in the text box with "undefined" in the dialog box. Type a number and click OK. I typed **50**, as you can see in the following illustration. (tt is the name of the server on which this code is running.)

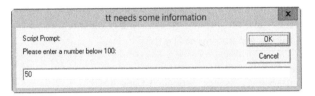

5. Click OK. You see a page like the following:

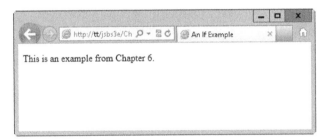

6. Reload the page in the browser, and this time, when prompted, type a number greater than 100. You receive an alert like this one:

Aside from the Hypertext Markup Language (HTML) and opening script tags, which you've seen in previous examples, the code works as follows:

■   The first line within the body's *<SCRIPT>* tag establishes a variable, *inputNum*, and then sets it equal to the result from the *prompt()* function:

```
var inputNum = prompt("Please enter a number below 100:");
```

- The next lines of code use an *if* statement to examine the value in the *inputNum* variable. If the value is greater than 99, an alert is shown:

```
if (inputNum > 99) {
    alert("That number, " + inputNum + ", is not below 100.");
}
```

This example needs improvements in many areas, and later examples show how to improve the code, taking advantage of what you've already learned and using some new techniques you learn later on in this chapter.

Compound conditions

Often, you need to test for more than one condition within the same *if* statement. Consider the previous example. Suppose you wanted to have the visitor enter a number between 51 and 99 inclusive. You could combine those tests within one *if* statement like this:

```
if ((inputNum < 51 ) || (inputNum > 99)) {
    alert("That number, " + inputNum + ", is not between 50 and 100.");
}
```

> **Note** You could also write that *if* statement without the extra parentheses around each evaluation on the first line; however, I find that adding them improves readability.

You can see the full code from the earlier example, with a compound *if* statement shown in bold-face, in Example 6-1.

EXAMPLE 6-1 A compound *if* statement

```
<!doctype html>
<html>
<head>
    <title>An If Example</title>
</head>
<body>
<script type="text/javascript">
var inputNum = prompt("Please enter a number between 50 and 100:");
if ((inputNum < 51) || (inputNum > 99)) {
    alert("That number, " + inputNum + ", is not between 50 and 100.");
}
</script>
<p>This is an example from Chapter 6.</p>
</body>
</html>
```

The statement in Example 6-1 uses the logical OR operator and reads, "If *inputNum* is less than 51 or *inputNum* is greater than 99, do this."

Consider again the example we've been using for much of this chapter. If you enter a number greater than 99 or less than 51, you receive an alert. But what if the input is not a number at all? What if you entered the word *boo*? You wouldn't receive the alert because the condition being used checks only whether the variable is above or below specified numbers.

Therefore, the code should check whether the value contained in the variable is a number. You can accomplish this task with the help of the *isNaN()* function and by nesting the decision, like this:

```
if (isNaN(inputNum) || ((inputNum > 99) || (inputNum < 51))) {
    alert("That number, " + inputNum + ", is not between 50 and 100.");
}
```

The conditional is now evaluated to first check whether the value in the *inputNum* variable is a number. If this initial check proves true (the user did not enter a number), no further processing is done, preventing the rest of the statement from being evaluated. If the user did enter a number, the *isNaN* check fails, and the *if* statement performs the checks for the range of numbers, which are nested together between parentheses, creating their own conditional set. The result, when run with the input value of *boo*, is shown in Figure 6-2.

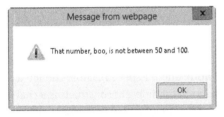

FIGURE 6-2 Running the example with the *isNaN()* function in a nested conditional.

The full code is shown in Example 6-2 (in the ifexample2.html file in the companion content). The nested condition is shown in boldface.

EXAMPLE 6-2 A nested *if* statement

```
<!doctype html>
<html>
<head>
    <title>An If Example</title>

</head>
<body>

<script type="text/javascript">
var inputNum = prompt("Please enter a number between 50 and 100:");
```

```
if (isNaN(inputNum) || ((inputNum > 99) || (inputNum < 51))) {
    alert("That number, " + inputNum + ", is not between 50 and 100.");
}

</script>

<p>This is an example.</p>

</body>
</html>
```

Using *else if* and *else* statements

The next problem with the code example used so far is that the alert dialog box text in Figure 6-2 always indicates that a number was entered. That obviously isn't always the case—I entered the word *boo*. What you really need is a way to perform multiple separate conditional checks. How can you do this? Here's where *else if* and *else* become useful.

> ### *Else if*
>
> Most modern programming languages have the *if/else if/else* conditional constructs, but they differ in how they use those constructs, especially the way they spell or construct the *else if* statement. Some languages define it as *elsif*, all one word (and misspelled). Others define it as *elseif*—all one word but spelled correctly. Remembering these different constructs is a challenge, and this discussion hasn't even considered the different ways that languages use braces to define the code to be executed. In JavaScript programming, you use *else if*—two words, both spelled correctly.

Using *else if* and *else*, you can create multiple levels of conditions, each of which is tested in turn. The code within the first matching condition is executed. If nothing matches, the code inside the *else* condition, if present, is executed. Example 6-3 (ifexample3.html in the companion content) shows code that first checks to see whether the *inputNum* variable contains a number. If the value is indeed a number, the *else if* statement performs the checks to make sure the input value is within the appropriate range. The code calls an appropriate *alert()* function based on the matching condition. If you've entered a number, the *else* condition fires and displays an alert showing the number.

EXAMPLE 6-3 Using an *else if* and *else* condition

```
<!doctype html>
<html>
<head>
    <title>An If Example</title>

</head>
<body>

<script type="text/javascript">
var inputNum = prompt("Please enter a number between 50 and 100:");

if (isNaN(inputNum)) {
    alert(inputNum + " doesn't appear to be a number.");
}
else if ((inputNum > 99) || (inputNum < 51)) {
    alert("That number, " + inputNum + ", is not between 50 and 100.");
}
else {
    alert("You entered a number: " + inputNum);
}

</script>

<p>This is an example from Chapter 6.</p>

</body>
</html>
```

In the same way that you can use *else if* and *else* to test several conditions, you can (sometimes even must) use multiple levels of conditions. For example, you can test for a certain condition, and when successful, execute additional conditions. Here's an example that takes advantage of the *match()* function and a regular expression. For more information about regular expressions, see Chapter 4, "Working with variables and data types."

Using multiple levels of conditionals and a regular expression

1. Open an editor and—if you followed the earlier procedure in this chapter—open the file you updated, ifexample.htm (in the companion content).

    The file should have the following code. (If you didn't follow the earlier example, just create an empty file, paste in the following code, and go on to the next step.)

    ```
    <!doctype html>
    <html>
    <head>
        <title>An If Example</title>
    </head>
    ```

```
<body>

<script type="text/javascript">
var inputNum = prompt("Please enter a number below 100:");

if (inputNum > 99) {
    alert("That number, " + inputNum + ", is not below 100.");
}

</script>

<p>This is an example from Chapter 6.</p>

</body>
</html>
```

2. Save the file with a different file name, such as myexample.html.

3. In the newly saved file, enter the following code shown in boldface. Note that I've included the changes from the earlier example in boldface:

```
<!doctype html>
<html>
<head>
    <title>A Multi-Level Example</title>

</head>
<body>
<script type="text/javascript">
var inputNum = prompt("Please enter a number between 50 and 100:");
if (isNaN(inputNum)) {
    if (inputNum.match(/one|two|three|four|five|six|seven|eight|nine|ten/)) {
        alert("While this is a number, it's not really a number to me.");
    } else {
        alert(inputNum + " doesn't appear to be a number.");
    }
} else if ((inputNum > 99) || (inputNum < 51)) {
    alert("That number, " + inputNum + ", is not between 50 and 100.");
}

</script>

<p>This is an example from Chapter 6.</p>

</body>
</html>
```

4. Test all these conditions. Start by visiting the page in a web browser. You are prompted to enter a number. For this first test, type the word **four**, as follows:

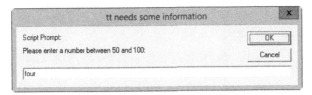

Click OK. The first *if* condition matches, and then the nested *if* examines the input. The input matches the string "four", resulting in this dialog box:

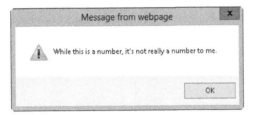

5. Click OK to close the dialog box. Reload the page. Now type the word **pizza**, as shown here:

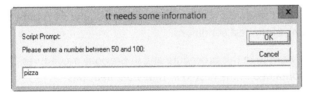

6. Click OK. As with the previous load of the page, the first condition (*isNaN()*) matches. However, because the inner *if* test doesn't match the phrase *pizza*, the *else* condition of the nested *if* will match, resulting in this dialog box:

7. Click OK to close the dialog box, and once again, reload the page. This time, type the numeral **4** into the text box, as shown here:

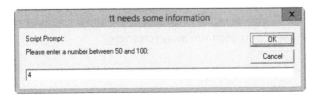

8. Click OK. Now the first *if* condition fails because the number 4 really is a number. Therefore, the *else if* condition is evaluated. Because the number 4 is less than 51 and not greater than 99, the *else if* condition is a match and displays this alert:

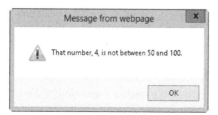

9. Good testing practices dictate that you also test a number above 99. Feel free to do so. When you're ready, just click OK to close the dialog box and reload the page once more. This time, type the number **64**, like this:

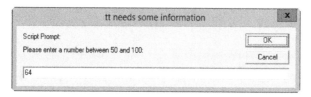

10. When you click OK, you won't receive any alerts because the number 64 is between 50 and 100 and doesn't match any of the test conditions.

I explained the code you're reviewing in this procedure and in previous procedures, but I did not address the regular expression contained in the nested *if*. That statement was:

```
if (inputNum.match(/one|two|three|four|five|six|seven|eight|nine|ten/) {
```

The regular expression is used with the *match()* function (or property) of the *inputNum* variable. The *match()* function accepts a regular expression as its argument. In this case, the argument is this:

```
/one|two|three|four|five|six|seven|eight|nine|ten/
```

The expression is delineated with two forward slashes (/), one on each end (like quote characters delineate a string). After that, the regular expression looks for any one of the strings *one, two, three, four, five, six, seven, eight, nine,* or *ten*. The pipe character (|) between each string indicates a logical OR, meaning that this regular expression will match any one of those strings but not more than one.

Interestingly, although this regular expression is very simple, it's also very flawed. For this regular expression to be better, it would need to mark, or anchor, the position of the matching strings. As the code is written now, the string *sixty* would match just as the word *six* matches now.

My intention here wasn't to show a perfect regular expression, but rather to expose you to one so that when you need to work with them, you don't run away screaming!

Working with ternary conditionals

Another style of conditional construct is called a *ternary conditional*. This type of conditional uses the question mark (?) operator to create a compact *if/else* construct. The basic structure of a ternary conditional expression is quite simple:

```
(name == "steve") ? "Hello Steve" : "Hello Unknown Person";
```

This statement might read as follows, "If name is steve, then "Hello Steve," else "Hello Unknown Person.""

You might use a ternary expression in a statement like the following (this code is in the ternary.txt file in the companion content):

```
var greeting = (name == "steve") ? "Hello Steve" : "Hello Unknown Person";
alert(greeting);
```

This code sets the variable *greeting* to the value from the outcome of the ternary test. If the value of the *name* variable is "steve", the *greeting* variable gets the string value "Hello Steve"; otherwise, the *greeting* variable gets the string value "Hello Unknown Person". Here's that same code in the traditional *if/else* form:

```
if (name == "steve") {
    var greeting = "Hello Steve";
}
else {
    var greeting = "Hello Unknown Person";
}

alert(greeting);
```

The ternary construct can sometimes be confusing if you've never seen it before. There's no shame in sticking to the traditional *if/else* syntax if you think it will help the readability of your programs in the future—especially if the person reading them doesn't know about the ternary construction!

Testing with *switch*

The *switch* statement is an easy and efficient way to test a variable for several values and then execute code based on whichever case matches. Although you can accomplish the task by using *if/else if* statements, doing so can be cumbersome; the *switch* statement is more useful for this situation.

Consider the example of a website that needs to execute certain code based on the language that the user chooses. For this exercise, assume that the visitor has chosen his or her language through a form. (Chapter 9, "The Browser Object Model," examines a way to detect the default language of the visitor's browser.)

If this site needed to execute code for several languages, we could use a giant set of *if/else if/else* conditionals. Assuming a variable called *languageChoice* with the value of the chosen language, the code might look like this:

```
if (languageChoice == "en") {
    // Language is English, execute code for English.
}
else if (languageChoice == "de") {
    // Language is German, execute code for German.
}
else if (languageChoice == "pt") {
    // Language is Portuguese, execute code for Portuguese.
}
else {
    // Language not chosen, use Swedish.
}
```

This code works OK when only a few languages are selected, but imagine this scenario with 20 or more languages selected. Then add more code to be executed for each condition, and it quickly becomes a maze. Here's the same code within a *switch* statement:

```
switch(languageChoice) {
    case "en":
        // Language is English, execute code for English.
        break;
    case "de":
        // Language is German, execute code for German.
        break;
    case "pt":
        // Language is Portuguese, execute code for Portuguese.
        break;
    default:
        // Language not chosen, use Swedish.
}
// Back to code outside the switch statement
```

The *switch* statement looks for each language case and then executes code for that case. The *break* statement indicates the end of the code that executes when a matching case is found. The *break* statement causes the code execution to break out of the *switch* statement entirely and continue executing after the closing brace of the *switch* statement.

For example, if the variable *languageChoice* was *de* and the *break* statement was missing, the code for German would be executed, but the *switch* statement would continue executing the code for the subsequent languages until it encountered a *break* statement or reached the end of the *switch* statement.

You almost always use the *break* statement with each case in a *switch* statement. However, part of the elegance of the *switch* statement is apparent when you have multiple cases that *should* execute the same code. Consider an example where a visitor chooses which country or region he or she is from. On such a site, visitors from the United States, Australia, and Great Britain would probably want their page to be displayed in English, even though people in these three countries spell (and pronounce) many words differently. Here's an example *switch* statement for this scenario:

```
switch(countryChoice) {
    case "US":
    case "Australia":
    case "Great Britain":
        // Language is English, execute code for English
        break;
    case "Germany":
        // Language is German, execute code for German.
        break;
    case "Portugal":
        // Language is Portuguese, execute code for Portuguese.
        break;
    default:
        // Locale not chosen, use Swedish.
}
// Back to code outside the loop
```

 Note As my friends from Montreal would point out and as I would recommend, visitors from any country should be able to choose another language that the site supports, such as French. Ignore that feature for this example, but take it into account when designing your site.

If the visitor chooses Australia as her country, the case for Australia will match, thus executing the code for English. Thanks to the *break* statement, JavaScript then breaks out of the *switch* statement and executes the first line of code following the *switch* statement.

Looping with *while*

The *while* statement creates a loop in which code is executed as long as some condition is true. This section examines the *while* statement and the related *do...while* statement.

The *while* statement

A *while* loop executes the code contained within its braces until a condition is met. Here's an example:

```
var count = 0;
while (count < 10) {
    // Do something in here.
    // Multiple lines are fine.
    // Don't forget to increment the counter:
    count++;
}
```

Always keep in mind two important aspects of *while* loops, listed here and discussed in turn:

- The code contained within a *while* statement might never execute, depending on the starting value of the variable or condition being tested.

- The condition being tested by the *while* statement must be changed within the loop.

Making sure the code executes at least once

In the preceding code example, the variable *count* is initially set to the number *0*. The *while* statement then runs as follows: the evaluation of the *while* statement examines the value of the *count* variable to see whether it is less than *10*. Because it is, the code within the braces executes. (However, if the value of the *count* variable was *not* less than *10*, the code within the *while* statement's braces would never execute—not even once.)

In JavaScript, the *do...while* loop executes code once, no matter what the initial condition is. The *do...while* loop is discussed a little later in this chapter.

Changing the condition

As previously stated, the evaluation of the *while* statement in the example examines the variable to see whether it's less than *10*. If *count* is less than *10*, the code within the *while* loop executes.

One of the lines of code within the *while* loop increments the *count* variable using the ++ unary operator, as follows:

```
count++;
```

When the code in the *while* statement finishes executing, the evaluation repeats. Without the code to increment the *count* variable, *count* would always be less than *10*, so you would have an endless loop on your hands—not what you want.

 Tip When you use a generic counter variable, as I did in the example, where you increment that variable is not important as long as you do it within the *while* statement's braces or within the *while* statement test. Here's an example: *while (i++ < 10)*. See Chapter 5 for more information about the postfix operator.

The moral of this story is to make sure that you increment or change whatever condition that you evaluate in the *while* statement.

The *do...while* statement

Unlike the *while* statement, the *do...while* statement executes the code contained in its braces at least once. The *while* statement might read like this: "While the condition is met, run this code." However, the *do...while* statement might read like this: "Do (or run) this code while the condition is met." Consider the following code:

```
<!doctype html>
<html>
<head>
    <title>Do While</title>
</head>
<body>
<script type="text/javascript">
var count = 0;
do {
    alert("Count is " + count);
    count++;
}
while (count < 3);

</script>
</body>
</html>
```

When this code executes, three dialog boxes appear. During the first run, the *count* variable holds a value of *0* because the variable is still set to the initial value, and the dialog box indicates that, as shown in Figure 6-3.

FIGURE 6-3 The *count* is zero during the first execution.

After running once, the *count* variable gets incremented. When the *while* statement is evaluated, *count* is still less than *3*, so the code is executed again, resulting in the dialog box shown in Figure 6-4.

FIGURE 6-4 When running, the code increments the counter and shows the result of the next execution.

The same process occurs again. The *count* variable is incremented, and the *while* condition is evaluated. The value of *count* is still less than *3*, so the code within the braces runs again, showing another dialog box that looks like Figure 6-5.

FIGURE 6-5 The *count* variable after another run.

Experiment with *while* and *do...while* statements until you're comfortable with the differences between them.

Using *for* loops

A *for* loop is frequently used in the same way a *while* loop is, namely, to execute code a certain number of times. The *for* loop has two cousins in JavaScript: the *for...in* loop and the *for each...in* loop. This section examines both loop types.

The *for* loop

You use a *for* loop to create a loop in which the conditions are initialized, evaluated, and changed in a compact form. Here's an example:

```
for (var count = 0; count < 10; count++) {
    // Execute code here
}
```

A *for* statement has three clauses in parentheses. The first clause sets the initial expression, as shown in the preceding example and also here:

```
var count = 0;
```

The next clause of a *for* statement specifies the test expression, represented by the following code from the example:

```
count < 10;
```

The final expression is usually used to increment the counter used for the test. In the code example, this expression is the final clause in the parentheses:

```
count++
```

Note The last expression in a *for* loop construct does not require a semicolon.

Here's an example that you can try. It uses a *for* loop to iterate over an array.

Using a *for* loop with an array

1. Using Microsoft Visual Studio, Eclipse, or another editor, edit the forloop.html file in the Chapter06 sample files folder in the companion content.

2. Within the page, replace the TODO comment with the following boldface code (you can find the code in the forloop.txt file in the companion content):

```html
<!doctype html>
<html>
<head>
    <title>For Loop Example</title>
</head>
<body>
<script type="text/javascript">
var myArray = ["Vega","Deneb","Altair"];
var arrayLength = myArray.length;
for (var count = 0; count < arrayLength; count++ ) {
    alert(myArray[count]);
}
</script>
</body>
</html>
```

3. Save the page, and view it in a web browser. You receive three successive *alert()* dialog boxes:

As you can see from the dialog boxes, the code iterates through each of the values within the *myArray* array. I'd like to highlight some of the code from this example. Recall from Chapter 4, where you learned how to create an array, that arrays in JavaScript are indexed by integer values beginning at 0. (This knowledge will come in handy in a little while.) Here's the pertinent line from the preceding code example:

```
var myArray = ["Vega","Deneb","Altair"];
```

The code creates a variable called *arrayLength* and sets it to the length of the array. Obtaining the length of the *myArray* array illustrates the use of the array object property named *length*. (I explain objects in more depth in Chapter 8, "Objects in JavaScript.") Obtaining the length within a separate variable (*arrayLength* in this case, as shown in the following code) rather than by using the *length* property within the *for* loop improves performance.

```
var arrayLength = myArray.length;
```

The *for* loop first creates and initializes the *count* variable and next checks whether the *count* variable is less than the length of the *myArray* array as set in the *arrayLength* variable. Finally, it increments the value of the *count* variable after the body of the loop is executed. The code within the body of the *for* loop shows an alert, using the value of the *count* variable to iterate through the indexes of the *myArray* array. Here's the code:

```
for (var count = 0; count < arrayLength; count++ ) {
    alert(myArray[count]);
}
```

The *for...in* loop

The *for...in* loop iterates through the properties of an object, returning the names of the properties themselves. Here's an example:

```
for (var myProp in myObject) {
    alert(myProp + " = " + myObject[myProp]);
}
```

In this code, the variable *myProp* gets set to a new property of *myObject* each time the loop is executed. Here's a more complete example that you can try.

Using a *for...in* loop

1. Using Microsoft Visual Studio, Eclipse, or another editor, edit the forinloop.html file in the Chapter06 sample files folder, which you can find in the companion content.

2. Within the page, replace the TODO comments with the following code shown in boldface (the code is in the forinloop.txt file in the companion content):

```
<!doctype html>
<html>
<head>
    <title>For In Loop Example</title>
</head>
<body>
<script type="text/javascript">
    var star = new Object;

    star.name = "Polaris";
    star.type = "Double/Cepheid";
    star.constellation = "Ursa Minor";

    for (var starProp in star) {
        alert(starProp + " = " + star[starProp]);
    }
</script>

</body>
</html>
```

3. Save the file, and view it in a web browser. You receive three dialog boxes:

As you can see from the code in the example, the variable *starProp* receives the name of the property, whereas using *starProp* as the index of the *star* object yields the value of that property.

Tip You sometimes see *for...in* loops used to iterate through an array in much the same way you saw them used in the previous section. However, using *for...in* to iterate through an array can have mixed results. One of the more visible problems of this approach is that a *for...in* loop doesn't return the properties in any particular order. This behavior can be troublesome, especially when you want to write text to a webpage with JavaScript! The point here is that when you want to loop through a simple array, use the *for* loop rather than the *for...in* loop.

The *for each...in* loop

A newer construct available in JavaScript is the *for each...in* loop. Because it's new, this construct is not yet supported in all browsers—notably, it's not supported in Internet Explorer 10 and earlier. However, it is supported in Firefox 2.0 and later.

Whereas the *for...in* construct returns the name of the property, the *for each...in* loop returns the value of the property. The syntax is essentially the same, but with the addition of the word *each*:

```
for each (var myValue in myObject) {
    alert(myValue " is in the object.");
}
```

Replacing the *for...in* loop from the earlier example with a *for each...in* loop results in the following code:

```
<!doctype html>
<html>
<head>
    <title>For Each In Loop Example</title>
</head>
<body>
<script type="text/javascript">

    var star = new Object;

    star.name = "Polaris";
    star.type = "Double/Cepheid";
```

```
        star.constellation = "Ursa Minor";

    for each (var starValue in star) {
        alert(starValue + " is in the star object.");
    }
</script>

</body>
</html>
```

When you view the page in Internet Explorer, you see an error screen (or maybe just a blank screen). However, viewing the page in Firefox 3.0 or greater (or Chrome) reveals the correct behavior.

You might want to refrain from using the *for each...in* loop construction because it is not supported in (still widely used) versions of Internet Explorer.

Validating forms with conditionals

Earlier in this chapter, you used the *prompt()* function to obtain input from the user. Using the *prompt()* function is somewhat uncommon, and it's fast becoming even less common because Internet Explorer 7 blocks it. This section previews using web forms with JavaScript. Web forms can be used (things like validation, changing the form, and so on) by JavaScript without having to be posted back to the server. All of Chapter 15, "Using JavaScript with web forms," is devoted to this subject.

Using an *if else... if else* conditional to validate input is a common task, so let's do that.

Validating input with a conditional statement

1. Open Microsoft Visual Studio, Eclipse, or another editor and create a new webpage. Name this one form1example.htm.

2. Within the page, enter the following markup and add the code shown in boldface, replacing the TODO comment:

```
<!doctype html>
<html>
<head>

    <title>Just Your Basic Form</title>
    <script type="text/javascript">
    function alertName() {
        var name = document.forms[0].nametext.value;
        if (name == "steve") {
            alert("Hello Steve.  Welcome to Machine");
        }
        else if (name == "tim") {
            alert("Hello Tim.");
        }
```

```
        else {
            alert("Hello " + name);
        }
        return true;
    }  //end function

    </script>
</head>
<body>
<form id="myform" action="#" onsubmit="return alertName();">
<p>Username: <input id="nametext" name="username" type="text" /></p>
<p><input type="submit" /></p>
</form>
</body>
</html>
```

3. Save the page, and view it in a web browser. You should see a page like this:

4. In the form, type the name **steve**, being sure to use lowercase letters. Click Submit Query, and you receive a dialog box like this:

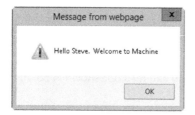

5. Click OK, and now type in the name **tim**, again without the quotation marks and in lowercase letters. When you click Submit Query, you receive a dialog box like this:

6. Click OK to close the dialog box. Type your name (or an entirely different name if your name happens to be one of those already tested), and click Submit Query. You receive this dialog box:

7. Click OK to close this dialog box.

You created a basic web form, accessed that form using JavaScript, and used a conditional to take an action based on user input. Don't worry if everything used in this example doesn't quite make sense yet. The main goal of the example was just to give some context for the conditionals you learned about in this chapter.

Chapter 7, "Working with functions," examines using functions within JavaScript. Chapter 15 shows additional form validation with JavaScript.

Exercises

1. Use a *prompt()* function to collect a person's name. Use a *switch* statement to execute a dialog box displaying the phrase "Welcome *<the entered name>*" if the name entered is yours, "Go Away" if the name entered is *Steve*, and "Please Come Back Later *<the entered name>*" for all other cases.

2. Use a *prompt()* function to collect the current temperature as input by the visitor. If the temperature entered is above *100*, tell the visitor to cool down. If the temperature is below *20*, tell the visitor to warm up.

3. Use a ternary statement to accomplish the same task as in Exercise 2.

4. Use a *for* loop to count from *1* to *100*. When the number is at *99*, display an alert dialog box.

5. Use a *while* loop to accomplish the same task described in Exercise 4.

CHAPTER 7

Working with functions

After reading this chapter, you'll be able to

- Understand the purpose of functions in JavaScript.

- Define your own functions.

- Call functions and receive data back from them.

- Understand some of the built-in functions in JavaScript.

What's in a function?

A JavaScript function is a collection of statements, either named or unnamed (anonymous), that can be called from elsewhere within a JavaScript program. Functions can accept arguments, which are input values passed into the function. Within a function, those arguments passed into the function can be acted upon and the results returned to the caller of the function via a *return* value.

Functions are perfect when you have something that needs to happen multiple times within a program. Rather than defining the same code multiple times, you can use a function (which is really just like a mini-program inside a program) to perform that action. Even if you have bits of code that are very similar—but not identical—throughout the program, you might be able to abstract them into a single function.

A good example of abstracting similar code is using a function to verify that required form fields have been filled in. You could write JavaScript code to verify each individual named field in the form, or you could use a function.

You've already seen functions at work through examples in earlier chapters. A function is defined with the keyword *function*, usually followed by the name of the function, and then by parentheses that contain optional parameters to be used. Use braces to surround the statements to be executed as part of the function:

```
function functionName() {
    // Statements go here;
}
```

> **Tip** It's important to note that when a function is defined (you can see this in the preceding basic function definition), the code isn't actually executed until the function is invoked, or called. You see how to call a function later in this chapter.

Function parameters

Place parameters passed to a function within the parentheses of the function definition. Here's a brief example of using function arguments:

```
function myFunction(parameter1, parameter2, ..., parameterN) {

}
```

Here's an example with two parameters:

```
function myFunction(parameter1, parameter2) {
    // Do something
}
```

Calling, or invoking, the function is as simple as:

```
myFunction(val1,val2);
```

One of the differences between JavaScript (the ECMA-262 specification) and other languages is that in JavaScript you don't need to specify the number of parameters or arguments being passed into a function, and the number of arguments being passed in does not need to match those that are defined in the function definition. When invoked, the function is given an array object named *arguments*. The *arguments* object holds the arguments sent into the function, which can be helpful when you don't know the number of arguments being sent in. Here's an example of how this is done:

```
function myFunction() {
    var firstArg = arguments[0];
    var secondArg = arguments[1];
}
```

Better still, you could get the length of the *arguments* object and loop through each argument, as follows (also in the functionbasics.txt file in the companion content):

```
function myFunction() {
    var argLength = arguments.length;
    for (var i = 0; i < argLength; i++) {
    // Do something with each argument (i)
    }
}
```

Here's a more complete example showing the results from a simple use of the *arguments* object:

```
<!doctype html>
<html>
<head>
    <title>Arguments Array</title>
</head>
<body>
<script type="text/javascript">
function myFunction() {
    var firstArg = arguments[0];
    var secondArg = arguments[1];
    alert("firstArg is: " + firstArg);
    alert("secondArg is: " + secondArg);
}
myFunction("hello","world");
</script>
</body>
</html>
```

When the code executes, it displays two alerts, as depicted in Figures 7-1 and 7-2.

FIGURE 7-1 Using the *arguments* object within a function to access the first argument.

FIGURE 7-2 Using the *arguments* object within a function to access the second argument.

Using the *arguments* object and its length property as in the previous example, you can extrapolate to any number of arguments, not only to the two shown in this example.

Variable scoping revisited

Function parameters are variable names and shouldn't be named the same as the variables that are used to invoke the functions. I purposefully use "shouldn't" rather than "can't," because you *could* use the same name for the variables in the function and the variables in function invocation, but doing that could create some confusing code and confusing scoping, as you'll learn.

Chapter 4, "Working with variables and data types," contains a section about variable scoping, including an exercise dealing with scoping inside and outside functions. The page from one of the variable scoping examples in Chapter 4 looks like this:

```html
<!doctype html>
<html>
<head>
    <title>Scoping Example</title>
    <script type="text/javascript">
        var aNewVariable = "is global.";
        function doSomething(incomingBits) {
            alert("Global variable within the function: " + aNewVariable);
            alert("Local variable within the function: " + incomingBits);
        }
    </script>
</head>
<body>
<script type="text/javascript">
    doSomething("is a local variable");
    alert("Global var outside the function: " + aNewVariable);
    alert("Local var outside the function: " + incomingBits);
</script>
</body>
</html>
```

This example shows how you can globally and locally declare and scope variables from inside and outside a function. However, the example keeps the variables logically separate, in that it doesn't use the same variable name, and then changes the variable's value. Here's an example in which using the same variable name might cause confusion. I find that the code I wrote years ago is confusing enough without introducing weird scoping issues, so try to avoid code like this:

```javascript
function addNumbers() {
    firstNum = 4;
    secondNum = 8;
    result = firstNum + secondNum;
    return result;
}
result = 0;
sum = addNumbers();
```

You might already have spotted the problem with this code. The *var* keyword is missing everywhere. Even though the code explicitly initializes the *result* variable to *0* outside the function, the variable gets modified by the call to the *addNumbers()* function. This in turn modifies the *result* variable to *12*, the result of adding *4* and *8* inside the function.

If you added an alert to display the *result* variable right after the initialization of the *result* variable, the alert would show *0*. And if you added another alert to display the *result* variable after the call to the *addNumbers()* function, the result would show *12*. I leave it to you in an exercise later to add these alerts in the right places.

The bottom line is that your life is easier when you use different names for variables inside and outside functions and always use the *var* keyword to initialize variables. Depending on the code contained in the function, the function might or might not have a return value. That *return* value is passed back to the caller, as you see in the next section.

Return values

When a function finishes executing its code, it can return a value to the caller by using the *return* keyword. Take a look at Example 7-1 (in the listing7-1.html file in the companion content).

EXAMPLE 7-1 A simple *return* value example

```
function multiplyNums(x) {
    return x * 2;
}
var theNumber = 10;
var result = multiplyNums(theNumber);
alert(result);
```

Example 7-1 creates a function called *multiplyNums* with an intended input value, which will be assigned to the variable *x*. The function performs one task: it returns its argument multiplied by *2*, as follows:

```
function multiplyNums(x) {
    return x * 2;
}
```

The code then creates a variable called *theNumber*, as follows:

```
var theNumber = 10;
```

Next, the code creates another variable called *result*. This variable holds the result of the call to the *multiplyNums* function. The *multiplyNums* function uses the variable *theNumber* as an argument:

```
var result = multiplyNums(theNumber);
```

When run, the code results in a dialog box, like the one shown in Figure 7-3.

FIGURE 7-3 This alert shows the return value from the function call.

You can place the return value anywhere within a function, not just at the end. Using a *return* within a conditional or after a loop is common, as shown here:

```
function myFunction(x) {
    if (x == 1) {
        return true;
    } else {
        return false;
    }
}
```

However, be careful where you place the *return* statement, because when the function execution gets to the *return* statement, the function returns immediately and won't execute any code after that. For example, code such as this (you can find this in the morereturnexamples.txt file in the companion content) probably won't do what you want:

```
function myFunction() {
    var count = 0;
    var firstNum = 48;
    return;
    var secondNum = 109;
}
```

This code never reaches the initialization of the variable *secondNum*.

More on calling functions

You nearly always invoke a function with some arguments or with empty parentheses, like this:

```
var result = orderFruit();
```

If arguments were required for that function, the function might look like this:

```
var result = orderFruit(type,quantity);
```

Omitting the parentheses to call a function can result in actions that are entirely different from what you want. Calling a function without parentheses results in the function *name* being returned, rather than whatever the function was supposed to return. Just as important, the function isn't actually executed.

Here's an example. Example 7-2 (which you can find in the listing7-2.html file in the companion content) shows some basic JavaScript code.

EXAMPLE 7-2 Invoking a function

```
<!doctype html>
<html>
<head>
    <title>Order Fruit</title>
```

```
        <script type="text/javascript">
        function orderFruit() {
            var total = 0;
            // Call another function to place order
            return total;
        }
        </script>
    </head>
    <body>
    <script type="text/javascript">
        var result = orderFruit();
        alert("The total is " + result);
    </script>
    </body>
    </html>
```

When executed, this code invokes the *orderFruit()* function. The *orderFruit()* function invokes another function (not shown) to place an order. The total is then calculated and sent back to the caller. As written, the code works fine and results in a dialog box like that shown in Figure 7-4.

FIGURE 7-4 Invoking the *orderFruit()* function with parentheses yields the results you'd expect.

A slight modification to the code—specifically, changing the function call to remove the parentheses—changes the entire result:

```
var result = orderFruit;
```

The result is shown in Figure 7-5.

FIGURE 7-5 Calling *orderFruit* without parentheses probably doesn't turn out the way you want.

Regardless of whether a function returns a value or accepts any arguments, calling the function by using parentheses to execute its code is important.

Anonymous/unnamed functions (function literals)

The functions you've seen so far are formally defined. However, JavaScript doesn't require functions to be formally defined in this way. For example, with a function literal—also known as an unnamed, or anonymous, function—the function is defined and tied to a variable, like this:

```
var divNums = function(firstNum,secondNum) { return firstNum / secondNum; };
```

You can easily test this functionality with the *javascript* pseudo-protocol. Type the following code in the address bar of your browser:

```
javascript:var divNums = function(firstNum,secondNum) { return firstNum / secondNum; };
alert(divNums(8,2));
```

Anonymous functions are frequently used in object-oriented JavaScript and as handlers for events. You see an example of this usage in Chapter 8, "Objects in JavaScript," and in later chapters.

Closures

In JavaScript, nested functions have access to the outer function's variables. *Closures* refer to the existence of variables outside a function's normal execution context. Closures are frequently created by accident and can cause memory leak problems in Internet Explorer if they're not handled properly. However, closures are one of the more powerful (and advanced) areas of JavaScript.

Here's an example of a closure:

```
function myFunction() {
    var myNum = 10;
    function showNum() {
        alert(myNum);
    }
    return showNum;
}
var callFunc = myFunction();
callFunc();
```

In this example, the function *showNum* has access to the variable *myNum* created in the outer (*myFunction*) function. The variable *callFunc* is created in the global context and contains both the variable *myNum* and the function *showNum()*.

When the *callFunc* variable is created, it immediately has access to the *myNum* variable.

Closures can be used to emulate private methods inside objects, and they have other uses, such as in event handlers. Closures are one of the more powerful and advanced concepts in JavaScript and as such aren't appropriate to discuss at length in an introductory book. You can find more information about closures at *http://msdn.microsoft.com/en-us/scriptjunkie/ff696765.aspx* and elsewhere on the Internet.

Methods

The easiest way to think about methods is that they are functions defined as part of an object. That's an oversimplification, but it suffices for now. You access a method of an object by using the dot operator ("."). Built-in objects, such as the *Math*, *Date*, and *String* objects, all have methods that you've seen (or will soon see) in this book. Functions such as the *alert()* function are actually just methods of the *window* object, and could be written as *window. alert()* rather than just *alert()*. Chapter 8 covers objects and methods in greater detail.

Note In much of the book, I use the terms *method* and *function* interchangeably. I'll continue to do so just so that you better understand that the line between these two is blurry for most uses. When a function is used in an object-oriented manner, using the term *method* is often clearer. When not used directly in an object-oriented manner—for example, the way you use the *alert()* function—using the term *function* is acceptable.

Defining your own functions vs. using built-in functions

As you've seen throughout the book, JavaScript has numerous built-in functions, or methods. In addition to using these built-in functions, you will frequently find yourself defining your own functions. Except for trivial scripts, most scripts you write will involve your own functions.

In some cases, however, you might define a function and then later discover that JavaScript already has an equally good built-in function for that same purpose. If you find that a JavaScript built-in function performs the same task as your own function, using the JavaScript function is usually a better idea.

A look at dialog functions

By now, you know all about the *alert()* function in JavaScript because you've seen many examples of it in previous chapters. You've also learned that the *alert()* function is just a method of the *window* object. This section looks at the everyday use of the *alert()* function in JavaScript, and two related functions of the *window* object.

More Info The *window* object is important enough to get some additional attention in Chapter 9, "The Browser Object Model." That chapter discusses numerous other methods of the *window* object.

Although the *window* object has several methods, for now I'd just like to highlight these three (which I call functions): *alert()*, *confirm()*, and *prompt()*. Because you've already seen too many *alert()* dialog boxes in the book, I won't include another one here (thank me later). Although the *prompt()* function is blocked by default beginning with Internet Explorer 7 , the *confirm()* function is still available in Internet Explorer.

The *confirm()* function displays a modal dialog box with two buttons, OK and Cancel, like the one shown in Figure 7-6. (A modal dialog box prevents other activity or clicks in the browser until the visitor closes the dialog box—in this case, by clicking OK or Cancel.)

FIGURE 7-6 The *confirm()* JavaScript function provides a dialog box for confirming user actions.

When you click OK, the *confirm()* function returns *true*. As you might guess, when you click Cancel, the *confirm()* function returns *false*.

Like *alert()* and *prompt()*, the *confirm()* function creates a modal dialog box on most platforms. This can get annoying if these functions are overused or used in the wrong place. But used properly, to provide important feedback and obtain vital information, these functions can be quite useful.

 Tip Don't use the *confirm()* function in place of a web form to obtain user input. The web form is much better for navigation and will keep your visitors happier.

The next exercise walks you through using the *confirm()* function to obtain input and make a decision based on that input.

Obtaining input with *confirm()*

1. Using Microsoft Visual Studio, Eclipse, or another editor, edit the file confirm.html in the Chapter07 sample files folder in the companion content.

2. In the page, replace the TO DO comments with the following code shown in boldface (you can find this code in the confirm.txt file in the companion content):

```
<!doctype html>
<html>
<head>
    <title>Confirming Something</title>

    <script type="text/javascript">
```

```
        function processConfirm(answer) {
            var result = "";
            if (answer) {
                result = "Excellent.  We'll play a nice game of chess.";
            } else {
                result = "Maybe later then.";
            }
            return result;
        }
    </script>
</head>
<body>
<script type="text/javascript">
var confirmAnswer = confirm("Shall we play a game?");
var theAnswer = processConfirm(confirmAnswer);
alert(theAnswer);
</script>
</body>
</html>
```

3. Save the page, and view it in a web browser. You are presented with a dialog box that looks like this:

4. Click OK. You see an *alert()* dialog box:

5. Click OK, and then reload the page.

6. You are again shown the original dialog box from the *confirm()* function, which asks if you'd like to play a game. This time, click Cancel. You are presented with a different *alert()* dialog box:

7. Click OK to close the dialog box.

The code has two major areas to examine, one within the *<HEAD>* portion and the other within the *<BODY>* portion. The function *processConfirm(answer)* is created in the *<HEAD>* portion of the page:

```
function processConfirm(answer) {
    var result = "";
    if (answer) {
        result = "Excellent.  We'll play a nice game of chess";
    } else {
        result = "Maybe later then.";
    }
    return result;
}
```

This function evaluates the value contained in the argument held in the variable *answer*. If the value in the *answer* variable evaluates to *true,* as it does when the visitor clicks OK, the function creates the variable *result* and assigns to *result* a string value of "Excellent. We'll play a nice game of chess." But, if the value in the *answer* variable evaluates to *false,* as it does when the visitor clicks Cancel, the function still creates the *result* variable but now assigns it the value of "Maybe later then." Regardless of what's held in the *answer* variable, *processConfirm* returns the *result* variable to the caller by using the *return* statement within the function. You could write this function more succinctly as:

```
function processConfirm(answer) {
    if (answer) {
        return "Excellent.  We'll play a nice game of chess.";
    } else {
        return "Maybe later then.";
    }
}
```

And even more succinctly as:

```
function processConfirm(answer) {
    var result;
    (answer) ? result = "Excellent.  We'll play a nice game of chess." : result = "Maybe
later then.";
    return result;
}
```

Note In all likelihood, I would use the last function example to perform this task. However, I've found many programmers who aren't comfortable with the ternary logic of the last example. So for readability, I'd choose the more explicit of the two:

```
function processConfirm(answer) {
    if (answer) {
        return "Excellent.  We'll play a nice game of chess.";
    } else {
        return "Maybe later then.";
    }
}
```

The JavaScript contained within the *<BODY>* section of the code creates the confirmation dialog box, calls the *processConfirm()* function, and displays the result:

```
var confirmAnswer = confirm("Shall we play a game?");
var theAnswer = processConfirm(confirmAnswer);
alert(theAnswer);
```

Like the *alert()* function, the *confirm()* function accepts a single argument, which is the message to be displayed in the dialog box. Although not necessary with the *alert()* function, with the *confirm()* function, phrasing your prompt in the form of a question or other statement that gives the visitor a choice is best. If the user really doesn't have a choice, use the *alert()* function instead. An even more succinct version combines all three lines, like this:

```
alert(processConfirm(confirm("Shall we play a game?")));
```

Exercises

1. Define a function that takes one numeric argument, increments that argument, and then returns it to the caller. Call the function from within the *<BODY>* section of a page, and display the result on the screen.

2. Define a function that accepts two numeric parameters. If the value of the first parameter is greater than the second, show an alert to the visitor. If the value of the first parameter is less than or equal to the second, return the sum of both parameters.

3. Add appropriate *alert()* functions to the following code so that you can see the value in the *result* variable both before and after the function call:

```
function addNumbers() {
    firstNum = 4;
    secondNum = 8;
    result = firstNum + secondNum;
    return result;
}
result = 0;
result = addNumbers();
```

4. Create an array with seven string values, initialized to the names of the following stars: Polaris, Aldebaran, Deneb, Vega, Altair, Dubhe, and Regulus. Create an array with seven additional string values, initialized to the names of the constellations in which the stars are found: Ursa Minor, Taurus, Cygnus, Lyra, Aquila, Ursa Major, and Leo. Next, create a function that accepts a single string parameter. Within the function, iterate through the first array, searching for the star. When the star is found, return the value contained in that index within the second array. That is, return the constellation name for that star. Within the *<BODY>* section of the page, use a prompt to gather the name of the star from the visitor, and then call the function with that input. Don't forget to include code that executes when the star isn't found. Display the result on the screen.

CHAPTER 8

Objects in JavaScript

After completing this chapter, you will be able to

- Understand objects in JavaScript, including object properties, object methods, and classes.

- Create objects.

- Define properties and methods for objects.

- Understand arrays in JavaScript.

- Use several array methods.

Object-oriented development

For those who are new to object-oriented programming concepts or might need a refresher, read on. If you're already comfortable with object-oriented programming, skip ahead to the section titled "Creating objects."

A programming paradigm describes a methodology for solving the problems you encounter. More than 25 different programming paradigms exist, some of which might be challenging to find used in an actual program. You might have heard of others or even used them without knowing it. Among these paradigms are functional programming, event-driven programming, component-oriented programming, and structured programming.

Programming paradigms come and go. However, object-oriented programming is one that has been around for many years and doesn't appear to be going away any time soon. This section can't do much more than give you an overview of this subject, but you need to be familiar with object-oriented techniques and terminology so that you're comfortable with the subset of those typically used by a JavaScript programmer.

Objects

Objects are things. In the real world—as opposed to the virtual and sometimes surreal world of computer programming—a ball, a desk, and a car are all objects. An object is something that has describable characteristics, that you can affect, and that behaves in a particular way. An object in the object-oriented programming paradigm is a combination of code and data that exhibits characteristics and behavior in a similar manner.

Properties

Objects have *properties*—defined as their attributes. Going back to the real world again, a ball has a color property—perhaps red, white, or multicolored. It also has a size property—perhaps it is small like a baseball or bigger like a basketball, or like something else entirely. These properties might be represented like this:

```
ball.color
ball.size
```

Methods

Just as objects can have properties, they can also have methods. *Methods* define the way an object behaves. A ball might have a *roll* method, which calculates how far the ball will roll. In theory, not all objects have methods and not all objects have properties, although in practice most objects have at least one method or one property.

Remember from Chapter 7, "Working with functions," that a method is just a function that belongs to an object. A method definition that uses a function *literal* for the *roll* method might look like this:

```
ball.roll = function() {
    var distance = this.size * this.forceApplied;
}
```

What's *this*?

The *ball.roll* example used something new—the keyword *this*, which refers to the object to which the current function or property belongs. In the context of objects, the keyword *this* refers to the calling object. The keyword *this* can be used to set properties of objects within a function call.

The *this* keyword is a boon to JavaScript developers looking to validate web forms, of which you see more in Chapter 11, "An introduction to jQuery," and Chapter 15, "Using JavaScript with web forms."

Classes

In object-oriented programming, an *object* is an instance of a *class,* which defines the set of properties and methods it exposes. Classes simplify the creation of multiple objects of the same type. However, ECMA-262 has no concept of classes in its object interface. Therefore, to take advantage of the benefits of class-based programming, you have to use a pattern to create pseudo-classes.

Consider the star example, which I used in earlier chapters. Example 8-1 (in the listing8-1.txt file in the companion content) shows what you need for a comprehensive webpage that includes information about 14 important stars.

EXAMPLE 8-1 Assembling a *star* object

```
var star = {};

star["Polaris"] = new Object;
star["Mizar"] = new Object;
star["Aldebaran"] = new Object;
star["Rigel"] = new Object;
star["Castor"] = new Object;
star["Albireo"] = new Object;
star["Acrux"] = new Object;
star["Gemma"] = new Object;
star["Procyon"] = new Object;
star["Sirius"] = new Object;
star["Rigil Kentaurus"] = new Object;
star["Deneb"] = new Object;
star["Vega"] = new Object;
star["Altair"] = new Object;

star["Polaris"].constellation = "Ursa Minor";
star["Mizar"].constellation = "Ursa Major";
star["Aldebaran"].constellation = "Taurus";
star["Rigel"].constellation = "Orion";
star["Castor"].constellation = "Gemini";
star["Albireo"].constellation = "Cygnus";
star["Acrux"].constellation = "Crux";
star["Gemma"].constellation = "Corona Borealis";
star["Procyon"].constellation = "Canis Minor";
star["Sirius"].constellation = "Canis Major";
star["Rigil Kentaurus"].constellation = "Centaurus";
star["Deneb"].constellation = "Cygnus";
star["Vega"].constellation = "Lyra";
star["Altair"].constellation = "Aquila";

star["Polaris"].type = "Double/Cepheid";
star["Mizar"].type = "Spectroscopic Binary";
star["Aldebaran"].type = "Irregular Variable";
star["Rigel"].type = "Supergiant with Companion";
star["Castor"].type = "Multiple/Spectroscopic";
star["Albireo"].type = "Double";
star["Acrux"].type = "Double";
star["Gemma"].type = "Eclipsing Binary";
star["Procyon"].type = "Double";
star["Sirius"].type = "Double";
star["Rigil Kentaurus"].type = "Double";
star["Deneb"].type = "Supergiant";
star["Vega"].type = "White Dwarf";
star["Altair"].type = "White Dwarf";
```

```
star["Polaris"].spectralClass = "F7";
star["Mizar"].spectralClass = "A1 V";
star["Aldebaran"].spectralClass = "K5 III";
star["Rigel"].spectralClass = "B8 Ia";
star["Castor"].spectralClass = "A1 V";
star["Albireo"].spectralClass = "K3 II";
star["Acrux"].spectralClass = "B1 IV";
star["Gemma"].spectralClass = "A0 V";
star["Procyon"].spectralClass = "F5 IV";
star["Sirius"].spectralClass = "A1 V";
star["Rigil Kentaurus"].spectralClass = "G2 V";
star["Deneb"].spectralClass = "A2 Ia";
star["Vega"].spectralClass = "A0 V";
star["Altair"].spectralClass = "A7 V";

star["Polaris"].mag = 2.0;
star["Mizar"].mag = 2.3;
star["Aldebaran"].mag = 0.85;
star["Rigel"].mag = 0.12;
star["Castor"].mag = 1.58;
star["Albireo"].mag = 3.1;
star["Acrux"].mag = 0.8;
star["Gemma"].mag = 2.23;
star["Procyon"].mag = 0.38;
star["Sirius"].mag = -1.46;
star["Rigil Kentaurus"].mag = -0.01;
star["Deneb"].mag = 1.25;
star["Vega"].mag = 0.03;
star["Altair"].mag = 0.77;
```

As you can see, Example 8-1 contains a lot of repeated code. Each star is defined as an element of the "star" object, essentially making it an array that contains other objects. Each of those objects is then given four properties: the constellation in which it appears; the star's type; its spectral class; and its magnitude (represented by the word *mag* in the code listing).

Consider the code in Example 8-2 (in the listing8-2.txt file in the companion content). It accomplishes the same result as the code in Example 8-1 but with the help of a constructor pattern to create a pseudo-class.

EXAMPLE 8-2 Assembling a *Star* object using a pseudo-class

```
var star = {};
function Star(constell,type,specclass,magnitude) {
    this.constellation = constell;
    this.type = type;
    this.spectralClass = specclass;
    this.mag  = magnitude;
}

star["Polaris"] = new Star("Ursa Minor","Double/Cepheid","F7",2.0);
```

```
star["Mizar"] = new Star("Ursa Major","Spectroscopic Binary","A1 V",2.3);
star["Aldebaran"] = new Star("Taurus","Irregular Variable","K5 III",0.85);
star["Rigel"] = new Star("Orion","Supergiant with Companion","B8 Ia",0.12);
star["Castor"] = new Star("Gemini","Multiple/Spectroscopic","A1 V",1.58);
star["Albireo"] = new Star("Cygnus","Double","K3 II",3.1);
star["Acrux"] = new Star("Crux","Double","B1 IV",0.8);
star["Gemma"] = new Star("Corona Borealis","Eclipsing Binary","A0 V",2.23);
star["Procyon"] = new Star("Canis Minor","Double","F5 IV",0.38);
star["Sirius"] = new Star("Canis Major","Double","A1 V",-1.46);
star["Rigil Kentaurus"] = new Star("Centaurus","Double","G2 V",-0.01);
star["Deneb"] = new Star("Cygnus","Supergiant","A2 Ia",1.25);
star["Vega"] = new Star("Lyra","White Dwarf","A0 V",0.03);
star["Altair"] = new Star("Aquila","White Dwarf","A7 V",0.77);
```

The *Star* function, shown in boldface in Example 8-2, creates an interface for constructing *Star* objects quickly.

When called, the function returns a new *star* object:

```
star["Polaris"] = new Star("Ursa Minor","Double/Cepheid","F7",2.0);
```

Even though Example 8-1 and Example 8-2 are functionally equivalent, the code in Example 8-2 is much shorter and easier to understand. Imagine an object that had nine properties instead of just the four shown here.

The creation of a class-like interface in this section used the constructor pattern. The constructor pattern is helpful but results in multiple instances of the same method being created each time the object is instantiated. A better and more advanced way to create multiple objects is to use a *prototype* pattern. For more information about creating objects using prototypes, see *http://msdn.microsoft. com/en-us/magazine/cc163419.aspx*.

Creating objects

You can create an object in JavaScript in two ways:

- Using the new keyword, as shown here:

  ```
  var star = new Object;
  ```

- Using curly braces, as shown here:

  ```
  var star = {};
  ```

The version you use depends largely on personal preference; they both accomplish the same task.

Adding properties to objects

After creating an object, you can start assigning properties and methods to it. If you have just one *star* object, you could assign properties directly to it, like this:

```
star.name = "Polaris";
star.constellation = "Ursa Minor";
```

When you need to create multiple related objects, you can assign properties efficiently by following the example shown in the previous section.

Displaying object properties

With a *for...in* loop, you can loop through each of the properties in an object. Try it out.

Looping through object properties

1. Using Microsoft Visual Studio, Eclipse, or another editor, edit the file proploop.html, which you can find in the Chapter08 sample files folder in the companion content.

2. In the page, replace the TO DO comment with the *for* loop shown here in boldface (you can find this code in the proploop.txt file in the companion content):

```
<!doctype html>
<html>
<head>
<title>Properties</title>

<script type="text/javascript">
    var star = {};

    function Star(constell,type,specclass,magnitude) {
        this.constellation = constell;
        this.type = type;
        this.spectralClass = specclass;
        this.mag = magnitude;
    }

    star["Polaris"] = new Star("Ursa Minor","Double/Cepheid","F7",2.0);

    star["Vega"] = new Star("Lyra","White Dwarf","A0 V",0.03);
    star["Altair"] = new Star("Aquila","White Dwarf","A7 V",0.77);

</script>
</head>
<body>
<script type="text/javascript">
for (var element in star) {
        for (var propt in star[element]) {
        alert(element + ": " + propt + " = " + star[element][propt]);
        }
    }
</script>
```

```
    </script>
    </body>
    </html>
```

3. View this page in a web browser. You are presented with an *alert()* dialog box for each of the properties for each of the elements in the *Star* object. (Yes, it's a lot of clicking. Sorry about that.) Here's an example of the type of dialog box you see:

This step-by-step exercise builds on the earlier example of using pseudo-classes to define properties of objects. In this case, a *Star* object was created with the following code:

```
var star = {};
```

That object was then given several elements, each containing a star name, which then was created as an object by using a call to create a new *Star* object (using the pseudo-class):

```
star["Polaris"] = new Star("Ursa Minor","Double/Cepheid","F7",2.0);
```

Each element of the original *Star* object, now essentially an array, in this case the name of each star, was then enumerated within the *<BODY>* section of the code by using a *for...in* loop:

```
for (var element in star) {
```

With each element (each individual star) now represented by the *element* variable, that individual element's properties could be enumerated. This enumeration is accomplished with another *for...in* loop. Within that loop, the *alert* is generated, showing the star's name, the property name, and the value of the property:

```
for (var propt in star[element]) {
alert(element + ": " + propt + " = " + star[element][propt]);
}
```

Looking for a property

Sometimes you don't want or need to loop through every property. Sometimes you just want to know whether a given property already exists within an object. You can use the *in* operator to test for the property, as in this pseudo-code:

```
if (property in object) {
    // do something here
}
```

This *in* operator also works when examining an array to see whether there's a given element within it. Example 8-3 shows a more complete example (available in the listing8-3.txt file in the companion code). It examines the *Star* object's elements for one of the star names, "Polaris," and if found, adds a new property to it. The example then iterates through each of the stars in a *for...in* loop looking for the new property called *aka* (an abbreviation for "also known as"). If the *aka* property is found, some information is sent in an alert.

EXAMPLE 8-3 Looking for a property

```
var star = {};

function Star(constell,type,specclass,magnitude) {
    this.constellation = constell;
    this.type = type;
    this.spectralClass = specclass;
    this.mag  = magnitude;
}

star["Polaris"] = new Star("Ursa Minor","Double/Cepheid","F7",2.0);
star["Mizar"] = new Star("Ursa Major","Spectroscopic Binary","A1 V",2.3);
star["Aldebaran"] = new Star("Taurus","Irregular Variable","K5 III",0.85);
star["Rigel"] = new Star("Orion","Supergiant with Companion","B8 Ia",0.12);
star["Castor"] = new Star("Gemini","Multiple/Spectroscopic","A1 V",1.58);
star["Albireo"] = new Star("Cygnus","Double","K3 II",3.1);
star["Acrux"] = new Star("Crux","Double","B1 IV",0.8);
star["Gemma"] = new Star("Corona Borealis","Eclipsing Binary","A0 V",2.23);
star["Procyon"] = new Star("Canis Minor","Double","F5 IV",0.38);
star["Sirius"] = new Star("Canis Major","Double","A1 V",-1.46);
star["Rigil Kentaurus"] = new Star("Centaurus","Double","G2 V",-0.01);
star["Deneb"] = new Star("Cygnus","Supergiant","A2 Ia",1.25);
star["Vega"] = new Star("Lyra","White Dwarf","A0 V",0.03);
star["Altair"] = new Star("Aquila","White Dwarf","A7 V",0.77);

if ("Polaris" in star) {
    star["Polaris"].aka = "The North Star";
    alert("Polaris found and is also known as " + star["Polaris"].aka);
}

for (var element in star) {
    if ("aka" in star[element]) {
        alert(element + " is in " + star[element].constellation);
    }
}
```

Note There are other approaches for checking property existence that aren't covered in this book, such as the *!==* operator.

Adding methods to objects

In the same way you can add properties to self-defined objects, you can add methods. For example, suppose you want to extend the *Star* pseudo-class used in earlier examples to include a method called *show()*, which just presents an *alert()* dialog box. You could add to this method to do whatever you need it to do. For example, look at this code:

```
function Star(constell,type,specclass,magnitude) {
    this.constellation = constell;
    this.type = type;
    this.spectralClass = specclass;
    this.mag  = magnitude;
    this.show = function() {
        alert("hello, this is a method.");
    }
}
```

To call the method, you write code that looks like this:

```
star["Polaris"].show();
```

Object-oriented programming in JavaScript doesn't end here. More advanced features of the object-oriented programming paradigm, such as inheritance, super-classing, and prototypes, are all possible with JavaScript, but they are beyond the scope of this book. MSDN Magazine published an article about some of the more advanced concepts, and you can find that article at *http://msdn. microsoft.com/en-us/magazine/cc163419.aspx.*

Finding out more about arrays

Chapter 4, "Working with variables and data types," introduced arrays and provided some examples of ways to define them. With arrays, you can group a set of values into an object and then access those values through a numbered index value. For example, you can use the *new Array()* explicit constructor as follows:

```
var star = new Array();
star[0] = "Polaris";
star[1] = "Deneb";
star[2] = "Vega";
star[3] = "Altair";
```

You also can perform the same task using the implicit array constructor (denoted by square brackets), like so:

```
var star = ["Polaris", "Deneb", "Vega", "Altair"];
```

The *length* property

The *length* property of an array returns the number of elements in the array. There's an important distinction between how many elements the array contains and how many have been defined. Here's a simple example. Consider the implicit star array definition discussed previously. You can count four star names: Polaris, Deneb, Vega, and Altair. The *length* property returns the same result:

```
var numStars = star.length;    // star.length is 4.
```

Elements can be counted by the *length* property that have not yet been defined or initialized. Here's an example that creates an array with more elements than were assigned:

```
var myArray = new Array(5);
```

Array methods

This section introduces you to some of the methods of the *array* object. You can find more information within the ECMA-262 specification at *http://www.ecma-international.org/publications/files/ECMA-ST/Ecma-262.pdf*.

You can add elements to an array by using two different methods, by either *prepending* them to the front of the array or appending them to the end of it.

Using *concat()* to add elements

The *concat()* method appends elements to the end of the array on which it is invoked. To use it, you supply the *concat()* method with arguments containing the items to append. The method returns a new array, as follows:

```
var myArray = new Array();
myArray[0] = "first";
myArray[1] = "second";
var newArray = myArray.concat("third");
// newArray is now [first,second,third]
```

You can also concatenate one array to another, like this:

```
var myFirstArray = [51,67];
var mySecondArray = [18,"hello",125];
var newArray = myFirstArray.concat(mySecondArray)
// newArray is [51,67,18,"hello",125]
```

Adding elements with *concat()*

1. Using Visual Studio, Eclipse, or another editor, edit the concat.html file in the Chapter08 sample files folder in the companion content.

2. Within the page, add the code shown in boldface type (found in concat.txt):

```
<!doctype html>
<html>
<head>
    <title>Concat</title>
    <script type="text/javascript">

    var star = ["Polaris", "Deneb", "Vega", "Altair"];

    for (var i = 0; i < star.length; i++) {
        alert(star[i]);
    }

    </script>
</head>
<body>

</body>
</html>
```

3. Save the page, and view it in a web browser. You receive an *alert()* dialog box (like the one shown here) for each of the four star names defined in the star array.

4. Alter the code to concatenate some additional stars onto the star array. (Yes, I realize that you could just add them directly to the star array, but that's cheating.) Here's the code (the changes are shown in boldface and are found in concat2.txt file):

```
<!doctype html>
<html>
<head>
    <title>Concat</title>
    <script type="text/javascript">

    var star = ["Polaris", "Deneb", "Vega", "Altair"];

    var newstars = ["Aldebaran", "Rigel"];
    var morestars = star.concat(newstars);
    var mStarLength = morestars.length;
    for (var i = 0; i < mStarLength; i++) {
        alert(morestars[i]);
    }

    </script>
</head>
<body>

</body>
</html>
```

5. Save and view the page in a web browser. You receive six *alert()* dialog boxes (sorry!), one for each star, like this one for Aldebaran:

Joining and concatenating with *join*

The *join()* method converts all the elements of an array to a joined string. This method is unlike the *concat()* method, which concatenates elements to an array and does not perform any type conversions. Here's the code (also found as starstring.html in the companion content):

```
var star = ["Polaris", "Deneb", "Vega", "Altair"];
var starString = star.join();
```

The *starString* variable contains *Polaris,Deneb,Vega,Altair*, as shown in Figure 8-1.

FIGURE 8-1 Using *join()* to join an array.

The *join()* method enables you to specify the join delimiter as well. Instead of just using a comma, you might want to use an asterisk, like this (found as aststring.html in the companion content):

```
var star = ["Polaris", "Deneb", "Vega", "Altair"];
var starString = star.join("*");
```

The result would be *Polaris*Deneb*Vega*Altair*, as shown in Figure 8-2.

FIGURE 8-2 Joining with a different delimiter.

 Tip The *join()* method is a quick way to see the contents of an array without creating an entire *for* loop structure.

Using *push* and *pop* to add and remove elements

Whereas *concat()* concatenates two arrays, *push()* and *pop()* add and remove individual elements. The *push()* method returns the length of the new array, and *pop()* returns the removed element. The methods *push()* and *pop()* operate on the end of the array, as shown in the following code:

```
var star = ["Polaris", "Deneb", "Vega", "Altair"];
star.push("Aldebaran");
```

Running the preceding code results in the *star* object containing five elements: Polaris, Deneb, Vega, Altair, and Aldebaran.

The *pop()* method removes the last element and returns the element that is removed:

```
var star = ["Polaris", "Deneb", "Vega", "Altair"];
var removedElement = star.pop();
```

The *removedElement* variable contains the string "Altair" because that was the last element of the array. The length of the array is also shortened (or decremented) by 1.

Using *shift* and *unshift* to add and remove elements

The *push()* and *pop()* methods operate on the end of the array. The *shift()* and *unshift()* methods perform the same functions as *push()* and *pop()*, except the former do it at the beginning of the array. In this code, the *unshift()* method adds an element to the beginning of an array:

```
var star = ["Polaris", "Deneb", "Vega", "Altair"];
star.unshift("Aldebaran");
```

The *star* array is:

```
["Aldebaran", "Polaris", "Deneb", "Vega", "Altair"]
```

Use *shift()* to remove an element from the beginning of an array. Notice that *shift()* returns the removed element, just like *pop()*:

```
var star = ["Polaris", "Deneb", "Vega", "Altair"];
var removedElement = star.shift();
```

The *star* array now contains:

```
["Deneb", "Vega", "Altair"]
```

Using *slice()* to return parts of an array

The *slice()* method is useful when you need to return specific portions of an array, but you must be careful because unless you make a copy of the array, *slice()* does not change the original array. For example, the following code returns and places into the *cutStars* variable the value *"Vega,Altair"*, because *Vega* and *Altair* are the third and fourth elements of the *star* array (remember that arrays start counting from zero) and *slice()* ends at but doesn't include the end argument.

```
var star = ["Polaris", "Deneb", "Vega", "Altair"];
var cutStars = star.slice(2,4);
```

Sorting elements with *sort()*

It's sometimes helpful to sort the elements of an array. Look at this code:

```
var star = ["Polaris", "Deneb", "Vega", "Altair"];
var sortedStars = star.sort();
```

The result is shown in Figure 8-3 (and produced with sort.html in the companion content), and as you can see, the elements of the star array are sorted alphabetically, even though they weren't ordered alphabetically in the array initializer. Notice that both the original *star* array and the *sortedStars* variable contain the sorted list.

FIGURE 8-3 The result of a sorted array using the *sort()* method.

Be careful not to use the *sort()* method to sort numbers. Consider this code:

```
var nums = [11,543,22,111];
var sortedNums = nums.sort();
```

You might expect the *sortedNums* variable to contain 11,22,111,543, but instead it sorts the values alphabetically, as shown in Figure 8-4.

11,111,22,543

FIGURE 8-4 Attempting to sort numbers with *sort()* doesn't work—at least not if you want them sorted in numerical order.

Iterating through arrays

Two primary methods exist for iterating through array elements in JavaScript. As of this writing, the primary cross-browser method for doing so is the *for()* method, which you've seen throughout the book so far. Here's a quick reminder of its syntax:

```
var candies = ["chocolate","licorice","mints"];
for (var i = 0; i < candies.length; i++) {
    alert(candies[i]);
}
```

Introduced with ECMA-262 edition 5 and supported in all major browsers with the exception of Internet Explorer 8 and earlier and Firefox 1.5 and earlier, the *forEach()* method walks through array elements as well. The syntax for *forEach()* is similar to that of a *for* loop (found as foreach.html in the companion content):

```
var candies = ["chocolate","licorice","mints"];
candies.forEach(function(candy) {
    alert(candy);
});
```

> **Note** Use the *forEach()* method (and other new methods) with caution because they aren't yet widely supported and aren't supported at all by older browsers.

The array object has other methods that you should know about. Some that you might encounter are listed in Table 8-1, but you should refer to the ECMA-262 specification available at *http://www.ecma-international.org/publications/files/ECMA-ST/ECMA-262.pdf* for a full list. Methods that are new to the ECMA-262 edition 5 standard are noted.

TABLE 8-1 Select methods of the array object

Method	Description	New to ECMA-262 Edition 5
reverse()	Reverses the order of the elements.	No
map()	Executes a function on each array item and returns an array.	Yes
indexOf()	Returns the index of the first occurrence of the argument.	Yes
lastIndexOf()	Returns the last index of the argument in the array.	Yes
every()	Executes a function on each array item and returns *true* while every element in the array satisfies the provided testing function.	Yes
filter()	Executes a function on each array item and returns an array containing only the items for which the function returns *true*.	Yes
some()	Executes a function and returns *true* if at least one element in the array satisfies the function.	Yes
splice()	Inserts or removes elements from an array. Returns an array containing the deleted items.	No

Taking advantage of built-in objects

The JavaScript language makes several useful objects available to assist with tasks common to the JavaScript program. You've already seen some of these, such as the *Date*, *Number*, and *Math* objects, which were covered in Chapter 4.

JavaScript has a *global object*, named *window*, that contains some of the methods already discussed, such as *isNaN()*. Another three commonly used global object methods are *encodeURI()*, *encodeURIComponent()*, and *eval()*, which are discussed in this section.

Making URIs safe

The *encodeURI()* method takes a Uniform Resource Identifier (URI) that contains characters that are not allowed in a given URI scheme, and it encodes them so that they can be used according to the standard. For example, RFC (Request For Comments) 2396 defines a generic syntax for URIs. The *encodeURI()* method can be used to correct the following URI:

```
http://www.braingia.org/a uri with spaces.htm
```

The preceding URI contains spaces—which are not allowed in an HTTP URI—and therefore the URI needs to be encoded (found as encode.html in the companion content):

```
alert(encodeURI("http://www.braingia.org/a uri with spaces.htm"));
```

Figure 8-5 shows the result.

FIGURE 8-5 Using the *encodeURI()* method to properly encode a URI in JavaScript.

Whereas the *encodeURI()* method works on an entire URI, like the one shown in Figure 8-5, the *encodeURIComponent()* method also encodes special characters such as slash (/), question mark (?), ampersand (&), and others.

Both the *encodeURI()* and *encodeURIComponent()* methods have decoding counterparts, *decodeURI()* and *decodeURIComponent()*, respectively.

Using the *eval()* method

The *eval()* method is one of the most powerful and dangerous methods you can use in JavaScript because it executes the code passed to it using the privileges of the caller. The *eval()* method takes a single argument that is interpreted as JavaScript and executed, for example:

```
eval("alert('hello world')");
```

The *eval()* method executes the *alert* code, just as it would if the code were executed directly. Typically, you use the *eval()* method during Asynchronous JavaScript and XML (AJAX) calls, but doing so poses a security problem because the code returned from the AJAX call is executed just as if it were normal code, and that code could be malicious.

Exercises

1. Create code to loop through a simple array of four objects, shown here, and display those in an *alert()* dialog box, one for each element of the array:

   ```
   var star = ["Polaris", "Deneb", "Vega", "Altair"];
   ```

2. Create an object to hold the names of three of your favorite songs. The objects should have properties containing the artist, the song length, and the title for each song.

3. The first step-by-step exercise in this chapter used a list of stars and a class to populate those objects, shown here:

   ```
   function Star(constell,type,specclass,magnitude) {
       this.constellation = constell;
       this.type = type;
   ```

```
        this.spectralClass = specclass;
        this.mag  = magnitude;
}
star["Polaris"] = new Star("Ursa Minor","Double/Cepheid","F7",2.0);
star["Mizar"] = new Star("Ursa Major","Spectroscopic Binary","A1 V",2.3);
star["Aldebaran"] = new Star("Taurus","Irregular Variable","K5 III",0.85);
star["Rigel"] = new Star("Orion","Supergiant with Companion","B8 Ia",0.12);
star["Castor"] = new Star("Gemini","Multiple/Spectroscopic","A1 V",1.58);
star["Albireo"] = new Star("Cygnus","Double","K3 II",3.1);
star["Acrux"] = new Star("Crux","Double","B1 IV",0.8);
star["Gemma"] = new Star("Corona Borealis","Eclipsing Binary","A0 V",2.23);
star["Procyon"] = new Star("Canis Minor","Double","F5 IV",0.38);
star["Sirius"] = new Star("Canis Major","Double","A1 V",-1.46);
star["Rigil Kentaurus"] = new Star("Centaurus","Double","G2 V",-0.01);
star["Deneb"] = new Star("Cygnus","Supergiant","A2 Ia",1.25);
star["Vega"] = new Star("Lyra","White Dwarf","A0 V",0.03);
star["Altair"] = new Star("Aquila","White Dwarf","A7 V",0.77)
```

The code then used a simple *for* loop to move through each of the star objects and displayed the names of the stars, as shown here:

```
for (var element in star) {
        for (var propt in star[element]) {
        alert(element + ": " + propt + " = " + star[element][propt]);
        }
}
```

Your task is to modify this code to display one single dialog box containing all the star names rather than display one dialog box for each star.

CHAPTER 9

The Browser Object Model

After completing this chapter, you will be able to

- Understand the different objects available as part of the *window* object.

- Use the *navigator* object to view properties of the visitor's browser.

- Obtain information about the visitor's screen, including available height and width.

- Use JavaScript to detect whether Java is enabled in the browser.

- Parse the query string sent by the browser.

Introducing the browser

Until this chapter in the book, you reviewed JavaScript mainly in the abstract. This chapter starts to examine JavaScript as you'd apply it in the real world.

I feel rather silly about writing this, but it's important, so I'm going to say it anyway: *the browser is central to JavaScript programming*. Projects like Rhino *(http://www.mozilla.org/rhino/)* want to change that, but understanding the environments that browsers provide is central to writing good JavaScript code that works well on multiple browsers running on multiple platforms. This section introduces you to the Browser Object Model.

The browser hierarchy

The Browser Object Model creates a tree-like hierarchy of objects, many of which provide properties and methods for the JavaScript programmer. The browser itself is represented by one object, called the *window* object. The *window* object is the parent of several child objects:

- *document*

- *frames*

- *history*

- *location*

- *navigator*

- *screen*

- *self/window/parent*

The *document* child of the *window* object is special because it has several child and even grand-child objects that provide access to all HTML elements within a page. The *window* object, its children, and their place in the browser hierarchy are illustrated in Figure 9-1.

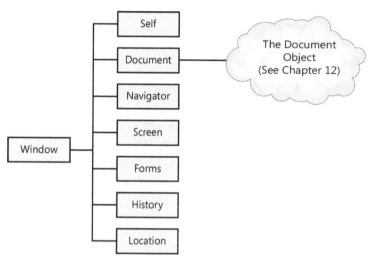

FIGURE 9-1 The *window* object and its children.

I discuss the *document* object in Chapter 12, "The Document Object Model." You learn about the other children of the *window* object in the remainder of this chapter.

Events

Events are briefly described in Chapter 1, "JavaScript is more than you might think." You use events in many areas of JavaScript programming, and quite a bit when working with web forms. Events are triggered when actions occur. The action can be initiated by users, when they click a button or link or move the mouse into or out of an area, or by programmatic events, such as when a page loads. Chapter 13, "JavaScript events and the browser," goes into detail about events related to the *window* object; Chapter 15, "Using JavaScript with web forms," provides more information about web forms.

A sense of *self*

The *window* object is a global object that represents the currently open window in the browser. The *window* object has several properties, methods, and child objects. You already used some of these methods, such as *alert()* and *prompt()*. Because the *window* object is a global object, you don't need to preface its properties and methods with *window*. Instead, you can call them directly, as you already saw done in the examples that made calls to the *alert()* method.

Direct descendants of the *window* object don't require the *window* prefix, but when you deal with objects beyond the *window* object's direct descendants, you need to precede them with the *window* object name. For example, the *document* object is a direct descendant of the *window* object and therefore doesn't need the *window* prefix, but descendants of the *document* object do need it, as shown in the following example:

```
alert("something");  // note no window. prefix.
document.forms[0]  // note the document. prefix but still no window. Prefix.
```

 Note You often see child objects of the *window* object referred to as properties of the *window* object—for example, the *screen* property rather than the *screen* object.

The *window* object also has properties and methods. Among its properties is the *self* property, which refers to the *window* object (and gave me the idea for the title for this section). Table 9-1 lists some of the widely used properties of the *window* object. You examine many of these in examples throughout the book.

TABLE 9-1 Selected properties of the *window* object

Property	Description
closed	Set to *true* when the window has been closed
defaultStatus	Used to set the text that appears by default in the status bar of a browser
name	The name of the window as set when the window is first opened
opener	A reference to the window that created the window
parent	Frequently used with frames to refer to the window that created a particular window or is one level up from the frame
status	Frequently used to set the text in the status bar when a visitor hovers over an element such as a link
top	Refers to the highest or topmost parent window

Tables 9-2 and 9-3 describe some of the *window* object's methods. You see examples of how to use many of these throughout the remainder of this book.

TABLE 9-2 Selected methods of the object

Method	Description
addEventListener()	Cross-browser (with support added in Internet Explorer 9) method to add event handlers. See Chapter 11, "An introduction to jQuery," for more information.
attachEvent()	The version of *addEventListener()* in Internet Explorer. See Chapter 11 for more information.
blur()	Changes the focus of keyboard input away from the browser window.
focus()	Changes the focus of keyboard input to the browser window.
close()	Closes the browser window.
detachEvent()	The version of *removeEventListener()* in Internet Explorer.

Method	Description
removeEventListener()	Cross-browser event handler removal method. Internet Explorer versions 9 and later support this.
open()	Opens a window.
print()	Causes the browser's print function to be invoked; behaves just as though someone clicked Print in the browser.

Some methods of the *window* object deal with moving and resizing the window and are described in Table 9-3.

TABLE 9-3 Selected methods of the object for moving and resizing

Method	Description
moveBy()	Used to move the window to a relative location
moveTo()	Used to move the window to a specific location
resizeBy()	Used to change the size of the window by a relative amount
resizeTo()	Used to change the size of the window to a certain size

Timers are found in some JavaScript applications and are discussed in Chapter 11. The *window* object methods related to timers are the following:

- *clearInterval()*

- *clearTimeout()*

- *setInterval()*

- *setTimeout()*

The rest of the chapter looks more closely at some of the direct children of the *window* object.

Getting information about the screen

The *screen* object provides a way to obtain information about the visitor's screen. You might need this information to determine which images to display or how large the page can be. Whether or not you use the *screen* object, you need to create a good CSS-based design (CSS stands for Cascading Style Sheets) that gracefully handles screens of all sizes.

The available properties of the *screen* object are as follows:

- *availHeight*

- *availWidth*

- *colorDepth*

- *height*

- *width*

You might be wondering what the difference is between the *availHeight* and *availWidth* properties and the *height* and *width* properties. The *availHeight* and *availWidth* properties return the available height and width of the screen minus the space used by other controls, such as the taskbar in Microsoft Windows. The *height* and *width* properties return the gross height and width. This might make more sense with an example.

Determining a visitor's screen height and width

1. Using Microsoft Visual Studio, Eclipse, or another editor, edit the screen.html file in the Chapter09 sample files folder in the companion content.

2. In the page, add the boldface code shown here (you can find this in the screen.txt file in the companion content):

```
<!doctype html>
<html>
<head>
    <title>Screen</title>

</head>
<body>

    <script type="text/javascript">
        alert("Available Height: " + screen.availHeight);
        alert("Total Height: " + screen.height);
        alert("Available Width: " + screen.availWidth);
        alert("Total Width: " + screen.width);
    </script>

</body>
</html>
```

3. Save and view the page in a web browser. You receive four *alert()* dialog boxes, one for each of the properties called. The following sample screen shots reflect a 1,024 × 768 pixel display.

As you can see from these screen shots, the total width and height are 1,027 pixels and 768 pixels, respectively. Notice that the available width remains 1,024, whereas the available height is reduced to 728 from 768 because of the taskbar.

Using the *navigator* object

The *navigator* object provides several properties that assist in the detection of various elements of the visitor's browser and environment. One of the most popular operations JavaScript can perform is detecting which browser the visitor is using. (Well, this section isn't about that—but it could be. See the sidebar "Problems with browser detection" for more information.)

Problems with browser detection

For a long time, websites used the *navigator* object to detect which browser the visitor was using. (Well, a long time in Internet years—which could be several years or as short as a few months, depending on the technology you're talking about.) Browser detection was used so that browser-specific JavaScript code could be executed. Although simple browser detection had its uses, some poorly designed sites used this technique as a means to lock out visitors who had particular browsers.

Little did they know that the information sent by a browser can be easily fooled. The User Agent Switcher add-on for Firefox is one such way to alter this information, thus rendering browser detection with the *navigator* object useless.

Tip I've said it before in this book and I'll say it now (and probably will repeat it again later): never rely on anything sent from the visitor's browser to your website. Always verify. Assuming that the browser is Internet Explorer just because it says so is not sufficient. Chapter 13 provides a better method for detecting whether the browser is capable of handling the JavaScript on your website.

When you use the *navigator* object to detect the visitor's browser, you encounter another problem because there are so many browsers out there. A web developer can spend too much time keeping track of which browsers might support which functions and trying to account for all those browsers in the code. However, all is not lost for the *navigator* object—it's still useful, as you will soon see.

In this exercise, you walk through the properties of the *navigator* object and their values.

Looking at the *navigator* object

1. Using Visual Studio, Eclipse, or another editor, edit the naviprops.html file in the Chapter09 sample files folder in the companion content.

2. Within the page, replace the TODO comment with the boldface code shown here (this code is in the naviprops.txt file in the companion content):

```
<!doctype html>
<html>
<head>
    <title>The navigator Object</title>
</head>
<body>
    <script type="text/javascript">
        var body = document.getElementsByTagName("body")[0];
        for (var prop in navigator) {
            var elem = document.createElement("p");
            var text = document.createTextNode(prop + ": " + navigator[prop]);
            elem.appendChild(text);
            body.appendChild(elem);
        }
    </script>

</body>
</html>
```

3. Save and view the page in a web browser of your choice. If you chose Firefox, you see a page like this:

4. If you chose Internet Explorer, the page will look similar to this; however, note the difference in the available properties:

I just couldn't bring myself to use yet another *alert()* dialog box for this exercise, so I had to use some functions that I haven't yet introduced. (The elements in this example are introduced in Chapters 12 and 13.)

The code for this exercise employs a function that uses the *document* object to create Hypertext Markup Language (HTML) elements within the webpage. A *for* loop is used to iterate through each of the properties presented by the *navigator* object:

```
var body = document.getElementsByTagName("body")[0];
    for (var prop in navigator) {
        var elem = document.createElement("p");
        var text = document.createTextNode(prop + ": " + navigator[prop]);
        elem.appendChild(text);
        body.appendChild(elem);
    }
```

If the JavaScript you're using doesn't work for a certain version of a web browser, you could detect the browser by implementing a workaround based on using the *navigator* object, but understand that this strategy isn't reliable and you really shouldn't use it as standard practice. But sometimes, you just need to use it.

If your site uses Java, you can use the *navigator* object to check whether Java is enabled. The following exercise shows you how.

Using the *navigator* object to detect Java

1. Using Visual Studio, Eclipse, or another editor, edit the file javatest.html in the Chapter09 sample files folder.

2. Within the page, replace the TODO comment with the boldface code shown here (also located in the javatest.txt file in the companion content):

```
<!doctype html>
<html>
<head>
    <title>Java Test</title>
    <script type="text/javascript">
        if (navigator.javaEnabled()) {
            alert("Java is enabled");
        } else {
            alert("Java is not enabled");
        }
    </script>
</head>

<body>

</body>
</html>
```

3. Save the page, and view it in Internet Explorer (if you have it installed). By default, Java is enabled in Internet Explorer, so you should see a dialog box like this:

4. Switch to Firefox, if you have it available, and disable Java. (In the Windows version of Firefox, you can do this by selecting Add-Ons, clicking Plugins, and then clicking Disable For The Java Plugins.) When you disable Java and refresh the page, you see a dialog box like this:

The *location* object

The *location* object gives you access to the currently loaded Uniform Resource Identifier (URI), including any information about the query string, the protocol in use, and other related components. For example, a URI might be:

http://www.braingia.org/location.html

If the webpage at that URI contains the JavaScript code to parse the URI that is presented in the next example, the output would look like that shown in Figure 9-2.

FIGURE 9-2 The *location* object being used to display the various properties.

The protocol in this case is *http:*, the host is *www.braingia.org* (as is the host name), and the path-name is *location.html*. Nothing was entered as a query string, so the search value remains empty. The port is not explicitly specified (it uses the standard port for HTTP traffic, tcp/80), so that, too, is empty.

Here's an exercise that examines the query string.

Looking at the *location* object

1. Using Visual Studio, Eclipse, or another editor, edit the location1.html file in the Chapter09 sample files folder in the companion content.

2. This first bit of HTML and JavaScript creates the page that you saw in Figure 9-2. (Actually, it steals the code from an earlier exercise that used the *navigator* object but with a slight modi-fication for the *location* object.) We build upon that code for this exercise, so add the boldface code shown here to the location1.html page:

```
<!doctype html>
<html>
<head>
    <title>Location, Location, Location</title>
</head>
<body>
    <script type="text/javascript">
        var body = document.getElementsByTagName("body")[0];
        for (var prop in location) {
            var elem = document.createElement("p");
```

```
                      var text = document.createTextNode(prop + ": " + location[prop]);
                      elem.appendChild(text);
                      body.appendChild(elem);
                  }
          </script>
    </body>
</html>
```

3. View the page in a web browser. Your results will vary, depending on how you set up your web server. This example shows that the webpage was retrieved from a server named tt. Also note that my example uses a file called location1-full.html, which contains all of the code for this exercise.

4. Modify the URI that you use to call the page by adding some query string parameter value pairs. For example, the URI used for my local environment is *http://tt/jsbs3e/Chapter09/ location1-full.html*. (Your environment and the location from which you serve the file will likely be different from this.) I'm going to modify the URL and add two parameters, *name=Steve* and *country=US*. Feel free to change the value for the *name* parameter to your name and change the *country* value to your home country (if you're not from the United States, that is). The values you choose aren't all that important here—what matters is that you use more than one parameter/value pair. Here's my final URI: *http://tt/jsbs3e/Chapter09/location1-full. html?name=Steve&country=US*.

5. When you load the page with the parameters you added, the *search* property has a value, as shown here:

6. Open the location1.html file again, and save it as **location2.html**.

7. Alter the code in location2.html so that it examines the *search* property, like this (the changes are shown in boldface type and are in the location2.txt file in the companion content):

```
<!doctype html>
<html>
<head>
    <title>Location, Location, Location</title>

</head>
<body>
    <script type="text/javascript">
            var body = document.getElementsByTagName("body")[0];
            for (var prop in location) {
                var elem = document.createElement("p");
                var text = document.createTextNode(prop + ": " + location[prop]);
                elem.appendChild(text);
                body.appendChild(elem);
            }
            if (location.search) {
                var querystring = location.search;
                var splits = querystring.split('&');
                for (var i = 0; i < splits.length; i++) {
                    var splitpair = splits[i].split('=');
                    var elem = document.createElement("p");
                    var text = document.createTextNode(splitpair[0] + ": "
```

```
        +splitpair[1]);
                        elem.appendChild(text);
                        body.appendChild(elem);
                }
        }
    </script>
</body>
</html>
```

8. Execute this code by pointing your browser to *location2.html?name=Steve&country=US*. (Alter the name and country as appropriate.) Again, note that the location2-full.html version is the full version. If you've followed along with the exercise, yours will still be called location2.html. When viewed in a browser, you now receive a page that lists the normal properties that you saw earlier but also lists (near the bottom) the parameter/value pairs parsed from the query string, like this:

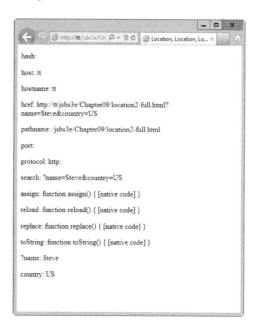

9. Notice that the first parameter, *name*, contains the question mark (*?*) from the query string, which is not what you want. You can solve this problem in several ways. One of the simplest is to use the *substring()* method. Change the *querystring* variable definition line to read:

```
var querystring = location.search.substring(1);
```

The *substring()* method returns the string starting at the point specified. In this case, the first character of *location.search* (at index *0*) is the question mark; therefore, use *substring()* starting at index *1* to solve the problem. The final code (with the change shown in boldface type) looks like the following (you can find this in the location3.html file in the companion content):

```
<!doctype html>
<html>
<head>
```

```
        <title>Location, Location, Location</title>

  </head>
  <body>
      <script type="text/javascript">
              var body = document.getElementsByTagName("body")[0];
              for (var prop in location) {
                  var elem = document.createElement("p");
                  var text = document.createTextNode(prop + ": " + location[prop]);
                  elem.appendChild(text);
                  body.appendChild(elem);
              }
              if (location.search) {
                  var querystring = location.search.substring(1);
                  var splits = querystring.split('&');
                  for (var i = 0; i < splits.length; i++) {
                      var splitpair = splits[i].split('=');
                      var elem = document.createElement("p");
                      var text = document.createTextNode(splitpair[0] + ": " +
                                      splitpair[1]);
                      elem.appendChild(text);
                      body.appendChild(elem);
                  }
              }
      </script>
  </body>
</html>
```

10. Save this code as **location3.html**, and run it again. You see from the results that you've solved the problem of the question mark:

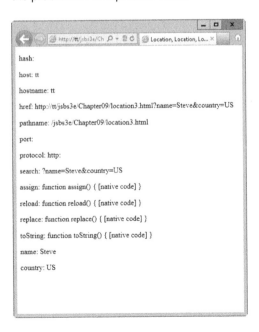

The URI that the browser displays can also be set using JavaScript and the location object. Typically you accomplish this using the *assign()* method of the *location* object. For example, to redirect to my website (always a good idea), I might use this code:

```
location.assign("http://www.braingia.org");
```

Calling the *assign()* method is essentially the same as setting the *href* property:

```
location.href = "http://www.braingia.org";
```

You can also change other properties of the location object, such as the port, the query string, or the path. For example, to set the path to */blog,* you can do this:

```
location.pathname = "blog";
```

To set the query string to *?name=Steve,* do this:

```
location.search = "?name=Steve";
```

You can reload the page by calling the *reload()* method:

```
location.reload();
```

When you call *location.reload()*, the browser might load the page from its cache rather than re-request the page from the server; however, if you pass a Boolean *true* to the method, the browser reloads the page directly from the server:

```
location.reload(true);
```

 Note Be careful using the *reload()* method. Trying to reload the page within a script, as opposed to through a function call triggered by an event, is likely to cause a loop condition.

The *history* object

The *history* object provides ways to move forward and backward through the visitor's browsing history. (However, for security reasons, JavaScript cannot access the URIs for sites that the browser visits.) Specifically, you can use the *back()*, *forward()*, and *go()* methods. It probably goes without saying, but *back()* and *forward()* move one page backward and forward, respectively. The *go()* method moves to the index value specified as the argument.

 Note If an application doesn't go to a different page or location in the address bar, the application won't be part of the browser's history and thus won't be accessible with these functions.

Here's some example code for moving backward and forward that can be adapted as needed. Examples in later chapters show more detail about how this kind of code might be used in the real world.

```
<!doctype html>
<html>
<head>
    <title>History</title>
    <script type="text/javascript">
        function moveBack() {
            history.back();
            return false;
        }
        function moveForward() {
            history.forward();
            return false;
        }
    </script>
</head>
<body>
<p><a href="#" onclick="return moveBack();">Click to go back</a></p>
<p><a href="#" onclick="return moveForward();">Click to go forward</a></p>
</body>
</html>
```

This code uses an inline event handler (*onclick*), which is not recommended for use in unobtrusive JavaScript, because the event handler inserts behavior in the page markup. The use of *onclick* here is for illustrative purposes only, to avoid introducing the event handler concept, which gets its own chapter—Chapter 13.

Registering handlers

HTML 5.0 introduced two new methods of the navigator object: *registerContentHandler()* and *registerProtocolHandler()*. Using these methods, a website can register a URI for handling certain types of information, such as an RSS feed. However, these methods are not yet widely supported and therefore aren't covered in this book.

Exercises

1. Use the *availHeight* and *availWidth* methods to determine whether a screen is at least 768 pixels high and 1,024 pixels wide. If it's not, display an *alert()* dialog box stating the size of the available screen.

2. Alter the step-by-step exercise that used the *location* object to display an *alert()* dialog box based on the values of the query string. Specifically, display the word "Obrigado" if the country is specified as Brazil, and display "Thank you" if the country is Great Britain. Test these conditions.

3. Install the User Agent Switcher add-on to Firefox or a similar add-on to Internet Explorer. Then use the code from the "Looking at the navigator object" exercise earlier in this chapter to experiment with the different values that you find. This exercise helps show why using the *navigator* object as the sole means of determining compatibility is not recommended. Bonus: Define your own user agent.

CHAPTER 10

An introduction to JavaScript libraries and frameworks

After completing this chapter, you will be able to

- Understand the role of JavaScript programming libraries and frameworks.

- Understand how to define your own library.

- Understand the role of third-party JavaScript libraries and frameworks and how to find more information about them.

Understanding programming libraries

In programming terms, a *library* is a grouping of code that provides common or additional functionality. Typically, libraries consist of one or more files that expose objects and functions. Within a program, a developer includes or calls the library to use these additional objects and functions. In this way, JavaScript libraries and frameworks are useful because they offload the maintenance and development of additional and enhanced functions. They help make common programming tasks easier and can also aid in smoothing out the differences and nuances in cross-browser development.

This chapter explores libraries in JavaScript, including the process of defining your own library, and takes a look at some of the more popular JavaScript libraries and frameworks available.

Defining your own JavaScript library

Developers working in any language find themselves performing common functions repeatedly in many of their coding tasks, so creating a personal library, or grouping, of common functions that you can use in future projects is helpful.

Libraries don't have to be large to be useful. In this next example, you create your own library.

Creating a library

1. Using Microsoft Visual Studio, Eclipse, or the editor of your choice, open the library.js file, which you can find in the Chapter10 folder of this book's companion content.

2. Within library.js, add the following code (replacing the TODO comment), and then add a function:

```
var MyLibrary = {};
```

```
MyLibrary.sendAlert = function(mesg, elm) {
        alert(mesg);
};
```

3. Save the file and close it.

4. Open the file librarypage.html. Within librarypage.html, add the boldface code shown here (replacing the TODO comment):

```
<!doctype html>
<html>
<head>
<title>A Basic Example</title>
<script type="text/javascript" src="library.js"></script>
</head>
<body>
<script type="text/javascript">

    MyLibrary.sendAlert("hello, this is the message");

</script>
</body>
</html>
```

5. Load the page librarypage.html in a web browser. You should receive an alert like this:

Tip If you don't receive an alert like the one just shown, be sure you have specified the path to the library.js file correctly. The example shown in the preceding librarypage.html code assumes that the JavaScript file library.js is in the same directory as the HTML file.

Take care when defining and using your own libraries so that you don't overlap or collide with existing functions and reserved words from the ECMA-262 specification. Additionally, if you use an external library or framework such as jQuery or YUI, you need to make sure that your library doesn't collide with the naming conventions used for those.

Looking at popular JavaScript libraries and frameworks

There are numerous publicly available libraries and frameworks for JavaScript. Their goal is to take difficult tasks and make them easier for programmers developing JavaScript-centric web applications.

Web developers spend a great deal of time trying to make pages look and act the same way across browsers. A significant advantage to using many JavaScript libraries or frameworks is that they remove the cross-browser compatibility headaches. All the popular JavaScript libraries and frameworks include code to make their respective functions work across all the browsers they support.

jQuery

jQuery provides a rich feature set, powerful options, extensibility, and excellent community support. Using jQuery, which is contained in a single JavaScript file, you can add effects to your webpages, enhance usability, and make processing of data with Asynchronous JavaScript and XML (AJAX) easier. Additionally, Microsoft shipped jQuery beginning with Visual Studio 2010. Chapter 11, "An introduction to jQuery," examines jQuery in greater detail. You can find more information about jQuery at *http://jquery.com*.

Modernizr

Modernizr enables developers to use some of the more advanced features of HTML5 and CSS3 in older browsers. It uses feature detection to determine whether a given browser supports a certain widget or effect and provides an alternative means of accomplishing the task at hand. More information about Modernizr can be found at *http://modernizr.com/*.

Yahoo! User Interface

Yahoo! User Interface (YUI) provides both JavaScript and Cascading Style Sheets (CSS), which simplifies developing web applications. Like jQuery, YUI includes features for enhancing usability and improving the web application. As an added bonus, YUI's documentation is excellent. You can find more information about YUI at *http://developer.yahoo.com/yui/*.

MooTools

MooTools is a very small, highly optimized library for JavaScript. MooTools differs from YUI and jQuery because it is an object-oriented framework that concentrates on providing greater modularity and code reuse, whereas YUI and jQuery focus on effects, CSS, and direct user-experience interactions. That's definitely not to say that MooTools doesn't have effects—MooTools also offers many of the same effects (such as an accordion and a slider) that you find in YUI and jQuery. MooTools is recommended for intermediate to advanced JavaScript programmers and is available from *http://mootools.net/*.

Other libraries

There are numerous other libraries and frameworks available for JavaScript—too many to cover or even mention in this book. As a starting point, see *http://en.wikipedia.org/wiki/Comparison_of_JavaScript_frameworks* to find out more information about JavaScript frameworks.

Exercises

1. Examine each of the libraries and frameworks shown in this chapter. Which do you think is easiest for the new JavaScript programmer to learn? Why?

2. Create your own JavaScript library with an external JavaScript file. Include that file in an HTML page and call it.

CHAPTER 11

An introduction to jQuery

After completing this chapter, you will be able to

- Understand how to include jQuery in your HTML.

- Understand important jQuery concepts and syntax.

- Use jQuery with your webpages.

jQuery primer

jQuery is a popular and easy-to-use JavaScript framework. jQuery makes difficult JavaScript tasks easy, often by taking the pain out of cross-browser JavaScript.

The entire jQuery library consists of only a single JavaScript file, which simplifies its inclusion in your JavaScript. jQuery syntax is also easy to learn; it uses a simple namespace and consistent functionality. Used together with the jQuery User Interface (UI) add-on (covered in Chapter 18, "Mobile development with jQuery Mobile)," you can create powerful, highly interactive web applications.

This chapter provides an introduction to jQuery, including how to download and use it in your JavaScript.

Using jQuery

You can obtain jQuery from *http://www.jquery.com/*. In this section, you'll see how to download jQuery and integrate it into a webpage.

The two jQuery downloads

On the jQuery home page, two downloads are available: a production version and a development version. Unless you're planning to develop jQuery plug-ins or need to look at the internals of jQuery, you should download and use the minified production version.

As another viable option, especially for working through this chapter, you could use a content delivery network (CDN) to access a hosted version of jQuery. Google hosts jQuery and other libraries through its API website. This means that you can include jQuery in your webpages and JavaScript programs without having to host the file locally on your server. See *http://code.google.com/apis /libraries/devguide.html* for more information.

> **Note** For almost all scenarios in which you are working with jQuery, I recommend downloading and hosting the jQuery file locally. Using the local version can be faster and more reliable than using the CDN version. For example, if you use a CDN-hosted version and the CDN server goes down, anything on your site that uses the library won't work! However, for development tasks in this chapter, using a CDN-hosted file is perfectly acceptable.

Performing the exercises and following along in this chapter requires that you have jQuery downloaded to your local development computer or are connected to it from a CDN.

Including jQuery

You include jQuery in a webpage in the same manner as you would any other external JavaScript file—with a *<SCRIPT>* tag pointing to the source file. Consider the code in Example 11-1, found in the companion content as listing11-1.html.

EXAMPLE 11-1 Including jQuery in a webpage

```
<!doctype html>
<html>
<head>
<title>Adding jQuery</title>
<script type="text/javascript" src="jquery-1.7.2.min.js"></script>
</head>
<body>
</body>
</html>
```

Now that you have jQuery downloaded or referenced from a CDN site and you've looked at the preceding example showing how to include jQuery in a file, it's time to move into learning jQuery syntax.

> **Important** Version 1.7.2 is the latest as of this writing. However, the version available from the jQuery website will almost certainly be different by the time you read this, so you'll need to change the *src* attribute appropriately for the version of the jQuery script that you download.

Basic jQuery syntax

When you include the jQuery library in a page, jQuery adds a function called *jquery()*. You might think that you'd make all calls to jQuery functions through this *jquery()* function interface, but there's a shortcut to the *jquery()* function: *$()*. Rather than typing **jquery()** each time, you access the jQuery library by using a dollar sign followed by parentheses, as shown in the examples in Table 11-1. Don't worry if this syntax doesn't quite make sense yet; you'll see more about selectors a little later in this chapter.

TABLE 11-1 A few jQuery selectors

Syntax	Description
$("a")	All <a> elements in the document
$(document)	The entire document, frequently used to access the *ready()* function shown later in this chapter
$("#elementID")	The element identified by ID *elementID*
$(".className")	The element or elements that have the *className* class

Like all JavaScript code, jQuery statements should end with a semicolon. It is also worth noting that you can use either single or double quotation marks as selectors within jQuery. For example, both of these statements are equally valid:

$("a")

$('a')

When you see examples of jQuery usage in the real world (not that this book isn't in the real world), both single and double quotation marks are used. Examples throughout this chapter use a mix of the two to get you familiar with seeing both cases; however, in your real-world programming, it's best to choose one style and stick with it.

Connecting jQuery to the *load* event

One of the most common ways to work with jQuery is by connecting to elements during the *load* (or *onload*) event of the page. (This chapter discusses events and functions in more detail later.) In jQuery, you do this through the *.ready()* utility function of the *document* element.

Recall from the brief example shown in the previous section that jQuery accesses elements with the *$()* syntax. Keeping that in mind, you can access the *document* element like this:

$(document)

And you can then access the *ready()* function like this:

$(document).ready()

The following exercise requires either that you have jQuery downloaded to your local development computer or that you use a CDN. The example shows version 1.7.2 of jQuery, but the version number will likely be different when you perform the exercise.

Using $(document).ready()

1. Using Microsoft Visual Studio, Eclipse, or another editor, edit the file docready.html in the Chapter11 sample files folder in the companion content.

2. Within that file, add the following code shown in boldface in place of the TODO comment:

```
<!doctype html>
<html>
<head>
<title>Document Ready</title>
<script type="text/javascript" src="jquery-1.7.2.min.js"></script>
</head>
<body>
<script type="text/javascript">
    $(document).ready(function() {
        alert('hi');
    });
</script>
</body>
</html>
```

3. Save the file, and view the page in a web browser. You'll see an alert like this one:

The code in this step-by-step exercise combines jQuery through the *$(document).ready()* function and also regular, plain old JavaScript, represented by the *alert()* function in this example. This mixture of jQuery and JavaScript is an important concept to understand: you use jQuery to supplement normal JavaScript. jQuery makes many of the difficult and sometimes mundane tasks easy—so easy, in fact, that you can spend your time building features rather than worrying about cross-browser nuances.

The *$(document).ready()* function removes the need for you to use the browser's *load* event or to insert a function call into the *load* event. With *$(document).ready()*, all the elements of the Document Object Model (DOM) are available before the *.ready()* function executes, although not necessarily all images.

Tip The *$(document).ready()* function is central to much of the programming that you do with jQuery.

Using selectors

Selectors are key to working with jQuery and the DOM. You use *selectors* to identify and group the elements on which a jQuery function is executed. As shown in Table 11-1, you use selectors to gather all the elements of a certain tag, of a certain ID, or with a certain class applied to them. You can also use selectors in much more powerful ways, such as to select a specified number of elements or to select only elements with a particular ancestry—for example, only those *<P>* tags that follow a *<DIV>* tag. This section introduces selectors in more detail.

Tip *Selectors* and the way they work in jQuery are based on selectors in CSS. If you are comfortable with using them in CSS (discussed in Chapter 16, "JavaScript and CSS"), you will feel right at home with this model.

Selecting elements by ID

The example in Table 11-1 showed the general syntax for selecting an element by its ID attribute:

```
$("#elementID")
```

For example, consider this bit of HTML:

```
<a href="#" id="linkOne">Link</a>
```

With normal JavaScript, you access this element like so:

```
getElementById("linkOne")
```

With jQuery, you access the element using this:

```
$("#linkOne")
```

Selecting elements by class

You select elements by class by prefixing a dot (.) to the class name. The syntax is this:

```
$(".className")
```

For example, here's a *<DIV>* element with a class applied:

```
<div class="specialClass">
```

You would access that element through jQuery like this:

```
$(".specialClass")
```

Bear in mind that you might not be accessing a single element; the class selector accesses *all* elements for which the specified class is applied. That is, if several elements in the page have the *"specialClass"* class applied, jQuery accesses all of them using the *$(".specialClass")* selector. You see more about this later when working with functions that iterate through each element retrieved with such a selector.

Selecting elements by type

You can also use selectors to access elements by type, such as all *<DIV>* elements, all *<A>* elements, and so on. For example, you would access all *<DIV>* elements in a document like this:

```
$('div')
```

Similarly, to access all the *<A>* elements, you would write:

```
$('a')
```

Using a type selector provides access to all the elements of the specified type on a page. Like the class selector, type selectors can return multiple elements.

Selecting elements by hierarchy

As mentioned earlier, you can select elements by their position in relation to other elements on the page. For example, to select all the *<A>* elements that are within *<DIV>* elements, you use this syntax:

```
$("div a")
```

You can get more specific than that as well. For example, if you want all the anchors within a specific *<DIV>* element, you combine the type selector with the ID selector syntax. Consider this HTML:

```
<div id="leftNav">
<a href="link1.html">Link 1</a>
<a href="link2.html">Link 2</a>
</div>
```

Here's the jQuery selector syntax to retrieve the two anchor elements within the *leftNav* *<DIV>* element:

```
$("#leftNav a")
```

More generically, if you want only the direct descendants of an element, use the greater-than sign:

```
$("div > p")
```

This syntax yields all the *<P>* elements that are direct descendants of a *<DIV>* element but does not include any *<P>* elements within the selected *<P>* elements.

You can also choose the *n*th child in a set with the *:nth-child()* selector. This example chooses the third child of every *<P>* element:

```
$("p:nth-child(3)")
```

Several other hierarchical selectors exist. You can find more in the jQuery selector reference documentation at *http://api.jquery.com/category/selectors/*.

Selecting elements by position

As you've seen, the selectors in jQuery are greedy. For example, the *$('a')* syntax selects all anchor tags. jQuery offers several ways to select more specific elements within a group. One such method is to use the *first* and *last* selectors. The following code selects the first *<P>* element within the page:

```
$("p:first")
```

Likewise, the last element is selected like this:

```
$("p:last")
```

You can also select elements by their direct position. As another example, consider this HTML:

```
<p>First P</p>
<p>Second P</p>
<p>Third P</p>
```

To select the second *<P>* element, you use this syntax:

```
$("p")[1]
```

Note that the array index begins with *0* for this type of selector, so the first element is index *0*, the second is index *1*, and so on. Using this syntax is a little dangerous because it relies on the strict positioning of the elements within the hierarchy. If someone adds another *<P>* tag to the page before the element you're trying to select, the addition causes the array index to change, so you would be choosing the wrong element from the selector. When possible, it's better to use an ID selector to choose an individual or specific element than to rely on an element's position.

An alternative way of selecting by index is to use the *:eq* syntax. For example, to choose the third paragraph, you could write:

```
$("p:eq(3)")
```

Finally, another sometimes useful set of positional selectors are *even* and *odd*, which select every other element in a set:

```
$("p:even")
```

The *even* and *odd* selectors are quite helpful when working with tabular data to alternate row colors. Example 11-2 shows how to use the *odd* selector to differentiate the background color of alternating rows in a table. You can find this code as listing11-2.html in the companion content.

> **Note** The code from Example 11-2 uses two items that haven't yet been formally introduced: a user-defined function and the *.css()* function. Don't worry about that now. You examine each of these items in more detail later in the chapter.

EXAMPLE 11-2 Tabular data and jQuery

```
<!doctype html>
<html>
<head>
<title>Table Test</title>
<script type="text/javascript" src="jquery-1.7.2.min.js"></script>
</head>
<body>
<table>
  <tr>
    <td>Row 1 Column 1 of the table</td>
    <td>Row 1 Column 2 of the table</td>
  </tr>
  <tr>
    <td>Row 2 Column 1 of the table</td>
    <td>Row 2 Column 2 of the table</td>
  </tr>
  <tr>
    <td>Row 3 Column 1 of the table</td>
    <td>Row 3 Column 2 of the table</td>
  </tr>
  <tr>
    <td>Row 4 Column 1 of the table</td>
    <td>Row 4 Column 2 of the table</td>
  </tr>
  <tr>
    <td>Row 5 Column 1 of the table</td>
    <td>Row 5 Column 2 of the table</td>
  </tr>
  <tr>
    <td>Row 6 Column 1 of the table</td>
    <td>Row 6 Column 2 of the table</td>
  </tr>
</table>
<script type="text/javascript">
$(document).ready(function() {
    $('tr:odd').css("background-color", "#abacab");
});
</script>

</body>
</html>
```

This main portion of this code is contained in the JavaScript section within the body of the HTML:

```
$(document).ready(function() {
    $('tr:odd').css("background-color", "#abacab");
});
```

The code uses the *$(document).ready()* function along with the *:odd* selector to set the background color to hexadecimal *#abacab*—a light gray color. Figure 11-1 shows an example of the output.

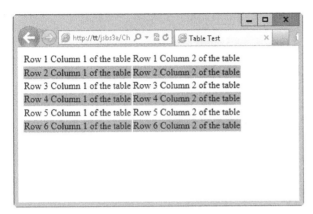

FIGURE 11-1 A table colorized with the help of jQuery.

You've seen some of the most common positional selectors, but there are many more positional selectors available. Refer to *http://api.jquery.com/category/selectors/* for more information.

Selecting elements by attribute

As you might suspect from the class selector you've already seen, jQuery lets you select elements that merely contain an attribute or those that contain an attribute with a specific value. For example, to select all images that have an *alt* attribute, you write this:

```
$("img[alt]")
```

Selecting only images that have an *alt* attribute set to a certain value looks like this:

```
$("img[alt='alternate text']")
```

The preceding code selects an image only if the *alt* text is the word *alternate text*. Note the use of alternating single and double quotation marks within this example. The *img* selector is wrapped in double quotation marks, whereas the internal *alt* attribute selector is wrapped in single quotation marks, but the example could just as easily have been in the reverse, with single quotation marks used on the *img* selector and double quotation marks used on the *alt* attribute selector:

```
$('img[alt="alternate text"]')
```

You could also use the same quotation mark scheme for both, but if you do that, you need to escape the internal quotation marks, as follows:

```
$("img[alt=\"alternate text\"]")
```

 Important This type of selector expects an exact match. In the preceding example, the *alt* attribute needs to be the string *"alternate text"*. Any variation of that, such as *"alternate text 2"* or *"alternate text2"* would not match.

jQuery includes wildcard selectors that don't require an exact match on attributes. Consider the examples in Table 11-2.

TABLE 11-2 Attribute selector matching

Syntax	Description
attribute*=value	Selects elements that contain the attribute for which the attribute value contains the specified value as a substring
attribute~=value	Selects elements that contain the attribute for which the attribute value contains the specified value as a word delimited by spaces
attribute!=value	Selects elements that either do not contain the attribute or for which the attribute value does not match the specified value
attribute$=value	Selects elements that contain the specified attribute for which the attribute's value ends with the specified string
attribute^=value	Selects elements that contain the attribute for which the attribute's value begins with the specified string

Selecting form elements

jQuery contains native selectors related to web forms. Table 11-3 lists some of these selectors, some of which are used in remainder of this chapter.

TABLE 11-3 Form-related selectors

Selector	Description
:checkbox	Selects all check boxes
:checked	Selects all elements that are checked, such as check boxes
:input	Selects all input elements on a page
:password	Selects all password inputs
:radio	Selects all radio button inputs
:reset	Selects all input types of reset
:selected	Selects all elements that are currently selected
:submit	Selects all input types of submit
:text	Selects all input types of text

More selectors

There are many more selectors in jQuery, such as those that select all hidden elements (*:hidden*) or all visible elements (*:visible*) as well as enabled elements, disabled elements, and others. See *http://api.jquery.com/category/selectors/* for a complete and up-to-date list of selectors in jQuery.

> **Tip** Rather than devising a complex and fragile selector syntax to get at a certain element, refer to the jQuery selector reference (*http://api.jquery.com/category/selectors/*) to see whether someone has already solved the selector problem.

Functions

So far, you've seen a lot of examples that select elements with jQuery, but only a couple of examples that show what you can do with those elements after selecting them. jQuery uses functions to perform actions on selected elements. Functions can be built in to jQuery or user-defined. You almost always end up using both at the same time.

Traversing the DOM

The nature of programming on the web using JavaScript and now jQuery frequently requires looping or iterating through several elements—for example, the *.each()* function takes a list of selected elements and iterates over each of them, doing something (or nothing) to each as it loops through the list. jQuery contains numerous functions for looping and iterating. This process is known in jQuery parlance as *traversing*. You can find more information about the traversing-related functions at *http://api.jquery.com/category/traversing/*.

When using traversal functions, you almost always do so with the help of a user-defined wrapper function along with the *$(this)* selector. Like the *this* keyword in object-oriented programming, the *$(this)* selector refers to the current object—in this case, the item currently being traversed.

An example might be useful here. The following HTML builds a standings page for a fictitious volleyball league:

```
<!doctype html>
<html>
<head>
<title>Iteration Test</title>
<script type="text/javascript" src="jquery-1.7.2.min.js"></script>
</head>
<body>
<table>
  <th>Team Name</th>
  <th>W-L Record</th>
  <th>Win Percentage</th>
  <tr>
    <td>Team 1</td>
```

```
      <td>12-8</td>
      <td class="percentage">.600</td>
    </tr>
    <tr>
      <td>Team 5</td>
      <td>11-9</td>
      <td class="percentage">.550</td>
    </tr>
    <tr>
      <td>Team 4</td>
      <td>10-10</td>
      <td class="percentage">.500</td>
    </tr>
    <tr>
      <td>Team 2</td>
      <td>9-11</td>
      <td class="percentage">.450</td>
    </tr>
    <tr>
      <td>Team 6</td>
      <td>6-14</td>
      <td class="percentage">.300</td>
    </tr>
    <tr>
      <td>Team 3</td>
      <td>2-18</td>
      <td class="percentage">.100</td>
    </tr>
</table>
<script type="text/javascript">
$(document).ready(function() {
    $('tr:odd').css("background-color", "#abacab");
});
</script>

</body>
</html>
```

When viewed in a web browser, the page looks like Figure 11-2.

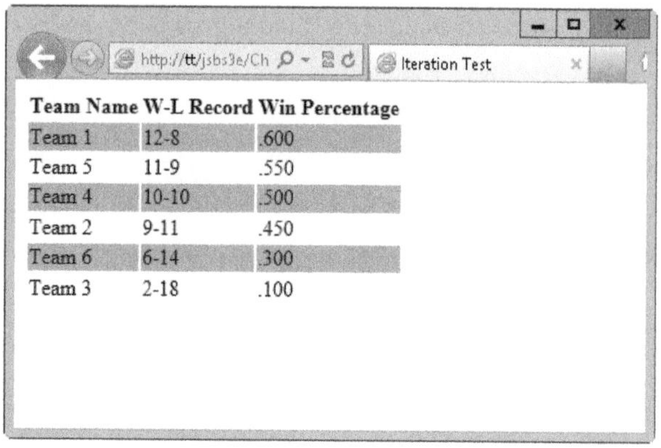

FIGURE 11-2 Standings page for a fictitious volleyball league.

So far, this example does essentially the same thing as Example 11-2. The next example iterates through all the elements that contain a *class* attribute called *percentage*—a *class* that's applied to the cells in the Win Percentage column in the table. For any team whose win/loss percentage is at or above .500 (meaning the team won at least half of its games), this example applies a boldface font to its field. You can accomplish this with the following jQuery code, added just below the other jQuery code already in the page:

```
$('.percentage').each(function() {
    if ($(this).text() >= .5) {
        $(this).css('font-weight', 'bold');
    }
});
```

This code uses a selector to gather all the elements that have the *percentage* class applied to them. It then accesses each of these elements using the *.each()* function in jQuery. Within the *.each()* function, a user-defined function performs a conditional to determine whether the value in the Win Percentage column is greater than or equal to .5. If it is, the code calls the *.css()* function to add a *font-weight* property set to *bold* for that element. After adding this code to the page, the result looks like Example 11-3, found as listing11-3.html in the companion content.

EXAMPLE 11-3 Adding jQuery to the volleyball league page

```
<!doctype html>
<html>
<head>
<title>Iteration Test</title>
<script type="text/javascript" src="jquery-1.7.2.min.js"></script>
</head>
<body>
<table>
  <th>Team Name</th>
  <th>W-L Record</th>
  <th>Win Percentage</th>
  <tr>
    <td>Team 1</td>
    <td>12-8</td>
    <td class="percentage">.600</td>
  </tr>
  <tr>
    <td>Team 5</td>
    <td>11-9</td>
    <td class="percentage">.550</td>
  </tr>
  <tr>
    <td>Team 4</td>
    <td>10-10</td>
    <td class="percentage">.500</td>
  </tr>
```

```
    <tr>
        <td>Team 2</td>
        <td>9-11</td>
        <td class="percentage">.450</td>
    </tr>
    <tr>
        <td>Team 6</td>
        <td>6-14</td>
        <td class="percentage">.300</td>
    </tr>
    <tr>
        <td>Team 3</td>
        <td>2-18</td>
        <td class="percentage">.100</td>
    </tr>
</table>
<script type="text/javascript">
$(document).ready(function() {
    $('tr:odd').css("background-color", "#abacab");
    $('.percentage').each(function() {
        if ($(this).text() >= .5) {
            $(this).css('font-weight', 'bold');
        }
    });
});
</script>

</body>
</html>
```

When you view this page in a browser, you see that the Win Percentage column is now boldface for those teams that have won at least half of their games, as depicted in Figure 11-3.

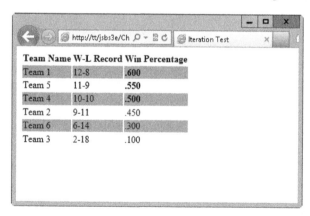

FIGURE 11-3 Some Win Percentage column entries are now boldface with the help of jQuery.

Looking at the output from Figure 11-3, you see that it would be even nicer to apply the boldface font weight to the entire table row rather than to just the Win Percentage column. Doing that might seem difficult, because logically the code is already past that HTML table row by the time the test is applied to find out the win percentage. Fortunately, jQuery has a function that can help: the .*parent()* function. (Actually, there are several ways to accomplish this. The .*parent()* function is just one way.)

Applying the *parent()* function essentially moves up the DOM tree to find the parent tag that encloses this particular *<TD>* element, which is the *<TR>* element. By applying the CSS style change to the *<TR>* element, you can make the entire row boldface. The new code looks like this, with the change highlighted in boldface:

```
$('.percentage').each(function() {
    if ($(this).text() >= .5) {
        $(this).parent().css('font-weight', 'bold');
    }
});
```

When added to the code from Example 11-3, the output becomes similar to that in Figure 11-4.

Team Name	W-L Record	Win Percentage
Team 1	12-8	.600
Team 5	11-9	.550
Team 4	10-10	.500
Team 2	9-11	.450
Team 6	6-14	.300
Team 3	2-18	.100

FIGURE 11-4 Applying CSS style at the table row level.

Note This revised code is available in the listing11-4.html file in the companion content.

The use of the .*parent()* function introduces a new concept called chaining. *Chaining* is a powerful construct in jQuery because it enables additional levels of selection and multilevel application of functions. In this example, the *$(this)* selector is chained to the .*parent()* function, which selects the parent element of the tag referenced by *$(this)*. Only then does the code execute the .*css()* function.

With the power of chaining comes a bit of danger. It's quite possible to chain your way into difficult-to-read and difficult-to-maintain code. In addition, chaining can create fragile code when the elements in a chained selector change. Chaining is powerful, so I recommend using it when possible but not at the expense of readability or maintainability.

The examples shown so far in the chapter have all accessed and changed the CSS directly, using JavaScript. As you'll see in Chapter 16, changing the style or presentational aspects of a webpage through JavaScript is not recommended. It's better practice to apply or remove styles through CSS rather than change attributes directly. Several methods exist to work with CSS style classes using jQuery, including *.hasClass()*, *.addClass()*, *.removeClass()*, and *.toggleClass()*. See *http://api.jquery.com/category/css/* for more information about working with classes by using these and other functions.

Working with attributes

In addition to the class-related attribute functions, jQuery has functions to work with attributes of the DOM. The most generic of these is the *.attr()* function, although others, such as *.html()* and *.val()*, are useful as well. This section looks at the *.attr()* function, saving *.html()*, *.val()*, and others for a later section.

You use the *.attr()* function to both retrieve and set attributes. For example, you can both retrieve and set an image's *alt* attribute using this syntax:

```
// Get the alt attribute:
$("#myImageID").attr("alt")
// Set the alt attribute:
$("#myImageID").attr("alt", "new text")
```

Note Retrieving the value of the element before setting it is unnecessary.

Changing text and HTML

You can completely rewrite a page using functions such as *.text()* and *.val()*. Of course, just because it's possible doesn't mean it's a good idea. However, you sometimes find that you need to rewrite portions of HTML within a page or change text or values.

The *.html()* function retrieves or changes the entire HTML within a selected element. For example, consider this HTML:

```
<div id="myDiv">Here is a div; it's quite nice</div>
```

And here's the jQuery:

```
$("#myDiv").html('<span class="redStyle">This is the new content of the div</span>');
```

The outcome of this bit of jQuery is that the *<DIV>* element identified by *myDiv* would now contain a *<SPAN>* element with new text in it, as shown in the code example. This is a rather simplistic example, but imagine that the *<DIV>* element contained an entire content section. Using jQuery, you could essentially rewrite that entire section, HTML and all.

Like the *.html()* function, the *.text()* function supports both retrieval and setting of the text within a selected element. Unlike HTML, the *.text()* function gets or sets only text, so it's not possible to alter the actual HTML of the selected element, although it is possible to replace any HTML within the element itself.

```
<div id="myDiv">Here is a div; it's quite nice</div>
$("#myDiv").text('This is the new content of the div');
```

In the preceding example, only the text changed; the code didn't add a span or apply styling. In fact, any HTML added using text would actually be encoded and wouldn't be very helpful at all.

Inserting elements

You can easily use jQuery to add elements to a page. Two primary functions for doing this are the *.after()* and *.before()* functions. As their names suggest, they add HTML either after or before a selected element, respectively.

For example, here's that *<DIV>* element again:

```
<div id="myDiv">Here is a div, it's quite nice</div>
```

And here's some jQuery that inserts another *<DIV>* element before it:

```
$("#myDiv").before("<div>This is a new div</div>");
```

The *.after()* function works in a similar fashion:

```
$("#myDiv").after("<div>This is a new div, it appears after myDiv</div>");
```

When run, the page containing this code would have three *<DIV>* elements:

```
<div>This is a new div</div>
<div id="myDiv">Here is a div, it's quite nice</div>
<div>This is a new div, it appears after myDiv</div>
```

The examples shown insert additional *<DIV>* elements—but of course you could use any valid element within these functions.

The *.append()* function works in much the same manner as the *.after()* function, with the difference being that the *.append()* function inserts the HTML within the element to which it's appended. Consider this code:

```
$(document).ready(function() {
    $('body').append('<div id="myDiv">Adding an element</div>');
});
```

This example produces the HTML output with the *<DIV>* element inside the *<BODY>* element:

```
<body>
    <div id="myDiv">Adding an element</div>
</body>
```

Here's that example code using the *after()* function:

```
$(document).ready(function() {
    $('body').after('<div id="myDiv">Adding an element</div>');
});
```

This produces the following HTML:

```
<body>
</body>
<div id="myDiv">Adding an element</div>
```

As you can see, *.after()* places the *<DIV>* element outside the *<BODY>* element, which is probably not desirable for this particular example.

Callback functions

Sometimes you need to run a function when another function completes, a construct called a *callback function*. A callback function is a function that is passed as an argument to another function that executes after its parent function completes. jQuery uses callback functions heavily, especially in AJAX. You already saw an example of a callback function when iterating using the *.each()* function.

For more information about callback functions, see *http://docs.jquery.com/Tutorials:How_jQuery_Works*.

For those of you who are beginner or intermediate JavaScript programmers, it's important that you don't *overthink* callback functions. They're merely a grouping of code that gets called within another function.

More jQuery

You've seen only a small portion of what jQuery can do. As you learn more about JavaScript and how it can help activate your websites, consider using jQuery or another JavaScript library to help you with those development efforts. Later chapters will show how to use jQuery for event handling and to retrieve data, as well as several other uses.

For more jQuery learning and reference material, see the resources at *http://www.jquery.com*.

Exercises

1. Using the code in listing11-1.html (from the chapter's first example) as a base, add a *<DIV>* HTML element using jQuery.

2. Using the code from Exercise 11-1, change the background color of the *<DIV>* element to any color other than white.

PART II

Integrating JavaScript into Design

This part of the book focuses on JavaScript and its use in the web browser. This section begins with a look at the Document Object Model (DOM), which is central to JavaScript programming. Browser events are discussed next, which leads into a discussion of images and web forms and how to work with those using JavaScript.

CSS is integral to design, and you can manipulate CSS using JavaScript. That's shown in this section, as is the use of jQuery Mobile and jQuery UI.

CHAPTER 12

The Document Object Model

After completing this chapter, you will be able to

- Use the Document Object Model (DOM) to retrieve elements from a document.

- Create new elements in a document.

- Make changes to elements in a document.

- Remove elements from a document.

The Document Object Model defined

The Document Object Model (DOM) provides a way to access and alter the contents of Hypertext Markup Language (HTML) documents. The DOM is a standard defined by the World Wide Web Consortium (W3C). Most Internet browsers implement the DOM in various forms—and with varying degrees of success.

Like many other standards, especially those related to web programming, the DOM has evolved over the years. It has three specifications, known as *levels* in DOM-speak, with a fourth specification on the way.

The DOM is much more powerful than this chapter or even this book can convey, and there's much more to it than I attempt to cover. You can use the DOM for more than just JavaScript programming. This book focuses on how you can use JavaScript to access and manipulate the DOM.

When I refer to the DOM in this chapter (and throughout this book), I emphasize how it relates to the current task rather than to the broader relevant concepts or what might be possible with the DOM. For example, this book concentrates on how the DOM represents HTML documents as trees. The DOM does so for HTML and Extensible Markup Language (XML) alike, but because this is a book about JavaScript, it's most important that you understand the DOM's relation to HTML.

For more information about the DOM, refer to its specification at the W3C site: *http://www.w3.org/DOM/.*

Note Some of the examples in this chapter use the inline event handlers, such as the *onload* event attached directly to the *<BODY>* tag, and the *onclick* event handler attached to various HTML tags. Use of inline event handlers is not best practice, and they are used here for illustrative purposes only. Chapter 13, "JavaScript events and the browser," introduces a better approach for attaching events to HTML.

DOM Level 0: The legacy DOM

DOM Level 0 is also known as the legacy DOM. DOM Level 0 was implemented before formal specifications of the DOM. After DOM Level 1 was specified, the previous technology related to document scripting was codified (although not in any formal way by any standards body) as the legacy DOM Level 0. Today, every major browser supports DOM Level 0 components for downward compatibility. You don't want all those scripts you wrote back in 1998 to break!

The DOM Level 0 concentrated mainly on giving access to form elements, but it also incorporated providing access to links and images. Chapter 15, "Using JavaScript with web forms," covers forms and how you access them with the DOM. Rather than spend time on examples of DOM Level 0, I concentrate on DOM Levels 1 and 2, which you're more likely to use when you program in JavaScript.

DOM Levels 1 through 3

The W3C issued Level 1 of the DOM as a specification in 1998. Like the legacy DOM, Level 1 is supported, in various forms, by all the major browsers. Level 2 of the DOM was formally released in 2000. Support of Level 2 DOM varies more widely among browsers. Finally, Level 3 of the DOM was codified in 2004 and has various levels of support in the major browsers. However, support of all DOM levels varies from browser to browser and from version to version.

Versions of Windows Internet Explorer prior to version 9 claim to support the DOM, but they do so differently from other browsers. As a result, you need to be aware that the DOM feature or function you're using or attempting to use in your JavaScript code might not work in Internet Explorer or might work only in Internet Explorer and nowhere else (and no, that's not acceptable). Windows Internet Explorer version 9 is a step in the right direction, but you still need to account for compatibility issues among browsers. Where applicable, I point out the places where browsers implement the DOM differently and some workarounds for such events.

Luckily, jQuery helps reduce much of the effort necessary in working with the DOM by making access to elements easy. You saw examples of this in the previous chapter and will continue to see jQuery used in this chapter and beyond.

The DOM as a tree

The DOM represents HTML documents in a tree-like structure—or rather, an uprooted tree-like structure—because the root of the tree is on top. For example, consider the simple HTML document shown in Example 12-1.

EXAMPLE 12-1 A simple HTML document

```
<!doctype html>
<html>
<head>
<title>Hello World</title>
</head>
<body>
<p>Here's some text.</p>
<p>Here's more text.</p>
<p>Link to the <a href="http://www.w3.org">W3</a></p>
</body>
</html>
```

Figure 12-1 shows the HTML from Example 12-1 when viewed in the tree structure of the DOM.

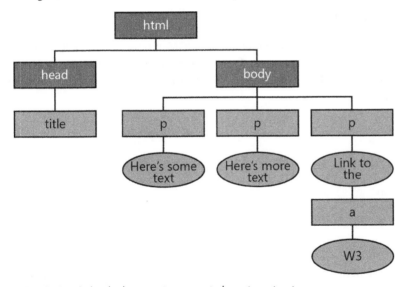

FIGURE 12-1 A simple document represented as a tree structure.

Many HTML elements can have attributes, such as the *href* attribute of the *<A>* element shown in Example 12-1. You can both retrieve and set these attributes using the DOM, as you will see later in this chapter.

When working with the DOM, you should be aware of the distinction among retrieving elements, setting elements and items related to elements, and removing or deleting elements. The methods for working with DOM elements reflect this distinction.

Working with nodes

The elements within the tree structure are sometimes referred to as *nodes* or *node objects*. Nodes at the level below a given node are known as *children*. For example, in the structure shown in Figure 12-1, the *<BODY>* node has three child nodes, all *<P>* elements, and one of the *<P>* elements has a child of its own, an *<A>* element. The *<BODY>* node is said to be a parent of the *<P>* nodes. Any nodes under a given node are known as *descendants* of that node. The three *<P>* nodes in Figure 12-1 are known as *siblings* because they're on the same level.

In the same way you use methods to work with elements of the DOM, you use methods to work with nodes that reflect the parent/child and sibling relationships. For example, you can use methods such as *appendChild()*, shown later in this chapter, to add nodes to an existing parent.

Retrieving elements

Retrieving the elements of a document is an essential way you use the DOM when programming with JavaScript. This section examines two of the primary methods you use to retrieve elements: *getElementById()* and *getElementsByTagName()*.

Retrieving elements by ID

The *getElementById()* method is a workhorse method of the DOM. It retrieves a specified element of the HTML document and returns a reference to it. To retrieve an element, it must have an *id* attribute. For example, you can modify the HTML from Example 12-1 to add an *id* attribute to the *<A>* element, as shown in boldface here:

```
<!doctype html>
<html>
<head>
<title>Hello World</title>
<body>
<p>Here's some text.</p>
<p>Here's more text.</p>
<p>Link to the <a id="w3link" href="http://www.w3.org">W3</a></p>
</body>
</html>
```

Now that the *<A>* element has an *id* attribute, you can retrieve it using the *getElementById()* method, as follows:

```
var a1 = document.getElementById("w3link");
```

The reference for the element with the ID *w3link* would be placed inside the JavaScript variable *a1*.

All HTML elements support *id* attributes, which makes them all retrievable by JavaScript. In this example, all the *<P>* elements get IDs, thus making them retrievable using the *getElementById()* method, too. Take a look at this code:

```
<!doctype html>
<html>
<head>
<title>Hello World</title>
<body>
<p id="sometext">Here's some text.</p>
<p id="moretext">Here's more text.</p>
<p id="linkp">Link to the <a id="w3link" href="http://www.w3.org">W3</a></p>
</body>
</html>
```

You can retrieve the <P> elements in the same way:

```
var p1 = document.getElementById("sometext");
var p2 = document.getElementById("moretext");
var plink = document.getElementById("linkp");
```

But what can you do with those elements after you retrieve them? For elements such as <A>, you can access their attributes by retrieving the value of the *href* attribute, as in this example:

```
<!doctype html>
<html>
<head>
    <title>Get By Id</title>
    <script type="text/javascript">
    function checkhref() {
        var a1 = document.getElementById("w3link");
        alert(a1.href);
    }
    </script>
</head>
<body onload="checkhref();">
<p id="sometext">Here's some text.</p>
<p id="moretext">Here's more text.</p>
<p id="linkp">Link to the <a id="w3link" href="http://www.w3.org">W3</a></p>
</body>
</html>
```

The page containing this code displays a dialog box showing the *href* attribute from the <A> element, like the one in Figure 12-2. This code can be found as example2.html in the companion content.

FIGURE 12-2 The *href* attribute retrieved with the help of *getElementById()*.

Later in this chapter, you see how to change elements and attributes.

A note on the *innerHTML* property

One way to change the text of elements is to use the *innerHTML* property. The *innerHTML* property enables fast and simple access to the HTML in such elements as a *<P>* element. This property generally works well—so well, in fact, that although it wasn't well liked in many web programming circles for some time, I find it difficult to skip it entirely in this book. So I won't.

The problem with *innerHTML* is that it wasn't formally defined as a standard by the W3C, so it's not necessarily supported in all browsers in the way that other DOM-specified objects are. However, *innerHTML* is a part of the HTML 5.0 specification, and with the sometimes unpredictable implementations of the actual DOM specification, *innerHTML* is still desirable. The major browsers support *innerHTML*—and they do so fairly consistently.

Take a look at this example, found as getbyid.html in the companion content.

```
<!doctype html>
<html>
<head>
    <title>Get By Id</title>
    <script type="text/javascript">
    function changetext() {
        var p1 = document.getElementById("sometext");
        alert(p1.innerHTML);
        p1.innerHTML = "Changed Text";
    }
    </script>
</head>
<body onload="changetext()">
<p id="sometext">Here's some text.</p>
<p id="moretext">Here's more text.</p>
<p id="linkp">Link to the <a id="w3link" href="http://www.w3.org">W3</a></p>
</body>
</html>
```

The *changetext()* function retrieves the element with an ID of *sometext* and places a reference to it in the variable *p1*, using this code:

```
var p1 = document.getElementById("sometext");
```

Next, it calls the *innerHTML* property, sending the result to an *alert()* dialog box.

Notice not only the *alert()* dialog box but also the text of the first line in the background window. When the user clicks OK, the *alert()* dialog box disappears, and the next line of JavaScript executes, using the *innerHTML* property to change the text of the first *<P>* element to *"Changed Text"*. The result is shown here:

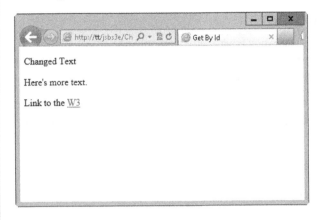

Here's that same code, except this time with jQuery. This code is similar to that which you saw in Chapter 11, "An introduction to jQuery," retrieving an element by its ID and then changing HTML on the element.

```
<!doctype html>
<html>
<head>
    <title>Get By Id</title>
    <script type="text/javascript" src="jquery-1.7.2.min.js"></script>
    <script type="text/javascript">
    $(document).ready(function() {
        function changetext() {
            alert($("#sometext").html());
            $("#sometext").html("Changed Text");
        }
        changetext();
    });
    </script>
</head>
<body>
<p id="sometext">Here's some text.</p>
<p id="moretext">Here's more text.</p>

<p id="linkp">Link to the <a id="w3link" href="http://www.w3.org">W3</a></p>
</body>
</html>
```

Notable changes in the jQuery version of this code, which can be found as getbyid-jquery.html in the companion content, include the addition of the jQuery script itself and then the use of the *ready()* function instead of the *onload* method. The *changetext()* function has been changed to simply alert the results of the *text()* function and to then change the text.

Retrieving by tag name

The *getElementById()* method works well when you're retrieving only one or just a few elements, but when you need to retrieve more than one element at a time, you might find the *getElementsByTagName()* method to be more appropriate.

The *getElementsByTagName()* method returns all the elements of the specified tag type in an array or in a list format. For example, to retrieve all the images (*<IMG>* tags) in a document, you write the following code:

```
var images = document.getElementsByTagName("img");
```

You could then examine the properties of the *<IMG>* elements stored in the *images* variable by looping through them.

Here's an example that modifies a table. This code changes the background color of each *<TD>* element within the table when the user clicks the Click To Change Colors link. You can find this code in the companion content, in the file getbytag.html:

```
<!doctype html>
<html>
<head>
    <title>Tag Name</title>
    <script type="text/javascript">
    function changecolors() {
        var a1 = document.getElementsByTagName("td");

        var a1Length = a1.length;
        for (var i = 0; i < a1Length; i++) {
            a1[i].style.background = "#aaabba";
        }
    }

    </script>
</head>
<body>
<table id="mytable" border="1">
<tr><td id="lefttd0">Left column</td><td id="righttd0">Right column</td></tr>
<tr><td id="lefttd1">Left column</td><td id="righttd1">Right column</td></tr>
<tr><td id="lefttd2">Left column</td><td id="righttd2">Right column</td></tr>
</table>
<a href="#" onclick="return changecolors();">Click to Change Colors</a>
</body>
</html>
```

Figure 12-3 shows how this page looks when viewed in a web browser.

FIGURE 12-3 Using *getElementsByTagName()* to format elements from a table.

Clicking the link causes the table elements to change background color, which you can see in Figure 12-4.

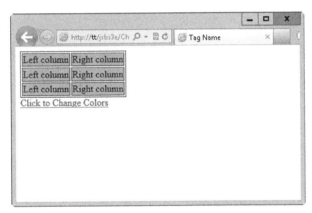

FIGURE 12-4 After a user clicks the link, the table elements change background color.

Examining the code, you see that the JavaScript in the *<HEAD>* portion of the page creates a function called *changecolors()*:

```
function changecolors() {
```

That function retrieves all the *<TD>* elements by using the *getElementsByTagName()* method, placing them into the *a1* array:

```
var a1 = document.getElementsByTagName("td");
```

The code then enumerates this array using a *for* loop, starting at element *0*, and continuing to the end of the array. It uses the *a1Length* variable, which obtained the length of the *a1* array in the line preceding the *for* loop.

Within the *for* loop, one line of code changes the background style of each element to #*aaabba*, a shade of blue. It's normally better to change the actual style by applying it through CSS (Cascading Style Sheets) than to explicitly change an attribute, as shown in the example. However, until you read about CSS and JavaScript in Chapter 16, "JavaScript and CSS," this approach suffices:

```
for (var i = 0; i < a1Length; i++) {
    a1[i].style.background = "#aaabba";
}
```

The link calls the *changecolors()* function because of an *onclick* event:

```
<a href="#" onclick="return changecolors();">Click to Change Colors</a>
```

 Note The *onclick* event, along with *onload* and other events, are covered in detail in Chapter 13.

Here's the same code using jQuery:

```
<!doctype html>
<html>
<head>
    <title>Tag Name</title>
    <script type="text/javascript" src="jquery-1.7.2.min.js"></script>
    <script type="text/javascript">
            function changecolors() {
                $("td").each(function() {
                    $(this).css("background-color","#aaabba");
                });
            }
    </script>
</head>
<body>
<table id="mytable" border="1">
<tr><td id="lefttd0">Left column</td><td id="righttd0">Right
column</td></tr>
<tr><td id="lefttd1">Left column</td><td id="righttd1">Right
column</td></tr>
<tr><td id="lefttd2">Left column</td><td id="righttd2">Right
column</td></tr>
</table>
<a href="#" onclick="return changecolors();">Click to Change Colors</a>
</body>
</html>
```

This code changes the *changecolors()* function to use jQuery. Specifically, the *each()* function is used to iterate through the elements collected with the *$("td")* selector. It then changes the background color using the *css()* function that you saw in Chapter 11.

Note This code still uses the legacy *onclick* handler. Chapter 13 will show you how to handle click events more gracefully with jQuery.

HTML collections

A number of objects contain groups of elements from a document. These include the following:

- **document.anchors** A group containing all the named *<A>* elements (that is, those with a *name* attribute assigned to them)

- **document.forms** A group containing all the *<FORM>* elements within a document

- **document.images** A group containing all the *<IMG>* elements

- **document.links** A group containing all the *<A>* and *<AREA>* elements that contain an *href* attribute

Working with siblings

JavaScript contains methods and properties for working with the parent/child and sibling relationship of an HTML document. For example, the *childNodes* property contains a group of nodes comprising the children of the given element. The group is similar to an array, though it's not a true *Array* type in JavaScript—for example, assume a *<DIV>* element with an ID of *mydiv* and several *<A>* anchor elements as its children. The following line of code retrieves the first child and places it into the *childOne* variable:

```
var childOne = document.getElementById("mydiv").childNodes[0];
```

Just as the parent node can have one or more children, each child has a parent node, which you retrieve using its *parentNode* property. You can iterate through a set of child nodes using the their *nextSibling* and *previousSibling* properties. If there are no more siblings, the property returns *null*. For example, the *previousSibling* property returns *null* when used on the first child, and the *nextSibling* property returns *null* when used on the last child.

Finally, the *firstChild* and *lastChild* properties contain the first child (*childNodes[0]*) and last child of a given element, respectively. When an element contains no children, these properties are both *null*.

In jQuery, the *children()* function returns the children of the matched element, while the *next()* and *prev()* functions return the next sibling and previous sibling, respectively. The *parent()* function returns the parent. jQuery has several traversal functions that are helpful for working with the DOM tree. See *http://api.jquery.com/category/traversing/tree-traversal/* for more information about the tree traversal functions in jQuery.

Working with attributes

The attributes of elements are both gettable and settable through JavaScript. This section looks at both tasks.

Viewing attributes

Sometimes, especially when first programming with JavaScript, you might not know what attributes are available for a given element. But you don't have to worry about that, because of a loop that calls the *getAttribute()* method. Here's a generic function that displays all the attributes of a given element:

```
function showattribs(e) {
    var e = document.getElementById("braingialink");
    var elemList = "";
    for (var element in e) {
        var attrib = e.getAttribute(element);
        elemList = elemList + element + ": " + attrib + "\n";
    }
    alert(elemList);
}
```

A little JavaScript with the *getElementById()* method is all you need to invoke this function, as you see in this exercise.

Retrieving element attributes

1. Using Microsoft Visual Studio, Eclipse, or another editor, edit the file showattribs.html in the Chapter12 sample files folder in the companion content.

2. Within the page, replace the TODO comment with the following code shown in boldface type. (The code is in the showattribs.txt file in the companion content.)

```
<!doctype html>
<html>
<head>
    <title>Show Attribs</title>
    <script type="text/javascript">
    function showattribs(e) {
        var e = document.getElementById("braingialink");
        var elemList = "";
        for (var element in e) {
```

```
                var attrib = e.getAttribute(element);
                elemList = elemList + element + ": " + attrib + "\n";
            }
            alert(elemList);
        }
    </script>
</head>
<body>
<a onclick="return showattribs();" href="http://www.braingia.org"
id="braingialink">Steve Suehring's Web Site</a>
<script type="text/javascript">

</script>
</body>
</html>
```

3. Save the code, and view it in a web browser. You see a page like this:

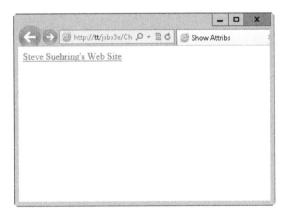

4. Click the link. The JavaScript function executes. The function retrieves the *<A>* element's attributes and loops through them, appending them to a variable. Finally, that variable displays in an *alert()* dialog box, like the partial one shown here:

Setting attributes

You saw how the *getAttribute()* method retrieved the values of attributes. You can also set attribute values using the *setAttribute()* method.

The *setAttribute()* method takes two arguments or parameters: the name of the attribute you want to change and the intended value for that attribute. Here's an example that changes the *href* attribute value, which you can also find in the companion code in the setattrib.html file:

```
<!doctype html>
<html>
<head>
    <title>Set Attrib</title>
```

```
</head>
<body>
<a href="http://www.braingia.org" id="braingialink">Steve Suehring's Web Site</a>
<script type="text/javascript">
    var a1 = document.getElementById("braingialink");
    alert(a1.getAttribute("href"));
    a1.setAttribute("href","http://www.microsoft.com");
    alert(a1.getAttribute("href"));
</script>
</body>
</html>
```

When you view this page in a web browser, you see an *alert()* dialog box that displays the current value of the *href* attribute, as shown in Figure 12-5.

FIGURE 12-5 The initial value of the *href* attribute.

When the dialog box closes, the *setAttribute()* method executes and the *href* attribute changes, as shown in Figure 12-6.

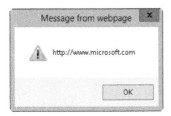

FIGURE 12-6 The new value of the *href* attribute.

The *setAttribute()* method doesn't work consistently in Internet Explorer prior to version 8.0, so a reliable way to set attributes is to use dot notation to access the element's properties. For example, you can set the *href* in the following code in the same way you used it in the previous code example:

```
a1.href = "http://www.braingia.org";
```

If your web application doesn't support earlier versions of Internet Explorer, using the *setAttribute()* and *getAttribute()* methods is preferable. Additionally, you can use the *removeAttribute()* method to remove an attribute entirely from an element. The same caution about support in earlier versions of Internet Explorer applies.

You've already seen examples of jQuery's method for setting attributes, the *attr()* function. Here's the same page written using jQuery:

```
<!doctype html>
<html>
<head>
    <title>Set Attrib</title>
    <script type="text/javascript" src="jquery-1.7.2.min.js"></script>
</head>
<body>
<a href="http://www.braingia.org" id="braingialink">Steve Suehring's Web
Site</a>
<script type="text/javascript">
    alert($("#braingialink").attr("href"));
    $("#braingialink").attr("href","http://www.microsoft.com");
    alert($("#braingialink").attr("href"));
</script>
</body>
</html>
```

This code uses the *attr()* function in jQuery to both retrieve and set the *href* attribute.

Creating elements

You aren't limited to interacting with the elements that already exist on a page. You can add elements to a document using the DOM. This section examines some ways to do that.

Adding text

In its most basic form, the *createElement()* method of the *document* object creates or adds an element to a document. Here's some example code:

```
var newelement = document.createElement("p");
```

The variable *newelement* now has a reference to the new element. To make the element visible, you need to append the element to the document—although usually only after adding text to it. You add an element to a document using the *appendChild()* method, as follows:

```
document.body.appendChild(newelement);
```

But what good is a *<P>* element if it doesn't have any text? The *appendChild()* element can help there, too, in conjunction with the *createTextNode()* method. You can append a text node to the *<P>* element, as follows:

```
newelement.appendChild(document.createTextNode("Hello World"));
```

You can use the three lines of code you've seen so far at any time after the body of the document has been declared. Here's the code in the context of a webpage. You can find this example in the companion code in the file create.html:

```
<!doctype html>
<html>
<head>
    <title>Create</title>

</head>
<body>
    <script type="text/javascript">
    var newelement = document.createElement("p");
    document.body.appendChild(newelement);
    newelement.appendChild(document.createTextNode("Hello World"));
    </script>
</body>
</html>
```

When viewed in a browser, the result is a simple *<P>* element containing the text Hello World, as shown in Figure 12-7.

FIGURE 12-7 Using *createElement*, *createTextNode*, and *appendChild()* to create an element.

Adding an element and setting an ID

The previous example showed how to add an element. Usually you want to set some attributes, such as the *ID* for that element, as well. This code expands on the previous example to add an *id* attribute (you can find this code in the companion code in the file createid.html):

```
<!doctype html>
<html>
<head>
    <title>Create</title>
</head>
```

```
<body>
    <script type="text/javascript">
    var newelement = document.createElement("p");
    newelement.setAttribute("id","newelement");
    document.body.appendChild(newelement);
    newelement.appendChild(document.createTextNode("Hello World"));
    </script>
</body>
</html>
```

Chapter 11 shows how to create an element using jQuery. Setting an ID would then be simply a matter of using the *attr()* function on the element.

Deleting elements

You can remove nodes from a document by using the *removeChild()* method. Recall the code from the previous section, which added an element. Expanding on that code by adding a few *<P>* elements simplifies your work with it:

```
<!doctype html>
<html>
<head>
    <title>Create</title>

</head>
<body>
    <script type="text/javascript">
    for (var i = 0; i < 3; i++) {
        var element = document.createElement("p");
        element.setAttribute("id","element" + i);
        document.body.appendChild(element);
        element.appendChild(document.createTextNode("Hello World, I'm Element " + i + "."));
    }
    </script>
</body>
</html>
```

When viewed in a web browser, the document creates a page that looks like the one in Figure 12-8.

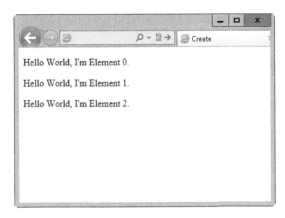

Hello World, I'm Element 0.

Hello World, I'm Element 1.

Hello World, I'm Element 2.

FIGURE 12-8 Creating and adding three elements using a *for* loop and the DOM.

You can then add a couple lines of code that remove one of the newly created elements. You can use *removeChild()* to remove any element from your documents, not just elements that you create. The two added lines of code are:

```
var removeel = document.getElementById("element1");
document.body.removeChild(removeel);
```

For this example, add the lines of code right after the code that creates the elements. In practice, you can place the call to *removeChild()* anywhere, as long as the element has already been created. The final code with the new lines shown in boldface type follows. You can find it in the companion code as del.htm:

```
<!doctype html>
<html>
<head>
    <title>Del</title>
</head>
<body>
    <script type="text/javascript">
    for (var i = 0; i < 3; i++) {
        var element = document.createElement("p");
        element.setAttribute("id","element" + i);
        document.body.appendChild(element);
        element.appendChild(document.createTextNode("Hello World, I'm Element " + i + "."));
    }
    var removeel = document.getElementById("element1");
    document.body.removeChild(removeel);
    </script>
</body>
</html>
```

Figure 12-9 shows the result. The *for* loop still creates three elements, but the code above in bold removes the middle one immediately.

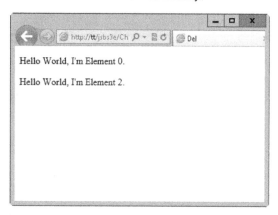

FIGURE 12-9 Using *removeChild()* to remove an element from a document.

Here's the final code written using jQuery. jQuery uses the *remove()* function to delete an element.

```
<!doctype html>
<html>
<head>
    <title>Del</title>
    <script type="text/javascript" src="jquery-1.7.2.min.js"></script>
</head>
<body>
    <script type="text/javascript">
    $(document).ready(function() {
    for (var i = 0; i < 3; i++) {
        $("body").append("<p id=\"element" + i + "\">Hello World, I'm Element " + i + ".</p>");
    }

    $("#element1").remove();
    });
    </script>
</body>
</html>
```

Note The jQuery *empty()* function clears child elements as well.

Exercises

1. Create a document containing a paragraph of text that you create and append using the DOM. Create a link immediately after this paragraph that links to a site of your choice, also using the DOM. Make sure that all the elements have *id* attributes.

2. Create a document with any elements you like, or use an existing HTML document that contains *id* attributes in its elements. Retrieve two of those elements, make changes to them, and put them back into the document. The type of change you make depends on the type of element you choose. For example, if you choose an *<A>* element, you might change the *href*; if you choose a *<P>* element, you might change the text.

3. Create a document by using the DOM that contains a table with at least two columns and two rows. Add some text in the table cells.

CHAPTER 13

JavaScript events and the browser

After completing this chapter, you will be able to

- Understand the legacy event model.

- Understand the W3C JavaScript event model.

- Add event handlers to a webpage by using JavaScript.

- Open new windows by using JavaScript.

- Open new tabs in a web browser.

- Create a timer by using JavaScript.

Understanding window events

You've seen event handling used a few times in earlier chapters to respond to user actions or document events. To review, the *window* object's events include *mouseover()* and *mouseout()*, and *load()* and *click()*. These events are fairly well standardized across all browsers, but other events and event handling are not as easy to implement. This section explores events and how you use them in JavaScript programming.

The event models

Your first challenge in understanding events is to understand the two distinct models: the model used by Windows Internet Explorer versions prior to version 9 and the model defined by the World Wide Web Consortium (W3C). An older model—the earlier Document Object Model 0 (DOM 0)—includes the events you saw throughout earlier chapters. (You can learn a little about DOM 0 in Chapter 12, "The Document Object Model.") DOM 0 is the most cross-browser-compatible model and is supported by all JavaScript-capable browsers. In this discussion, I provide a brief overview of the DOM 0 event model and then explore the competing W3C and Internet Explorer event models.

Using the DOM 0 model

The DOM 0 event model is by far the easiest model to use (as you learned in previous chapters), and it is the most compatible one to use for event handling in JavaScript. (As mentioned earlier, it is supported in all major web browsers.) So why not just use the DOM 0 event model everywhere? The reason is simple: it lacks the flexibility needed for complex event handling. For example, the DOM 0 model can't handle multiple event actions on the same element. Still, there's nothing wrong with using it for simple scripts, as shown throughout the book so far.

The DOM 0 event model includes several events that multiple Hypertext Markup Language (HTML) tags raise in response to various user actions or state changes. Table 13-1 describes each event.

TABLE 13-1 DOM 0 events

Event Name	Description
onblur()	The element lost focus. (That is, it is no longer selected by the user.)
onchange()	The element has changed (for example, a user typed into a text field) and lost focus.
onclick()	The mouse clicked an element.
ondblclick()	The mouse double-clicked an element.
onfocus()	The element got focus.
onkeydown()	A keyboard key is pressed (as opposed to released) while the element has focus.
onkeypress()	A keyboard key is pressed while the element has focus.
onkeyup()	A keyboard key is released while the element has focus.
onload()	The element is loaded (a document, a frameset, or an image).
onmousedown()	A mouse button is pressed while the element has focus.
onmousemove()	The mouse is moved while the pointer is over the element.
onmouseout()	The mouse is moved off or away from an element.
onmouseover()	The mouse is over an element.
onmouseup()	A mouse button is released.
onreset()	The form element is reset, such as when a user presses a form reset button.
onresize()	The window's size is changed.
onselect()	The text of a form element is selected (for file, password, text, and textarea types).
onsubmit()	The form is submitted.
onunload()	The document or frameset is unloaded.

Newer event models: W3C and Internet Explorer

The W3C codified an event model that allows powerful event handling, and almost all later versions of major browsers support it, with the notable exception of Internet Explorer prior to version 9, which uses a different model. Because the standard W3C event model and the earlier Internet Explorer event model differ, you must account for each in any JavaScript that uses either event handling approach rather than only the approach provided by the DOM 0 event model.

Conceptually, the process of event handling is similar in the W3C model and Internet Explorer model. In both models, you register the event first, associating a function with the event.

When a registered event gets triggered, the event's function gets called. However, the location at which the event occurs is one important difference between them.

To understand this difference, imagine a document with a *<BODY>* element and another element in the body, for example, an *<IMG>* element. If a visitor moves the mouse over the image, should the *onmouseover()* event be handled first by the *<IMG>* element or by the *<BODY>* element? The two models diverge in determining where the event should be processed first.

The W3C model supports two forms for locating where the event should be handled: *Event Capture* and *Event Bubbling*. With *Event Capture*, the search for a handler begins at the top level (the document level) and proceeds downward through the DOM tree to more specific elements. If you used *Event Capture* in the example from the last paragraph, an event would be processed first by the *<BODY>* element and then by the *<IMG>* element. Processing occurs in exactly the reverse order for *Event Bubbling*; the element in which the event occurred gets searched for a handler first, and the search proceeds upward from there.

As previously stated, the W3C model—and therefore all browsers that adhere to it (that is, all browsers except older versions of Internet Explorer)—can use both forms of event handling (you learn about this soon), whereas older versions of Internet Explorer use only *Event Bubbling*. With the W3C model, you register an event by using the *addEventListener()* method. With the earlier Internet Explorer model, you use *attachEvent()* for the same purpose. In practical terms, this means that you need to use both methods in every script you write that handles events, choosing at runtime the one appropriate for the browser in which the script is running—or use a library like jQuery. In practical terms, most event handling that I see in the wild today uses a library to abstract these nuances (and repetitive code) away. However, this being a book on JavaScript, you should see the JavaScript way.

The basic structure of the *addEventListener()* method is this:

```
addEventListener(event,function,capture/bubble);
```

The *capture/bubble* parameter is a Boolean value, where *true* indicates that the event should use top-down capturing and *false* indicates that the event should use bubbling. Here's a typical call to the *addEventListener()* method for a Submit button. The call registers the *submit* event, specifying a function named *myFunction()* (that would be defined elsewhere in the code), and uses top-down event capturing:

```
window.addEventListener("submit",myFunction(),true);
```

To register the same event using bubbling, you write this:

```
window.addEventListener("submit",myFunction(),false);
```

The *attachEvent()* method used in the earlier Internet Explorer model doesn't require the third argument, because you don't have to decide whether to use capturing or bubbling; the earlier Internet Explorer model offers only bubbling.

Here's an example of registering the *submit* event in earlier versions of Internet Explorer, associating it with *myFunction()* by calling *attachEvent()*:

```
window.attachEvent("onsubmit",myFunction());
```

You might have noticed a subtle difference in the name of the event to which the event handlers were added—*submit,* as opposed to *onsubmit* in the DOM Level 0 model. Many of the events in the DOM Level 2 changed names. Table 13-2 shows the names of several DOM Level 0 events and their W3C DOM Level 2 counterparts. The DOM 2 events simply remove the word "on" from the event name. (The earlier Internet Explorer model uses the DOM 0 names.)

TABLE 13-2 DOM Level 0 and DOM Level 2 events

DOM 0 Event	DOM 2 Event
onblur()	Blur
onfocus()	Focus
onchange()	Change
onmouseover()	Mouseover
onmouseout()	Mouseout
onmousemove()	Mousemove
onmousedown()	Mousedown
onmouseup()	Mouseup
onclick()	Click
ondblclick()	Dblclick
onkeydown()	Keydown
onkeyup()	Keyup
onkeypress()	Keypress
onsubmit()	Submit
onload()	Load
onunload()	Unload

Both the W3C and earlier Internet Explorer models include methods to remove event listeners. In the W3C model, the method is called *removeEventListener()* and takes the same three arguments as *addEventListener()*:

```
removeEventListener(event,function,capture/bubble)
```

The earlier Internet Explorer model uses *detachEvent()* for this same purpose:

```
detachEvent(event,function);
```

You might find it necessary to stop event handling from propagating upward or downward after the initial event handler is executed. The W3C model uses the *stopPropagation()* method for this purpose, whereas the earlier Internet Explorer model uses the *cancelBubble* property.

A generic event handler

Adding event listeners for each event that you need to handle quickly can become too cumbersome. Instead, you can use a generic event handler for this purpose so that you can abstract the cross-browser incompatibilities. Example 13-1 shows a generic event handler. You can find this code in the companion content, in the ehandler.js file in the Chapter13 folder.

EXAMPLE 13-1 A generic event handler

```
var EHandler = {};
if (document.addEventListener != "undefined") {
    EHandler.add = function(element, eType, eFunc) {
        if (eType == "load") {
            if (typeof window.onload == "function") {
                var existingOnload = window.onload;
                window.onload = function() {
                    existingOnload();
                    eFunc();
                } //end existing onload handler
            } else {
                window.onload = eFunc;
            }
        } else {
            element.addEventListener(eType, eFunc, false);
        }
    };

    EHandler.remove = function(element, eType, eFunc) {
        element.removeEventListener(eType, eFunc, false);
    };
}
else if (document.attachEvent) {
    EHandler.add = function(element, eType, eFunc) {
        if (eType == "load") {
            if (typeof window.onload == "function") {
                var existingOnload = window.onload;
                window.onload = function() {
                    existingOnload();
                    eFunc();
                } //end existing onload handler
            } else {
                window.onload = eFunc;
```

```
        }
    } else {
        element.attachEvent("on" + eType, eFunc);
    }
};
EHandler.remove = function(element, eType, eFunc) {
    element.detachEvent("on" + eType, eFunc);
};
}
```

This generic event handler creates an object called *EHandler* (which stands for *event handler*), which then has two methods added to it, *add()* and *remove()*, both available in the W3C and the earlier Internet Explorer models. The *add()* method in each model determines whether the event type is a load event, meaning that the function needs to be executed on page load. If the function does, the *add* handler needs to determine whether any existing *onload* functions are already defined. If they are, the handler must set the *onload* functions to run with the newly defined function.

Luckily, Windows Internet Explorer 9 uses the W3C compatible model, and as that new browser version becomes more popular in the market, *attachEvent* will slowly be replaced. However, sites that support earlier browsers will still need to use the older Microsoft model for years to come.

You can improve on this event handler script so that it is more suitable for situations you might encounter when building more powerful JavaScript applications. (You can find more information about this topic at John Resig's website: *http://ejohn.org/blog/flexible-javascript-events/.*) However, a better solution is to use a JavaScript framework or library, such as jQuery, to abstract the event model even more.

jQuery event handling

jQuery can also be used for event handling without the need for creating your own event handling library. Of course, you have to load up jQuery, but you were going to be doing that anyway, right?

Binding and unbinding

The *.on()* function connects an event handler to an event, such as a mouse click:

```
.on(event [, selector][, data], handler(eventObject))
```

In this instance, *event* is the event to which you want to respond, *selector* is an optional filter used on the descendants of the selected element(s), *data* is an optional object containing additional data to be passed into the event handler, *handler* is the function that you want to run in response to this event, and *eventObject* is the event object being handled.

For example:

```
<a href="/link1.html" id="myLink">A link</a>
$("#myLink").on("click", function() {
```

```
alert("clicked the link");
});
```

The result of this code is that after the *click* event is captured for the anchor tag, the page displays an alert. Notice that this example didn't use the optional *data* parameter within the call to the *.on()* function.

The ehandler.js script that you saw earlier in this chapter is essentially what jQuery's *.on()* function is doing. The difference is that jQuery's *.on()* function is much better at cross-browser event handling and much more powerful than the ehandler.js script.

Although you can use *.on()* for event handling, jQuery also provides shortcut functions that perform the same way as *.on()*. Instead of writing *.on("click", function())...*, you can just write *.click(function()....* For example, you could rewrite the earlier *.on()* example as:

```
$("#myLink").click(function() {
alert("clicked the link");
});
```

To stop responding to events, you can unbind them using the *.off()* function:

```
.off(events, [selector], handler(eventObject)])
```

The *events* argument is the event or events to which you want to stop responding, and both *selector* and *handler(eventObject)* match the respective items used with the call to the *.on()* function.

Not only can you respond to events such as clicking a link, but you can also trigger events. The *trigger()* function is used for this purpose. For example, consider the code in Example 13-2.

EXAMPLE 13-2 Responding to events

```
<!doctype html>
<html>
<head>
<title>Trigger Test</title>
<script type="text/javascript" src="jquery-1.7.2.min.js"></script>
</head>
<body>
<div id="myDiv">
Here is some text.<br>
It goes inside this div<br>
</div>
<p>
<a id="braingiaLink" href="http://www.braingia.org">Steve Suehring</a>
</p>
<script type="text/javascript">
$(document).ready(function() {

$('#braingiaLink').on("click", function() {
    alert("hello");
    });
```

```
$('#myDiv').on("click",function() {
    $('#braingiaLink').trigger("click");
});
});
</script>

</body>
</html>
```

When this page is loaded into a web browser, clicking anywhere within the *<DIV>* element triggers the click event for the anchor as if you had clicked the anchor itself.

> **Note** You can pass data into the *trigger()* function, and you can bind multiple event handlers to the same event by calling *.on()* multiple times for that event. See *http://api. jquery.com/on/* for more information about the *.on()* function and similar event handling functions.

Detecting visitor information

JavaScript programming often requires *browser detection*—that is, the detection of which browser a visitor to a website is using. For several years, browser detection was accomplished largely by using the *userAgent* property of the *navigator* object. The *userAgent* property is available through the *navigator* object and shows information about the user's browser. However, relying on the *userAgent* property is no longer recommended, because visitors can so easily forge it. In addition, maintaining accurate *userAgent* information for every version of every browser is incredibly difficult. Even so, *userAgent* detection is frequently used for redirecting to mobile sites.

With its use for mobile in mind, the *userAgent* property is discussed, albeit only briefly, and then the discussion moves on to show the newer methods for determining whether the JavaScript that you're using will work in the visitor's browser. This section also examines other properties of the *navigator* object that are helpful, if not 100 percent reliable.

A brief look at the *userAgent* property

As mentioned, the *userAgent* string is a property of the *navigator* object. It contains information about the user's browser. The following code, found as useragent.html in the companion content, displays the user agent information:

```
<!doctype html>
<html>
<head>
<title>user agent</title>
</head>
<body>
```

```
<script type="text/javascript">

    alert(navigator.userAgent);

</script>
</body>
</html>
```

If you're using Windows Internet Explorer 10, you might see an alert like the one in Figure 13-1.

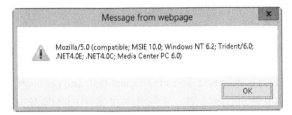

Message from webpage

Mozilla/5.0 (compatible; MSIE 10.0; Windows NT 6.2; Trident/6.0; .NET4.0E; .NET4.0C; Media Center PC 6.0)

OK

FIGURE 13-1 The *userAgent* property of the *navigator* object.

Other browsers report different information. For example, one version of Firefox reports itself as this:

```
Mozilla/5.0 (Windows NT 6.2; rv:12.0) Gecko/20100101 Firefox/12.0
```

This string usually changes as each new version of a browser is released, which in the case of Firefox seems like daily. If you tried to track each released version of each browser and then tried to track which version of each browser supported which feature of JavaScript, you'd be spending a lot of time (and possibly a lot of your employer's or client's time as well) maintaining that list.

A much better way to track what is and is not supported in the visitor's browser is a technique known as feature testing, discussed in the next section.

Feature testing

Using *feature testing,* sometimes referred to as *object detection,* a JavaScript program attempts to detect whether the browser that is visiting the webpage supports a given feature.

Fortunately, you don't have to test whether *every* function and method you want to use is supported in the visitor's browser. The DOM Level 0 model and other earlier functions of JavaScript are so widely supported, and their cross-browser implementations are so close, that testing for particular features isn't necessary. However, you must still test whether JavaScript is available, because not all browsers support JavaScript and not all visitors have the JavaScript support option turned on.

The *typeof* operator is the primary mechanism used to implement feature testing. In general terms, you use the operator as follows:

```
if (typeof featureName != "undefined") {
    // Do Something Fun With That Feature
}
```

Try an example. To test for the existence of the *getElementById()* method, which indicates that the browser supports the more advanced DOM interface, you might use this code:

```
if (typeof document.getElementById != "undefined") {
    alert("getelembyid is supported");
} else {
    alert("no getelembyid support");
}
```

You might be tempted to skip the use of *typeof* within the test, and you might see examples on the web where a feature test looks like this:

```
if (document.getElementById) { ... }
```

Unfortunately, this method of feature testing isn't as reliable as the *typeof* test. The problem is that the shorter syntax runs the method. When you omit *typeof*, the method or property being tested might return *0* or *false* by default, which makes the test fail; that is, it appears that the browser doesn't support that method or property—when it actually does. Therefore, testing using *typeof* is safer and more reliable.

Another way to accomplish this task that looks a bit cleaner is to use the *ternary* operator to set a flag early in the code. Script that runs later can use a standard *if* conditional to check the flag, as shown here:

```
// test for getElmementById, set getElem to the result
var getElem = (typeof document.getElementById == "function") ? true : false;

// now you can test getElem
if (getElem) {
    // We know getElementById is supported,
    // so let's use it.
}
```

Keeping JavaScript away from older browsers

One of the most discouraging problems you face as a web programmer is dealing with the presence of older browsers. Writing webpages that have any sort of current look and feel and still display reasonably well in older browsers is becoming increasingly difficult. What defines an older browser? Ask three different web designers, and you'll probably get three different answers. To me, an older browser is one that is more than three years old, although I lean toward saying two years rather than three.

By this definition, Firefox 3.0 is an older browser, even though most webpages display fine, and almost all the JavaScript code you write will probably work perfectly in that version of Firefox. A more general rule is that any version of Internet Explorer or Netscape earlier than version 5 tends to have many, many quirks that web designers must take into account. And that doesn't even take into account the horrible mess that is Internet Explorer 6 (IE6). Microsoft even acknowledges that IE6 should be retired on its site at *http://www.ie6countdown.com/*.

Given the fact that browsers even older than Microsoft Internet Explorer 6.0 are sometimes still in use, accepting that your code might fail in these browsers is a good idea. However, you can try to make your code fail gracefully, although doing even that might not always be possible. I recently installed a copy of Netscape 3 (which, if I remember correctly, was released in 1997). The browser had trouble with most JavaScript and also had problems displaying HTML and CSS (Cascading Style Sheets) on basic websites. This was to be expected, because that version of Netscape was released well before many of the standards in use today were codified. The point is that no matter how hard you try, your website is probably never going to fail gracefully in really old versions of browsers. I recommend that you choose a minimum browser level to support and design for that target, keeping in mind that the later the minimum level, the more visitors you shut out of the site. The goal is to strike a balance between being a welcoming site and being a cutting-edge site.

There are two primary techniques for keeping JavaScript away from older browsers: inserting HTML-style comments into the JavaScript and using the *<NOSCRIPT> </NOSCRIPT>* tags.

To use HTML comments in your JavaScript, you surround them within *<!--* and *-->* marks, as shown in this example:

```
<script type="text/javascript">
<!-- //Begin Comment
var helloelem = document.getElementById("hello");
alert(helloelem.innerHTML);
// End Comment-->
</script>
```

Unfortunately, not every browser obeys these HTML comments, so you still encounter errors sometimes. This style of commenting, or protection, is becoming less and less common. As the old browsers slowly get cycled out, this type of workaround isn't really necessary.

Whatever falls between the *<NOSCRIPT> </NOSCRIPT>* tag pairs is displayed only when the page detects no JavaScript support in the browser. Here's an example of *<NOSCRIPT>*:

```
<noscript>
<p>This Web Page Requires JavaScript</p>
</noscript>
```

When visitors whose browsers don't accept JavaScript visit the webpage, they see whatever falls between the *<NOSCRIPT> </NOSCRIPT>* tag pair. In this example, they'd see the text "This Web Page Requires JavaScript." Note that using *<NOSCRIPT>* doesn't halt execution or parsing of the remainder of the document, so other HTML within the page is displayed, but using it does provide you with a good opportunity to fail gracefully by offering a text-only page or a site map link.

I recommend keeping the use of *<NOSCRIPT>* to a minimum, using it only in those applications where JavaScript is an absolute necessity for functionality, rather than in applications where your JavaScript provides only behavioral aspects, such as rollovers. You can easily overuse JavaScript or use it incorrectly, hindering the user experience rather than enhancing it. There's nothing worse than to have visitors come to your site only to have their browsers crash, lock up, or become otherwise unresponsive because of some unnecessary JavaScript widget.

Tip Remember that there are several legitimate reasons that a visitor might not have JavaScript capability, not the least of which is that she or he is using an accessible/assistive browser or text reader. You should strive to allow text capabilities on your site and provide a site map for usability.

Other *navigator* properties and methods

Although the *userAgent* string is falling out of favor, the *navigator* object does provide some helpful information that JavaScript programmers can retrieve. Chapter 9, "The Browser Object Model," explores the *navigator* object in detail, showing all the *navigator* object's properties and how to determine whether Java is enabled in the browser.

Note Use the *navigator* object with caution. Sometimes the results might not be entirely accurate. Worse yet, the *navigator* object might not be available when JavaScript isn't supported on the visitor's browser. For example, relying on *navigator* object properties for the functionality of your page would definitely be a problem!

Opening, closing, and resizing windows

One of the most maligned uses of JavaScript is its ability to open, close, and resize browser windows. The act of opening a browser window in response to or as part of the *onload* event was one of the most frequent and annoying operations that Internet advertisers employed (and still do). Mozilla Firefox, Opera, and others give their users the ability to block all these annoyances by default without sacrificing usability. Windows Internet Explorer 6.0 with Service Pack 2 and later has that capability as well.

I have yet to see an automatic pop-up window that actually enhances the usability of a website without being intrusive. If you believe that your site requires a component that opens a new window, I recommend rethinking the navigation before creating that component. Not only will your visitors thank you because your site has simplified navigation and is more intuitive, but your site will also work better because it will rely less on JavaScript, which might be disabled. Additionally, pop-up windows typically don't play nice in a mobile environment, possibly not working at all or making it impossible for the user to navigate.

Despite those annoying windows, your visitors sometimes might want to open new windows in response to events like a mouse click. For example, clicking a link might open a small side window that allows visitors to choose an option from a menu or that displays Help text about the various options.

The *window* object contains several methods helpful for opening, closing, and resizing browser windows. The *open()* method, as you might guess, is used to open a new browser window. The basic syntax of the *open()* method is this:

```
window.open(url, name, features)
```

The *url* parameter is a string representing the Uniform Resource Locator (URL) to load. If this parameter is left blank, the browser opens a default *about:blank* page. The *name* parameter is a string representing the name of the window to open. If a window with the same name is already open, the URL opens in that named window; otherwise, a new window opens.

The *features* parameter is a string of comma-separated options that represents various features you want the new window to have, such as the window's height and width, and a scroll bar. Table 13-3 lists some of the features available. This list is not comprehensive, because browsers support different features and feature names. See *http://msdn2.microsoft.com/library/ms536651.aspx* for information about Internet Explorer, and *https://developer.mozilla.org/en/DOM/window.open* for information about Firefox and the Mozilla family.

TABLE 13-3 Some features used in the method of the object

Feature	Description
height	The height in pixels of the new window.
left	The location in pixels from the left edge of the screen where the new window is to be placed.
location	Determines whether the location bar will be displayed. This is always displayed in Internet Explorer 9 and earlier and can be changed to always be displayed in other major browsers..
menubar	Determines whether the menu bar appears in the new window but has special behavior in Internet Explorer 7 and later where the menu bar is hidden unless revealed by the ALT key.
resizable	Determines whether the window is resizable by the visitor. Firefox always allows the window to be resized for accessibility (and just general friendliness, too).
scrollbars	Determines whether scroll bars are displayed.
status	Determines whether the status bar is displayed in the new window. User-configurable in Firefox.
toolbar	Determines whether the toolbar appears in the new window.
top	The location in pixels from the top edge of the screen where the new window is to be placed.
width	The width in pixels of the new window.

Some browsers give users control over whether the options in Table 13-3 have any effect. For example, attempting to hide the location bar from a new window doesn't work in Internet Explorer or in Firefox (depending on how the user has configured Firefox).

The *close()* method of the *window* object has no parameters. To use *close()*, just call it like this:

```
window.close()
```

This method doesn't always work reliably, so you should never assume that the window was actually closed. At best, you can hope it was.

Window opening best practices

Include in any new open windows the menus, navigational elements, and the address bar. Firefox, Chrome, and increasingly Internet Explorer don't allow JavaScript to disable functionality such as resizing and interface components such as the status bar. Those elements are important for enabling visitors to use the site and application in a way that works for them based on their needs rather than on the developer's needs. Including those options and designing your pages and site so that visitors aren't affected by those user interface elements is the best approach.

You'll find *window.open()* increasingly unnecessary. With the advent of tabbed browsing, *window.open()* is near the end of its useful life. The next section moves outside the realm of a JavaScript book to show how you can open a new tab without any JavaScript.

Opening tabs: no JavaScript necessary

Actually, you don't need any JavaScript to open a new tab, which is really what most developers are looking for anyway. Instead, you can open a new tab using the *target* attribute of anchor (*<A>*) elements. Using the *target* attribute is preferable, because it won't interfere with the visitor's experience in later browsers such as Firefox, Chrome, Safari, and Internet Explorer 7 or later. It also works well in a mobile environment. However, Internet Explorer 10 in the new Windows 8 user interface will open a new window.

Here's an example of the *target* attribute in action:

```
<a target="Microsoft" href="http://www.microsoft.com" id="mslink">Go To Microsoft</a>
```

Another example to open the page in a new unnamed tab:

```
<a target="_blank" href="http://www.microsoft.com" id="mslink">Go To Microsoft</a>
```

Resizing and moving windows

JavaScript also supports resizing the browser window. However, browsers like Firefox include an option to prevent window resizing by JavaScript. For this reason, I strongly recommend against resizing windows using JavaScript, and this book introduces you to the methods and properties for doing so only briefly. For more information about resizing or moving browser windows, refer to *http://support.microsoft.com/kb/287171*.

Chapter 9 includes a section titled "Getting information about the screen," which shows properties of the window's *screen* object, including *availHeight* and *availWidth*. These properties are sometimes used to assist with changing the size of a browser window. Other helpful properties and methods in the *window* object related to resizing and moving windows are listed in Table 13-4.

TABLE 13-4 Selected properties and methods related to moving and resizing windows

Property/Method	Description
moveBy(x,y)	Move the window by the amount of *x* and *y* in pixels.
moveTo(x,y)	Move the window to the coordinates specified by *x* and *y*.
resizeBy(x,y)	Resize the window by the amount of *x* and *y* in pixels.
resizeTo(x,y)	Resize the window to the size specified by *x* and *y*

Timers

JavaScript includes functions called *timers* that (as you might guess) time events or delay execution of code by a given interval.

Four global functions are involved in JavaScript timers:

- *setTimeout()*

- *clearTimeout()*

- *setInterval()*

- *clearInterval()*

At their most basic, the two timer-related functions for setting the timer—*setTimeout()* and *setInterval()*—expect two arguments: the function to be called or executed and the interval. With *setTimeout()*, the specified function is called when the timer expires. With *setInterval()*, the specified function is called each time the timer interval has elapsed. The functions return an identifier that you can use to clear or stop the timer with the complementary *clearTimeout()* and *clearInterval()* functions.

Timer-related functions operate in milliseconds rather than in seconds. Keep this in mind when using the functions. There's nothing worse than setting an interval of 1, expecting it to execute every second, only to find that it tries to execute 1,000 times a second.

 Tip One second is 1,000 milliseconds.

Examples 13-3 and 13-4 (in the example13-3.html and example13-4.html files in the companion content) show an example of the *setTimeout()* function set to show an alert after three seconds. Example 13-3 uses the ehandler.js script, and Example 13-4 uses jQuery's *.on()* function.

EXAMPLE 13-3 An example of *setTimeout()*

```
<!doctype html>
<html>
<head>
<title>timer</title>
<script type="text/javascript" src="ehandler.js"></script>
</head>
<body id="mainBody">
<p>Hello</p>
<script type="text/javascript">
function sendAlert() {
    alert("Hello");
}
function startTimer() {
    var timerID = window.setTimeout(sendAlert,3000);
}
var mainBody = document.getElementById("mainBody");
EHandler.add(mainBody, "load", function() { startTimer(); });
</script>
</body>
</html>
```

Example 13-3 includes two functions, *sendAlert()* and *startTimer()*. The *onload* event of the page calls the *startTimer()* function, which has one line that calls the *setTimeout()* function. The *setTimeout()* function in this case calls another function called *sendAlert()* after 3 seconds (3,000 milliseconds).

The *timerID* variable contains an internal resource that points to the *setTimeout()* function call. You could use this *timerID* variable to cancel the timer, like this:

```
cancelTimeout(timerID);
```

The *setTimeout()* function can accept raw JavaScript code rather than a function call; however, using a function call is the recommended approach. Choosing to include raw JavaScript code rather than a function call can result in JavaScript errors in some browsers.

EXAMPLE 13-4 The jQuery version of the timer example

```
<!doctype html>
<html>
<head>
<title>timer</title>
<script type="text/javascript" src="jquery-1.7.2.min.js"></script>
</head>
<body id="mainBody">
<p>Hello</p>
```

```
<script type="text/javascript">
function sendAlert() {
    alert("Hello");
}
function startTimer() {
    var timerID = window.setTimeout(sendAlert,3000);
}
$(window).load(function() {
    startTimer();
});
</script>
</body>
</html>
```

The jQuery version of the file begins in much the same way as Example 13-3, although obviously loading jQuery instead of the ehandler.js file. The primary difference is in the code:

```
$(window).load(function() {
    startTimer();
});
```

This code uses the *load()* event of the window to start the timer by calling *startTimer()*. The *load()* event handler function is different from the traditional *$(document).ready()* function that you've seen throughout the book. The *load()* function is like *ready()* except that *ready()* waits only for the DOM to be available, but *load()* waits for the DOM and all of the other elements, like images, to be available.

Events

You've now seen several examples of selectors and scratched the surface of functions in jQuery. The final piece of your initial look at jQuery involves a couple more events. Just like the event handling you already saw in JavaScript, jQuery enables your programs to respond to mouse clicks, form submissions, keystrokes, and more. Unlike JavaScript, cross-browser event handling in jQuery is quite easy. jQuery thrives in a cross-browser environment. This is especially true in event handling, which saves you the hassle of trying to figure out how each browser will respond to certain functions.

Mouse events and hover

You already saw how to bind and handle the *click* event in the preceding examples, but you can also work with mouse events such as *mouseover* and *mouseout*. One fun thing to do is to make items disappear when a user moves the mouse over them (although doing so can lead to user frustration, so you shouldn't use it on a live site). Example 13-5 shows some code that makes an anchor disappear when the mouse moves over its containing paragraph.

EXAMPLE 13-5 Working with mouse events

```
<!doctype html>
<html>
<head>
<title>Trigger Test</title>
<script type="text/javascript" src="jquery-1.7.2.min.js"></script>
<style type="text/css">
#braingiaLink {
    border: solid 1px black;
    padding: 3px;
}
#wrapperP {
    padding: 50px;
}
</style>
</head>
<body>
<div id="myDiv">
Here is some text.<br>
It goes inside this div<br>
</div>
<p id="wrapperP">
<a id="braingiaLink" href="http://www.braingia.org">Steve Suehring</a>
</p>
<script type="text/javascript">
$(document).ready(function() {
$('#braingiaLink').click(function() {
    alert("hello");
    return true;
});

$('#myDiv').click(function() {
    $('#braingiaLink').click();
});

$('#wrapperP').mouseover(function() {
    $('#braingiaLink').hide();
});

$('#wrapperP').mouseout(function() {
    $('#braingiaLink').show();
});

});
</script>

</body>
</html>
```

The keys to this code are the *.mouseover()* and *.mouseout()* event handlers, which in turn use two additional jQuery functions, *.hide()* and *.show()*. The *.mouseover()* and *.mouseout()* events are connected to the paragraph with ID *wrapperP*. When the mouse enters this paragraph, the anchor identified by *braingiaLink* disappears, only to reappear when the mouse leaves the paragraph area. It's worth noting that the link can still be activated using keyboard navigation. Always keep in mind that there's more than one way around a webpage.

jQuery also has a *.hover()* function that performs much like a combination of the *.mouseover()* and *.mouseout()* events. See *http://api.jquery.com/hover/* for more information about the *.hover()* function.

Many more event handlers

As the earlier list shows, there are numerous other event handlers in jQuery—too many to cover in a single introductory chapter on jQuery. I recommend the excellent documentation on jQuery events available at *http://api.jquery.com/category/events/*.

Exercises

1. Create a webpage that contains an *onclick* event handler connected to a link using a DOM 0 inline event. The event handler should display an alert stating "You Clicked Here."

2. Change the webpage created in Exercise 1 to use the jQuery *.on()* style of event handling and connect the same *click/onclick* event to display the alert created in Exercise 1.

3. Create a webpage with a link to *http://www.microsoft.com*. Make that link open in a new tab.

CHAPTER 14

Working with images in JavaScript

After completing this chapter, you will be able to

- Understand both new and old methods for creating rollover or hover images using JavaScript.

- Preload images using JavaScript.

- Create a slide show of images.

- Enhance image maps using JavaScript.

Working with image hovers

The term *image rollover* refers to changing an image when a user moves the mouse over it, to provide visual feedback about the mouse location on the screen. The more common term for rollover is now *hover*. Although this technique has been largely supplanted by Cascading Style Sheets–based solutions, because this is a JavaScript book, I show you only the JavaScript methods for creating hovers. You can still benefit from learning how JavaScript-based hovers work, even if you use Cascading Style Sheets to create them.

Hovers take advantage of certain events that relate to mouse movement on a computer, primarily *mouseover* and *mouseout*.

A simple hover

Placing *mouseover* and *mouseout* event handlers within the *<IMG>* tag creates the hover effect. The handlers display images that differ only slightly from each other. The following HTML creates a hover effect using the old DOM event handling model:

```
<!doctype html>
<html>
<head>
<title>hover example</title>
</head>
<body>
<img id="home" name="img_home" src="home_default.png" alt="Home"
onmouseover="window.document.img_home.src='home_over.png'"
```

```
onmouseout="window.document.img_home.src='home_default.png'">
</body>
</html>
```

The important parts of this *<IMG>* tag are its name (*img_home*); the *mouseover* and *mouseout* events; and code that runs when those events fire. The tag's name allows you to access the image easily through the *window.document* object call, and the *mouseover* and *mouseout* events make the action happen. When viewed in a web browser, the preceding code loads the image called home_default.png, as shown in Figure 14-1.

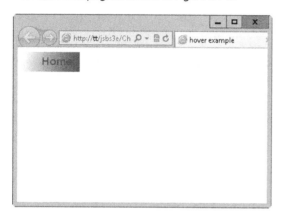

FIGURE 14-1 The initial load of the default graphic through a webpage.

When you move the mouse over the graphic, the *mouseover* event fires, and the following code changes the source of the graphic to home_over.png:

```
window.document.img_home.src='home_over.png'
```

While the mouse is over the graphic, the image changes to the one shown in Figure 14-2, in which the direction of the gradient is reversed.

FIGURE 14-2 The graphic changes when the mouse moves over it.

When the mouse moves away from the graphic, the image changes back to home_default.png, thanks to the *mouseout* event, which calls this JavaScript:

```
window.document.img_home.src='home_default.png'
```

Modern hovers with jQuery

A newer method for creating hovers with JavaScript is to use the Document Object Model (DOM) and the *load* event of the *window* object. (The *load* event of the *window* object was covered in Chapter 13, "JavaScript events and the browser.") With the DOM in use, when the page calls the *load* event, the *load* handler calls a JavaScript function that populates the *mouseover* and *mouseout* events for all the images in the document.

Using Modern Hovers

Although using the DOM with the *load* event is called "modern hovers," and it does accomplish the goal of unobtrusive scripting, the technique can be somewhat cumbersome. Using the DOM with the *load* event can also be slightly less compatible when used across various browsers and platforms.

The pragmatist in me wants to say that using the example that was just shown is acceptable, especially if your webpage has just a few graphics, but I feel like I'm teaching a bad practice if I tell you to use it. Therefore, I leave it up to you to choose which approach works best for you. If you have a lot of graphics that require the hover effect, you'll find that this second, more current approach, which uses a generic function to handle the hover events, is easier to maintain.

Example 14-1 works exactly the same as the example in the preceding section, but uses different code. (See listing14-1.html in the sample code in the companion content.)

EXAMPLE 14-1 A different approach to hover

```
<!doctype html>
<html>
<head>
<title>hover example</title>
<script type="text/javascript" src="jquery-1.7.2.min.js"></script>
</head>
<body>
<img id="home" name="img_home" src="home_default.png" alt="Home" />
<script type="text/javascript">
$(window).load(function () {
    $('#home').hover(function() {
        $("#home").attr("src","home_over.png");
    }, function() {
        $("#home").attr("src","home_default.png");
```

```
        });
    });
    </script>
    </body>
    </html>
```

The preceding code, coupled with a *load* event handler, creates a simple *mouseover* effect. The jQuery *hover()* function gets called during the *load* event to make sure that all of the images are ready. The *hover()* function takes two arguments, the function to handle the *mouseover* event and the function to handle the *mouseout* event. With that in mind, the code loads two anonymous functions, both named *function()*, which merely change the *src* attribute of the image.

Even though the functionality is the same as the preceding example, the code in Example 14-1 is not very portable. This is fine if all you have is one image and its accompanying hover state, as in this example. However, if you have a page full of images, as is more likely the case in the real world, this code breaks. Therefore, the script needs improving.

This example code does show the basic *theory* of how to implement hovers. Retrieve the image with its ID and set the *hover()* function to use specific functions, which in turn should set the *src* attribute to the name of the image to use for that event. Now it's your turn to make the function more portable so that you can use it in the future.

This exercise uses six images (three graphics, each of which has a default and a hover image), but the code is written to support any number of images. I included the images used in this exercise with the downloadable code for this book, so you don't have to reinvent the wheel just to make this exercise work.

Creating portable hovers

1. Using Microsoft Visual Studio, Eclipse, or another editor, edit the file hover.html in the Chapter14\hover sample files folder in the companion content. This folder includes six images: home_default.png, home_over.png, about_default.png, about_over.png, blog_default.png, and blog_over.png. The file names containing *_default* are the images to display initially; the file names containing *_over* are the hover images.

2. Within the webpage, add the boldface code shown here into hover.html (to replace the TODO comments):

```
<!doctype html>
<html>
<head>
<title>hover exercise</title>
<script type="text/javascript" src="jquery-1.7.2.min.js"></script>
</head>
<body>
```

```
<img id="home" name="img_home" src="home_default.png" alt="Home" /><br />
<img id="blog" name="img_blog" src="blog_default.png" alt="Blog" /><br />
<img id="about" name="img_about" src="about_default.png" alt="About" /><br />
<script type="text/javascript">
$(window).load(function () {
    $('img').hover(function() {
        $(this).attr("src",$(this).attr("id") + "_over.png");
    }, function() {
        $(this).attr("src",$(this).attr("id") + "_default.png");
    });
});
</script>
</body>
</html>
```

3. View the page in a browser. You should see a page similar to the following screen shot. If you run into problems, make sure that each of the images and jQuery are located in the current directory, because that's where the <IMG> tag is looking for them.

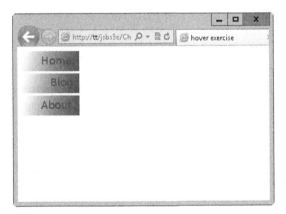

4. Move the mouse over the buttons one at a time. Each image should change to its corresponding hover image. Here's what the screen looks like when the mouse is over the Blog graphic:

A closer look at the exercise

The portable hover exercise you performed in the preceding section shows a better hover implementation. Like the example that preceded it, the code used in the exercise creates a function and then calls it using the *window.load* event. Unlike the preceding example, the exercise's code gathers all the images using the jQuery *$('img')* selector and then adds a *mouseover* and a *mouseout* event handler to each through the *hover()* function. This code, as shown in the exercise, is as follows:

```
$('img').hover(function() {
    $(this).attr("src",$(this).attr("id") + "_over.png");
}, function() {
    $(this).attr("src",$(this).attr("id") + "_default.png");
});
});
```

This code still changes the *src* attribute of the image, now by using the *$(this)* selector. A notable change is that the *id* attribute is retrieved and used as the name of the *src* attribute.

Making sure that the file names and the *<IMG>* tags' *id* attributes match is important. For example, here's one of the *<IMG>* tags from the example:

```
<p><img id="about" name="img_about" src="about_default.png" alt="About"></p>
```

Because these file names are generated in the event handlers based on the element IDs, the file names for the About graphic must be about_default.png and about_over.png. Similarly, the image file names must be home_default.png and home_over.png for the Home graphic, and so on.

> **Note** Of course, you could use an entirely different naming convention—the important issue is that the naming convention you use for the hover graphics files must match what you coded in the JavaScript.

The *hover()* function shown in the exercise gathers all the images on the page. For real-world pages, that means there's a good chance that the *images* collection list contains graphics and images that don't have a hover action. Therefore, a further improvement on this script is to create a conditional to check whether the graphic should be a hover. One of the simplest solutions is to refine the naming convention for hover graphics to include the word *hover* in the *<IMG>* tag's name attribute, like this:

```
<p><img id="about" name="hover_about" src="about_default.png" alt="About"></p>
```

The new code iteration uses a jQuery selector to examine whether the name attribute starts with the word *hover*. If it does, the code continues the hover action; otherwise, it simply returns. Figure 14-3 shows an example page with four images, three of which have hover behavior.

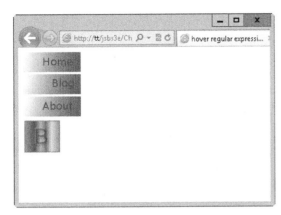

FIGURE 14-3 An example with only certain images being hover capable.

When you move the mouse over any of the top three images on the page, the hover image loads. However, because the name of the last image doesn't contain the word *hover*, it doesn't get a *mouseover* or *mouseout* event handler. Here's the full code (but note that the script still needs a little more improvement before it's done). This code is included in the companion content sample files in as hover-jquery.html.

```
<!doctype html>
<html>
<head>
<title>hover regular expression</title>
<script type="text/javascript" src="jquery-1.7.2.min.js"></script>
</head>
<body>
<img id="home" name="hover_home" src="home_default.png" alt="Home" /><br />
<img id="blog" name="hover_blog" src="blog_default.png" alt="Blog" /><br />
<img id="about" name="hover_about" src="about_default.png" alt="About" /><br />
<img id="logo" name="logo" src="logo.png" alt="Logo" /><br />
<script type="text/javascript">
$(window).load(function () {
        $('img[name^=hover]').hover(function() {
                $(this).attr("src",$(this).attr("id") + "_over.png");
        }, function() {
                $(this).attr("src",$(this).attr("id") + "_default.png");
        });
});
</script>
</body>
</html>
```

The differences between this code and the earlier code are slight and exist within the selector and the *<IMG>* elements in the HTML. Instead of simply *$('img')* as the selector, the selector is now *$('img[name^=hover]')*, which indicates that the name needs to begin with the string "hover" to match.

See Also *See http://api.jquery.com/category/selectors/ for more information about selectors with jQuery.*

Preloading images

You might have noticed an issue when you first began working with the hover examples in the previous section. When the hover image is first loaded, it can take a second to render. This delay occurs because the image has to be loaded through the web server and network before it is displayed in the browser.

This isn't a huge issue; it's more of an annoyance when using the application across a super-fast network connection. However, the lag is noticeable in real-world web applications, especially for users who might be running on slow dial-up connections or through a mobile device. Luckily, you can preload the images using a little JavaScript. *Preloading* stores the images in the browser's cache so that they are available almost instantly when a visitor moves the mouse over an image.

The basic premise behind preloading an image is to create an *image* object and then set the *src()* property on that object, pointing to the image you'd like to preload. What you do with that object after you set the *src()* property isn't important. JavaScript makes the call to load the image asynchronously, so the rest of the script continues to execute while the image loads in the background.

The asynchronous nature of preloading does have an important implication when you're working with multiple images: you must create a new *image* object for each image that you need to preload. If you have a batch of hover images, as is often the case, each image needs its own object and its own *src()* property set.

The final version of the hover code incorporates preloading. Example 14-2 shows the hover script and the HTML page for context; the preload elements of the code are shown in boldface. This code is included in the companion content sample files in the hover\preload folder.

EXAMPLE 14-2 Preloading images with jQuery

```
<!doctype html>
<html>
<head>
<title>hover regular expression</title>
<script type="text/javascript" src="jquery-1.7.2.min.js"></script>
</head>

<body>
<img id="home" name="hover_home" src="home_default.png" alt="Home" /><br />
<img id="blog" name="hover_blog" src="blog_default.png" alt="Blog" /><br />
<img id="about" name="hover_about" src="about_default.png" alt="About" /><br />
<img id="logo" name="logo" src="logo.png" alt="Logo" /><br />
<script type="text/javascript">
```

```
$(window).load(function () {
        $('img[name^=hover]').each(function() {
            var image = $('<img />').attr('src',$(this).attr("id") + "_over.png");
        });

        $('img[name^=hover]').hover(function() {
                $(this).attr("src",$(this).attr("id") + "_over.png");
        }, function() {
                $(this).attr("src",$(this).attr("id") + "_default.png");
        });
});
</script>
</body>
</html>
```

Example 14-3 shows the same preload script, written with the use of the ehandler.js script and JavaScript, for environments where jQuery is not available. This code is found in the preload-js folder in Chapter 14's companion content.

EXAMPLE 14-3 Preloading and hover

```
<!doctype html>
<html>
<head>
<title>Rollover</title>
<script type="text/javascript" src="ehandler.js"></script>
<script type="text/javascript">
function rollover() {
    var images = document.getElementsByTagName("img");
    var imgLength = images.length;
    var preLoad = [];
    for (var i = 0; i < imgLength; i++) {
        if (images[i].id.match(/rollover/)) {
            preLoad[i] = new Image();
            preLoad[i].src = images[i].id + "_over.png";
            EHandler.add(images[i],"mouseover", function(i) {
                return function() {
                    images[i].src = images[i].id + "_over.png";
                };
            }(i));
            EHandler.add(images[i],"mouseout", function(i) {
                return function() {
                    images[i].src = images[i].id + "_default.png";
                };
            }(i));
        }
    }
}
```

```
    </script>
    </head>
    <body>
    <p><img id="rollover_home" name="img_home" src="rollover_home_default.png"
        alt="Home"></p>
    <p><img id="rollover_about" name="img_about" src="rollover_about_default.png"
        alt="About"></p>
    <p><img id="rollover_blog" name="img_blog" src="rollover_blog_default.png"
        alt="Blog"></p>
    <p><img id="logo" name="img_logo" src="logo.png" alt="Braingia Logo"></p>
    <script type="text/javascript">
    var bodyEl = document.getElementsByTagName("body")[0];
    EHandler.add(bodyEl,"load", function() { rollover(); });
    </script>
    </body>
    </html>
```

To review, the code from Example 14-3 uses the image tag naming convention to construct the image names, so all the same warnings about synchronizing the *id* attributes with your JavaScript code discussed earlier in this chapter apply.

Working with slide shows

You can use JavaScript to create a "slide show" effect in which one image is swapped for another in the browser window. For the purposes of this chapter, you build a visitor-controlled slide show—that is, one in which the visitor controls the image changes by clicking buttons to move forward and backward through them, as opposed to a timed slide show, in which the application swaps the images automatically after a certain interval.

Creating a slide show

You can implement slide show functionality through JavaScript in several ways. One approach might be to use a *for* loop to iterate through the images, but this section illustrates another, more straight-forward slide show variation.

Most slide shows are rather simple in design, although I've seen some overly complex ones. Example 14-4, which I explain, shows the slide show in its first version, with just forward capability. The first versions of the slide show use simple JavaScript along with the ehandler.js script. A later version in this chapter will utilize jQuery.

EXAMPLE 14-4 A basic (but slightly incomplete) slide show

```
<!doctype html>
<html>
<head>
<title>Slideshow</title>
<script type="text/javascript" src="ehandler.js"></script>
<script type="text/javascript">
var images = ['home_default.png','about_default.png','blog_default.png','logo.
png'];
function nextImage() {
    var img = document.getElementById("slideimage");
    var imgname = img.name.split("_");
    var index = imgname[1];
    if (index == images.length - 1) {
        index = 0;
    } else {
        index++;
    }
    img.src = images[index];
    img.name = "image_" + index;
}
</script>
</head>
<body>
<p><img id="slideimage" name="image_0" src="home_default.png" alt="Home"></p>
<form name="slideform">
<input type="button" id="nextbtn" value="Next">
</form>
<script type="text/javascript">
var nextBtn = document.getElementById("nextbtn");
EHandler.add(nextBtn,"click",function() { nextImage(); });
</script>
</body>
</html>
```

I might as well discuss the HTML portion of this code, because it's short. Here it is:

```
<p><img id="slideimage" name="image_0" src="home_default.png" alt="Home"></p>
<form name="slideform">
<input type="button" id="nextbtn" value="Next">
</form>
```

This HTML code displays an image and sets its ID and name to specific values that will be used later by the JavaScript. Next, it creates a form button that has a value of *Next*. That's all there is to it.

The JavaScript portion of the code first links to the *EHandler* object script developed in Chapter 13:

```
<script type="text/javascript" src="ehandler.js"></script>
```

The heart of the code that moves forward through the slide show is next:

```
var images = ['home_default.png','about_default.png','blog_default.png','logo.png'];
function nextImage() {
    var img = document.getElementById("slideimage");
    var imgname = img.name.split("_");
    var index = imgname[1];
    if (index == images.length - 1) {
        index = 0;
    } else {
        index++;
    }
    img.src = images[index];
    img.name = "image_" + index;
}
```

The JavaScript creates an array of images.

> **Note** The image array created in the preceding script contains only the file names, so the image files must be located in the same directory as the JavaScript being executed. Otherwise, the image file names within this array will also need to include the appropriate path(s).

Next, a script in the body of the document connects the *nextImage()* function to the *click* event of the Next button by using the *EHandler.add()* method:

```
<script type="text/javascript">
var nextBtn = document.getElementById("nextbtn");
EHandler.add(nextBtn,"click",function() { nextImage(); });
</script>
```

At this point, when a user clicks the Next button, the script will call the *nextImage()* function. The *nextImage()* function retrieves the image object from the *<IMG>* HTML tag, using the *getElementById()* function. Next, it splits the *name* attribute of that image at the underscore character, so the function can obtain the number from the ending characters of the *name* attribute. It stores that number in the *index* variable.

The next portion of the code performs a conditional test that checks whether the *index* value equals the length of the *images* array minus 1. If this condition is true, the user has reached the end of the slide show, so the script sets the *index* value back to *0* to start over. If the slide show has not yet reached the end of the available images, the code increments the *index* value by 1.

The final two lines of JavaScript set the *src* attribute to the new image and set its name appropriately so that the next time the code goes through the function, the current index can be determined.

Moving backward

You might think that adding a button to enable backward traversal through the slide show should just be a matter of copying and pasting the code you just created, altering it slightly to implement the Previous button's functionality. In most instances, you'd be right. However, consider the special case of trying to go backward from the first image. Contending with that scenario makes using a Previous button a bit more challenging.

This next exercise reuses some of the graphics you've already seen in previous exercises and examples in this chapter. They might make the slide show rather boring, so feel free to replace them with whatever other images you have handy. I didn't select four images for this example for any special reason, so you're welcome to use more. However, be sure to use at least three images so that you can fully test the backward and forward capabilities of the JavaScript.

Creating a Previous button

1. Using Visual Studio, Eclipse, or another editor, edit the file slideshow.html in the Chapter14 \slideshow-js sample files folder, which you can find in the companion content.

2. Within that page, replace the TODO comments in slideshow.txt with the boldface code shown here:

```
<!doctype html>
<html>
<head>
<title>Slideshow</title>
<script type="text/javascript" src="ehandler.js"></script>
<script type="text/javascript">
var images = ['home_default.png','about_default.png','blog_default.png','logo.png'];
function nextImage() {
    var img = document.getElementById("slideimage");
    var imgname = img.name.split("_");
    var index = imgname[1];
    if (index == images.length - 1) {
        index = 0;
    } else {
        index++;
    }
    img.src = images[index];
    img.name = "image_" + index;
}
</script>
</head>
<body>
<p><img id="slideimage" name="image_0" src="home_default.png" alt="Home"></p>
<form name="slideform">
<input type="button" id="nextbtn" value="Next">
</form>
<script type="text/javascript">
var nextBtn = document.getElementById("nextbtn");
EHandler.add(nextBtn,"click",function() {
    nextImage();
```

```
});
</script>
</body>
</html>
```

3. View the page in a web browser. You should see a page like this:

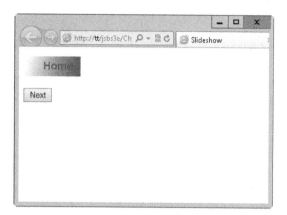

4. Click Next to scroll through all the images. Notice that the slide show wraps back to the first image after the slide show gets to its end.

5. Now alter the code to add a Previous button (the new code and HTML is shown in boldface):

```
<!doctype html>
<html>
<head>
<title>Slideshow</title>
<script type="text/javascript" src="ehandler.js"></script>
<script type="text/javascript">
var images = ['home_default.png','about_default.png','blog_default.png','logo.png'];
function nextImage() {
    var img = document.getElementById("slideimage");
    var imgname = img.name.split("_");
    var index = imgname[1];
    if (index == images.length - 1) {
        index = 0;
    } else {
        index++;
    }
    img.src = images[index];
    img.name = "image_" + index;
}
function prevImage() {
    var img = document.getElementById("slideimage");
    var imgname = img.name.split("_");
    var index = imgname[1];
    if (index == 0) {
        index = images.length - 1;
    } else {
        index--;
    }
```

```
        img.src = images[index];
        img.name = "image_" + index;
    }

</script>
</head>
<body>
<p><img id="slideimage" name="image_0" src="home_default.png" alt="Home"></p>
<form name="slideform">
<input type="button" id="prevbtn" value="Previous">
<input type="button" id="nextbtn" value="Next">
</form>
<script type="text/javascript">
var nextBtn = document.getElementById("nextbtn");
var prevBtn = document.getElementById("prevbtn");
EHandler.add(nextBtn,"click",function() {
    nextImage();
});
EHandler.add(prevBtn,"click",function() {
    prevImage();
});
</script>
</body>
</html>
```

6. View the page in a browser again. You see that there's a Previous button.

7. Test the page's functionality by using both buttons in any combination to move backward and forward through the slide show.

The code for this exercise added a new button within the HTML for the *Previous* function:

```
<input type="button" id="prevbtn" value="Previous">
```

In addition, the JavaScript added a new function called *prevImage()* to go backward through the images:

```
function prevImage() {
    var img = document.getElementById("slideimage");
    var imgname = img.name.split("_");
```

```
        var index = imgname[1];
        if (index == 0) {
            index = images.length - 1;
        } else {
            index--;
        }
        img.src = images[index];
        img.name = "image_" + index;
}
```

The code is strikingly similar to the *nextImage()* function, except for the conditional. If the index is *0*, the slide show is at the first image; therefore, the function needs to loop back to the last image. Otherwise, the code moves backward by one index, showing the previous image.

A jQuery slide show

There are many versions of slide show plugins for jQuery, offering varying levels of functionality and complexity. The one shown here mirrors the functionality seen in the previous section to provide a Previous button and a Next button. The code shown in Example 14-5 still creates a function for loading the next and previous images but does so with the help of a jQuery selector. Two other notable changes are to the *id* and *name* attributes of the *<IMG>* element and to the use of the jQuery *on()* function for event handling.

EXAMPLE 14-5 A simple jQuery slide show

```
<!doctype html>
<html>
<head>
<title>Slideshow</title>
<script type="text/javascript" src="jquery-1.7.2.min.js"></script>
<script type="text/javascript">
var images = ['home_default.png','about_default.png','blog_default.png','logo.
png'];
function nextImage() {
    var index = $('img[name=slideimage]').attr("id");
    if (index == images.length - 1) {

        index = 0;
    } else {
        index++;
    }
    $('img[name=slideimage]').attr("src",images[index]);
    $('img[name=slideimage]').attr("id",index);
}
function prevImage() {
    var index = $('img[name=slideimage]').attr("id");
    if (index == 0) {
        index = images.length - 1;
    } else {
        index--;
```

```
        }
        $('img[name=slideimage]').attr("src",images[index]);
        $('img[name=slideimage]').attr("id",index);
    }
    </script>
    </head>
    <body>
    <p><img id="0" name="slideimage" src="home_default.png" alt="Home"></p>
    <form name="slideform">
    <input type="button" id="prevbtn" value="Previous">
    <input type="button" id="nextbtn" value="Next">
    </form>
    <script type="text/javascript">
    $(window).load(function() {
        $("#prevbtn").on("click",function() {
            prevImage();
        });
        $("#nextbtn").on("click",function() {
            nextImage();
        });
    });
    </script>
    </body>
    </html>
```

See Also *I've had good luck deploying the jQuery Cycle plug-in for more advanced slide shows. See http://jquery.malsup.com/cycle/ for more information about Cycle. Another popular slide show is SlidesJS at http://slidesjs.com/.*

Working with image maps

Image maps are images that have particular areas defined to behave in specific ways, such as linking to another document. Image maps are frequently used in maps to pick out the country or region in which the visitor resides. They also are used within menus, although less so with the advent of Cascading Style Sheets.

Unfortunately, I'm not nearly a good enough artist to draw a map of the Earth. Instead, I created a wildly out-of-scale representation of a small piece of the night sky facing north from 44.52 degrees North latitude, -89.58 degrees West longitude, during the summer months. This graphic is included within the sample code for this chapter (in the companion content) and is called nightsky_map_default.gif.

In the illustration shown in Figure 14-4 are four constellations: Ursa Minor, Cepheus, Draco, and Cassiopeia.

FIGURE 14-4 A small piece of the night sky as seen from Stevens Point, Wisconsin.

I made this graphic into an image map so that when visitors click any of the constellations, they're taken to the Wikipedia page about that constellation. The code for this image map is shown in Example 14-6 (and is included in the sample files in the Chapter 14 folder in the companion content).

EXAMPLE 14-6 An image map for the night sky graphic

```
<!doctype html>
<html>
<head>
<title>Night Sky</title>
<script type="text/javascript">
</script>
</head>
<body>
<p><img id="nightsky" name="nightsky" src="nightsky_map_default.gif" isMap
useMap="#sky" alt="The Night Sky"></p>
<p><map name="sky">
<area coords="119,180,264,228" alt="Ursa Minor" shape="RECT"
 href="http://en.wikipedia.org/wiki/Ursa_Minor">
<area coords="66,68,193,170" alt="Draco" shape="RECT"
 href="http://en.wikipedia.org/wiki/Draco">
<area coords="36,170,115,246" alt="Draco" shape="RECT"
 href="http://en.wikipedia.org/wiki/Draco">
<area coords="118,249,174,328" alt="Draco" shape="RECT"
 href="http://en.wikipedia.org/wiki/Draco">
```

```
<area coords="201,47,298,175" alt="Draco" shape="RECT"
 href="http://en.wikipedia.org/wiki/Cepheus_(constellation)">
<area coords="334,95,389,204" alt="Cassiopeia" shape="RECT"
 href="http://en.wikipedia.org/wiki/Cassiopeia_(constellation)">
</map></p>
</body>
</html>
```

Example 14-6 creates a simple image map using pixel coordinates that represent small rectangular shapes for each constellation and using three rectangles to account for the constellation Draco's shape and tail. This code alone is functional and creates a working image map, but you can enhance it with JavaScript.

The *<AREA>* tag of an image map supports *mouseover* and *mouseout* events. Using these events and some JavaScript, you can improve the usability of the image map. For example, when a visitor moves the mouse over one of the mapped areas, you could load a new image that highlights the constellation. The following code demonstrates using the *mouseover* and *mouseout* events in this manner. Example 14-7 shows the code.

EXAMPLE 14-7 An image map with JavaScript functionality

```
<!doctype html>
<html>
<head>
<title>Night Sky</title>
<script type="text/javascript" src="ehandler.js"></script>
<script type="text/javascript">
function loadConst() {
    var areas = document.getElementsByTagName("area");
    var areaLength = areas.length;
    for (var i = 0; i < areaLength; i++) {
        EHandler.add(areas[i],"mouseover", function(i) {
                    return function() {
                        document.getElementById("nightsky").src = "nightsky_
map_" +
                            areas[i].id + ".gif";
                    };
                }(i));
        EHandler.add(areas[i],"mouseout", function(i) {
                    return function() {
                        document.getElementById("nightsky").src =
                            "nightsky_map_default.gif";
                    };
                }(i));
    }  //end for loop
}  // end function loadConst
</script>
</head>
<body>
```

```
<p><img id="nightsky" name="nightsky" src="nightsky_map_default.gif" isMap
useMap="#sky"
alt="The Night Sky"></p>
<p><map name="sky">
<area id="ursaminor" coords="119,180,264,228" alt="Ursa Minor" shape="RECT"
 href="http://en.wikipedia.org/wiki/Ursa_Minor">
<area id="draco" coords="66,68,193,170" alt="Draco" shape="RECT"
 href="http://en.wikipedia.org/wiki/Draco">
<area id="draco" coords="36,170,115,246" alt="Draco" shape="RECT"
 href="http://en.wikipedia.org/wiki/Draco">
<area id="draco" coords="118,249,174,328" alt="Draco" shape="RECT"
 href="http://en.wikipedia.org/wiki/Draco">
<area id="cepheus" coords="201,47,298,175" alt="Cepheus" shape="RECT"
 href="http://en.wikipedia.org/wiki/Cepheus_(constellation)">
<area id="cassie" coords="334,95,389,204" alt="Cassiopeia" shape="RECT"
 href="http://en.wikipedia.org/wiki/Cassiopeia_(constellation)">
</map></p>
<script type="text/javascript">
var bodyEl = document.getElementsByTagName("body")[0];
EHandler.add(bodyEl,"load", function() { loadConst(); });
</script>
</body>
</html>
```

When you view the page in a web browser, as you move the mouse over each constellation, the constellation's outline appears, as shown in Figure 14-5. The JavaScript that enhances the image map is really just a variation of the mouseover code you saw earlier in this chapter, although it reacts to moving the mouse over <AREA> elements rather than <IMG> elements:

```
var areas = document.getElementsByTagName("area");
```

An obvious improvement to this script would be to preload all the rollover images for the image map. (You do this later in one of the chapter exercises.) Another improvement would be to convert this to jQuery.

Note The HTML used in this example isn't entirely valid according to the HTML standard, because the <AREA> tags for the Draco constellation all use the same *id* value. To make this HTML valid, each tag would need its own *id* value. However, this would complicate the JavaScript because each ID would need to be split or otherwise parsed to make sure that Draco's outline is loaded; otherwise, you'd need to load three different images or find some other workaround.

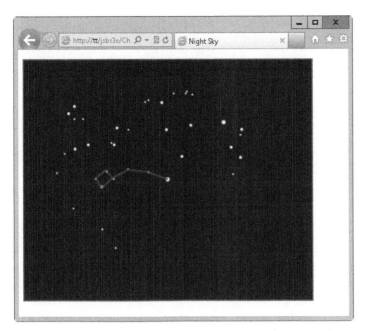

FIGURE 14-5 Adding JavaScript to the image map to implement a rollover.

Exercises

1. Create a preloaded rollover image, making sure to keep the JavaScript functions separate from the HTML.

2. Using the image map example from this chapter (or an image map of your own if you prefer), preload all the images used within the image map so that they don't need to be downloaded when the visitor moves the mouse over the different areas of the map.

CHAPTER 15

Using JavaScript with web forms

After completing this chapter, you will be able to

- Understand how to validate the input to a web form using JavaScript.

- Work with radio buttons, select boxes, and check boxes, both to get their values and to set their state.

- Provide feedback based on validation, both through an *alert()* dialog box and inline within the document.

- Understand the limitations of JavaScript form validation, and see an example of validation gone wrong.

JavaScript and web forms

JavaScript has been used with web forms for a long time—typically, to quickly verify that a user has filled in form fields correctly before sending that form to the server, a process called *client-side validation*. Prior to JavaScript, a browser had to send the form and everything in it to the server to make sure that all the required fields were filled in, a process called *server-side validation*.

 Important When using JavaScript, you must perform server-side validation, just in case a user has disabled JavaScript or is purposefully doing something malicious.

Validation with JavaScript

Remember the *alert()* function you examined in earlier chapters, which was used to illustrate simple examples? It's back. The *alert()* function is sometimes used to provide user feedback during form validation, although newer techniques use Cascading Style Sheets (CSS) and the Document Object Model (DOM) to display friendlier feedback.

A webpage with a basic form might look like the one in Figure 15-1.

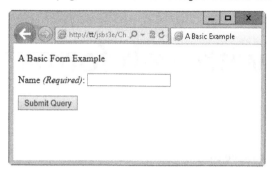

FIGURE 15-1 A basic web form.

When a user submits this form, the JavaScript code in the background checks to make sure that the Name text box was filled in. When filled out correctly, with the name "Steve," for example, the page displays the entered name, as shown in Figure 15-2.

FIGURE 15-2 When the web form is filled out correctly, the alert displays a greeting.

If a user fails to enter any data in the Name text box, the script displays an *alert()* dialog box indicating that the field is required, as you can see in Figure 15-3.

FIGURE 15-3 The form displays an alert when the Name text box is empty.

The code that does all this follows. You can find it in the example1.html file in the companion content. The file includes the Hypertext Markup Language (HTML) shown here:

```
<!doctype html>
<html>
<head>
<title>A Basic Example</title>
<script type="text/javascript" src="ehandler.js"></script>
```

```
<script type="text/javascript">
function formValid(eventObj) {
        if (document.forms[0].textname.value.length == 0) {
            alert("Name is required.");
            if (eventObj.preventDefault) {
                eventObj.preventDefault();
            } else {
                window.event.returnValue = false;
            }
            return false;
        } else {
            alert("Hello " + document.forms[0].textname.value);
            return true;
        }
}
</script>
</head>
<body>
<p>A Basic Form Example</p>
<form action="#">
<p>Name <em>(Required)</em>: <input id="textbox1" name="textname" type="text" /></p>
<p><input id="submitbutton1" type="submit" /></p>
<script type="text/javascript">
var formEl = document.getElementsByTagName("form")[0];
EHandler.add(formEl,"submit", function(eventObj) { formValid(eventObj); } );
</script>
</form>
</body>
</html>
```

The JavaScript within the *<HEAD>* element first links to the event handler script ehandler.js, which was developed in Chapter 13, "JavaScript events and the browser." Next, it defines a function called *formValid()* to process the input from the simple form, as shown in the following code:

```
function formValid(eventObj) {
        if (document.forms[0].textname.value.length == 0) {
            alert("Name is required.");
            if (eventObj.preventDefault != "undefined") {
                eventObj.preventDefault();
            } else {
                window.event.returnValue = false;
            }
            return false;
        } else {
            alert("Hello " + document.forms[0].textname.value);
            return true;
        }
}
```

Within the *formValid()* function, an *if* conditional test uses the *document.forms[]* array. By examining the first index value (*0*) of that array, the code finds the only form on this webpage. The conditional tests whether the length of the input element's *value* property on the form is *0*. If it is, the script indicates the error using an *alert()* dialog box. If it is not, it displays whatever is in the input element's *value* property.

The return value is important. When the *submit* or *click* event handlers are called and return *false*, the browser halts the form submission process. This is why returning *false* is important when validation fails. Without returning *false*, the default action is to continue and submit the form. You can stop the default action in most browsers by calling the *preventDefault()* method. However, *preventDefault()* is not available in Windows Internet Explorer prior to version 9, so the script executes a conditional test to see first whether the *preventDefault()* method is available. If it is, the script calls *preventDefault()*; otherwise, the script sets the *returnValue* property of the *window.event* object to *false* to account for Internet Explorer.

The next bit of JavaScript, which appears in the *<BODY>* HTML element, adds the *submit* event to the form by using the *EHandler* event handler script:

```
var formEl = document.getElementsByTagName("form")[0];
EHandler.add(formEl,"submit", function(eventObj) { formValid(eventObj); } );
```

Notice that to retrieve the form, the *formValid()* function uses the first index value of the *document.forms[]* list, whereas the *var formEl* definition uses the *getElementsByTagName* method. Both of these approaches work fine when only one form is on the page. You'll also frequently see script that accesses the form through its name, as shown in the next section.

Validation with jQuery

jQuery form validation is a bit less complex than validation with plain JavaScript. Recreating the same functionality from example1.html by using jQuery results in the code you see here (found as example1-jquery.html in the companion content).

```
<!doctype html>
<html>
<head>
<title>A Basic Example</title>
<script type="text/javascript" src="jquery-1.7.2.min.js"></script>
<script type="text/javascript">
$(document).ready(function() {
    $("#myForm").submit(function(eventObj) {
        if ($("#textbox1").val() == "") {
            alert("Name is required.");
            eventObj.preventDefault();
            return false;
        } else {
            alert("Hello " + $("#textbox1").val());
            return true;
        }
    });
});
</script>
</head>
<body>
<p>A Basic Form Example</p>
<form id="myForm" action="#">
<p>Name <em>(Required)</em>: <input id="textbox1" name="textname" type="text" /></p>
<p><input id="submitbutton1" type="submit" /></p>
```

```
</form>
</body>
</html>
```

This code first includes jQuery instead of ehandler.js, and then the code attaches a function that is fired when the document has been loaded. This function is the *ready()* function, and you'll use it frequently. Within the *ready()* function, another function is attached to the form's *submit* event. (An *id* attribute was added to the form tag to help make the jQuery selector easier.) The *if* conditional is essentially the same as you saw in the first example. The exception is that the jQuery *preventDefault()* function is used, along with returning *false*, to prevent the form from submitting. However, in Internet Explorer prior to version 9, you should check for the existence of the *preventDefault()* function. You can do so with a conditional such as `if (eventObj.preventDefault != "undefined")`. Doing so will keep the browser from showing a JavaScript error.

Notable also is use of the *val()* function. The *val()* function in jQuery enables you to either retrieve the value, as is the case in the *if* conditional, or set the value too, as you'll see in the next section.

Working with form information

You can access all individual elements of web forms through the DOM. The exact method for accessing each element differs depending on the type of element. For text boxes and select boxes (also known as *drop-downs*), the *value* property holds the text that a visitor types in or selects. This is accessed using the *value* property when using JavaScript or with the *val()* function when using jQuery.

You use a somewhat different approach from *value* to determine the state of radio buttons and check boxes, which this section explains.

Working with select boxes

A select box holds groups of options. Here's an example of the HTML used to create a select box. The full page will be shown later.

```
<form id="starform" action="">
Select A Constellation:
<select name="startype" id="starselect">
<option selected="selected"> </option>
<option value="Aquila">Aquila</option>
<option value="Centaurus">Centaurus</option>
<option value="Canis Major">Canis Major</option>
<option value="Canis Minor">Canis Minor</option>
<option value="Corona Borealis">Corona Borealis</option>
<option value="Crux">Crux</option>
<option value="Cygnus">Cygnus</option>
<option value="Gemini">Gemini</option>
<option value="Lyra">Lyra</option>
<option value="Orion">Orion</option>
<option value="Taurus">Taurus</option>
<option value="Ursa Major">Ursa Major</option>
<option value="Ursa Minor">Ursa Minor</option>
```

```
</select>
</form>
```

This code produces a select box like the one shown in Figure 15-4.

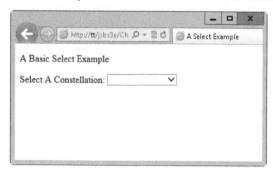

FIGURE 15-4 A select box based on the HTML example.

When a user selects an option, the select box's *value* property is set to the value of the particular option chosen. For this example, the select box named *startype* holds in its *value* property whatever the visitor selects. With JavaScript, you can access this property as follows:

```
document.forms["starform"].startype.value
```

With jQuery, you access the value like this:

```
$("#starselect").val();
```

For this particular example, you need to connect an event handler to the *change* event of the select box, which you can do with the help of the *change* event handler function in jQuery. The *change* event triggers a function each time the selection in the select box changes, such as when the user selects an option using the drop-down menu. The page attaches the *change* event to the *<SELECT>* element.

EXAMPLE 15-1 Attaching a *change* event to a *<SELECT>* element using jQuery

```
$(document).ready(function() {
    $("#starselect").change(function(eventObj) {
        alert($("#starselect").val());
    });
});
```

This code uses the jQuery *ready()* function and the jQuery *change()* function to add a function to the *change* event of the *<SELECT>* element. The code then retrieves the value through the *<SELECT>* element's ID, *starselect*, and displays it in an alert.

This bit of JavaScript simply shows the value selected from the drop-down menu. For example, choosing Ursa Minor from the drop-down menu causes the *alert()* dialog box in Figure 15-5 to be shown.

FIGURE 15-5 Choosing a constellation through a form and then sending an *alert()* dialog box.

 Note The finished code for this example is in the selectbox.html file, which is included with the Chapter 15 companion code.

The HTML for the select box includes an attribute named *selected*, which indicates which option is shown. The example selects an empty option so that the initial value of the select box is blank:

```
<option selected="selected"> </option>
```

It's also possible to select an option using JavaScript and the DOM. Programmatically selecting options is common on forms that have multiple inputs, where one choice automatically causes other options to be selected.

In the following exercise, you build a web form that a pizza company might use to take orders. The company makes just a few special pizzas: one with vegetables; one with a variety of meats; and one that is Hawaiian style, with ham and pineapple toppings. The company would like a webpage with three buttons to help their pizza makers keep track of the pizza types ordered. The buttons preselect the main topping on the pizza.

Selecting an option with JavaScript

1. Using Microsoft Visual Studio, Eclipse, or another editor, edit the file pizza.html in the Chapter14 sample files folder (in the companion content).

2. Within the page, add the code shown here in boldface type (this is in pizza.txt in the companion content):

```
<!doctype html>
<html>
<head>
    <title>Pizza</title>
    <script type="text/javascript" src="jquery-1.7.2.min.js"></script>
    <script type="text/javascript">
    function flip(pizzatype) {
        if (pizzatype.value == "Veggie Special") {
          $("#topping").val("veggies");
        } else if (pizzatype.value == "Meat Special") {
            $("#topping").val("meat");
        } else if (pizzatype.value == "Hawaiian") {
```

```
                    $("#topping").val("hampineapple");
                }
            }
        </script>
    </head>
    <body>
    <form id="pizzaform" action="#">
    <p>
    <input id="vegbutton" type="button" name="special_veg" value="Veggie Special">
    <input id="meatbutton" type="button" name="special_meat" value="Meat Special">
    <input id="hawbutton" type="button" name="special_hawaiian" value="Hawaiian">
    </p>
    Main Topping: <select id="topping" name="topping">
    <option value="cheese" selected="selected">Cheese</option>
    <option value="veggies">Veggies</option>
    <option value="meat">Meat</option>
    <option value="hampineapple">Ham & Pineapples</option>
    </select>
    </form>
    <script type="text/javascript">
        $(document).ready(function() {
            $('input[name^=special]').each(function() {
                $(this).on("click",function() {
                    flip(this);
                });
            });
        });
    </script>
    </body>
    </html>
```

3. View the page within a web browser. You'll see a page like this:

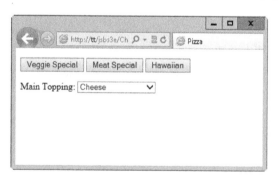

4. Choose one of the buttons. (Notice that the select box for Main Topping changes accordingly.)

The heart of the example is twofold, the click event handler and the *flip()* function. Each input element that begins with the string special is selected with a jQuery selector. These are then looped through with the jQuery *each()* function, and a click event handler is added to each using the jQuery *on()* function. The click event handler calls the *flip()* function. The resulting code looks like this:

```
$(document).ready(function() {
    $('input[name^=special]').each(function() {
        $(this).on("click",function() {
            flip(this);
        });
    });
});
```

The flip() function looks like this:

```
function flip(pizzatype) {
    if (pizzatype.value == "Veggie Special") {
        $("#topping").val("veggies");
    } else if (pizzatype.value == "Meat Special") {
        $("#topping").val("meat");
    } else if (pizzatype.value == "Hawaiian") {
        $("#topping").val("hampineapple");
    }
}
```

This function examines the value of the *pizzatype* variable that gets passed into the function and then, using the conditional, changes the value of the select box, called *topping,* accordingly.

The preceding example shows how to obtain information from a form and how to set information within a form. Although the form doesn't look like much, and the pizza company isn't making many pizzas right now, it's growing because of the popularity of its pizzas. Future examples in this chapter expand on this form.

Working with check boxes

The previous example showed select boxes, and you saw text boxes used earlier in this chapter, too. Another type of box—a check box—allows users to select multiple items. The pizza-ordering scenario introduced in the previous section serves as a good example for illustrating the check box.

Recall that in the initial pizza ordering system, when the pizza order taker selected one of three pizza types, the *"Main Topping"* select box changed to reflect the main ingredient of the pizza. However, allowing more flexibility, such as more pizza types, would be nice.

Figure 15-6 shows a new pizza prep form. The order taker can now select from a variety of ingredients, in any combination.

FIGURE 15-6 Changing the order prep form to include check boxes.

Selecting the various ingredients and clicking the Prep Pizza button displays the selected pizza toppings on the screen, as shown in Figure 15-7.

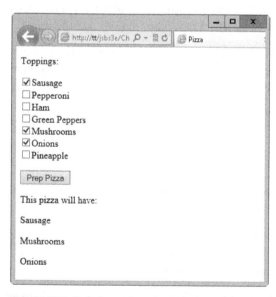

FIGURE 15-7 Ordering a pizza through the new form and adding elements by using jQuery.

The code for this functionality is shown in Example 15-2 (pizza-checkbox.html in the companion content).

EXAMPLE 15-2 Using check boxes with the order form

```
<!doctype html>
<html>
<head>
    <title>Pizza</title>
    <script type="text/javascript" src="jquery-1.7.2.min.js"></script>
    <script type="text/javascript">
    function prepza() {
        $("#orderheading").text("This pizza will have:");
        $("input[name=toppingcheck]:checked").each(function() {
            $("#orderheading").append('<p id="newelement' + $(this).val() + '">'
                                    + $(this).val() + '</p>');
        });
        return false;
    }
    </script>
</head>
<body>
<form id="pizzaform" action="#">
<p>Toppings:</p>
<input type="checkbox" id="topping1" value="Sausage"
    name="toppingcheck">Sausage<br>
<input type="checkbox" id="topping2" value="Pepperoni"
    name="toppingcheck">Pepperoni<br>
<input type="checkbox" id="topping3" value="Ham"
    name="toppingcheck">Ham<br>
<input type="checkbox" id="topping4" value="Green Peppers"
    name="toppingcheck">Green Peppers<br>
<input type="checkbox" id="topping5" value="Mushrooms"
    name="toppingcheck">Mushrooms<br>
<input type="checkbox" id="topping6" value="Onions"
    name="toppingcheck">Onions<br>
<input type="checkbox" id="topping7" value="Pineapple"
    name="toppingcheck">Pineapple<br>
<p><input type="button" id="prepBtn" name="prepBtn" value="Prep Pizza"></p>
<p id="orderheading"></p>
</form>
<script type="text/javascript">
    $(document).ready(function() {
        $("#prepBtn").on("click",function() {
            return prepza(this);
        })
    });
</script>
</body>
</html>
```

The heart of the page is the function *prepza()*, which starts by gathering the number of check boxes contained within the form *pizzaform*. These are selected using the *name* attribute *toppingcheck* along with the *:checked* filter, all part of a jQuery selector, as follows:

```
$("input[name=toppingcheck]:checked").each(function() {
```

Each of the checked elements is looped through, and a new *<P>* element is created. Like the previous example, a click event handler is added using jQuery's *on()* function.

Keep this example in mind, because one of the exercises at the end of the chapter asks you to combine it with functionality that automatically selects toppings when a user presses a button, as in the select box example you saw earlier.

Working with radio buttons

Radio buttons also create a group of options, but unlike check boxes, only one radio button from the group can be selected at any given time. In the context of the pizza restaurant example, visitors might use a radio button to select the type of crust for the pizza: thin, deep dish, or regular. Because a pizza can have only one kind of crust, using radio buttons for this selection type makes sense. Adding radio buttons to select a crust type results in a page like that shown in Figure 15-8.

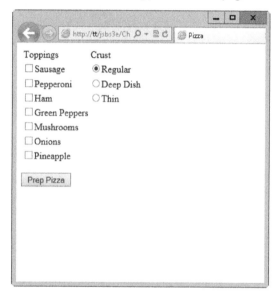

FIGURE 15-8 Adding radio buttons for selecting the crust type.

The HTML that adds these radio buttons and a simple table to hold them looks like this (the full code for this example is found in pizza-radio.html in the companion content):

```
<table>
<tr><td>Toppings</td><td>Crust</td></tr>
<tr>
  <td><input type="checkbox" id="topping1" value="Sausage"
    name="toppingcheck">Sausage</td>
  <td><input type="radio" name="crust" value="Regular"
    checked="checked" id="radio1">Regular</td>
</tr>
<tr>
  <td><input type="checkbox" id="topping2" value="Pepperoni"
    name="toppingcheck">Pepperoni</td>
```

```
<td><input type="radio" name="crust" value="Deep Dish"
   id="radio2" />Deep Dish</td>
</tr>
<tr>
  <td><input type="checkbox" id="topping3" value="Ham"
    name="toppingcheck">Ham</td>
  <td><input type="radio" name="crust" value="Thin" id="radio3">Thin</td>
</tr>
<tr>
  <td><input type="checkbox" id="topping4" value="Green Peppers"
    name="toppingcheck">Green Peppers</td>
  <td></td>
</tr>
<tr>
  <td><input type="checkbox" id="topping5" value="Mushrooms"
    name="toppingcheck">Mushrooms</td>
  <td></td>
</tr>
<tr>
  <td><input type="checkbox" id="topping6" value="Onions"
    name="toppingcheck">Onions</td>
  <td></td>
</tr>
<tr>
  <td><input type="checkbox" id="topping7" value="Pineapple"
    name="toppingcheck">Pineapple</td>
  <td></td>
</tr>
</table>
```

The code that processes the radio buttons is similar to the code you saw that processed the check boxes. The main difference is that radio buttons all share the same name and logical grouping, meaning that they are grouped together and only one can be checked at a time. The code for processing the radio buttons is added to the *prepza()* function, like this:

```
$("#orderheading").append('<p>' + $("input[name=crust]:checked").val() + ' Crust</p>');
```

Pre-validating form data

JavaScript is frequently used to validate that a given form field is filled in correctly. You saw an example of this behavior earlier in this chapter, when a form asked you to fill in a name. If you didn't put anything in the field, an error alert appeared. JavaScript is good at pre-validating data to make sure that it resembles valid input. However, JavaScript is poor at actually validating the data that makes it to your server.

You should never assume that what gets to the server is valid. I can't count the number of web developers whom I've heard say, "We have a JavaScript validation on the data, so we don't need to check it on the server." This assumption couldn't be further from the truth. People can and do have JavaScript disabled in their browsers; and people also can send POST-formatted and GET-formatted data to the server-side program without having to follow the navigation dictated by the browser interface. No matter how many client-side tricks you employ, they're just that—tricks. Someone will find a way around them.

The bottom line is that you can and should use JavaScript for pre-validation. Pre-validation is a small sanity check that can be helpful for providing quick feedback to users when your code notices something blatantly wrong with the input. But you *must* perform the actual validation of all input on the server side, after users have submitted their input completely.

This section looks at some ways to use JavaScript for pre-validation, but to frame that discussion, I first illustrate the dangers of using JavaScript as the sole validator for your site.

Hacking JavaScript validation

This section uses a server-side program to create a catalog order system that has three simple elements: a product, a quantity, and a price. The items to be sold are blades of grass from my lawn. My area has had an extremely dry summer, so there's not much lawn left at this point—lots of weeds and sand, but not much of what I would call proper lawn. Because blades of grass from my lawn are so rare, orders are limited to three blades per household, and the price is high. I limit the order quantity by using some JavaScript code.

I created a page to sell the blades of grass. When viewed in a browser, the page looks like Figure 15-9.

FIGURE 15-9 A small catalog order form.

Here's the HTML and JavaScript to produce the page (also present in the /validating folder in the file grass.html file, in the companion content). Note also that you won't be able to submit the form because the form action, catalog.php, doesn't actually exist. The action of the form isn't that important to this example.

```
<!doctype html>
<html>
<head>
<title>Catalog Example</title>
<script type="text/javascript" src="jquery-1.7.2.min.js"></script>
</head>
<body>
<form name="catalogform" id="catalogform" action="catalog.php" method="POST">
<p>Order Blades of Grass From Steve Suehring's Lawn</p>
<div id="lawndiv"><img alt="steve suehring's lawn is dead" src="lawn.png"
id="lawnpic"><br></div>
<p>Description: Steve is terrible at lawn care, therefore there's not much
   grass on his lawn.  Quantities are extremely limited.</p>
<p>Price:  $100.00 per blade</p>
<p>Quantity to order (Limit 3 per Household): <input type="text" name="quantity"></p>
<p><input type="submit" value="Place Order"></p>
</form>
<script type="text/javascript">
    $(document).ready(function() {
        $("#catalogform").on("submit",function(event) {
            if ($("input[name=quantity]").val() > 3) {
                alert("Limit 3 per Household.");
                event.preventDefault();
                return false;
            } else {
                return true;
            }
        });
    });
</script>
</body>
</html>
```

 Note One improvement you could make to this validation would be to ensure that the visitor doesn't try to order fewer than one blade of grass, either!

With JavaScript enabled in my browser, the user's attempt to order a quantity of three or fewer blades of grass is acceptable, so the form gets submitted to the server-side script, which handles the request and returns an order total, shown in Figure 15-10.

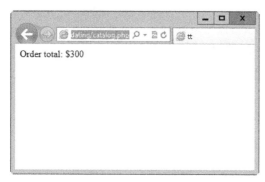

FIGURE 15-10 Ordering a quantity of three blades of grass or fewer gives the expected results, including an order total.

If the user goes back to the page, still with JavaScript enabled, and attempts to order a quantity of four blades of grass, he or she sees an *alert()* dialog box, like the one shown in Figure 15-11.

FIGURE 15-11 An error occurs through JavaScript when the user attempts to order more than three blades.

So far, so good. Now imagine that I disabled JavaScript in my browser. There's no noticeable change in the page when I go to the order form, so the page looks exactly like the one in Figure 15-9. However, I'm now able to order a quantity of 1,500. Simply entering 1500 into the quantity and clicking Place Order results in the server-side web form happily receiving and processing the order, as shown in Figure 15-12.

FIGURE 15-12 Because JavaScript is disabled, nothing validated this order before it hit the server.

Because no validation existed on the server side, this input was perfectly valid, and the order could be processed. The only problem is that I don't have 1,500 blades of grass on my lawn (I counted), so I can't possibly fulfill this order.

You might be tempted to dismiss this scenario as contrived, but it represents an all-too-common occurrence in web applications. In fact, this example is relatively tame compared to some situations in which a site actually lets a visitor change the price of an item during the ordering process and never bothers to validate that input—because "no one will ever do that." Well, people have done that before, and they will again—if you don't stop them.

You might be tempted to try to solve the problem by requiring that all visitors have JavaScript enabled in their browsers before they can place an order—but that doesn't work. You can attempt to figure out if JavaScript is enabled, but you can never be 100 percent certain.

The only correct way to solve this issue is to validate and to enforce valid rules on the server side. The back-end script should check the business rule of the quantity limitation. Doing this won't be a problem the vast majority of the time, but it takes only that one time—and then I'd be outside trying to dig up 1,500 blades of grass for my customers.

This section showed how easy it is to bypass JavaScript validation by simply turning off JavaScript in the browser. The next section shows you how to use JavaScript for pre-validation. JavaScript should be used only for pre-validation and never as the sole means of ensuring that input is valid.

 Note If you've disabled JavaScript in your browser, now's a good time to turn it back on.

Validating a text field

At the beginning of this chapter, you saw one example of how to validate a text field. If the field wasn't filled in, an *alert()* dialog box appeared. In this section, you see how to provide feedback inline, next to the form field, rather than using an *alert()* dialog box.

The following code achieves this. (You can find this code in the sample file grass-inline.html in the companion content.) If you followed the previous section's example and turned off JavaScript, be sure to turn it back on before trying this example!

```
<!doctype html>
<html>
<head>
<title>Catalog Example</title>
<script type="text/javascript" src="jquery-1.7.2.min.js"></script>
</head>
<body>
<form name="catalogform" id="catalogform" action="catalog.php" method="POST">
<p>Order Blades of Grass From Steve Suehring's Lawn</p>
<div id="lawndiv"><img alt="steve suehring's lawn is dead" src="lawn.png"
id="lawnpic"><br></div>
```

```
<p>Description: Steve is terrible at lawn care, therefore there's not much
   grass on his lawn.  Quantities are extremely limited.</p>
<p>Price:  $100.00 per blade</p>
<p>Quantity to order (Limit 3 per Household): <input type="text" name="quantity"></p>
<p><input type="submit" value="Place Order"></p>
</form>
<script type="text/javascript">
    $(document).ready(function() {
        $("#catalogform").on("submit",function(event) {
            if ($("input[name=quantity]").val() > 3) {
                $("input[name=quantity]").after('<span id="errorSpan"> Limit 3 per \
                    household</span>');
                $("#errorSpan").css("background-color","grey");
                event.preventDefault();
                return false;
            } else {
                return true;
            }
        });
    });
</script>
</body>
</html>
```

> **Tip** It's worth noting that the JavaScript validation in these last examples uses the submit event to trigger validation. The submit event of the entire form is preferred over the click event of the Submit button, because the form's submit event fires regardless of whether the visitor clicks the Submit button or presses the Enter key on the keyboard. Welcome to JavaScript programming!

Basically, this code doesn't do anything that you haven't already seen done. The code just checks whether the form is valid. If the form is not valid, the code creates and appends an HTML span element with the text *"Limit 3 per Household,"* as shown in Figure 15-13, rather than show an *alert()* dialog box. The code does set a CSS property using the jQuery *css()* function, which provides a nice lead-in to the next chapter, which discusses CSS and JavaScript.

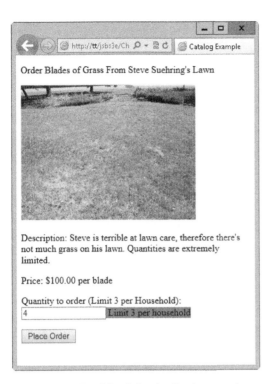

Order Blades of Grass From Steve Suehring's Lawn

Description: Steve is terrible at lawn care, therefore there's not much grass on his lawn. Quantities are extremely limited.

Price: $100.00 per blade

Quantity to order (Limit 3 per Household):

4   Limit 3 per household

Place Order

FIGURE 15-13 Providing inline feedback on a webpage rather than an *alert()* dialog box.

Exercises

1. Create a web form that displays an *alert()* dialog box based on a select box input type.

2. Add a set of radio buttons to the pizza form exercise seen earlier in this chapter to accept three pizza sizes: small, medium, and large. Display the results along with the result of the pizza order.

3. Redesign the pizza order system to add the buttons from the original pizza example, enabling the order taker to select the Veggie Special, Meat Special, or Hawaiian pizza types. These buttons should then select the correct topping check boxes for the particular type of pizza to be made. For the Veggie Special pizza, select Green Peppers, Mushrooms, and Onions. For the Meat Special pizza, select Sausage, Pepperoni, and Ham; and for the Hawaiian pizza, select Pineapple and Ham.

CHAPTER 16

JavaScript and CSS

After completing this chapter, you will be able to

■ Understand the basics of Cascading Style Sheets (CSS).

■ Understand the relationship between JavaScript and CSS.

■ Use JavaScript to change the style of an individual element.

■ Use JavaScript to change the style of a group of elements.

■ Use JavaScript to provide visual feedback on a web form using CSS.

What is CSS?

Using CSS, you can specify the look and feel of a webpage: you can apply color, fonts, and layout to the elements of a page.

Figure 16-1 shows a basic webpage. It's fairly boring—or at least the layout is.

FIGURE 16-1 A basic webpage with no styles applied.

By using CSS, you can add styling that improves the look of the page in Figure 16-1 without altering the page's content. For example, you can change the font for the heading and emphasize a particular portion of the page using some boldface text markup, as shown in Figure 16-2.

FIGURE 16-2 The same webpage from Figure 16-1 with CSS styles applied to it.

Using properties and selectors

The basic structure of a CSS statement is a list of CSS property names, each followed by a colon and then its value, as in the following example:

```
property: value
```

The *style* attribute is one of many different properties you can set. In Figure 16-2, for example, the *font-weight* CSS property changed to boldface for the second line. You can find a full list of properties and their acceptable values on the World Wide Web Consortium (W3C) website at *http://www. w3.org/TR/CSS21/propidx.html*.

You can apply CSS properties to a group of document elements based on the element type (*<P>*, *<H1>*, *<A>*, and so on), or to a subset of elements by specifying the *class* or *id* attribute values of the element(s). Collectively, these groupings are known as *selectors*.

A selector tells CSS to which element or elements the specified properties and values should be applied. The basic structure for CSS statements with a selector is as follows:

```
selector { property: value; }
```

For example, the code to apply the Arial font to all *<H1>* elements within the document looks like this:

```
h1 { font-family: arial; }
```

Although applying a style to a whole element type is often useful, you will run across situations in which you want to style some elements of a certain type but not others, or you want to style elements of the same type in different ways. You do this more selective styling by using the *class* or *id* attributes of an element. These attributes enable granular control over the display of any elements within the document. For example, the document might have many *<P>* elements, but you want to give only certain *<P>* elements a boldface font. By using a *class* attribute with the appropriate CSS, you can give the *<P>* elements belonging to that class a specific style. For example, to apply a boldface font to all elements with a class of *boldParagraphs*, you write the CSS like this:

```
.boldParagraphs { font-weight: bold; }
```

Notice that class selectors start with a period. The boldface style is then applied to any HTML element that includes a class attribute with the *"boldParagraphs"* value:

```
class="boldParagraphs"
```

Here's a complete tag example:

```
<p class="boldParagraphs">This would be bold text.</p>
```

You can gain even more granular control with the *id* attribute, which enables you to select a specific element with its particular ID and apply a style to it, as was done in the example shown in Figure 16-2. Both the text *"JavaScript Step by Step is a book by Steve Suehring, published by Microsoft Press"* and the text *"The book emphasizes standards-based JavaScript that works on multiple platforms through different browsers"* are enclosed within *<P>* elements. However, the first sentence is given an ID of *tagline*, which allows it to be given a boldface font through a CSS.

Here's the Hypertext Markup Language (HTML):

```
<p id="tagline">JavaScript Step by Step is a book by Steve Suehring, published by Microsoft
Press.</p>
```

And the CSS:

```
#tagline { font-weight: bold; }
```

```
Note that individual ID selectors start with a hash symbol (#).
```

Applying CSS

Several approaches exist for applying styles to a document using CSS, including the following:

- You can apply a style directly to an HTML element within the element itself.

- You can include a *<STYLE>* element within the *<HEAD>* portion of a document.

- You can link to an external CSS file, in much the same way you link to JavaScript in external files.

By far the best approach is to use an external CSS file—just as the best practice with JavaScript is to use an external JavaScript file. Using external CSS promotes reusability and greatly simplifies ongoing maintenance of the site. Suppose that you manage a site with hundreds of pages, and your boss calls telling you that the new design for the company now requires the font to change for page headings. If the site uses a common external CSS file, the change is quick and easy, and you can make the change by modifying only a single file. If the CSS is contained in each document, such a change can be quite time-consuming.

There's much more to the subject of CSS than a JavaScript book can realistically cover. If you're unfamiliar with CSS, you can find more information on the "CSS Overviews and Tutorials" page (*http://msdn2.microsoft.com/library/ms531212.aspx*) on the Microsoft website.

The relationship between JavaScript and CSS

You can use JavaScript to manipulate document styles dynamically using the Document Object Model (DOM) 2 (which you encountered earlier in Chapter 12, "The Document Object Model"). Using the DOM, you can retrieve an element by its tag name or ID and then set that element's *style* property.

For example, the heading text shown in Figure 16-1 is contained in an *<H1>* element. If you give that *<H1>* element a descriptive ID, such as *heading*, you can retrieve it using JavaScript's *getElementById()* method or with the # selector in jQuery. You then use the *style* property of the element to retrieve its *style* object, which is JavaScript's way of altering the style of an element. Here's an example that changes the style to use a different font:

```
var heading = document.getElementById("heading");
heading.style.fontFamily = "arial";
```

The jQuery way is to use the *css()* function, like so:

```
$("#heading").css("font-family","arial");
```

Setting element styles by ID

Using *getElementById()* and the *style* object to set the style for an element, as you just saw, is an easy and effective way to change a style, as is the *css()* function. You set styles individually by using their JavaScript style name, which is usually similar to—but not always the same as—the corresponding CSS property. In JavaScript, the style property name is usually the same as the official CSS style name when the property is a single word, such as *margin*; however, when the CSS property is a hyphenated word, such as *text-align*, the property name becomes *textAlign*. Notice that the hyphen was removed and an uppercase letter used to separate the main word from the subordinate words within the name. Spelling a property name in this way is called *camelCase*.

Table 16-1 shows selected CSS properties and their JavaScript counterparts.

TABLE 16-1 CSS and JavaScript property names compared

CSS Property	JavaScript Property
background	background
background-attachment	backgroundAttachment
background-color	backgroundColor
background-image	backgroundImage
background-repeat	backgroundRepeat
border	border
border-color	borderColor
color	color
font-family	fontFamily
font-size	fontSize
font-weight	fontWeight
height	height
left	left
list-style	listStyle
list-style-image	listStyleImage
margin	margin
margin-bottom	marginBottom
margin-left	marginLeft
margin-right	marginRight
margin-top	marginTop
padding	padding
padding-bottom	paddingBottom
padding-left	paddingLeft
padding-right	paddingRight
padding-top	paddingTop
position	position
float	styleFloat (in Windows Internet Explorer); cssFloat (in other browsers and beginning with Internet Explorer 9)
text-align	textAlign
top	top
visibility	visibility
width	width

One common use of JavaScript is to validate form entries. Using CSS with JavaScript can help you avoid using *alert()* dialogs and instead provide visual feedback directly in the page, right next to the area of the form that is filled out incorrectly. The next exercise shows you how to implement this feature.

1. Using Microsoft Visual Studio, Eclipse, or another editor, edit the file form.html in the Chapter16 sample files folder (in the companion content). That code looks like this:

```
<!doctype html>
<html>
<head>
<title>Form Validation</title>
</head>
<body>
<form name="formexample" id="formexample" action="#">
<div id="citydiv">
        City: <input id="city" name="city">
</div>
<div>
        <input id="submit" type="submit">
</div>
</form>
</body>
</html>
```

2. View the page in a web browser. The page should look like this:

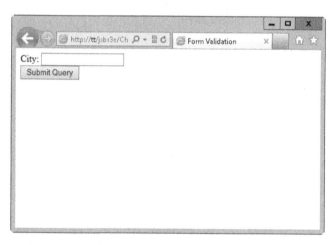

3. Create a JavaScript source file in the same folder where you saved the form.html file. Name this new JavaScript source file **form.js**.

4. Within form.js, place the following code (found as form_js.txt in the companion content). If you like, you can change the value against which the city is being validated to a city other than Stevens Point (my hometown). Save the file.

```
$(document).ready(function() {
    $("#formexample").on("submit",function(event) {
        if ($("#city").val() != "Stevens Point") {
            $("#citydiv").css("font-weight","bold");
            $("#citydiv").css("border","1px solid black");
```

```
            event.preventDefault();
            return false;
        } else {
            return true;
        }
    });
});
```

5. Reopen form.html, and alter it to add a reference to the external JavaScript file and jQuery. The form.html file should look like this (changes shown in boldface):

```
<!doctype html>
<html>
<head>
<title>Form Validation</title>
<script type="text/javascript" src="jquery-1.7.2.min.js"></script>
<script type="text/javascript" src="form.js"></script>
</head>
<body>
<form name="formexample" id="formexample" action="#">
<div id="citydiv">
        City: <input id="city" name="city">
</div>
<div>
        <input id="submit" type="submit">
</div>
</form>
</body>
</html>
```

6. Reload form.html in your browser. Within the *City* text field, type the word **test** and click Submit Query. You should immediately see the label City change to boldface and a border get added around the div.

7. Change the input for the *City* text field to **Stevens Point** (or whatever you used for the value in step 5), and click Submit Query. The background changes, and the field is empty. This is because the form continues along its submission path. (In this case, the form doesn't do anything.)

The code used in this example is merely a variation on code used earlier in the book with the addition of an external JavaScript file to perform the validation and provide the feedback through CSS. Inside the external JavaScript file is the validation code, which first retrieves the *text* input element from the form. Next, this field is examined to see whether its value matches *Stevens Point*. If the value isn't *Stevens Point*, the code changes the *font-weight* style property of the text field to boldface and adds a border property.

The problem with this approach is that the CSS styling for the element is now set within the JavaScript code. Maintenance is far easier when you keep markup, styles, and behavior separate. You can improve this example by setting a style with an element type selector or by creating a common error class in the CSS and then applying that error class using the JavaScript code. The next sections examine each of these approaches in turn.

Setting element styles by type

Although setting an element's style by ID is a common approach to changing styles in JavaScript, you might also find it necessary to set properties on all the elements of a particular type.

Recall the screenshots shown earlier in this chapter, Figure 16-2 in particular. Example 16-1 shows the HTML for that page, found in css1.html in the companion content.

EXAMPLE 16-1 The HTML for Figure 16-2

```
<!doctype html>
<html>
<head>
<title>JavaScript Step by Step</title>
<style type="text/css">
h1 { font-family: arial; }
#tagline { font-weight: bold; }
</style>
</head>
<body>
<h1 id="heading">JavaScript Step by Step</h1>
<p id="tagline">JavaScript Step by Step is a book by Steve Suehring, published
by Microsoft Press.</p>
<p>The book emphasizes standards-based JavaScript that works on multiple
platforms through different brow
ers.</p>
</script>
</body>
</html>
```

Notice two *<P>* elements in Example 16-1. The first *<P>* element has a style applied to it, *font-weight: bold*. You can use JavaScript to apply additional styles to all *<P>* elements. Consider the code in Example 16-2, which adds some JavaScript code (shown in boldface type) to change the *<P>* element's font family.

EXAMPLE 16-2 Using JavaScript plus HTML to change element style

```
<!doctype html>
<html>
<head>
<title>JavaScript Step by Step</title>
<style type="text/css">
h1 { font-family: arial; }
#tagline { font-weight: bold; }
</style>
</head>
<body>
<h1 id="heading">JavaScript Step by Step</h1>
```

```
<p id="tagline">JavaScript Step by Step is a book by Steve Suehring, published by
Microsoft Press.</p>
<p>The book emphasizes standards-based JavaScript that works on multiple
platforms
through different browsers.</p>
<script type="text/javascript">
    var pElements = document.getElementsByTagName("p");
    for (var i = 0; i < pElements.length; i++) {
        pElements[i].style.fontFamily = "arial";

    }
</script>
</body>
</html>
```

When viewed in a web browser, the page shows that the two <P> elements are in the Arial font, as depicted in Figure 16-3.

The JavaScript used for this example is rather simple insofar as it uses functions that you've already seen throughout the book. First, it retrieves the <P> elements using the DOM's getElementsByTagName() method and stores them in a variable called pElements. Then it iterates over the pElements variable list using a for loop, changing each element's style.fontFamily property to Arial.

FIGURE 16-3 Using JavaScript to change the font of several elements at once.

The code, written with jQuery, looks like this (found in css2-jq.html in the companion content):

```
$("p").css("font-family","arial");
```

Setting CSS classes with JavaScript

In keeping with the development guideline to separate content and markup from style (the CSS) and behavior coding (JavaScript), an even better solution for changing styles of elements is to create a class in the CSS markup and then, where necessary, apply that class using JavaScript rather than change specific attributes such as *font-weight* and *size* using JavaScript. This section shows how to both add and remove CSS classes from elements, using both JavaScript and jQuery.

Recall that you create a CSS class like this:

```
.errorClass {
    font-weight: bold;
    border: 1px solid black;
}
```

You can apply that class through JavaScript using the *className* property, like this:

```
var tagLineElement = document.getElementById("tagline");  //retrieve the tagline element
tagLineElement.className += "errorClass";
```

Notice the use of the += operator within this code. The operator causes the class to be *added* to any existing classes to which the element might already belong rather than *overwrite* classes that were already applied classes.

jQuery's *addClass()* function is used to add a class. Using jQuery to add a class for the HTML element with the *id* tagline looks like this:

```
$("#tagline").addClass("errorClass");
```

With JavaScript, removing a class from an element involves the *replace()* method and regular expressions. You retrieve the element as before, and then you retrieve the list of classes to which the element belongs by using the *className* property. Finally, you replace the class name you want to remove by using a regular expression:

```
var tagLineElement = document.getElementById("tagline");  //retrieve the tagline element
tagLineElement.className = tagLineElement.className.replace(/\berrorClass\b/,"");
```

This example removes the *errorClass* class name from the *className* property of the *tagLineElement* with the help of the regular expression. The regular expression looks for a word boundary (\b), followed by the string *errorClass*, followed by another word boundary (\b). It replaces any match with an empty string ("").

As you might expect, jQuery's version is simpler. The *removeClass()* function is used to remove a class. Again, using that tagline element as an example:

```
$("#tagline").removeClass("errorClass");
```

jQuery also has a function called *toggleClass()*, which either adds or removes the specified class, depending on whether the class is already applied to the element. For example, if the *errorClass* class wasn't already applied to the tagline element, this code would add it:

```
$("#tagline").toggleClass("errorClass");
```

However, if the class was already applied, it could be toggled off or removed with that same line of code.

Retrieving element styles with JavaScript

The aggregate styles applied to a given element are also accessible using JavaScript; however, the method for retrieving the styles differs between Internet Explorer and other browsers. For most browsers (including Internet Explorer 9 and later), you retrieve the styles using the *getComputedStyle()* method; for Internet Explorer earlier than version 9, you use the *currentStyle* array property. The style retrieved is the final style applied, because it is the composite style calculated from all possible CSS locations, including external style sheet files and all CSS styles applied within the document. You'll see the jQuery way shortly.

Example 16-3 shows an example of retrieving the computed CSS *color* property of an element with the ID of *heading*. In this example, the heading is an *<H1>* element:

```
<h1 style="font-family: arial; color: #0000FF;" id="heading">JavaScript Step by Step</h1>
```

In Example 16-3, an *alert()* dialog box displays the result.

EXAMPLE 16-3 Using JavaScript to retrieve a CSS *color* property

```
var heading = document.getElementById("heading");
if (typeof heading.currentStyle != "undefined") {
    var curStyle = heading.currentStyle.color;
else if (typeof window.getComputedStyle != "undefined") {
    var curStyle =
        document.defaultView.getComputedStyle(heading,null).
                getPropertyValue("color");
}
alert(curStyle);
```

When you view the result through a web browser, you see an *alert()* dialog box, as shown in Figure 6-4. The *getComputedStyle()* method accepts two parameters: the element to retrieve and a pseudo-element. In most cases, you use only the element itself, so you can ignore the second parameter by setting it to null, as shown in the example. This entire code is found as example16-3.html in the companion content.

FIGURE 16-4 The currently applied style for an element.

 Note Firefox returns *rgb(0, 0, 255)* for this same code to represent the *color* value.

jQuery uses the *css()* function to retrieve the current value for a given property. You've seen the *css()* function already used to set a given CSS property. The same JavaScript code that you saw for retrieving the current property is condensed to this with jQuery:

```
alert($("#heading").css("color"));
```

Exercises

1. Create a basic HTML document that uses a style sheet, either within the document itself or through an external file. Make sure the page has at least two *<P>* elements and one *<H1>* element. Give each of the elements ID attributes.

2. Use JavaScript to alter the style of one of the *<P>* elements, changing its *color* property to blue.

3. Use JavaScript or jQuery to alter the style of all the *<P>* elements to change their visibility to hidden. (Refer to Table 16-1 for assistance on the property for visibility.)

4. Use JavaScript or jQuery to retrieve the current style for the *<P>* element's visibility, and display the current visibility setting using an *alert()* dialog box.

jQuery effects and plug-ins

After completing this chapter, you will be able to

- Understand how to install jQuery UI.

- See how to create a sample jQuery UI page.

You've seen how jQuery is used to help JavaScript programming by alleviating many of the mundane tasks and helping to make some of the more difficult tasks easy. jQuery has a strong and active plug-in community as well. These plug-ins work alongside jQuery to provide specialized functionality to help solve specific problems. For example, there are plug-ins for helping with form validation, plug-ins for photo slide shows, and plug-ins to create enhanced visual effects. It's the enhanced visual effects that will be the focus of this chapter. The jQuery UI plug-in will be examined in this chapter.

Installing jQuery UI

jQuery UI is a set of customizable JavaScript and CSS files that enable advanced visual and behavioral effects on a webpage. Using jQuery UI, you can create enhanced drag-and-drop-like effects, sliders, and much more, all through an interface that operates just like other jQuery functions.

Because jQuery UI is a set of JavaScript and CSS files, installing it is a bit more involved than just installing jQuery, which is a single JavaScript file. That said, the installation is still relatively easy, and in this section you'll see just how to do it.

Obtaining jQuery UI

jQuery UI is downloaded from *http://jqueryui.com*. At the jQuery UI home page, you'll see a link to download. Inside that link you have the opportunity to build a custom download. You'd do this so that you can use only the effects that you need, thereby reducing the code footprint and, along with that, reducing the number of potential bugs and the size of the files themselves.

 Note Like jQuery itself, jQuery UI can also be used through a CDN.

For the testing you'll do in this chapter it's best to just grab the full download package from jQuery UI. This essentially means leaving all the components in their default (checked) state on the page, choosing a theme (UI Lightness will be the theme used in this chapter), and selecting Download. When you do so, the jQuery UI site will build a zip file containing the effects and widgets that you've specified, along with the theme that you specified.

Installing jQuery UI

Unzipping the downloaded file reveals three folders: css, development-bundle, and js. The CSS files for jQuery UI are included in the css folder, and the JavaScript, including a version of jQuery itself, is included in the js folder. The development-bundle folder contains samples, documentation, and other ancillary files for jQuery UI. When deploying jQuery UI to a live or production environment, the development-bundle directory doesn't need to (and probably shouldn't) be included.

The files for jQuery UI should be placed appropriately on your web server. This means that you place them in your document root or within your project. For example, Figure 17-1 shows the folder hierarchy for the default download of jQuery UI.

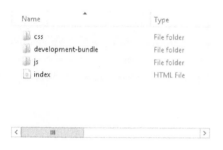

FIGURE 17-1 The folders within the jQuery UI download.

Adding the appropriate directories and files to a project in Microsoft Visual Studio typically involves the following steps:

1. Right-click within Solution Explorer, select Add, and then select Existing Item.

2. In the Add Existing Item dialog box, navigate to the file (for example, the jQuery or jQuery UI file) and select Add. You might need to select Script or All Files from the file type drop-down to see the appropriate file types.

3. Select the js and css folders to add all the files.

Building a jQuery UI demonstration page

jQuery UI has a number of different effects, widgets, and interface enhancements—enough that it's difficult to try to describe all of them in words. It's more effective to show you how to build a demonstration page that enables you to experiment with the various things that jQuery UI can do. The index.html page included with jQuery UI provides a good sample page as well, but implementing one for yourself will help you to learn the structure and usage pattern for jQuery UI.

With that in mind, the following exercise helps build a jQuery UI demonstration page. To complete this exercise, you should already have jQuery UI installed. This exercise assumes that jQuery and jQuery UI are installed in the js folder within your current folder or project and that the jQuery UI CSS is installed in a css folder within your current folder or project.

Building a demonstration page

1. Within Visual Studio, Eclipse, or another editor, open the file test.html in the Chapter17 companion content.

2. Inside test.html, add the code shown in bold, noting particularly to change the version numbers of jQuery UI's css and js file and the main jQuery JavaScript file's version, too.

```
<!DOCTYPE html>
<html>
<head>
    <title>jQuery UI Test Page</title>
    <link type="text/css" rel="stylesheet"
        href="css/ui-lightness/jquery-ui-1.8.22.custom.css" />
    <link type="text/css" rel="stylesheet"
        href="css/style.css" />
    <script type="text/javascript"
        src="js/jquery-1.7.2.min.js">
    </script>
    <script type="text/javascript"
        src="js/jquery-ui-1.8.22.custom.min.js">
    </script>
    <script type="text/javascript"
        src="js/custom.js">
    </script>
</head>
    <body>
        <div id="mainContainer">
        <div id="mainHeadingContainer">
            <div id="header">
                <h1>jQuery UI Test Page</h1>
                Here's some text!
            </div>
        </div>
        <form action="#" method="POST">
            <select name="effect">
            <option value="bounce">Bounce</option>
            <option value="drop">Drop</option>
            <option value="explode">Explode</option>
            <option value="fade">Fade</option>
            <option value="fold">Fold</option>
            <option value="highlight">Highlight</option>
            <option value="puff">Puff</option>
            <option value="pulsate">Pulsate</option>
            <option value="shake">Shake</option>
            <option value="slide">Slide</option>
            <option value="transfer">Transfer</option>
            </select>
```

```
            <input type="submit" name="submit" value="Run Effect">
            <input type="button" name="reset" value="Reset Page">

      <span id="trash"></span>
            </form>
            </div> <!-- end mainContainer -->
      </body>
</html>
```

3. Save test.html.

4. Create a new CSS file. If you're using an editor or integrated drive electronics (IDE) like Visual Studio that requires you to add a new file to the project, add it within the css folder.

5. Inside the CSS file, place the following contents:

```
body {
        font-family: arial, helvetica, sans-serif;
}
#mainContainer {
        border: 3px solid black;
        padding: 10px;
}
#mainHeadingContainer {
          width: 300px;
          background: #999999;
          text-align: center;
}
#header {
          width: 300px;
          height: 200px;
          background: #CCCCCC;
          margin-bottom: 25px;
}
.transfer {
        border: 2px solid black;
}
```

6. Save the file as style.css (within your css folder). This file can be found as style.css in the css folder of the Chapter 17 companion content.

7. Create a new JavaScript file. If you're using an editor or IDE like Visual Studio that requires you to add a new file to the project, add the file within the js folder.

8. Inside the JavaScript file, place the following JavaScript. This file can also be found as custom.js in the Chapter 17 companion content.

```
$(document).ready(function () {
        $("form").on('submit', function () {
            var effect = $(":input[name=effect]").val();
            var options = {};
            var effectTime = 1000;
            if (effect === "transfer") {
                options = { to: "#trash", className: "transfer" };
                effectTime = 500;
```

```
            }
        $("#header").effect(effect, options, effectTime);
        return false;
    });
    $(":input[name=reset]").on('click', function () {
        $("#header").removeAttr("style");
            });
});
```

9. Save the file as custom.js in your js folder.

10. View test.html in your browser. You should see a page like that shown here:

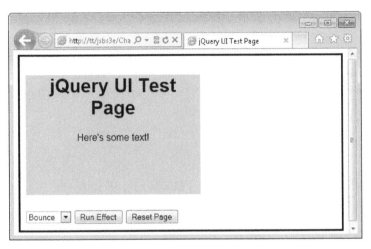

11. Use the drop-down menu to select different effects, and note how each interacts with the page.

If you don't receive the page shown, here are some troubleshooting tips:

■ Make sure that you have the right versions of jQuery UI's CSS and JS files, as well as the correct version of jQuery itself. The version numbers shown in the example will be out of date by the time you read this.

■ Make sure the paths to the files are correct. You should have the file test.html in your project or document root, and there should also be a css and js folder in the same directory. Inside the css folder are the jQuery UI CSS files as well as your own style.css created in this exercise. The js folder contains the main jQuery file as well as the jQuery UI JavaScript file and your custom.js file created as part of this exercise.

The custom JavaScript used for this page was contained in the file custom.js in your js folder. That JavaScript began with the jQuery *ready()* function called as part of *$(document)*.

```
$(document).ready(function () {
```

Within the *ready()* function, a *submit* event handler was added to the form:

```
$("form").on('submit', function () {
```

Within the *submit* event handler's function, the name of the effect being requested was obtained using the *:input[name=effect]* selector's *val()* function:

```
var effect = $(":input[name=effect]").val();
```

Many of the jQuery UI effects accept options as well as the amount of time (in milliseconds) to perform the effect. These variables are set up next:

```
var options = {};
var effectTime = 1000;
```

The "transfer" effect looks better with a quicker *effectTime* value and requires some additional options, such as the destination for the transfer effect. Therefore, a conditional tests whether the effect was *transfer* and if it was, the *options* and *effectTime* values were set accordingly:

```
if (effect === "transfer") {
    options = { to: "#trash", className: "transfer" };
    effectTime = 500;
}
```

With all the initial setup out of the way, the jQuery UI *effect()* function is called, using the name of the effect, any options, and the time to run the effect.

```
$("#header").effect(effect, options, effectTime);
```

The remaining area within the code sets a click event handler onto the reset button found on the page. This reset button removes any styles applied to the area of the page used by the jQuery UI *effect* function.

```
$(":input[name=reset]").on('click', function () {
    $("#header").removeAttr("style");
});
```

Creating a jQuery UI calendar

A common widget when building a webpage is a calendar to enable the visitor to select a date rather than having to type the date into the form manually. jQuery UI includes a type of calendar known as a datepicker. The jQuery UI datepicker lets you create a calendar that displays when the visitor clicks within the form field on the page, like the one shown in Figure 17-2.

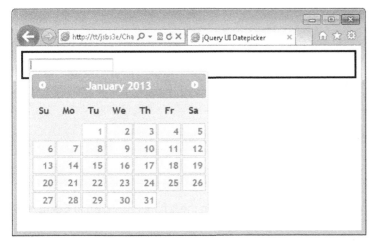

FIGURE 17-2 A jQuery UI datepicker.

Adding the jQuery UI datepicker is just about as easy as anything you'll do in JavaScript, assuming that you have jQuery UI and jQuery installed and ready to go. Assume that you have a text field in a form, like this:

```
<input type="text" name="cal" id="cal">
```

You turn this input into a datepicker by using one line of jQuery in your JavaScript:

```
$('#cal').datepicker();
```

Example 17-1 shows the HTML to create the page shown in Figure 17-2. You can also find this code in the file cal.html in the companion content.

EXAMPLE 17-1 HTML to create a basic datepicker page

```
<!DOCTYPE html>
<html>
<head>
    <title>jQuery UI Datepicker</title>
    <link type="text/css" rel="stylesheet"

        href="css/ui-lightness/jquery-ui-1.8.22.custom.css" />
        <link type="text/css" rel="stylesheet"
                href="css/cal.css" />
    <script type="text/javascript"
                src="js/jquery-1.7.2.min.js">
        </script>
    <script type="text/javascript"
                src="js/jquery-ui-1.8.22.custom.min.js">
        </script>
    <script type="text/javascript"
```

```
        src="js/cal.js">
    </script>
</head>
    <body>
        <div id="mainContainer">
        <form action="#" method="POST">
        <input type="text" name="cal" id="cal">
        </form>
        </div> <!-- end mainContainer -->
    </body>
</html>
```

The JavaScript used to create the page (saved as cal.js in the js folder) is shown in Example 17-2.

EXAMPLE 17-2 JavaScript to create a datepicker

```
$(document).ready(function () {
        $('#cal').datepicker();
});
```

The CSS, which is really used only to create the border, to make it easier to see in the book, is shown in Example 17-3.

EXAMPLE 17-3 CSS to add a border for the example

```
#mainContainer {
        border: 3px solid black;
        padding: 10px;
}
```

Customizing the calendar

The datepicker widget is highly customizable. You can change the format of the date, show the week of the year, show drop-down lists for the month and year for quicker navigation, show multiple months at once, and much more. Customizations are added by placing options (as an array) within the call to the datepicker function.

This section examines a few of the customizations. For more information about others, see the datepicker demo page at *http://jqueryui.com/demos/datepicker/.*

Adding buttons

You can add buttons for quick access to the current date and also to indicate that the visitor is done choosing a date. This is accomplished with the *showButtonPanel* option. The JavaScript shown in Example 17-2 to add the *showButtonPanel* option looks like this (note the addition of opening and closing braces within the *datepicker()* function):

```
$('#cal').datepicker({
    showButtonPanel: true
});
```

The result is a calendar that looks like Figure 17-3.

FIGURE 17-3 A datepicker with a button panel.

Displaying multiple months

For certain applications, it can be helpful to display multiple months at once. This is accomplished with the *numberOfMonths* option, which is then further configured to determine the number of months to display.

```
$('#cal').datepicker({
    showButtonPanel: true,
    numberOfMonths: 2
});
```

The resulting calendar looks like Figure 17-4.

FIGURE 17-4 A calendar displaying multiple months and buttons.

Adding month and year drop-down lists

You can add drop-down lists for the month and/or the year to make navigation across large date ranges easier. This is accomplished with the *changeMonth* and *changeYear* options, respectively:

```
$('#cal').datepicker({
    changeMonth: true,
    changeYear: true
});
```

The resulting calendar looks like Figure 17-5.

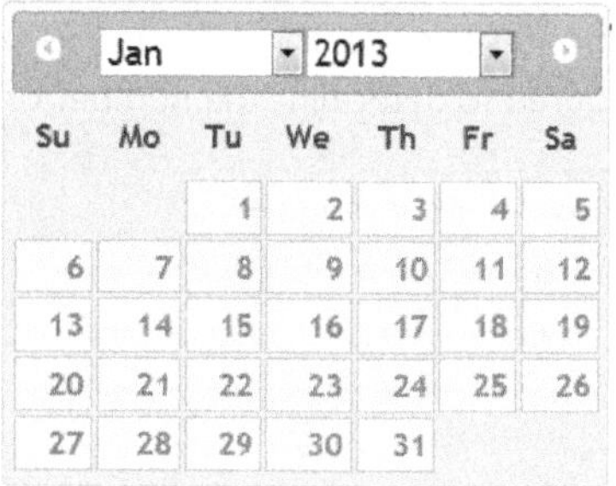

FIGURE 17-5 A calendar with drop-down lists for month and year.

Limiting the date range

If you attempt to use the year drop-down list from the previous example, you'll notice that you can choose dates from 10 years ago. However, calendars are frequently used in forward-looking mode only, where, for example, people can pick a date for a reservation in the future.

You can limit the date range for the calendar, both backward and forward. Doing so is a bit more complex than merely setting an option because you need to choose the date range from a number of formats.

To solve the immediate problem identified, where a date well into the past can be chosen, the *minDate* option is used with *-0D* as the option's value, to exclude dates previous to today. The code looks like this:

```
$('#cal').datepicker({
    changeMonth: true,
    changeYear: true,
    minDate: "-0D"
});
```

The resulting calendar looks just like the one in Figure 17-6. Notice that dates previous to today are no longer available for selection.

FIGURE 17-6 Excluding dates in the past with *minDate*.

Both the *minDate* and *maxDate* options accept values of *D* to indicate days, *M* to indicate months, and *Y* to indicate years. For example, allowing dates beginning with today (as you saw) and no later than one year and one day in the future looks like this:

```
$('#cal').datepicker({
    changeMonth: true,
    changeYear: true,
    minDate: "-0D",
    maxDate: "+1Y +1D"
});
```

Adding a dialog box

jQuery UI has various dialog boxes available through its *dialog()* function. The default dialog is an overlaid dialog with a title bar and main window for content. The default dialog is resizable and can be closed as well.

Example 17-4 shows the HTML involved in making a dialog. It's similar to that found in previous examples in this chapter, with the main change being the addition of a *<DIV>* element for the dialog itself. This HTML is found as dialog.html in the Chapter 17 companion content.

EXAMPLE 17-4 HTML to create a dialog with jQuery UI

```html
<!DOCTYPE html>
<html>
<head>
    <title>jQuery UI Dialog</title>
    <link type="text/css" rel="stylesheet"
               href="css/ui-lightness/jquery-ui-1.8.22.custom.css" />
    <script type="text/javascript"
               src="js/jquery-1.7.2.min.js">
    </script>
    <script type="text/javascript"
               src="js/jquery-ui-1.8.22.custom.min.js">
    </script>
    <script type="text/javascript"
        src="js/dialog.js">
    </script>
</head>
    <body>
        <div id="dialog" title="My Dialog">
            <p>Here's a dialog</p>
        </div>
    </body>
</html>
```

The JavaScript used to create the dialog is shown in Example 17-5.

EXAMPLE 17-5 JavaScript to create a dialog with jQuery UI

```javascript
$(document).ready(function () {
        $('#dialog').dialog();
});
```

When viewed in a browser, the result is shown in Figure 17-7.

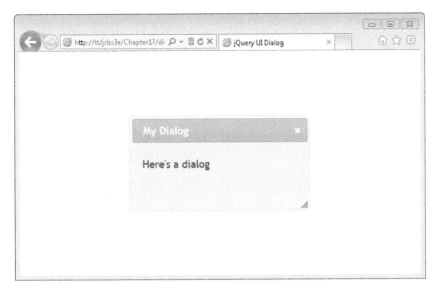

FIGURE 17-7 Creating a basic dialog.

Like the datepicker from the previous section, the *dialog()* function can also take advantage of options that customize its behavior and appearance.

Creating a modal dialog

A modal dialog is one that prevents the user from interacting with the parent window until the dialog is dismissed. Creating a modal dialog is accomplished using the modal option, as in this example:

```
$(document).ready(function () {
        $('#dialog').dialog({
                modal: true
            });
});
```

When added as an option, the resulting page and dialog are shown in Figure 17-8. Notice the effect applied to the background, graying it out to indicate that no input is allowed in that area of the page.

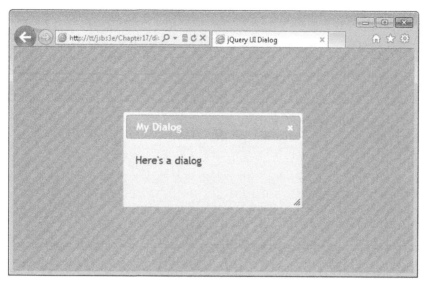

FIGURE 17-8 A modal dialog with jQuery UI.

Adding buttons

Buttons can be added to the dialog. This might be done to obtain a confirmation from the user. Consider this JavaScript:

```
$('#dialog').dialog({
    resizable: false,
    modal: true,
    buttons: {
        "Confirm": function() {
            // Perform actions here based on
            // receiving confirmation
            // Then close the dialog:
            $(this).dialog("close");
        },
        "Cancel": function() {
            $(this).dialog("close");
        }
    }  //end buttons option
});
```

This JavaScript uses the buttons option, which accepts an array of the buttons to add. When viewed through a browser, Figure 17-9 is the result.

FIGURE 17-9 Creating a confirmation dialog with jQuery UI.

When viewed in a browser, the dialog opens immediately. A more likely scenario is that the dialog will be opened when a visitor clicks an element within a page. The *dialog()* function can be opened and closed on a click of another element. Example 17-6 shows the HTML to create this scenario.

EXAMPLE 17-6 HTML for opening a dialog when a page element is clicked

```
<!DOCTYPE html>
<html>
<head>
    <title>jQuery UI Dialog</title>
    <link type="text/css" rel="stylesheet"
        href="css/ui-lightness/jquery-ui-1.8.22.custom.css" />
    <script type="text/javascript"
        src="js/jquery-1.7.2.min.js">
    </script>
    <script type="text/javascript"
        src="js/jquery-ui-1.8.22.custom.min.js">
    </script>

    <script type="text/javascript"
        src="js/dialog-open.js">
    </script>
</head>
    <body>
        <div id="opener">Click here to open the dialog</div>
        <div id="dialog" title="My Dialog">
            <p>Here's a dialog</p>
        </div>
    </body>
</html>
```

The JavaScript for this scenario is where the bulk of the additional work is needed. In JavaScript, the dialog is first told not to automatically open through its *autoOpen* option. Next, a click event handler is created and added to the "opener" *<DIV>* section on the page. This click event, when fired, sets up the dialog and then opens it. The JavaScript is shown in Example 17-7.

EXAMPLE 17-7 Opening a dialog with a click event

```
$(document).ready(function () {
        $("#dialog").dialog({ autoOpen: false,
                                resizable: false,
                                modal: true
                            });
        $('#opener').on('click', function() {

                $("#dialog").dialog("open");
        });
});
```

When viewed through a browser, the page looks like Figure 17-10.

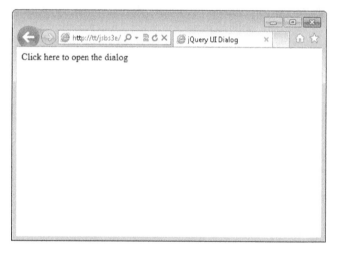

FIGURE 17-10 Creating a page to hold a dialog that displays with a click event.

Clicking anywhere within the text "Click here to open the dialog" shows the dialog, like that in Figure 17-11.

FIGURE 17-11 The dialog opened after clicking the text message.

Note This code can be found as dialog-open.html and dialog-open.js in the companion content.

More JQuery UI

There's quite a bit more to jQuery UI than this chapter could convey. For example, jQuery UI has an autocomplete function and several other widgets, with more being added all the time.

A good place to start for more information about jQuery UI, with a special focus on how to make things work, is on the jQuery UI demo site at *http://jqueryui.com/demos/*.

Exercises

1. Create a jQuery UI datepicker on a webpage and allow the date range to be from 1 month prior to the current date up to 12 months ahead of the current date.

2. Refer to the jQuery UI documentation and implement a page with at least one widget not shown in this chapter.

CHAPTER 18

Mobile development with jQuery Mobile

After completing this chapter, you will be able to

- Understand mobile development with jQuery Mobile.

- Create a mobile-friendly page.

Ask executives in an organization what they want their website to do, and they'll say "be mobile." Of course, they'll say that without any inkling of what exactly the phrase means, as if there's some magic potion to make a site work well in a mobile web browser, such as a phone or an iPad. Selling the magic potion to executives is already a multimillion-dollar business. Luckily for you, you'll soon find out that there's really no magic potion involved in making a site mobile. So when the boss wants to outsource the "mobile development project" for $250,000, you can step in and say, "I think we can do it for less."

This chapter looks at jQuery Mobile, which, like jQuery UI, is a complementary project to the main jQuery library. jQuery Mobile helps to make sites work well in a mobile environment. However, jQuery Mobile isn't the only way to go. You could also change the HTML and CSS in such a way as to make the site work better in a mobile environment. However, because this is a book on JavaScript, the focus will center on the JavaScript way to accomplish the task.

A walkthrough of jQuery Mobile

jQuery Mobile is a framework that enables advanced webpage design optimized for the touch experience that people would experience if they were using a website through a mobile phone or an iPad. jQuery Mobile takes care of the layout and the transition between pages of a site to make the site more like a mobile app. For example, Figure 18-1 shows a simple site created with jQuery Mobile. I use a page similar to this to store my personal bookmarks so that I can use them from a mobile device when I'm traveling.

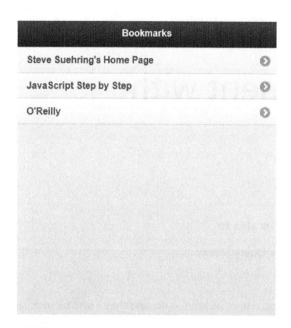

FIGURE 18-1 A simple bookmark page created with jQuery Mobile.

jQuery Mobile makes use of the HTML *data-* attributes. Example 18-1 shows the main portion of the HTML used to create the page for Figure 18-1.

EXAMPLE 18-1 HTML to create a bookmark page with jQuery Mobile

```
<div id="page1" data-role="page">
<div id="header" data-role="header">
<h1>Bookmarks</h1>
</div>
<div data-role="content">
<ul data-role="listview" id="bookmarkList">
<li><a href="http://www.braingia.org">Steve Suehring's Home Page</a></li>
<li><a href="http://www.javascriptstepbystep.com">JavaScript Step by Step</a></li>
<li><a href="http://www.oreilly.com">O'Reilly</a></li>
</ul>
</div> <!-- end content div -->
</div> <!-- end page1 main page div -->
```

Notice the use of four different *data-role* attributes in the HTML shown in Example 18-1. There's the *data-role* called "page", another called "header", one called "content", and another called "listview". jQuery Mobile uses these *data-role* attributes to apply special formatting and behavior. If there is any magic potion, that's where the magic happens: by applying different *data-role* (and other *data-*) attributes throughout a page, you control how jQuery Mobile renders the page and how the page behaves. You'll see other *data-* attributes throughout this chapter.

jQuery Mobile is available as a download or through a Content Delivery Network (CDN). Later in this chapter, you'll see how to download jQuery Mobile. Like jQuery UI (and jQuery, for that matter), jQuery Mobile is added to a page by placing references to its CSS and JavaScript within your page. This is the same concept that you've been using throughout the book, so no surprises here.

Example 18-2 shows the entire HTML used to create the page shown in Figure 18-1.

EXAMPLE 18-2 The entire HTML to create a bookmark page with jQuery Mobile

```
<!DOCTYPE html>
<html>
<head>
  <title>bookmarks</title>
  <link media="only screen and (max-device-width: 480px)" href="mobile-bookmarks.css"
        type="text/css" rel="stylesheet">
<link rel="stylesheet" href="http://code.jquery.com/mobile/1.0b1/jquery.mobile-
1.0b1.min.css" />
<script src="http://code.jquery.com/jquery-1.6.1.min.js"></script>
<script src="http://code.jquery.com/mobile/1.0b1/jquery.mobile-1.0b1.min.js"></
script>
</head>
<body>
<div id="page1" data-role="page">
<div id="header" data-role="header">
<h1>Bookmarks</h1>
</div>
<div data-role="content">
<ul data-role="listview" id="bookmarkList">
<li><a href="http://www.braingia.org">Steve Suehring's Home Page</a></li>
<li><a href="http://www.javascriptstepbystep.com">JavaScript Step by Step</a></
li>
<li><a href="http://www.oreilly.com">O'Reilly</a></li>
</ul>
</div> <!-- end content div -->
</div> <!-- end page1 main page div -->
</body>
</html>
```

 Note If you attempt to re-create this page, the version of jQuery and jQuery Mobile should be updated to the latest version. See *http://jquerymobile.com* for more information about the latest version.

There's also a CSS file used in Example 18-2. The CSS just increases the font size to account for my lack of skill at accurately tapping a small item through my phone! Here's the CSS:

```
body {
    font-size: 4em;
}
```

jQuery Mobile can also use themes, in much the same way that jQuery UI does. Themes change the appearance of jQuery Mobile to be more customized to the look and feel you'd like to present to the user.

Getting jQuery Mobile

jQuery Mobile can be downloaded from *http://jquerymobile.com*. Alternatively, jQuery Mobile can be used through a CDN, as shown in Example 18-2. This section looks at downloading and installing jQuery Mobile for use on your computer and in your websites.

Downloading jQuery Mobile

Downloading jQuery Mobile is very similar to the process used for jQuery UI. Refer to Chapter 17, "jQuery effects and plug-ins," for information about downloading and using jQuery UI. jQuery Mobile comes as a set of JavaScript and CSS and accompanies jQuery. Downloading jQuery Mobile means heading to *http://jquerymobile.com* and clicking the Download link.

At the time of this writing, the folks at jQuery Mobile are testing a Download Builder to enable you to select the various components to be included in your download. If you don't need a certain widget or effect, you don't need to include it, thus reducing the amount of code (and reducing the number of potential bugs) that you need to use to deliver your site to the browser. The Download Builder concept is similar to jQuery UI's download process.

Unfortunately, at the time of this writing, the resulting download built with Download Builder was incomplete. Therefore, the process described here recommends downloading the compressed zip file from the main Download page, shown in Figure 18-2, rather than using the Download Builder.

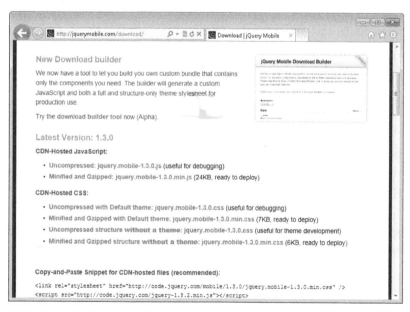

FIGURE 18-2 The jQuery Mobile Download page is used to download jQuery Mobile.

Within the Download page, look for the latest stable version. Within that section you'll see a link likely called "ZIP File." That's the one you want. Click it and the download will begin. jQuery Mobile is downloaded as a compressed zip file. Inside the file is a directory called jquery-mobile, along with the version number. Within that directory are the CSS, images, and JavaScript files for jQuery Mobile, shown in Figure 18-3.

Name	Type	Compresser
demos	File folder	
images	File folder	
jquery.mobile.structure-1.1.1.css	Cascading Style Sheet Do...	
jquery.mobile.structure-1.1.1.min.c...	Cascading Style Sheet Do...	
jquery.mobile.theme-1.1.1.css	Cascading Style Sheet Do...	
jquery.mobile.theme-1.1.1.min.css	Cascading Style Sheet Do...	
jquery.mobile-1.1.1.css	Cascading Style Sheet Do...	
jquery.mobile-1.1.1.js	JScript Script File	
jquery.mobile-1.1.1.min.css	Cascading Style Sheet Do...	
jquery.mobile-1.1.1.min.js	JScript Script File	

FIGURE 18-3 The jQuery Mobile files.

As you can see from Figure 18-3, the CSS and JavaScript files are all contained within the same folder; there's no hierarchical structure placing CSS in a css folder and JavaScript in a js folder. Therefore, placing the files correctly is up to the developer.

If you're using css and js folders, copy the CSS and JavaScript files to their respective folders within your project or server's document root and be sure to point to the appropriate place from within your code, too.

Note The versions of these files will change by the time you read this.

Testing jQuery Mobile

With jQuery Mobile downloaded, it's time to walk through an exercise to test jQuery Mobile.

Walking through a jQuery Mobile test exercise

1. Open the compressed (zip) file containing the jQuery Mobile files.

2. Unzip or uncompress the contents of the jQuery Mobile download. If you're using a css folder and a js folder to organize your CSS and JavaScript, place the CSS files into the css folder and JavaScript files into the js folder as appropriate. Otherwise, uncompress the files into your server's document root. Keep the images directory underneath the CSS files, hierarchically. The images directory should be within whatever folder in which you place the CSS files, as shown in Figure 18-3.

3. Place a copy of jQuery into your project or document root. For instructions about how to obtain jQuery, see Chapter 11, "An introduction to jQuery."

4. Open Visual Studio, Eclipse, or another editor. If you're using an editor that requires files to be added to the project (such as Visual Studio), add the CSS and JavaScript files from jQuery Mobile to the project. In Visual Studio, this is typically accomplished using the File | Add Existing Item menu option. Repeat this process as necessary to get all of the CSS and JavaScript files imported, and import the images directory and its contents, too.

5. Create a new HTML file or edit test.html in the Chapter18 companion content.

6. If you're using a new file, place the following HTML in the file. If you're editing test.html, add the HTML shown in boldface here. You'll likely need to change the version of jQuery Mobile and jQuery itself to match the version that you downloaded.

```html
<!doctype html>
<html>
<head>
    <title>Test Page for jQuery Mobile</title>
    <meta name="viewport" content="width=device-width, initial-scale=1">
    <link rel="stylesheet"
        href="jquery.mobile-1.1.1.css">
    <script type="text/javascript"
        src="jquery-1.7.2.min.js">
    </script>
    <script type="text/javascript"
        src="jquery.mobile-1.1.1.js">
    </script>
</head>
<body>
<div data-role="page">
    <div data-role="header">
        <h1>Test Page</h1>
    </div>
    <div data-role="content">
        <p>This is some nice content.</p>
    </div>
    <div data-role="footer">
        <h2>Footer content</h2>
    </div>
</div>  <!-- end page div -->
</body>
</html>
```

7. Save test.html.

8. View test.html in a web browser. You should see a page similar to that in the following graphic.

If your page didn't work as expected, here are some troubleshooting tips:

- Make sure the versions of jQuery's JavaScript file and the jQuery Mobile CSS and JavaScript files are all correct.

- Make sure that the paths to the files are correct. You could use Firebug's Net console tab to see whether all of the files were loaded.

- Make sure that the files are loaded in the correct order. The CSS files should be loaded before the JavaScript, and jQuery should be loaded before the jQuery Mobile JavaScript.

- Make sure that the data-roles are defined as shown in the HTML example.

With jQuery Mobile tested in your own web environment, it's time to see what else the framework can do.

Linking with jQuery Mobile

Links in pages within a jQuery Mobile site work essentially the same as links within a normal website. However, when the link is to a page within the same site, jQuery Mobile adds special animations called *transitions* while the page is being loaded. Transitions help the user experience by providing visual feedback that something is happening while the page loads. This section looks at the various forms of links in jQuery Mobile.

Creating a link

By default, links to other documents or pages within the same site are loaded using AJAX (Asynchronous JavaScript and XML). You'll learn more about AJAX in Chapter 19, "Getting data into JavaScript." For now, what you need to know is that when you link to another page, it can be loaded using a special method that will enable page transitions and animations—essentially, letting jQuery Mobile do what it's designed to do.

There's nothing special that you need to do to make links trigger the transition effect, because it's the default behavior. When an anchor tag (<A>) is clicked or tapped, jQuery Mobile takes over and attempts to fetch the page. While the page is loading, an animation will be displayed, and when loaded, the page will be displayed to the user.

Example 18-3 shows a page called link.html (in the companion content) that contains a link to the test.html page created in the previous exercise.

EXAMPLE 18-3 A jQuery Mobile page with a link

```
<!doctype html>
<html>
<head>
    <title>Test Page for jQuery Mobile</title>
    <meta name="viewport" content="width=device-width, initial-scale=1">
    <link rel="stylesheet"
        href="jquery.mobile-1.1.1.css">
    <script type="text/javascript"
        src="jquery-1.7.2.min.js">
    </script>
    <script type="text/javascript"
        src="jquery.mobile-1.1.1.js">
    </script>
</head>
<body>
<div data-role="page">
    <div data-role="header">
        <h1>Link Page</h1>
    </div>
    <div data-role="content">
        <p><a href="test.html">Load the test page</a></p>
    </div>
    <div data-role="footer">
        <h2>Footer content</h2>
    </div>
</div>   <!-- end page div -->
</body>
</html>
```

Loading this page in a browser reveals a page with a single link. When that link is clicked or tapped, the test.html page loads.

Changing the page transition

The default page transition is called *fade*, which fades the current page out of view and fades the new page into view quickly. This transition is configurable on a per-link or global basis. Some of the transitions that you can use include the following:

- fade (the default)
- flip
- flow
- none
- pop
- turn
- slide
- slidedown
- slideup
- slidefade

The type of page transition is changed with the *data-transition* attribute placed on a link. For example, the link from Example 18-3 was this:

```
<a href="test.html">Load the test page</a>
```

Changing the transition to something different, like turn, looks like this:

```
<a href="test.html" data-transition="turn">Load the test page</a>
```

You can also set the *data-transition* to *none*, for no transition effect on load.

> **Note** Changing the page transition globally involves working with the *auto-initialization* event. See *http://jquerymobile.com/demos/1.2.0/docs/api/globalconfig.html* for more information about the *mobileinit* function and how to use it, and see *http://jquerymobile.com/demos/1.2.0/docs/pages/page-transitions.html* for more information about the option to set for configuring the default transition.

Linking without AJAX

Certain links won't load with the AJAX behavior. For example, links outside the current site won't use AJAX. You can also change the default behavior so that the link, even if it's within the same site, won't use AJAX. The following four scenarios will prevent the link from using the AJAX load method:

- Links outside the site (to another domain)

- Links defined with the *rel="external"* attribute

- Links defined with the *data-ajax="false"* attribute

- Links defined with a *target* attribute

Example 18-4 shows the HTML to create five different links (also included as links.html in the companion content). The first link opens using the default AJAX method, while the next three all use methods for changing the default linking behavior to not use AJAX. The final link in the example won't load with AJAX because it goes to an external domain.

EXAMPLE 18-4 Loading links in various ways

```
<!doctype html>
<html>
<head>
    <title>Test Page for jQuery Mobile</title>
    <meta name="viewport" content="width=device-width, initial-scale=1">
    <link rel="stylesheet"
        href="jquery.mobile-1.1.1.css">
    <script type="text/javascript"
        src="jquery-1.7.2.min.js">
    </script>
    <script type="text/javascript"
        src="jquery.mobile-1.1.1.js">
    </script>
</head>
<body>
<div data-role="page">
    <div data-role="header">
        <h1>Link Page</h1>
    </div>
    <div data-role="content">
        <p><a href="test.html">Load the test page</a> (default behavior)</p>
        <p><a href="test.html" data-ajax="false">Load the test page</a> (data-
ajax = false)</p>
        <p><a href="test.html" rel="external">Load the test page</a> (rel =
external)</p>
        <p><a href="test.html" target="_blank">Load the test page</a> (in new
tab)</p>
        <p><a href="http://www.braingia.org">Braingia.org</a></p>
    </div>
```

```
        <div data-role="footer">
            <h2>Footer content</h2>
        </div>
    </div>  <!-- end page div -->
    </body>
</html>
```

When loaded in a browser, the page looks like that in Figure 18-5.

FIGURE 18-5 A jQuery Mobile page demonstrating link behaviors.

More Info See *http://jquerymobile.com/demos/1.2.0/docs/pages/page-links.html* for more information about page linking.

Enhancing the page with toolbars

Toolbars are commonly used to provide page-level and navigation information. In the examples you've seen in this chapter (Figure 18-5, for example), the header and footer are both toolbars, with the easy-to-remember *data-role* values of *header* and *footer*, respectively. You can also add a navigation bar. This section looks at just that. The examples in this section show navigation bars being added to the header and the footer, but there's nothing special that says you need to do that. You can add a navbar just about anywhere on the page using *data-role="navbar"* and the correct HTML.

Adding a navigation bar

The navigation bar uses the *data-role* of *"navbar"*, as in this example:

```
<div data-role="navbar">
    <ul>
        <li><a href="#">Link 1</a></li>
        <li><a href="#">Link 2</a></li>
    </ul>
</div>
```

jQuery Mobile automatically sizes the resulting buttons so that they fill the width of the screen, with each button taking up an equal portion of the size. Example 18-5 shows a full-page example with a two-item navbar in the header area. This is also included as navbar.html in the companion content.

EXAMPLE 18-5 Creating a top navbar

```
<!doctype html>
<html>
<head>
    <title>Test Page for jQuery Mobile</title>
    <meta name="viewport" content="width=device-width, initial-scale=1">
    <link rel="stylesheet"
        href="jquery.mobile-1.1.1.css">
    <script type="text/javascript"
        src="jquery-1.7.2.min.js">
    </script>
    <script type="text/javascript"
        src="jquery.mobile-1.1.1.js">
    </script>
</head>
<body>
<div data-role="page">
    <div data-role="header">
        <h1>Navbar Page</h1>
        <div data-role="navbar">
            <ul>
                <li><a href="#">Link 1</a></li>
                <li><a href="#">Link 2</a></li>
            </ul>
        </div>
    </div>
    <div data-role="content">
        <p>Content.  Yay!</p>
    </div>
    <div data-role="footer">
        <h2>Footer content</h2>
    </div>
</div>  <!-- end page div -->
</body>
</html>
```

The resulting page is shown in Figure 18-6. Notice the Link 1 and Link 2 buttons immediately below the header.

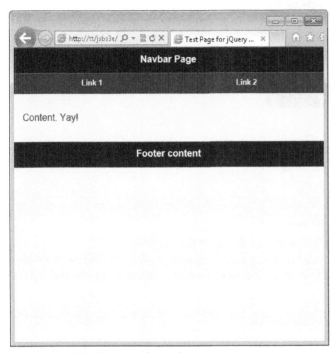

FIGURE 18-6 A basic page with a navbar.

Adding a footer navigation bar

A common item seen in mobile applications is a navigation or tab bar on the bottom of the screen. This effect can be created with jQuery Mobile. Adding the navbar in the footer is the same as adding it to the header section, except that the HTML goes into the footer section instead of the header:

```
<div data-role="footer">
    <h2>Footer content</h2>
    <div data-role="navbar">
        <ul>
            <li><a href="#">Link 1</a></li>
            <li><a href="#">Link 2</a></li>
        </ul>
    </div>
</div>
```

One common pattern in mobile apps is to have a tab bar or navigation bar on the bottom that contains icons and names. This effect can be created with the help of a couple additional attributes added to the footer. Specifically, the *data-icon* and *data-iconpos* attributes define the icons to use and their position relative to the text (top or bottom, for example). Figure 18-7 shows an example of this design pattern.

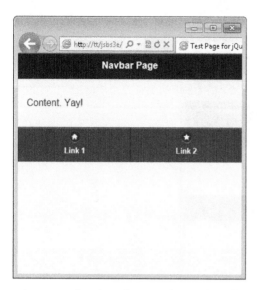

FIGURE 18-7 Creating a footer navigation bar effect with icons in jQuery Mobile.

Example 18-6 shows the HTML to create this effect. This is also included as footerbar.html in the companion content.

EXAMPLE 18-6 HTML to create an icon navigation bar

```
<!doctype html>
<html>
<head>
    <title>Test Page for jQuery Mobile</title>
    <meta name="viewport" content="width=device-width, initial-scale=1">
    <link rel="stylesheet"
        href="jquery.mobile-1.1.1.css">
    <script type="text/javascript"
        src="jquery-1.7.2.min.js">
    </script>
</head>
<body>
<div data-role="page">
    <div data-role="header">
        <h1>Navbar Page</h1>
    </div>
    <div data-role="content">
        <p>Content.  Yay!</p>
    </div>
```

```
        <div data-role="footer">
            <div data-role="navbar">
                <ul>
                    <li><a data-icon="home" data-iconpos="top" href="#">Link 1</a></
li>
                    <li><a data-icon="star" data-iconpos="top" href="#">Link 2</a></
li>
                </ul>
            </div>
        </div>
    </div> <!-- end page div -->
    </body>
</html>
```

There are numerous icons included with jQuery Mobile. See *http://jquerymobile.com/test/docs/ buttons/buttons-icons.html* for more information about the available icons and their names.

Adding buttons to toolbars

jQuery Mobile has built-in space for buttons to appear on both the left and right side of the header element. You add buttons by just placing links within the *<DIV>* element with the *data-role* of header. For example:

```
<div data-role="header">
    <a href="#" data-icon="back">Go Back</a>
    <h1>My Buttons</h1>
    <a href="#" data-icon="forward">Go Forward</a>
</div>
```

That HTML (when added to the HTML from Example 18-6) reveals a page like the one in Figure 18-8. Notice the addition of the buttons in the header section. This HTML is included as headerbutton.html in the companion content.

FIGURE 18-8 Adding header buttons with jQuery Mobile.

See the previous section for information about changing the icons used for the buttons.

Other toolbar enhancements

Toolbars have other enhancements that you can use to change the behavior of the toolbar. This section looks at two such enhancements.

Changing the toolbar color

You can change the theme or color of the navigation bar by applying the *data-theme* attribute to the elements. For example, changing the theme of the navbar buttons shown in Example 18-6 looks like this (also included as footerbarb.html in the companion content):

```
<ul>
    <li><a data-theme="b" data-icon="home" data-iconpos="top" href="#">Link 1</a></li>
    <li><a data-theme="b" data-icon="star" data-iconpos="top" href="#">Link 2</a></li>
</ul>
```

The resulting page looks like Figure 18-9.

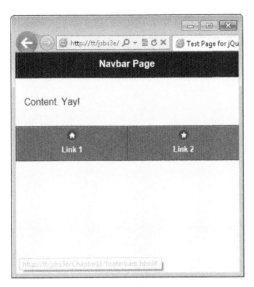

FIGURE 18-9 Changing the theme of footer elements.

There are currently five themes included in jQuery Mobile. They use letters *a* through *e* with the theme at letter *a* being the default. You can visit *http://jquerymobile.com/test/docs/toolbars/bars-themes.html* to see how each theme looks.

Persistent toolbar

One final toolbar customization covered in this chapter is a persistent toolbar. This design pattern is frequently used to make the footer navigation bar always stay on the bottom of the user's viewport, no matter how short or long the page's actual content. You'll work through an exercise to see this in action.

This exercise assumes that you've followed the earlier exercise in the chapter and have jQuery Mobile working in your development environment.

Creating a persistent toolbar

1. Open Visual Studio, Eclipse, or your text editor.

2. In your editor, create a new page or edit pers.html in the Chapter18 companion content.

3. In the pers.html file, add the code shown in bold:

```
<!doctype html>
<html>
<head>
    <title>Test Page for jQuery Mobile</title>
    <meta name="viewport" content="width=device-width, initial-scale=1">
```

```
        <link rel="stylesheet"
            href="jquery.mobile-1.1.1.css">
        <script type="text/javascript"
            src="jquery-1.7.2.min.js">
        </script>
        <script type="text/javascript"
            src="jquery.mobile-1.1.1.js">
        </script>
    </head>
    <body>
    <div data-role="page">
        <div data-role="header">
            <h1>Persistent Footer</h1>
        </div>
        <div data-role="content">
            <p>I love creating content.</p>
            <p>I love creating content.</p>
            <p>I love creating content.</p>
            <p>I love creating content.</p>
            <p>I love creating content.</p>
            <p>I love creating content.</p>
        </div>
        <div data-role="footer" data-id="persistent" data-position="fixed">
            <div data-role="navbar">
                <ul>
                    <li><a data-icon="home" data-iconpos="top" href="#">Link 1</a></li>
                    <li><a data-icon="star" data-iconpos="top" href="#">Link 2</a></li>
                </ul>
            </div>
        </div>
    </div>  <!-- end page div -->
    </body>
    </html>
```

4. Save the file as **pers.html**.

5. View pers.html in your browser.

You should see a page like that in Figure 18-10. You might need to resize your browser to see the scroll effect and how the bottom footer navbar sticks to the bottom no matter where you scroll.

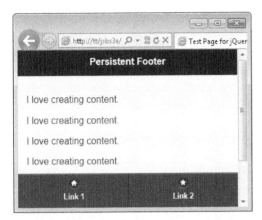

FIGURE 18-10 Creating a persistent footer.

This persistence was created by adding two attributes to the footer, *data-id* and *data-position*. Setting *data-position* to *fixed* created the effect, and the *data-id* attribute is used to share the same footer among several pages, as you might do if you have multiple pages in a site that need the same footer.

You can also change the appearance of one of the navigation elements to give a "current page" or "active item" look and feel, as shown in Figure 18-11.

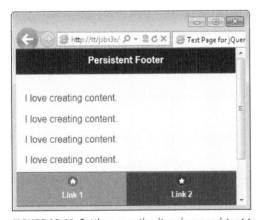

FIGURE 18-11 Setting an active item in a persistent toolbar.

This effect is accomplished by adding the class *ui-btn-active* and *ui-state-persistent* on the appropriate anchor, as in this example:

```
<a class="ui-btn-active ui-state-persist" data-icon="home" data-iconpos="top" href="#">
```

Even more jQuery Mobile

Like jQuery UI, jQuery Mobile is an expansive subject area, worthy of an entire book by itself. This chapter touched on jQuery Mobile and hopefully gave you enough information to get started so that you can see how valuable jQuery Mobile can be when creating a mobile website.

Additional areas that you can look into include creating buttons and button effects, adding forms and accepting input, creating lists, and formatting content, just to name a few. See *http://jquerymobile. com/test/* for more information about the various effects that can be created with jQuery Mobile.

Exercises

1. Use a different theme for jQuery Mobile to change the appearance of the header.

2. Change the code from the final exercise (persistent footer) to set one of the items as active.

3. Examine the jQuery Mobile site and implement a demo page for one of the areas identified and not covered in this chapter.

CHAPTER 19

Getting data into JavaScript

After completing this chapter, you will be able to

■ Understand the architecture of a JavaScript-based web application.

■ Understand the basics of AJAX.

The JavaScript you've seen so far in this book works with page events to change the behaviors and look and feel of pages, and does a little validation of forms. A widely used feature of JavaScript is to be able to obtain and work with data, sending it and receiving it from a server. The "data" in this case can be anything: flight times, prices, lists of the types of insects found in a region, or even entire webpages. This chapter examines Asynchronous JavaScript and XML, the method known as AJAX, to obtain and work with data to and from a server.

JavaScript application architecture

Building a browser-based application with the sophisticated look and feel of a desktop application frequently involves using JavaScript. Such an application has some of the same features and responsiveness of a desktop application, as though it were sitting on the local computer rather than operating through a web browser.

This brief chapter provides an overview of the components that constitute an application based on JavaScript. The goal is to help you understand the underlying architecture and some of the complexity necessary to create this type of application at the enterprise level.

The big three: display, behavior, data

Three primary components exist in a web application:

■ **Display**   The look and feel of the page

■ **Behavior**   What the application interface does—that is, what happens when the user clicks an element on the page or otherwise interacts with the page

■ **Data**   The server component that contains the data and performs the actions, the results of which appear on the page

JavaScript code typically handles the first two components in the preceding list—display and behavior—to affect the interface or react when a user performs an action on a page. JavaScript works with the data returned from the server as well, but usually does so only to alter the display in some manner. For example, a call to a web service that returns the current temperature or sky condition might use JavaScript to change an icon when the weather is sunny. The following sections examine each of these three elements in a little more detail.

Display: page layout

The webpage display encompasses the page layout and anything related to the look and feel of the page and site, including the color scheme, images, styling of menus (whether they have rounded corners or square ones, and so on), the placement of buttons and content, font colors, and use of images. JavaScript can affect all these items, as you've seen in previous chapters on Cascading Style Sheets (CSS) and form validation. These elements are the primary focus of web design and receive the most attention from users, and you should consider these elements when determining requirements for your site.

Behavior: controlling what happens when

One of the most important factors in determining the user experience is also one of the most often overlooked elements of a web application design: the behavior of the application interface, which controls what happens when users interact with a given element. Consider the following two simple scenarios:

- When a visitor clicks the Submit button on a web form, does that Submit button stay active or become disabled?

- When an input text field gains focus, should it change color or be highlighted?

Even these minor behaviors can greatly enhance the user experience when designed properly. However, when working through a design of a site, these behaviors are also frequently forgotten, ignored, or discounted in favor of the look and feel or raw design of the site.

Data: consume, display, and validate

JavaScript, at least its use as far as this book is concerned, doesn't interact directly with a database or server. Obviously, JavaScript does so through AJAX and through web services, but those processes require server-side code to return data back to the calling JavaScript.

Like the display portion of the site, the back-end server-side data components should receive a fair share of attention when you design a web application. From database design to programming the business logic, this back-end coding needs careful attention.

JavaScript and web interfaces

Programmers use JavaScript to create front ends that provide a quality user experience. Microsoft Bing Maps (formerly Live Search Maps) is an example of a web application that relies heavily on JavaScript.

With Bing Maps, and other applications like it, users can drag the map display around in much the same way they would when interacting with a desktop application. The map is composed of tiles at various resolutions. When a user drags the map, the browser sends several HTTP requests to the Virtual Earth web server, requesting additional tiles that the browser then quickly displays.

The Bing search engine also uses a type-ahead search similar to that of other search engines like Google. If you begin typing in the main text box on *http://www.bing.com*, the browser immediately sends an HTTP request to the server to find similar searches.

All of these elements from the Bing search engine use JavaScript. Countless other web interfaces rely on JavaScript to enhance the user experience by controlling the behavior layer of the page.

You've seen a lot about the first two parts of the application architecture, display and behavior. The remainder of this chapter and the next chapter examine the third element, data, in depth.

Introduction to AJAX

AJAX describes the programming paradigm that combines JavaScript and a web server. Developers use AJAX to create highly interactive web applications such as Microsoft Virtual Earth.

Without AJAX, a web application might make the visitor wait while a response is gathered from the web server. An AJAX-based application sends requests from the web browser to the web server in the background (asynchronously) while the visitor is using the application. This makes the application feel much more responsive to the user.

In an AJAX application, JavaScript processes the response and presents the data to users. When combined with CSS and a good layout, an AJAX application provides excellent usability and the portability that only a web application can.

As complex as some AJAX applications might seem, the actual process of sending a request and handling the response is not terribly complicated. Using AJAX revolves around a fundamental AJAX object: *XMLHttpRequest*.

One central concept in AJAX is that you call server-side applications to return data. The next chapter contains a brief overview of how to create such an application using both ASP.NET and PHP. (PHP is a recursive acronym for PHP Hypertext Preprocessor.) If you need additional assistance in creating the server-side portion of an AJAX application, you can get help from several sources.

If you're creating a server-side application using Microsoft technologies, the Microsoft Developer Network provides a great resource with many tutorials and an introductory article on AJAX (*http://msdn.microsoft.com/en-us/magazine/cc163363.aspx*). Microsoft Press also publishes several excellent books on building applications for the web. One such title is *Microsoft ASP.NET 4 Step By Step* (Microsoft Press, 2010). For others, look at *http://www.microsoft.com/mspress* for more information.

If you're developing a server-side application using other technologies such as the LAMP (Linux, Apache, MySQL, Perl/PHP/Python) stack, searching the web for tutorials is likely the easiest way to get up to speed quickly on development on the platform. The book *Learning Perl* (O'Reilly, 2011) is a great resource for learning the basics of the Perl programming language.

 Note If you like my writing style, I wrote *Beginning Perl Web Development* (Apress, 2005), which focuses on using Perl to work with web applications.

PHP's main website (*http://www.php.net*) is a good place to start for information about PHP, and for Python, take a look at the Python website (*http://www.python.org*).

AJAX with jQuery

The next chapter will show how to create, send, and receive data using the standard *XMLHttpRequest* object. However, a much more robust method for working with server-side data is to use jQuery's AJAX-related methods.

jQuery includes a built-in function called *$.ajax()* that greatly simplifies the process of sending and receiving data with JavaScript. The problem is that *XMLHttpRequest*, while simple to use for standard requests, starts to become cumbersome when nonstandard items need to be addressed.

When you begin to program with *XMLHttpRequest*, you'll soon find yourself wanting to create your own standard library to instantiate the *XMLHttpRequest* object and handle errors, and so on. Therefore, rather than walk down the path of reinventing the wheel, you'll see how to use jQuery for AJAX, which alleviates the need to create your own library just for AJAX.

AJAX without the X

Extensible Markup Language (XML) is a highly structured language for exchanging data. XML works very, very well for what it is. However, XML is very, very verbose. This verbosity means that there is a good amount of extraneous information exchanged for each and every request sent.

As the amount of data transferred using AJAX increases, so does this extra data. The more data exchanged, the more that needs to be downloaded by the user (especially noteworthy on slow mobile connections). Luckily there's another way.

JavaScript Object Notation (JSON) provides a lightweight way to exchange data over AJAX without losing any of the fidelity or descriptive nature provided by XML. For example, consider this XML to represent a person and the person's details:

```
<person>
    <firstname>Steve</firstname>
    <lastname>Suehring</lastname>
    <emailAddresses>
        <primaryEmail>suehring@braingia.com</primaryEmail>
    </emailAddresses>
    <twitter>@stevesuehring</twitter>
</person>
```

Represented through JSON, that same data is compacted down to this:

```
"person": {
    "firstname": "Steve",
    "lastname": "Suehring",
    "emailAddresses": {
        "primaryEmail": "suehring@braingia.com"
    },
    "twitter": "@stevesuehring"
}
```

While the JSON version is less verbose, it's still clear what each element represents. However, the same data was conveyed with about 25 percent less extraneous information. The example here is simple, with a small amount of data. Imagine this example expanded 100 times. Suddenly that 10 percent data savings starts to add up.

What's Next?

You've now seen some information about the overall architecture of a JavaScript-based web application. You've also been introduced to the concepts surrounding AJAX, including the *XMLHttpRequest* object and jQuery's *$.ajax()* function. Finally, you saw how JSON can be used to exchange information in a more efficient manner than XML for web applications. The next chapter expands on these concepts to show how to send and receive AJAX requests.

PART III

AJAX and Server-Side Integration

Asynchronous JavaScript and XML (AJAX) is a key technology for making responsive, dynamic web pages with JavaScript. This section focuses on AJAX and accompanying technologies.

CHAPTER 20

Using AJAX

After completing this chapter, you will be able to

- Create an AJAX Request.

- Retrieve data from the server using AJAX.

- Use jQuery's AJAX function to retrieve data from the server.

The *XMLHttpRequest* object

The *XMLHttpRequest* object is central to building an Asynchronous JavaScript and XML (AJAX) application. Although implementations of JavaScript differ, the ECMAScript and the World Wide Web Consortium (W3C) have standardized many aspects of it. Even with differences between browsers, since the release of Windows Internet Explorer 7, you use the *XMLHttpRequest* object in the same way across all major browsers.

Microsoft first implemented the *XMLHttpRequest* object in Microsoft Internet Explorer 5.0. If a visitor is using a browser version earlier than that, applications using *XMLHttpRequest* won't work. In Internet Explorer versions prior to version 7, the *XMLHttpRequest* object was instantiated as an *ActiveXObject* object, but other browsers implemented the *XMLHttpRequest* object as a JavaScript object built into the browser. This means that if your applications need to work with versions of Internet Explorer earlier than version 7, you need to instantiate the *XMLHttpRequest* object for those browsers in a different way, as I show you later in the chapter. The next section, "Instantiating the *XMLHttpRequest* object," shows how you can test for the existence of *XMLHttpRequest* and how to instantiate it in all versions of Internet Explorer.

Instantiating the *XMLHttpRequest* object

Internet Explorer 7 and later versions, and all other major browsers that support *XMLHttpRequest*, instantiate the *XMLHttpRequest* object in the same way:

```
var req = new XMLHttpRequest();
```

For Internet Explorer versions earlier than version 7, you must instantiate an *ActiveXObject* instead. However, the way you do this varies depending on the version of the XMLHTTP library installed on the client. Therefore, you need to do a bit of code juggling to instantiate an *XMLHttpRequest* object in these earlier versions of Internet Explorer.

The code in Example 20-1 is a cross-browser function that instantiates an *XMLHttpRequest* object across multiple browsers.

EXAMPLE 20-1 Instantiating an *XMLHttpRequest* object across browsers

```
function readyAJAX() {
    try {
        return new XMLHttpRequest();
    } catch(e) {
        try {
            return new ActiveXObject("Msxml2.XMLHTTP");
        } catch(e) {
            try {
                return new ActiveXObject("Microsoft.XMLHTTP");
            } catch(e) {
                return "A newer browser is needed.";
            }
        }
    }
}
```

The function in Example 20-1 uses multiple levels of *try/catch* blocks to instantiate an *XMLHttpRequest* object, regardless of whether the visitor is using Internet Explorer or another browser. If the native call to *XMLHttpRequest* fails, it means that the visitor is using an Internet Explorer browser older than version 7. In such a case, the error is caught and one of the methods for instantiating *XMLHttpRequest* that is based on *ActiveXObject* is tried. If none of these methods succeeds, the likely reason is that the browser is too old to support *XMLHttpRequest*.

Using *try/catch*

The *try* portion of the *try/catch* set of statements encapsulates a block of JavaScript. When the script executes, any exceptions that are thrown in the *try* block are caught by the *catch* statement. You can then handle the error within the JavaScript placed in the *catch* block. The code to do this follows this format:

```
try {
    // Execute some code
}
catch(errorObject) {
    //  Error handling code goes here
}
```

As the code within the *try* clause executes, any errors encountered cause processing to be immediately handed over to the *catch* clause. In Example 20-1, if *XMLHttpRequest* is not available, the catch clause executes, which creates another *try/catch* block. When using a *catch* clause, it's common to perform multiple tasks, such as call another function to log an error, or handle a condition using a general, or generic, approach. Using *catch* is particularly helpful in problematic areas of code or in areas where the nature of the code can lead to errors (such as in code that processes user input).

An optional complementary statement in JavaScript, called *finally*, works with *try/catch*. The *finally* statement contains code that gets executed regardless of whether the *try* statement's code succeeded or the *catch* handler executed. Typically, you use a *finally* block to make sure that some code (such as cleanup code) executes every time.

The article "About Native XMLHTTP" on MSDN describes some of the version history and security nuances of the *XMLHttpRequest* object in Internet Explorer. This article can be found at *http://msdn2. microsoft.com/en-us/library/ms537505.aspx*.

You call the *readyAJAX()* function shown in Example 20-1 like this:

```
var requestObj = readyAJAX();
```

The *requestObj* variable now contains the *XMLHttpRequest* object returned by the function, or, if the function couldn't create the object, the *requestObj* variable contains the string *"A newer browser is needed."*

Sending an AJAX request

With a newly created *XMLHttpRequest* object in hand, you can send requests to the web server and get responses. To send the request, you use a combination of the *open()* and *send()* methods of the *XMLHttpRequest* object.

There are two fundamentally different ways to send AJAX requests: synchronously and asynchronously. When sent in a synchronous manner, the requesting code simply waits for the response—a process called *blocking*. So, for a synchronous request, the requesting code will block, effectively preventing further processing or execution of other JavaScript while the script waits for the response from the web server. This process has obvious disadvantages when the request or response gets lost in transit or is just slow. With asynchronous requests, the requesting code doesn't block. Instead, the caller can check the request status to discover when the request has completed. You see more about asynchronous requests later in this chapter; it's easier to work with synchronous requests first.

Before you can send a request, you have to build it. To do that, you use the *open* method, which has three arguments: the request method (*GET, POST, HEAD*, or others), the Uniform Resource Locator (URL) to which the request will be sent, and a Boolean *true* or *false*, indicating whether you want to send the request asynchronously or synchronously, respectively.

Assuming that your request object has been retrieved using the *readyAJAX()* function and placed into a variable named *requestObj,* a typical asynchronous call to the *open* method might look like this:

```
var url = "http://www.braingia.org/getdata.php";
requestObj.open("GET", url, true);
```

That same call, sent synchronously, looks like this:

```
var url = "http://www.braingia.org/getdata.php";
requestObj.open("GET", url, false);
```

You actually send the request with the *send* method, as follows:

```
requestObj.send();
```

Note If the parameters sent with the request have any special characters, such as spaces or other characters reserved by the URI RFC, you must first escape those characters using the % notation. This is discussed further in RFC 3986, which you can find at *ftp://ftp.rfc-editor. org/in-notes/rfc3986.txt.* You can also find more information at *http://msdn2.microsoft.com/ en-us/library/aa226544(sql.80).aspx.*

How the web works in 500 words or fewer

The Hypertext Transfer Protocol (HTTP) is the language of the web. HTTP is currently defined by RFC 2616 and describes a protocol for exchanging information by using requests from clients and responses from servers.

Requests from clients such as web browsers contain a specific set of headers that define the method used for retrieval, the object to be retrieved, and the protocol version to be used. Other headers contain the web server host name, languages requested, the name of the browser, and other information that the client deems relevant to the request.

Here's a basic HTTP version 1.1 request that shows only the most important of these headers:

```
GET / HTTP/1.1
Host: www.braingia.org
```

This request specifies the *GET* method to retrieve the document located at the / (root) directory location using HTTP version 1.1. The second line, commonly called the *Host* header, is the URL *http://www.braingia.org*. This header tells the web server which website is being requested. Several different methods can be used in a request; the three most common are *GET, POST,* and *HEAD*. The client and server also exchange HTTP cookies as part of the headers. Cookies are sent in the request, and others might be received in the response.

When the web server for *http://www.braingia.org* receives a request like this, the web server sends response headers that indicate how it has handled the request. In this case, the web server sends response headers similar to these:

```
HTTP/1.1 200 OK
Date: Sat, 12 Mar 2011 01:04:34 GMT
Server: Apache/1.3.33 (Debian GNU/Linux) mod_perl/1.29 PHP/4.3.10-22
Transfer-Encoding: chunked
Content-Type: text/html; charset=iso-8859-1
```

The requested document follows the response headers. The first and most important header indicates the status of the response. In the example, the response is *200*, which is synonymous with OK. Other common responses include *404* (which indicates that the requested document was not found), *302* (which indicates a redirect), and *500* (which indicates that a server error occurred).

Understanding these basics of HTTP is important for understanding how to build AJAX requests and how to troubleshoot those requests when things go wrong. You can find more information about HTTP, including the various response codes, in RFC 2616 at *ftp://ftp.rfc-editor.org/in-notes/rfc2616.txt*.

Processing an AJAX response

It's easier to work with the response when the request is sent synchronously, because the script's execution stops while awaiting the response. The *requestObj* variable provides helpful methods for processing a response, including giving access to the status codes and text of the status sent from the server. Regardless of whether the request is synchronous or asynchronous, you should evaluate the status code to ensure that the response was successful (usually indicated by a status of *200*).

The *responseText* method contains the text of the response as received from the web server.

For example, assume a server application returns the sum of two numbers. Calling the application to add the numbers 2 and 56 looks like this:

```
http://www.braingia.org/addtwo.php?num1=2&num2=56
```

Here's a synchronous call and response retrieval:

```
requestObj.open("GET", "http://www.braingia.org/addtwo.php?num1=2&num2=56", false);
requestObj.send();
if (requestObj.status == 200) {
    alert(requestObj.responseText);
} else {
    alert(requestObj.statusText);
}
```

In this example, assume that the *requestObj* variable was created using the *readyAJAX()* function that you saw earlier. The preceding code then calls the *open* method using a *GET* request to the specified URL (*http://www.braingia.org/addtwo.php?num1=2&num2=56*). The request is sent synchronously because the last argument to the *open* method is *false*. Next, the code calls the *send* method, which actually sends the request to the web server.

When the client receives the response from the web server, it calls the status property to check the status value. If the response code is *200*, indicating success, the code displays the *responseText* method, which holds the response from the server. If the response status code is anything other than *200*, the code displays the status text.

Processing an asynchronous response is a bit more complex. When a request is sent asynchronously, script execution continues. Therefore, it is unpredictable when the script will be notified that the response has been received. To know the response status, you can use the *onreadystatechange* event to trigger code that checks the event's *readyState* property to determine the state of the request/response cycle. The *readyState* property has five states, as shown in Table 20-1.

TABLE 20-1 *readyState* properties

Value	Description
0	Uninitialized. Open but has yet to be called.
1	Open. Initialized but not yet sent.
2	Sent. The request has been sent.
3	Receiving. The HTTP response headers have been received, but the response body has not yet been completely received.
4	Loaded. The response has been fully received.

For practical purposes, the only state that matters to the JavaScript and AJAX programmer is state *4*—Loaded. Attempting to process a response that has a *readyState* value other than *4* results in an error.

You typically use an anonymous function to handle the *onreadystatechange* event for asynchronous AJAX calls. The function checks to see whether the *readyState* property has reached *4* and then checks to ensure that the status is *200*, indicating success. The code follows this format:

```
requestObj.onreadystatechange = function() {
    if (requestObj.readyState == 4) {
        if (requestObj.status == 200) {
            alert(requestObj.responseText);
        } else {
            alert(requestObj.statusText);
        }
    }
}
```

In this next exercise, you create an *XMLHttpRequest* object and send a request to a web server to retrieve a book title based on its ISBN. You need a web server and web server code to print the response, because requests sent using *XMLHttpRequest* are subject to the JavaScript same-origin policy.

The *same-origin policy* requires that requests go only to servers within the same domain from which the calling script was loaded. That is, because I'm executing the script in this exercise directly from my web server at *http://www.braingia.org*, my script can call that server and retrieve a response. However, if you tried to call a URL on another web server, the same-origin policy would prevent the script from retrieving the response.

> **Note** One way to get around the same-origin security feature is to use an HTTP proxy or to write the server-side program so that it sends a request on behalf of the calling program; however, learning how to do that is beyond the scope of this book.

For the upcoming exercise, the script or program running on the server needs to return the phrase *"JavaScript Step by Step"* when it receives a *GET* request with a *name/value* argument with the following value:

isbn=9780735624498

For example, at its most basic, the server-side program could look like this when implemented inside an Active Server Pages (ASP) page based on VBScript:

```
<%
dim isbn
isbn=Request.QueryString("isbn")
If isbn<>"" Then
    If isbn=="9780735624498" Then
        Response.Write("JavaScript Step by Step")
    End If
End If
%>
```

A functionally similar program looks like this if written in PHP:

```
<?php

$isbn = $_GET['isbn'];

if (! $isbn) {
    print "That request was not understood.";
} else if ($isbn == "9780735624498") {
    print "JavaScript Step by Step";
}

?>
```

In the following exercise, the URL to which the request will be sent is predefined, but you must replace that URL with the URL where your server-side program is located. Because of the same-origin policy, the server-side program needs to be within the same domain as the page that calls it.

1. Create your server-side program to return the book title when it receives the *isbn* argument shown earlier. You can do this in your choice of languages. (If you need to, look at the two examples shown earlier.)

2. Using Microsoft Visual Studio, Eclipse, or another editor, edit the file isbn.html in the Chapter20 sample files folder (in the companion content).

3. Within the webpage, replace the TODO comment with the following code shown in boldface. Be sure to replace the *url* variable with the appropriate URL for your server-side program:

```
<!doctype html>
<html>
<head>
<title>ISBN</title>
</head>
<body>
<div id="data"></div>
<script type="text/javascript">
function readyAJAX() {
    try {
        return new XMLHttpRequest();
    } catch(e) {
        try {
            return new ActiveXObject("Msxml2.XMLHTTP");
        } catch(e) {
            try {
                return new ActiveXObject("Microsoft.XMLHTTP");
            } catch(e) {
                return "A newer browser is needed.";
            }
        }
    }
}
var requestObj = readyAJAX();
var url = "http://www.braingia.org/isbn.php?isbn=9780735624498";

requestObj.open("GET",url,true);
requestObj.send();
requestObj.onreadystatechange = function() {
    if (requestObj.readyState == 4) {
        if (requestObj.status == 200) {
            alert(requestObj.responseText);
        } else {
            alert(requestObj.statusText);
        }
    }
}
</script>
</body>
</html>
```

4. Save and view the page in a web browser. You should receive an alert like the following:

Congratulations! You've now processed your first *XMLHttpRequest* object.

Processing XML responses

The AJAX example that you just saw used plain Hypertext Markup Language (HTML) and a text response from the web server, so you could retrieve them using the *XMLHttpRequest* object's *responseText* method. However, server applications can also return XML responses, which you can process natively using the *responseXML* method.

Earlier in this chapter, the sidebar titled "Describing how the web works in 500 words or fewer" discussed an example web server response. The server response contained this *Content-Type* header:

```
Content-Type: text/html; charset=iso-8859-1
```

To retrieve a response using the *responseXML* method, the web server needs to send a *Content-Type* of *text/xml* or *application/xml* (or really anything +xml) like this:

```
Content-Type: application/xml
```

When the *XMLHttpRequest* object receives native XML as the response, you can use Document Object Model (DOM) methods to process the response.

The *responseXML* method has been somewhat quirky historically, and using it can result in unexpected behavior, depending on the browser and operating system. In addition, *responseXML* isn't as widely supported as other JavaScript methods. Using *responseXML* means combining the *XMLHttpRequest* techniques already seen in this chapter with the XML parsing techniques described in Chapter 17, "jQuery effects and plug-ins." For example, consider this XML document (call it book. xml):

```
<?xml version="1.0" encoding="ISO-8859-1"?>
<book>
  <title>JavaScript Step by Step</title>
  <isbn>9780735624498</isbn>
</book>
```

Combining the *XMLHttpRequest* object and XML parsing leads to the following code, which retrieves and displays the ISBN from the book.xml document:

```
var requestObj = readyAJAX();
var url = "http://www.braingia.org/book.xml";
requestObj.open("GET",url,false);
requestObj.send();
```

```
if (requestObj.status == 200) {
    var xmldocument = requestObj.responseXML;
    alert(xmldocument.getElementsByTagName("isbn")[0].childNodes[0].nodeValue);
} else {
    alert(requestObj.statusText);
}
```

When the request completes successfully, *requestObj.responseXML* contains the requested XML document (book.xml). The *xmldocument.getElementsByTagName("isbn")* code retrieves an array of the *<ISBN>* tags in the document. There's only one of those in this document; the *[0]* indicates the first one. The *.childNodes[0]* portion of the code retrieves the first child node from that *<ISBN>* tag. In this case, that's the text node, which contains the ISBN number. Finally, the *.nodeValue* portion of the code retrieves the value of that text node, the ISBN itself, which the preceding code displays with an *alert* call.

Working with JSON

JavaScript Object Notation (JSON) is a way to pass data as native JavaScript objects and arrays, rather than encode data within XML (or HTML) responses. JSON is a more efficient way to pass data from server to client. Parsing XML using the DOM is more complex and thus slower, whereas parsing JSON-encoded data is done directly in JavaScript.

Recall the book.xml document from an earlier example in this chapter. That same data in JSON looks like this:

```
{
"book":
    {
    "title": "JavaScript Step by Step",
    "isbn": "9780735624498"
    }
}
```

Retrieving an individual element is somewhat easier with JSON than with XML. You use the JavaScript *eval()* function to parse the JSON-formatted response. For example, here's the code to retrieve and display the book title:

```
var requestObj = readyAJAX();
var url = "http://www.braingia.org/json.php";
requestObj.open("GET",url,false);
requestObj.send();
if (requestObj.status == 200) {
    var jsondocument = eval('(' + requestObj.responseText + ')');
    alert(jsondocument.book.title);
} else {
    alert(requestObj.statusText);
}
```

Using JSON carries an inherent security risk, because it uses the *eval()* function to parse the response. The *eval()* function essentially executes the JavaScript code received, so if that code were malicious, it would execute in the context of the application being run. It is your responsibility to ensure that the data your application is using with JSON is clean and free of malicious code that could cause problems when executed using *eval()*.

Using a JavaScript framework such as jQuery alleviates much of this concern, as does the addition of native JSON into ECMA-262 edition 5. You learn how to use jQuery and how to use it for processing JSON later in this chapter.

Processing headers

The *HTTP HEAD* method returns just the response headers from the server, rather than the headers and the body in the way the *GET* method does. The *HEAD* method is sometimes helpful for determining whether a given resource has been updated or changed.

One frequently sent HTTP header is *Expires*, which indicates when the client should request a refreshed copy of a document rather than read it from the client's cache. If the server sends the *Expires* header, the *HEAD* method is an efficient way to view and parse the *Expires* header because the *HEAD* method retrieves only the response header rather than the entire body of the requested resource.

To obtain only the response headers from the *XMLHttpRequest* object, whether using a *HEAD* request or any other type of request such as *GET* or *POST*, use the *getAllResponseHeaders()* method of the *XMLHttpRequest* object, as follows:

```
requestObj.getAllResponseHeaders();
```

Example 20-2 shows how to retrieve the response headers from the default page of my website.

EXAMPLE 20-2 Retrieving headers

```
<!doctype html>
<html>
<head>
<title>Response Headers</title>
</head>
<body>
<div id="data"></div>
<script type="text/javascript">
function readyAJAX() {
    try {
        return new XMLHttpRequest();
    } catch(e) {
        try {
            return new ActiveXObject("Msxml2.XMLHTTP");
        } catch(e) {
            try {
                return new ActiveXObject("Microsoft.XMLHTTP");
            } catch(e) {
                return "A newer browser is needed.";
```

```
                }
            }
        }
    }
    var requestObj = readyAJAX();
    var url = "http://www.braingia.org/";
    requestObj.open("HEAD",url,true);
    requestObj.send();
    requestObj.onreadystatechange = function() {
        if (requestObj.readyState == 4) {
            if (requestObj.status == 200) {
                alert(requestObj.getAllResponseHeaders());
            } else {
                alert(requestObj.statusText);
            }
        }
    }
}
</script>
</body>
</html>
```

> **Tip** The same-origin policy that you came across during the exercise earlier in the chapter
> applies equally to the *HEAD* method in Example 20-2. When writing Example 20-2, I forgot
> about the same-origin policy and originally set the *url* variable to *http://www.microsoft.
> com/,* thinking I'd get that site's default page. However, upon receiving an error, I realized
> the problem and changed the *url* variable to match the domain on which the script was
> running (my site). You are likely to encounter the same problem. Remember to change the
> *url* variable to your server of origin when attempting to run the code in Example 20-2.

Using the *POST* method

Up to this point, the examples you've seen have used the *GET* and *HEAD* methods to retrieve data
from the server. To submit queries through HTTP, you often use the *POST* method. Using the *POST*
method with *XMLHttpRequest* is a bit more complex than using either the *GET* or *HEAD* methods.
However, the *POST* method offers two specific advantages over the *GET* method. First, parameters
you send with a *POST* request are contained in the body of the request rather than in the URL, as they
are with the *GET* method, and therefore are less likely to be seen by the casual observer trying to find
ways into your application. Second, the *POST* method supports larger requests. Some servers limit the
amount or size of a *GET* request to a certain number of characters, and although those servers might
also limit the size of a *POST* request, the limitation for *POST* requests is almost always much greater.

The HTTP *POST* method requires an additional header to be set within the request. You set that
additional header with the *setRequestHeader()* method:

```
requestObj.setRequestHeader(header, value);
```

For example, to set the *Content-Type* header for a web form, as you would do for a *POST* request, you could write:

```
requestObj.setRequestHeader("Content-type", "application/x-www-form-urlencoded");
```

When you saw the AJAX requests sent earlier using the *GET* method, the URL included the parameters or *name/value* pairs for the application, like so:

```
http://www.braingia.org/books/javascriptsbs/isbn.php?isbn=9780735624498
```

In the preceding example, the *isbn* parameter has the value *9780735624498*. However, when working with *POST* requests, the URL contains only the document or resource requested—it doesn't contain any parameters. Therefore, you must send the parameters as part of the *send()* method.

Example 20-3 presents an AJAX request using the *POST* method, shown in boldface type. It uses two parameters—see whether you can spot them.

EXAMPLE 20-3 Constructing a *POST* request

```
<!doctype html>
<html>
<head>
<title>Post</title>
</head>
<body>
<div id="xmldata"></div>
<script type="text/javascript">
function readyAJAX() {
    try {
        return new XMLHttpRequest();
    } catch(e) {
        try {
            return new ActiveXObject("Msxml2.XMLHTTP");
        } catch(e) {
            try {
                return new ActiveXObject("Microsoft.XMLHTTP");
            } catch(e) {
                return "A newer browser is needed.";
            }
        }
    }
}
var requestObj = readyAJAX();
var url = "http://www.braingia.org/books/javascriptsbs/post.php";
var params = "num1=2&num2=2";
requestObj.open("POST",url,true);
requestObj.setRequestHeader("Content-type", "application/x-www-form-urlencoded");
requestObj.send(params);
requestObj.onreadystatechange = function() {
```

```
        if (requestObj.readyState == 4) {
            if (requestObj.status == 200) {
                alert(requestObj.responseText);
            } else {
                alert(requestObj.statusText);
            }
        }}
    </script>
    </body>
    </html>
```

Example 20-3 creates two parameters placed into a variable called *params*:

```
var params = "num1=2&num2=2";
```

After constructing the request object (*requestObj*), the parameters are passed as an argument to the *send()* method:

```
requestObj.send(params);
```

AJAX and jQuery

The previous section showed how to write and use AJAX. This section shows how to use AJAX with jQuery.

jQuery offers several functions for working with data from and sending data to a server. Among these are the *.load()* function, the *.post()* function, and the *.get()* function. jQuery also includes a specific AJAX function, aptly titled *.ajax()*.

Using the *.ajax()* function, you can set several parameters, including which HTTP method the call should use (*GET* or *POST*), the time-out, and what to do when an error occurs (as well as when the code succeeds, of course).

Note See *http://api.jquery.com/jQuery.ajax/* for a full list of the available parameters for use with the *.ajax()* function.

The basic syntax of the *.ajax()* function is:

```
$.ajax({
    parameter: value
});
```

You can pass a number of *parameter: value* pairs to the *.ajax()* function, but you typically specify the method, the URL, and a callback function. It's also quite common to specify the data type to be returned, whether to cache the response, the data to be passed to the server, and the function to call when an error occurs.

> **Note** The *.ajaxSetup()* function lets you set defaults for AJAX-related parameters, such as for caching, methods, and error handling, among others.

Here's a real-world example of the *.ajax()* function in action:

```
$.ajax({
    url:  "testajax.aspx",
    success:  function(data) {
        alert("Successful load");
    }
});
```

jQuery also includes a function called *.getJSON()* that performs the same essential function as the other AJAX-related functions, but it works specifically with JSON-encoded data from the server. The *.getJSON()* function is the equivalent of calling the *.ajax()* function with the additional parameter *dataType: 'json'*.

For example, consider this JSON-encoded list of a few states:

```
["Wisconsin","California","Colorado","Illinois","Minnesota","Oregon","Washington","New
York","New Jersey","Nevada","Alabama","Tennessee","Iowa","Michigan"]
```

For this example, assume that the JSON-encoded data is returned when the file json.php is called on the local server. The following use of the *.ajax()* function retrieves the data and calls a function named *showStates* when successful:

```
$.ajax({
    type: "GET",
    url: "json.php",
    dataType: "json",
    success: showStates
});
```

The function *showStates* creates a list and adds it to a form's *<SELECT>* drop-down box.

Using AJAX with jQuery

To complete this step-by-step exercise, you need to have a file called json.php available in the same directory as the file you'll use in this exercise. (A json.php file is included with the book's companion content.) Like the examples from the previous section, the json.php file must reside in the same domain as the file that's making the AJAX request. Additionally, you need jQuery available. This example assumes that jQuery resides in the same directory as the file.

1. Edit the file ajax.html file (included with this book's companion content) using your editor of choice.

2. Within the file, replace the TODO comment with the code shown in boldface (ajax.txt in the companion content):

```html
<!doctype html>
<html>
<head>
<title>AJAX Test</title>
<script type="text/javascript" src="jquery-1.7.2.min.js"></script>
</head>
<body>
<div id="states">
</div>
<script type="text/javascript">
$(document).ready(function() {

$.ajax({
    type: "GET",
    url: "json.php",
    dataType: "json",
    success: showStates
});
function showStates(data,status) {
    $.each(data, function(item) {;
        $("#states").append("<div>" + data[item] + "</div>");
    });}

});
</script>
</body>
</html>
```

3. Save the file, and view it in a web browser. You see a list of states, like the one shown here:

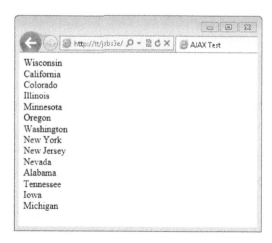

AJAX errors and time-outs

The *.ajax()* function lets you handle errors and time-outs gracefully. In addition to the success handler, you can specify an error handler with the *error* parameter. The value of the *error* parameter is usually a callback function. Here's an example, with the newly added error parameter in boldface:

```
$.ajax({
    type: "GET",
    url: "json.php",
    dataType: "json",
    success: successFunction,
    error: errorFunction
});
```

The callback function used for error handling (*errorFunction* in the code example) receives three arguments: the *XMLHTTPRequest* object; a string representing the error encountered; and string containing the HTTP error code, if there was one. Therefore, an error handler function should accept these three arguments and then do something with the results. This example shows an alert:

```
function errorFunction(xhr, statusMessage, httpErrorCode) {
    alert("An error was encountered " + statusMessage);
}
```

You might find it necessary to set a time-out for an AJAX request. You can set a generic AJAX time-out value through the default *$.ajaxSetup*, but you can also specify a time-out value for any individual call using the *timeout* parameter. Here's an example:

```
$.ajax({
    type: "GET",
    url: "json.php",
    dataType: "json",
    success: successFunction,
    error: errorFunction,
    timeout: 5000
});
```

It's important to realize that the time-out is in milliseconds. Therefore, the example shown sets the time-out at five seconds.

Sending data to the server

You not only need to receive data from a server in an AJAX call, but you also need to send data to a server and receive a response. You use the *data* parameter to the *.ajax()* function for this, sending data using either *GET* or *POST*.

You can format the data as ampersand-separated *key=value* pairs (*key1=value1&key2=value2*) or as mapped pairs *{key1: value1, key2: value2}*. The example here uses the *key=value* option, also known as the *query string option*.

This example calls a server-side program titled statefull.php, which, given a two-letter state abbreviation, returns the full name of the state.

```
$.ajax({
    type: "POST",
    url: "statefull.php",
    dataType: "json",
    success: successFunction,
    data: "state=WI"
});
```

Other important options

There are numerous options to the *.ajax()* function. You've seen how to use many of them already, but I'd like to highlight two more options:

- *async*

- *cache*

The *async* option, which is set to *true* by default, informs the script whether it should wait (and block further input in the browser) while the AJAX transaction is sent, received, and processed. When set to *true*, the AJAX transaction is done asynchronously, so it does not block.

The *cache* setting, which defaults to *true* in most instances, controls whether jQuery will cache the AJAX transaction. This is useful when the data being received doesn't change often, because *caching* speeds up the transaction, but caching can cause problems when your application is using older cached data that has changed on the server. I've found it helpful to set this option to *false* so that the response is not cached, especially in cases where you encounter problems when data is apparently not refreshing.

Exercise

1. Create a form with a *submit* event handler such that when the user enters a two-letter abbreviation for a state, the full name is returned using AJAX. The solution will require using some of the items you've learned throughout the book so far to create a form and add a handler. You can use jQuery for this exercise (that's how the solution will show it), or you can use the standard *XMLHttpRequest* object.

CHAPTER 21

Developing for Windows 8

After completing this chapter, you will be able to

- Understand apps in Windows 8.

- Understand the guidelines used when developing for Windows 8.

- Understand distribution mechanisms for Windows Apps.

Windows 8 introduces a new user interface to the operating system and simultaneously promotes JavaScript to a more prominent role within the operating system. This chapter looks at development for Windows 8 using JavaScript.

Windows 8 apps

Windows 8 introduces a new Start screen, shown in Figure 21-1, that changes the paradigm from one of a traditional desktop interface to one that's more touch and gesture friendly.

FIGURE 21-1 The Windows 8 Start screen.

Apps used through the Windows 8 interface utilize tiles, and these tiles are interesting in that they can be dynamically updated. For example, the Weather tile in Windows 8 automatically updates based on current conditions.

Developing Windows 8 apps

Developing and distributing apps has become much easier with Windows 8, especially for small developers. This section looks at some of the ins and outs of app development.

Development guidelines

Microsoft has developed a strong set of guidelines for Windows Apps that helps to ensure a positive and consistent user experience. As discussed within the "Windows 8 Product Guide for Developers" (*http://msdn.microsoft.com/windows/apps/hh852650*), the following principles govern apps in Windows 8:

- **Use strong content—content first.** The content of an app is the most important thing about the app and is the reason that users choose an app.

- **Responsive design.** Interactions with the user are designed to be intuitive and responsive.

- **State-aware.** The app should be able to run in various states, including as a full-screen app or in a snapped view where the app is secondary on the screen.

- **Contract support.** App contracts give multiple apps the ability to work together.

- **Live tiles.** Tiles can be updated in the background to enhance the user experience even when they're not working with the app.

- **Cloud support.** Windows 8 features cloud-based resources and settings prominently, and apps should take advantage of cloud support wherever possible.

When an app is submitted for approval in the Windows Store it goes through several tests, including a manual test, to ensure that the guidelines have been followed. The process for distribution is discussed later in this chapter. Microsoft does this to ensure a consistent and high-quality user experience for apps delivered in the Windows Store, much the same way that Apple performs testing of an app before distribution through its App Store.

The development process

The overall development process for apps is roughly the same as it is for all apps, with the exception of some extra steps necessary for approval if the app needs to be sold through the Windows Store. The overall steps are:

1. Plan and design the app.

2. Develop the app.

3. Package and test the app.

4. Distribute the app.

Planning and designing the app

Prior to jumping into development, Microsoft stresses the importance of following good design principles for apps. Doing so helps to ensure that the app will pass validation checks and ultimately provide a good user experience.

Microsoft has identified several planning steps when designing the user experience (UX) for apps. The first and foremost of these steps is deciding what the app will do and how users will interact with it. While this sounds obvious, when you start actually laying out (using pen and paper, for example) an app's design, you'll find out the best way to present information and how the user might best interact with the app.

> **Note** See "Designing UX for apps" at *http://msdn.microsoft.com/en-us/library/windows/apps/hh779072.aspx* for more information about the design recommendations for apps.

Developing the app

Apps are developed using the Windows 8 Software Development Kit (SDK). This SDK, available as a separate download or as part of Microsoft Visual Studio 2012, provides the interface through which apps interact with the Windows user interface. While Visual Studio isn't required for JavaScript development, it certainly does help when developing for Windows 8.

Using Visual Studio, apps can be developed in several different languages, including:

- Visual Basic
- Visual C++
- Visual C#
- JavaScript

This being a book on JavaScript, the focus will be on using JavaScript for app development. However, if you have expertise in any of the other languages, those also provide options for app development.

The use of JavaScript for app development is a great step forward for the language. Although so far this book has shown JavaScript being used in a browser, its use for Windows 8 moves JavaScript into the role of full-fledged client-side development language. This means that using nothing more than JavaScript, along with some HTML and CSS, you can create an app that can access all of the features available in Windows 8, such as the following:

- Access to media such as music, movies, and images
- Access to Internet-based resources
- Use of built-in Windows functions for controlling devices

When an app has been created, it gets assembled into an app package, which is a collection of files needed to run the file.

Packaging and testing the app

When development is complete, there is a packaging step that needs to occur with all apps, whether distributed through the Windows Store or within an organization. The app packaging process includes all of the files necessary for your app to run on another Windows 8–based computer. It's during the app packaging stage that you choose the architectures on which your program will run, such as the version number and so on.

You can also set several items about the app through its manifest file, part of which is shown in Figure 21-2. This manifest file is discussed in more detail in Chapter 22, "Using Visual Studio for Windows 8 development."

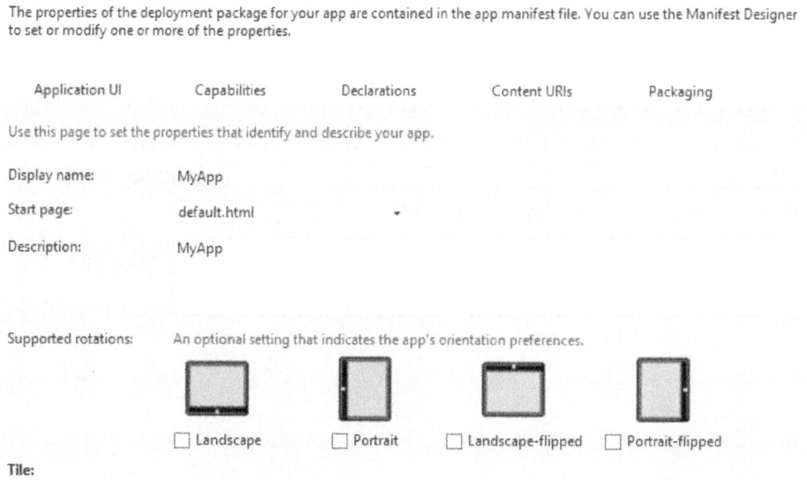

The properties of the deployment package for your app are contained in the app manifest file. You can use the Manifest Designer to set or modify one or more of the properties.

| Application UI | Capabilities | Declarations | Content URIs | Packaging |

Use this page to set the properties that identify and describe your app.

Display name: MyApp

Start page: default.html

Description: MyApp

Supported rotations: An optional setting that indicates the app's orientation preferences.

☐ Landscape   ☐ Portrait   ☐ Landscape-flipped   ☐ Portrait-flipped

Tile:

FIGURE 21-2 Setting items about the app through its manifest in Visual Studio.

App packaging is accomplished through the Create Your Package Wizard, the first step of which is shown in Figure 21-3.

The app package contains several files, including a security certificate and any dependencies necessary for your app to run. As you can see by the first step of the Create Your Package Wizard, you can choose whether the app will be distributed through the Windows Store or internally. App distribution is the focus of the next section.

After an app has been packaged, it can be tested on other devices and also by using the Windows App Certification Kit, which is part of the SDK. The Windows App Certification Kit is used by Microsoft during the app approval process but can also be used by the developer prior to submitting to the Windows Store or distributing internally. Doing so helps to ensure that the app will be approved by giving you a chance to eliminate any related errors prior to submittal.

FIGURE 21-3 Creating an app package in Visual Studio.

The Windows App Certification Kit, shown in Figure 21-4, runs several tests on the app, including executing it on the computer on which the wizard is run.

FIGURE 21-4 The Windows App Certification Kit.

When the wizard completes successfully, shown in Figure 21-5, the app is ready to be distributed, which is discussed in the next section.

 Note Microsoft has developed a checklist for app submission that you can use prior to submitting the app to the Windows Store. The checklist is available at *http://msdn.microsoft. com/library/windows/apps/hh694062.aspx*.

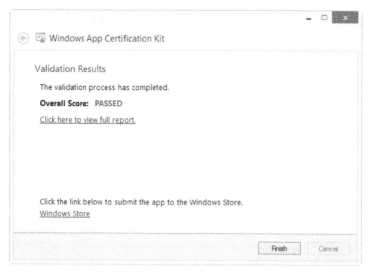

FIGURE 21-5 Results of app certification.

Distributing Windows apps

There are two means for distributing apps, through the Windows Store and by sideloading. The Windows Store is the primary means for distributing apps, and doing so makes your app available to the public. *Sideloading* is a process by which Line of Business (LOB) apps are distributed within an organization.

Distributing in the Windows Store

Distributing in the Windows Store means accepting the developer and other related licenses and agreements and submitting each app for an approval process. After the app has been built and tested locally, you can upload it to the Windows Store. When submitted, an app goes through the phases described in Table 21-1.

TABLE 21-1 App testing for the Windows Store

Phase	Description
Security Testing	Microsoft tests the app package for malware and other security issues.
Technical Compliance Testing	Microsoft uses the Windows App Certification Kit to test the app.
Content Compliance	The app is tested manually by Microsoft personnel and its content is examined.
Release	The app is queued for release to the public, either as soon as possible or at a time specified by you when the app was submitted.

When an app has been fully tested, it gets signed by Microsoft to prevent tampering, and you also receive a certification report on the results.

> **Note** See *http://msdn.microsoft.com/en-us/library/windows/apps/br230835.aspx* for an overview of the app submission process.

Distributing in an enterprise

As mentioned in the preceding section, another method for app distribution is by sideloading. In the context of Windows, sideloading refers to the process of installing an app within an enterprise. Sideloading is typically used for enterprises to distribute apps that are specific to the organization and that the enterprise wouldn't release to the public. When an app is sideloaded, it doesn't need to be submitted to Microsoft for approval, although the Windows App Certification Kit should still be used to ensure that the app is stable and usable.

Sideloading an app has several requirements, including changing Group Policy, using a specific version of Windows, and other related items. The process and requirements for doing so are discussed at *http://technet.microsoft.com/en-us/library/hh852635.aspx*. Explaining how to sideload an app is beyond the scope of this book.

Summary

This chapter doesn't have exercises for you to work through. By way of a summary, your takeaways from this chapter should be that Windows 8 changes the landscape on which apps are developed for Windows. JavaScript can be used to develop full-fledged, powerful apps for Windows 8.

Microsoft has developed numerous design principles surrounding good app development for Windows 8, and there are also overall platform requirements of which you should be aware when designing an app for Windows 8, especially if you want to distribute the app in the Windows Store.

Developing an app for Windows 8 is much like development for other programs. The app needs to be planned and designed, programmed, packaged, and tested. Visual Studio 2012 helps immensely with the tasks related to packaging and testing the app.

After the app has been tested, it can be submitted for approval through Windows Store. This process involves several stages including manual testing by Microsoft personnel. You can also distribute an app within an enterprise using a process called sideloading.

PART IV

JavaScript and Windows 8

The combination of HTML, CSS, and JavaScript can be used to build Windows 8 apps. This elevates JavaScript from more than a web-centric language and fully into the realm of cli-ent-side programming. The final section of the book looks at creating a Windows 8 app using HTML, CSS, and JavaScript.

CHAPTER 22

Using Visual Studio for Windows 8 development

After completing this chapter, you will be able to

- Install Visual Studio for Windows 8 development.

- Understand some of the Windows App templates available with Visual Studio.

- Create a new project and run a templated app.

The theme throughout the book has been that JavaScript development doesn't require an Integrated Development Environment (IDE) and that you should use whatever tool with which you're most comfortable for development. I tend to use Vim for writing HTML, CSS, and JavaScript for web applications. With the release of Windows 8, JavaScript can now be used to create full-fledged applications that run natively in Windows, freed from the web browser. Microsoft has updated Visual Studio to include tools that help in developing Windows 8 apps with JavaScript. Among the changes are templates for common layouts and packaging tools to help test apps and sell apps in the Windows Store. Therefore, when developing for Windows 8, it makes sense to use Visual Studio.

Installing Visual Studio 2012

Visual Studio comes in several forms, from a free version called Express to an enterprise-level version that stresses team-based development. This chapter will focus on the Express edition for Windows 8. There are actually several Express editions, including one focusing on web development and one focusing on Windows 8 development. For this chapter, you'll want the Express edition for Windows 8.

 Note Microsoft has a comparison of the different editions of the enterprise-level Visual Studio available at *http://www.microsoft.com/visualstudio/eng/products/compare*.

The various versions of Visual Studio can be downloaded at *http://www.microsoft.com/visualstudio/eng/downloads#d-2012-express*. When you find the edition you want, you can choose how to install it: either by clicking an Install Now link or a Download Now link. This chapter will show the use of the Download Now link, which downloads an entire installation package. This link is highlighted in Figure 22-1.

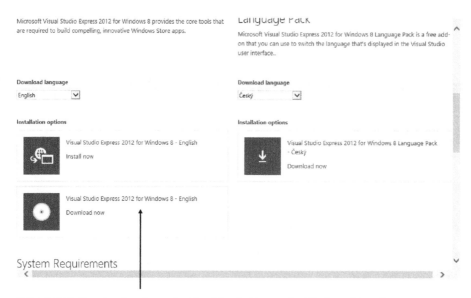

Microsoft Visual Studio Express 2012 for Windows 8 provides the core tools that are required to build compelling, innovative Windows Store apps.

Language Pack

Microsoft Visual Studio Express 2012 for Windows 8 Language Pack is a free add-on that you can use to switch the language that's displayed in the Visual Studio user interface..

Download language

English

Download language

Český

Installation options

Visual Studio Express 2012 for Windows 8 - English

Install now

Installation options

Visual Studio Express 2012 for Windows 8 Language Pack - Český

Download now

Visual Studio Express 2012 for Windows 8 - English

Download now

System Requirements

FIGURE 22-1 Downloading the entire Visual Studio Express for Windows 8 installer.

Installing Visual Studio 2012 Express for Windows 8

When the download completes, the next task is to install Visual Studio. The full download is an ISO file, which can be opened natively in Windows 8. Doing so reveals the ISOs contents, shown in Figure 22-2.

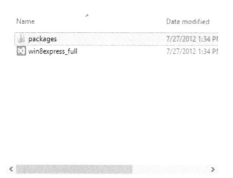

Name	Date modified
packages	7/27/2012 1:34 PM
win8express_full	7/27/2012 1:34 PM

FIGURE 22-2 The contents of the Visual Studio download file.

The following step-by-step exercise will walk you through installing Visual Studio 2012 Express for Windows 8.

1. With the ISO file opened in Windows 8, begin the installation process by double-clicking the win8express_full file. The first screen of the installation process is displayed, as in the following graphic:

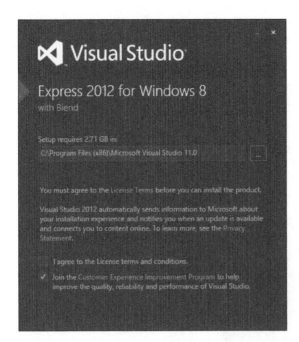

2. Within that first screen, read the license terms and, if you find them agreeable, mark your consent accordingly. When you do so, the "Install" area will become available, as shown in the following graphic:

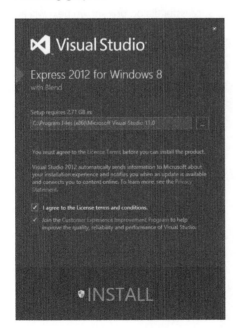

3. Click INSTALL to begin the installation process. If you're logged in as a normal user, you'll be prompted to allow the installation process to continue. Click Yes. The installation process will begin, with progress noted as shown in the following:

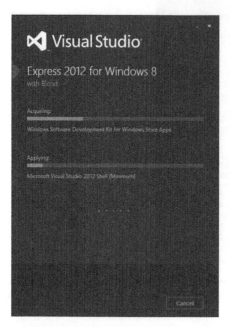

When the installation completes, the Setup Successful dialog box shown next will appear:

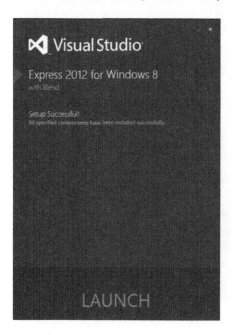

4. Click Launch. Visual Studio will start.

   Even though this edition of Visual Studio is free, you still must register it, so the registration process begins next, as shown in the following:

5. Click Register Online. Your browser will open, and you'll be directed to a Microsoft website where you can fill in your information and register to receive a product key.

6. Enter the product key that you receive from Microsoft into the dialog box from the preceding graphic, and click Next. If you're running as an account without administrative privileges you'll be prompted to allow the process to continue. If that's the case, click Yes.

7. After the key has been entered and you've clicked Next, a dialog box will be shown to confirm that a product key has been entered. This dialog box is shown in the following graphic:

Click Close to dismiss this dialog box.

8. Visual Studio will now begin a preparation, after which time it will open. Another dialog box will be displayed to obtain yet another license. This time the license is for Windows 8 development. The dialog box is shown in the following figure. Read through its terms, and if you agree, click I Agree. As before, if you're not logged in as administrator, you'll be prompted to allow this program to run. Click Yes.

9. To obtain the license, you need to log in with a Microsoft account, as shown here:

Enter your credentials, and click Sign In.

10. After you click Sign In, a license will be obtained and a confirmation dialog box will be shown. Click Close on that dialog box, and you'll (finally) be allowed into Visual Studio, shown here:

That's it! Enjoy your shiny new IDE. The next sections walk through Visual Studio to help get you familiar with the process of Windows 8 development. However, Visual Studio is a vast and powerful (and complex) piece of software. I encourage you to spend time in the Help section of Visual Studio, which is excellent.

Windows 8 app templates

Visual Studio includes multiple templates that help to kickstart the development process for Windows 8. The templates provide a good starting point, using common design patterns. This section looks at some of the templates available with Visual Studio 2012.

The templates are found by creating a new project, which is accomplished either by clicking New Project within the Start section of the Visual Studio's home screen (shown in the previous graphic) or by selecting New Project from the File menu. Doing so reveals the New Project dialog box, as shown in Figure 22-3.

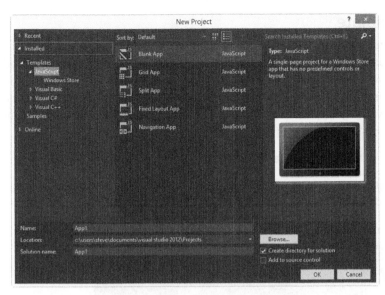

FIGURE 22-3 The New Project dialog box in Visual Studio 2012.

As you can see from Figure 22-3, there are four languages available and, within the JavaScript section, there are five templates currently installed. If you click to expand the Online section and then expand the Samples section, you can browse various code samples for JavaScript, shown in Figure 22-4.

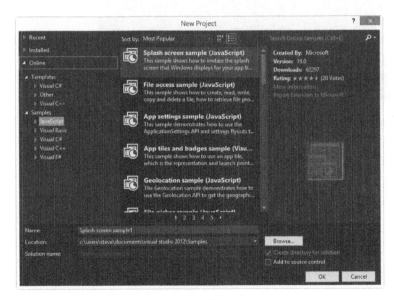

FIGURE 22-4 JavaScript samples are available online in Visual Studio.

Now, within the Installed JavaScript Templates section, it's time to explore a few of the various templates that are installed within Visual Studio.

Blank App template

The Blank App template creates just what it says, a blank app. The app has limited base functionality when compared with other templates but still includes base functionality to connect to the libraries and CSS necessary for an app. However, with the limited base functionality, you get greater flexibility to implement the features and the look and feel that you need for the app. The Blank App template also provides an easy way to get started with Windows 8 development because it contains a minimum number of files, so it'll be the focus of the following step-by-step exercise.

1. Begin the exercise from within Visual Studio 2012. Click File | New Project.

2. In the New Project dialog box, select Blank App from the JavaScript Templates. Name the app **BlankApp1** and click OK. This dialog box is shown in the following graphic:

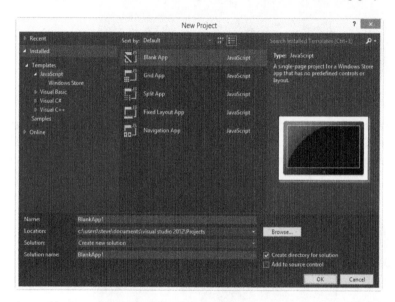

A new blank application will be created, and the default.js JavaScript file will be opened, as shown in the following:

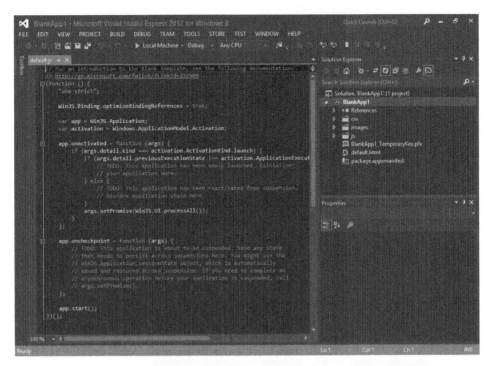

3. Run the app by selecting Start Debugging from the Debug menu or by pressing F5. The app will compile and start, showing the splash screen and finally the main page in full-screen mode, looking similar to this:

4. Close the app by dragging it from the top to the bottom of the screen. Switch back to the classic desktop to find Visual Studio.

5. Verify that the app has stopped, or select Stop Debugging from the Debug menu to stop the app.

6. Within the Solution Explorer, open default.html to reveal the HTML for the landing page for the app (from Figure 22-16).

7. In default.html, locate the *<P>*Content goes here*</P>* section within the *<BODY>* section, and delete it. In its place, add:

```
<h1>Here's my app!</h1>
```

The following graphic shows the new tag and its location:

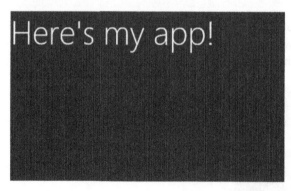

```
<!DOCTYPE html>
<html>
<head>
    <meta charset="utf-8" />
    <title>BlankApp1</title>

    <!-- WinJS references -->
    <link href="//Microsoft.WinJS.1.0/css/ui-dark.css" rel="stylesheet" />
    <script src="//Microsoft.WinJS.1.0/js/base.js"></script>
    <script src="//Microsoft.WinJS.1.0/js/ui.js"></script>

    <!-- BlankApp1 references -->
    <link href="/css/default.css" rel="stylesheet" />
    <script src="/js/default.js"></script>
</head>
<body>
    <h1>Here's my app!</h1>
</body>
</html>
```

8. Save default.html.

9. Run the solution by selecting Start Debugging from the Debug menu. The app will execute, and when it loads, you'll see your content, as shown here:

Here's my app!

10. Stop the project by dragging the app off the screen, switching to the desktop, and selecting Stop Debugging from the Debug menu.

Congratulations! You've created and slightly modified an app in Windows 8.

The real heart of the app is in the JavaScript. It's through JavaScript that you can make the app interactive, just like JavaScript does for webpages. In the next chapter, you'll build a more complex app. For now, feel free to experiment with the default.html and also to use the samples available with Visual Studio.

Grid App template

The Grid App template is used to convey information that needs to be grouped for ease of browsing by the user. For example, multiple items such as news stories would be a good candidate for a Grid app. The grid layout is shown in Figure 22-5.

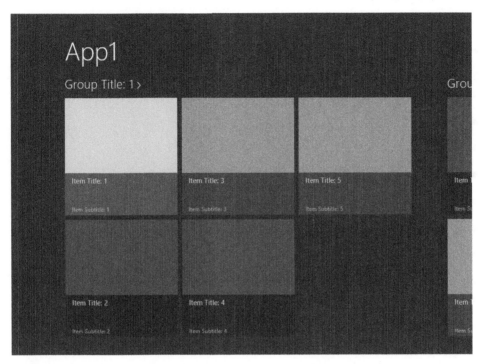

FIGURE 22-5 A Grid app in Windows 8.

You can see the grid layout in action by selecting New Project from the File menu and selecting Grid App from the templates. Just building the app by selecting Start Debugging from the Debug menu starts the app, and you can see how the various interactions take place within a Grid app.

Whereas the Blank App template included a single JavaScript file (default.js), a single CSS file (default.css), and a single HTML file (default.html), the Grid App template includes several other files that are used to create the layout.

The Grid App template includes four HTML files (three of which are found within their own folders in the pages folder):

- default.html

- groupDetail.html

- groupedItems.html

- itemDetail.html

Six JavaScript files are used, three of which are found alongside their corresponding HTML files within the pages folder hierarchy:

- default.js

- data.js

- navigator.js

- groupedItems.js

- groupDetail.js

- itemDetail.js

Four CSS files are used, one in the css folder and three with their corresponding HTML files in the pages folder hierarchy:

- default.css

- groupDetail.css

- groupedItems.css

- itemDetail.css

The design pattern that you see in this app is a good practice for your apps because it keeps each page or screen of the app and all of its code in separate containers, making it easy to maintain separation for each page.

When the Grid app loads, it first loads the default.html file. Within default.html, there's a *<DIV>* element that then references another page by using HTML *data-* attributes:

```
<div id="contenthost" data-win-control="Application.PageControlNavigator" data-win-
options="{home: '/pages/groupedItems/groupedItems.html'}"></div>
```

These *data-* attributes are custom attributes that can be used to define additional behavior. In this case, they load a *PageControlNavigator* attribute, which references the groupedItems.html page. In essence, default.html loads and then the page groupedItems.html is loaded within the Content Host *<DIV>* element.

> **Note** The page that loads by default can be changed using the app manifest, which will be discussed later in this chapter.

Split App template

The Split App template is useful for displaying a listing of information, such as products in a catalog or real estate listings. The Split app layout is shown in Figure 22-6.

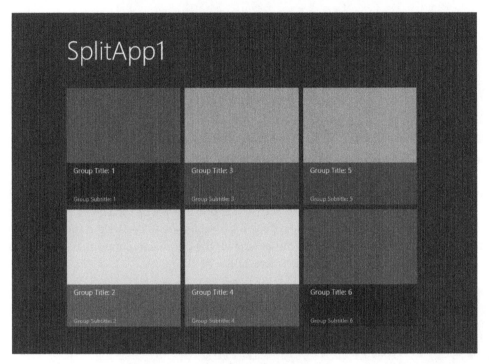

FIGURE 22-6 The Split app layout.

Like the Grid app layout, the Split app layout includes several HTML and CSS files, some of which are housed within the pages folder within the app. Also like the Grid app, the Split app layout loads default.html and then loads another file to take over control. An exercise at the end of this chapter asks you to determine which file is loaded from default.html.

Setting app details in the App Manifest

As previously stated, you can set the page that gets loaded first by using the app's Package Manifest, sometimes called the App Manifest, file. Visual Studio includes an editor for this file, which you can find within your solution as the file package.appxmanifest.

Double-clicking package.appxmanifest reveals the contents of the file loaded into a custom editor, like the one shown in Figure 22-7.

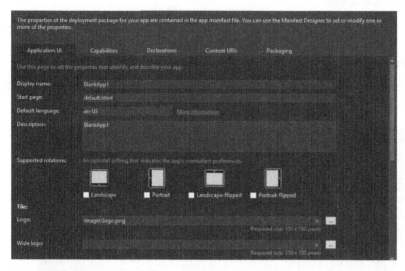

FIGURE 22-7 Editing the Package Manifest file in Visual Studio 2012.

As you can see from Figure 22-7, you can change the name of the app and its default page, along with several other items related to the app, such as the logo that will be used on its Start screen tile. There are several tabs in the editor, including one that enables you to declare the app's capabilities. For example, if your app needs to access the webcam or the Documents library, that needs to be declared on the Capabilities tab, shown in Figure 22-8.

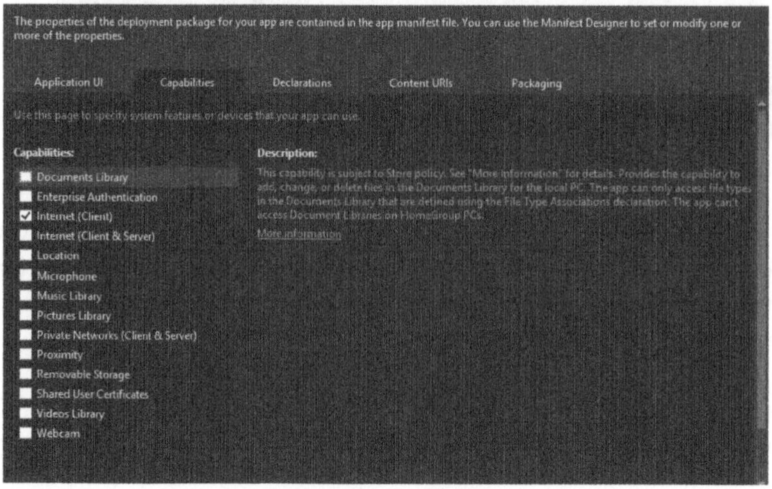

FIGURE 22-8 The Capabilities tab of the Package Manifest editor in Visual Studio 2012.

Using the Package Manifest editor is a common task when packaging your app for distribution through the Windows Store. That distribution is the subject of the next and last section of this chapter.

Packaging apps for the Windows Store

You've got your shiny new app ready, you've done all the testing you can locally, and you're ready to sell it to the world, or just about all of the world, anyway. Apps are sold through the Windows Store. The Windows Store has its own set of policies and procedures that need to be followed before your app can be sold. This chapter concentrates on the technical aspects of packaging an app. Refer to Chapter 21, "Developing for Windows 8," for more information about the overall process for app packaging and distribution.

Certification requirements

Selling an app in the Windows Store means getting the app approved by Microsoft. The approval process is similar to that for other storefronts, such as Apple's App Store. The approval and certification process ensures that apps provide a consistent and secure environment that's in line with the quality assurance standards for the Windows Store.

The certification process involves several requirements, as discussed at *http://msdn.microsoft.com /library/windows/apps/hh694083.aspx*. The highlights include the following:

- The app must provide value.

- Any ads displayed mustn't be the sole focus of the app.

- The app must be implemented in a manner consistent with the design principles set forth by Microsoft.

- The app must behave in a predictable manner.

- The app must have appropriate content.

Speaking in general terms, Microsoft wants to ensure the highest-quality experience for users of apps downloaded through the Windows Store. Apps that are clearly low quality, crash, or try to do unexpected things won't make it into the Windows Store.

How do I make money?

Apps in the Windows Store can be offered through numerous pricing models that enable you to make money. You can offer your app for free, completely free, which can be rewarding in its own way. You can also offer the app for sale, with various price tiers available. When offered this way, the users prepay for the app before using it. Apps can also be offered on a limited trial basis, with additional features becoming available through in-app purchases.

Another method for monetizing the app is to include advertisements within the app. When doing so, Microsoft allows you to use any ad platform that adheres to the Windows Store requirements. This gives you flexibility to use an ad network that has the highest return for you. If you've sold apps through another app store, you'll find that Microsoft offers the same types of options as the other app stores. See *http://msdn.microsoft.com/library/windows/apps/hh694084.aspx* for more information about making money with your app.

The technical process

The technical process for getting an app into the Windows Store involves several stages, beginning with the upload of the app to the Windows Store. During the upload phase, the package passes through some initial checks for compliance. When the upload phase is complete, the app begins its gauntlet of tests.

The first tests after upload are a series of security tests, where the package is checked for obvious malware and virus-related traits. Assuming you're not uploading a virus, the app will then pass into a series of technical compliance tests. The technical compliance tests should be easy for the app to pass because Microsoft uses the same tool, the Windows App Certification Kit, that you have in Visual Studio. So assuming that you ran (and passed) those tests when packaging your app, you should pass them again here.

Passing the technical compliance tests means the end of the automated testing processes. It also means the beginning of the manual processing test, known as content compliance. The content compliance phase is where a human inspector looks at your app to make sure that it meets the content criteria defined by Microsoft.

When your app passes content compliance, it gets signed and queued for release. The release can be immediate or on a certain date that you set during the submission of the app.

Exercises

1. Change the blank app created in this chapter's second exercise to add a link that opens a webpage, such as *http://www.microsoft.com*.

2. Create a Split app by using the Split App template, and determine which HTML file gets control from the default.html page.

CHAPTER 23

Creating a Windows app

After completing this chapter, you will be able to

■   Use Visual Studio 2012 to build a Windows app.

The previous chapters have shown what's involved in creating and distributing an app for Windows 8. You've seen a fair amount about the overall design process for apps, and you've seen how Visual Studio 2012 makes development of Windows apps easier through its use of templates and tight integration with the Windows Store. This chapter builds an app with Visual Studio 2012.

The app development process

In this chapter, you'll work through an extended example that will show how to customize one of the app templates included with Visual Studio. The app will use the U.S. National Weather Service data feeds to build a weather app that provides current conditions for six locations. As a step in the creation process, you'll customize the app's tile and splash screen, too. After the app has been created, it will be packaged and tested using the Windows App Certification Kit. The end result of the app will be something like the one shown in Figure 23-1.

FIGURE 23-1 The weather app when it's complete.

When building apps for Windows 8, you'll use a combination of HTML, CSS, and JavaScript. The primary focus of this example will be on JavaScript, but there's also a good amount of content devoted to making the CSS and HTML work with the JavaScript for the app.

In much of the web programming you've seen so far in this book, you used various JavaScript functions and sometimes the jQuery library. When programming for Windows 8, you'll still use the same JavaScript functions that you've seen in the book, but instead of jQuery, you'll use the WinJS library. The WinJS library provides an interface into core Windows functionality and also provides many helper functions and objects that aid in programming a Windows 8 app. For example, using the WinJS library, you can make AJAX calls or access the Documents library on a user's computer.

The process used here will be divided into several logical steps with checkpoints along the way so that you can verify everything's working. There will be no exercises at the end of this chapter; you'll be exhausted, and I'm not that cruel.

Starting the app design and programming

You'll begin the app's design and programming within Visual Studio, although there's not much to designing this app because it'll use a template, and the specification is to use the layout included within that template.

1. Begin by opening Visual Studio and selecting New Project from the File menu.

2. Within the New Project dialog box, select Split App from the JavaScript templates. Call the app MyWX, as shown in the following image, and click OK.

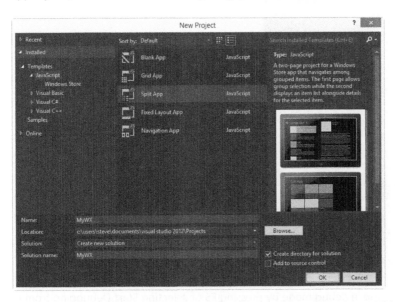

3. Visual Studio will open and show the default.js file. Your environment will look like this.

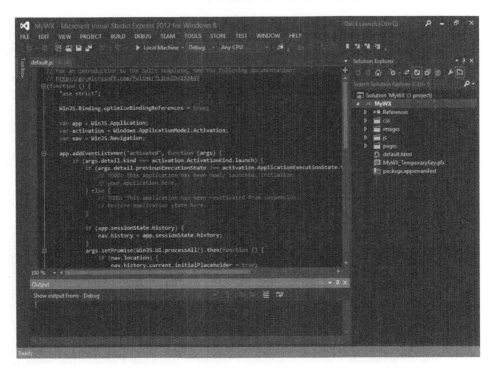

4. Close default.js.

5. Explore the files within this template by expanding the various folders within Solution Explorer. You'll see several JavaScript, HTML, and CSS files in the solution, as shown here.

6. Run the app in debug mode by pressing F5 or selecting Start Debugging from the Debug menu. You'll see a screen like the following.

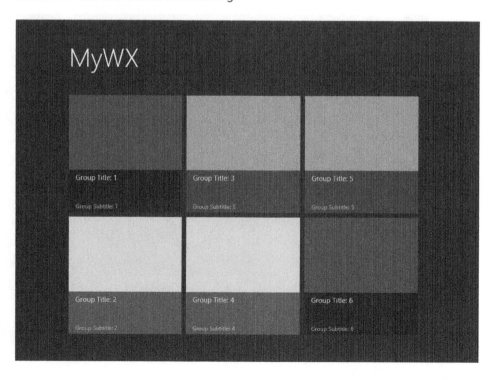

7. Stop the app by dragging it from the top to the bottom of the screen.

8. Switch back to the classic desktop, and, if the app hasn't stopped, select Stop Debugging from the Debug menu.

With that, the app's initial creation is complete. Time to customize the app.

Customizing the app

So far you've created the initial app and made sure that it can execute. This section will work through the customizations needed to grab current weather conditions and display them within the app. You'll add customizations to only four files as part of this process, with the bulk of the work being in JavaScript and HTML.

Customize the JavaScript

The first thing to do is to customize the JavaScript. This is the most detailed and complex piece of the app, but showing the simple CSS changes, for example, won't help to give you context, so it'll be good to see the app built from the foundation. The JavaScript is somewhat long for this example, so the exercise will have you add it in sections.

The following exercise assumes that you have Visual Studio open and that you have the MyWX solution open as well. If you don't, open the MyWX solution within Visual Studio before beginning this exercise.

1. Open data.js from within the js folder.

2. Within data.js, remove the *generateSampleData()* function. You won't need sample data, because you're going to be working with real data! That function looks like this (remember to remove the closing brace, too):

```
// TODO: Replace the data with your real data.
// You can add data from asynchronous sources whenever it becomes available.
generateSampleData().forEach(function (item) {
    list.push(item);
});
```

3. Within data.js, place the following code immediately below the "use strict" line:

```
var weatherStations;
var wxPromises = [];
var wxData = new WinJS.Binding.List();

function getWXData() {

    weatherStations = [
      {
        key: "kste",
        url: "http://w1.weather.gov/xml/current_obs/KSTE.xml",
```

```
            title: "Unavailable",   // To be filled in dynamically,
            summary: "Unavailable",   // To be filled in dynamically
            dataPromise: null,
            getData: callAJAX
        }
    ];

    weatherStations.forEach(function (station) {
        station.dataPromise = station.getData(station.url);
        wxPromises.push(station.dataPromise);
    }); //end foreach
    return WinJS.Promise.join(wxPromises);

} //end function getWXData
```

4. Save data.js.

> **Note** The JavaScript you just added sets up three variables for later use and then
> creates a function called *getWXData*. The *getWXData* function sets up an array
> with an object to hold the weather location from which the data will be gathered.
> Inside of that object is a key, the URL of the National Weather Service's XML for
> that location, along with the title and summary that will be filled in later. There's a
> *promise* object and *getData* function also added to this object, both of which will be
> explained after the exercise.
>
> After the *weatherStations* array has been created, a *forEach* loop is created for the
> members of the array. Each member is called "station" within the loop. Inside the
> *forEach* loop, a *promise* object is created to retrieve the weather data. These *promise*
> objects are pushed onto an array of *promise* objects. Finally, that array of *promise*
> objects is linked and returned to end the function. Essentially, what you've done
> here is set up a series of objects corresponding to each of the weather stations
> from which you'll gather information. For now, there's only one weather station, but
> there'll be more later.

5. Below the closing brace for the *getWXData* function, add the following function:

```
function callAJAX(url) {
    return WinJS.xhr({ url: url });
}
```

6. Save data.js

> **Note** This function issues a call to the *XHR* function, which is used to make AJAX
> requests. In this example, the *callAJAX* function is attached to the *weatherStations*
> object created in an earlier step. As you can see, the *callAJAX* function and the *XHR*
> function accept an argument of the URL to call.

7. The third and final (and most complex) function is a function to parse the weather data. Add this code after the closing brace of the *callAJAX* function that you just added in the previous step.

```
function parseWXData() {
    getWXData().then(function () {
        weatherStations.forEach(function (station) {
            station.dataPromise.then(function (wxResponse) {
                var wxDataItem = wxResponse.responseXML;

                station.title =
                    wxDataItem.querySelector("current_observation > location")
                        .textContent;

                var summary =
                    wxDataItem.querySelector("current_observation > weather")
                        .textContent;

                station.temp =
                    wxDataItem.querySelector("current_observation > temperature_
                        string") .textContent;

                station.summary = summary + " | " + station.temp;

                var imageBase =
                    wxDataItem.querySelector("current_observation > icon_url_base")
                        .textContent;

                var imageName =
                    wxDataItem.querySelector("current_observation > icon_url_name")
                        .textContent;

                station.wxImage = imageBase + imageName;

                station.updated =
                    wxDataItem.querySelector("current_observation > observation_time")
                        .textContent;

                station.wind = wxDataItem.querySelector("current_observation > wind_
                        string") .textContent;
            });   //end dataPromise

            wxData.push({
                group: station,
                key: station.key,
                title: station.title,
                wxImage: station.wxImage,
                summary: station.summary,
                temp: station.temp,
                updated: station.updated,
                wind: station.wind
            });   //end wxData.push
        });  // end forEach weatherStations
```

```
        }); //end getWXData call

        return wxData;

    } //end function parseWXData
```

8. Save data.js.

> **Note** This function is responsible for gathering all of the data from all of the
> weather stations in the *weatherStations* array. The function begins by calling the
> *getWXData()* function, which sets up the objects in the *weatherStations* array and
> issues the AJAX requests to the U.S. National Weather Service. When the AJAX
> requests have all completed (as denoted by the "then" statement attached to
> *getWXData*), each of the objects in the *weatherStation* array is looped using a
> *forEach* loop.
>
> During the loop, the response from the AJAX request is obtained from the *prom-*
> *ise* objects attached to each of the weather stations, and then (as denoted by the
> "then" statement attached to *station.dataPromise* in the code) the result is parsed.
> This is where the heart of the code exists. Each of the XML-formatted responses
> from the National Weather Service is examined for various elements within the XML.
> For example, the name of the weather station is found in the XML as *<LOCATION>*.
> This, and related items, are found and parsed using the *querySelector* method and
> *textContent* property. For certain areas, like the summary and the weather image, a
> bit of extra work is involved to format the item.
>
> Still within the loop for each of the weather stations, the results are pushed onto
> an array called *wxData*. The *wxData* variable is actually a data binding to a *listView*
> object, which is a special object available for Windows app programming. This vari-
> able was declared in an earlier step in this exercise. Finally, when the *forEach* loop is
> complete, the *wxData* variable is returned.

9. You'll make one last change to data.js. After the *parseWXData* object, you should see a line
that looks like this:

```
var list = new WinJS.Binding.List();
```

Comment that line out with two slashes in front of it, so it looks like this:

```
// var list = new WinJS.Binding.List();
```

10. Directly below that newly commented-out line, place the following code:

```
var list = parseWXData();
```

Note Now, instead of the list variable being set to a new instance of *WinJS.Binding.List()* as before, it'll be set to your *parseWXData()* function that returns *wxData*, which is itself a *WinJS.Binding.List* instance.

11. Save data.js.

12. Execute the app in debug mode by selecting Start Debugging from the Debug menu or by pressing F5. You should see a screen like the following.

You'll notice that the image is missing and that there's also an "undefined" listed in the app. That's because you haven't connected the data from the JavaScript to the HTML; you haven't told the HTML where to find the shiny new data that you have in JavaScript.

Customize the main HTML

Aside from the default.html file that simply loads another file, Split apps have two HTML files, items.html and split.html. When default.html is loaded, it immediately refers to items.html within the pages folder hierarchy. The items.html file is what displays the item or items that you see when you run the app.

As you can see from the final output of step 12 in the preceding exercise, there are some undefined items and the image is apparently missing. This is because the HTML for items.html is still related to the original data. Therefore, the task here is to update items.html to reflect the changes you've made to the source data, specifically to the names of the data elements. As it stands right now, items.html is trying to access data by variable names that no longer exist, so changing those is really all that needs to happen to make items.html work.

As before, the following exercise assumes that you have Visual Studio loaded and the MyWX project open. If not, now's a good time to do so.

1. Open items.html from within the pages -> items folder.

2. Within items.html, change the *data-win-bind* attribute in the first *<IMG>* element to use *wxImage* instead of *backgroundImage*. It should look like this when you've made the change:

    ```
    <img class="item-image" src="#" data-win-bind="src: wxImage; alt: title" />
    ```

3. Immediately below the *<IMG>* element, create a new element. The element will display the weather summary within the image itself. Add this HTML directly below the *<IMG>* tag and before the *item-overlay <DIV>*:

    ```
    <h3 id="summary" data-win-bind="textContent: summary"></h3>
    ```

4. Below the <DIV CLASS="item-overlay"> element, change the <H4> element to an <H3> element. It should look like this when you're done:

```
<h3 id="title" data-win-bind="textContent: title"></h3>
```

5. The final change is to the <H6> element. Instead of using *subTitle*, change it to use the variable *updated*. The HTML should look like this when you've made the change:

```
<h6 class="item-subtitle win-type-ellipsis" data-win-bind="textContent: updated"></h6>
```

6. Save items.html.

7. Run the solution by selecting Start Debugging from the Debug menu or by pressing F5. You should see a page similar to the following image.

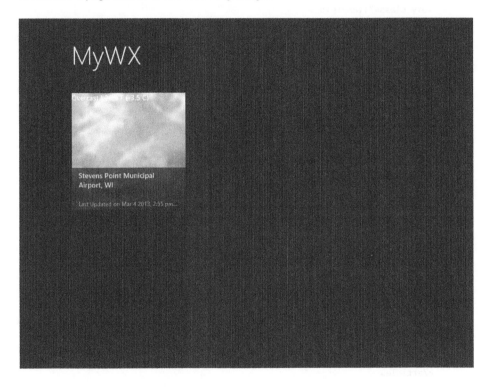

Customize the detail HTML

Each of the items inside the items.html file is clickable (or tappable). When clicked, the split.html page is loaded with additional information about each. The example we're building will use some of the data to show how it's done, but you could, as your own learning exercise, add even more information from the weather feed, such as the relative humidity, and so on.

As before, the following exercise assumes that you have Visual Studio loaded and the MyWX project open. If not, now's a good time to do so.

1. Open split.html, found within the pages -> split folder.

2. Within split.html, change the first *<IMG>* element to use *wxImage*, as you did in items.html:

```
<img class="item-image" src="#" data-win-bind="src: wxImage; alt: title" />
```

3. Below the *<DIV CLASS="item-info">* element, change the *<H6>* and *<H4>* elements to use the variables that you've set up as part of your data. This means changing the *data-win-bind* attributes as you've done before. When complete, the code should look like the following. (I've included the surrounding code for reference; the two changed lines are boldface.)

```
<div class="item-info">
    <h3 class="item-title win-type-ellipsis" data-win-bind="textContent: title"></h3>
    <h6 class="item-subtitle win-type-ellipsis" data-win-bind="textContent: updated"></h6>
    <h4 class="item-description" data-win-bind="textContent: summary"></h4>
</div>
```

4. Scroll down within the split.html file to locate the *<ARTICLE>* section. Within that section, remove the first *<DIV CLASS="text">* and all of its contents.

5. Change the *<IMG>* tag so that it uses *wxImage*.

6. After the closing *</HEADER>* tag, remove the *<DIV CLASS="article-content"* and add the following:

```
Temperature: <div class="article-content" data-win-bind="textContent: temp"></div>
Wind: <div class="article-content" data-win-bind="textContent: wind"></div>
```

That final section should look like this. Notice that none of other HTML around this changes; this is showing the contents of the *<ARTICLE>* element only:

```
<article>
    <header class="header">
        <img class="article-image" src="#" data-win-bind="src: wxImage; alt: title" />
    </header>
    Temperature: <div class="article-content" data-win-bind="textContent: temp"></div>
    Wind: <div class="article-content" data-win-bind="textContent: wind"></div>
</article>
```

7. Save split.html.

8. Run the project by selecting Start Debugging from the Debug menu or by pressing F5.

9. Click the icon for Stevens Point's weather conditions. Behind the scenes, split.html will load and you'll see a screen similar to the following.

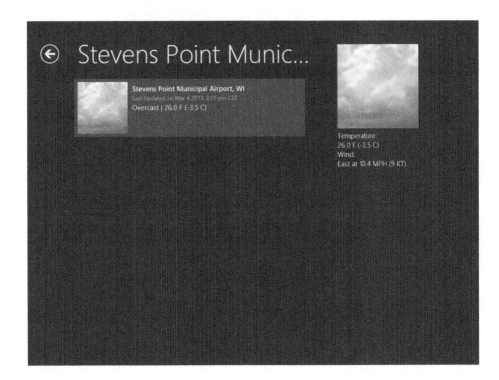

Customize the CSS

With the HTML and JavaScript working, it's time to tweak the layout a bit. Using CSS, you can make large-scale changes to the layout of the entire app. For our purposes, the change will merely show how to change some text positioning. In Figure 23-2, you'll notice that the current conditions and temperature are very close to the edge of the image. It would be nice to move this down and more toward the middle and maybe add a little color.

FIGURE 23-2 An expanded view of an individual item.

Moving this text can be accomplished by adding to the default.css file. When you changed items.html, you added an *<H3>* element like this:

```
<h3 id="summary" data-win-bind="textContent: summary"></h3>
```

As you can see, that *<H3>* has an ID already, so accessing it in CSS will be quite easy.

Before beginning the following exercise, open the MyWX project in Visual Studio.

1. Open default.css.

2. On the top of default.css, add the following code:

```
#summary {
    margin: 15px;
    color:  orangered;
}
```

3. Save default.css.

4. Run the app in Debug mode, as you've done in previous exercises.

You should see that the text has moved down and toward the middle slightly, as in the zoomed example shown here in Figure 23-3.

FIGURE 23-3 Moving the text using CSS.

Finalizing the app

With the CSS complete, the app's development is complete. However, one of the reasons for using the Split App template is so that more than one weather station can be shown in summary view. Therefore, one last change, should you elect to do it, is to add more weather stations to the *weatherStations* array found in data.js.

The example shown here adds five more weather stations from cities chosen by the author. Feel free to choose your own. You can find a listing of the sites and the corresponding URLs at *http:// w1.weather.gov/xml/current_obs/*.

Begin the following exercise by opening data.js in the MyWX project.

1. Within data.js, find the *getWXData* function. Change the *weatherStations* array to the following, being careful not to alter anything outside the *weatherStations* array:

```
weatherStations = [
        {
            key: "kste",
            url: "http://w1.weather.gov/xml/current_obs/KSTE.xml",
            title: "Unavailable",  // To be filled in dynamically,
            summary: "Unavailable",  // To be filled in dynamically
            dataPromise: null,
            getData: callAJAX
        },
        {
            key: "klax",
            url: "http://w1.weather.gov/xml/current_obs/KLAX.xml",
            title: "Unavailable",  // To be filled in dynamically,
            summary: "Unavailable",  // To be filled in dynamically
            dataPromise: null,
            getData: callAJAX
        },
        {
            key: "phnl",
            url: "http://w1.weather.gov/xml/current_obs/PHNL.xml",
            title: "Unavailable",  // To be filled in dynamically,
            summary: "Unavailable",  // To be filled in dynamically
            dataPromise: null,
            getData: callAJAX
        },
        {
            key: "kpdx",

          url: "http://w1.weather.gov/xml/current_obs/KPDX.xml",
            title: "Unavailable",  // To be filled in dynamically,
            summary: "Unavailable",  // To be filled in dynamically
            dataPromise: null,
            getData: callAJAX
        },
        {
            key: "pafa",
            url: "http://w1.weather.gov/xml/current_obs/PAFA.xml",
            title: "Unavailable",  // To be filled in dynamically,
            summary: "Unavailable",  // To be filled in dynamically
            dataPromise: null,
            getData: callAJAX
        },
        {
            key: "kbos",
            url: "http://w1.weather.gov/xml/current_obs/KBOS.xml",
            title: "Unavailable",  // To be filled in dynamically,
            summary: "Unavailable",  // To be filled in dynamically
            dataPromise: null,
            getData: callAJAX
        }
    ];
```

2. Save data.js.

3. Run the app. You should see a screen like the one shown here:

Customizing the Package Manifest

You might have noticed the intermediate screen that loads after you run the app but before the app's content actually loads. This is called the splash screen. It's a good practice to have a splash screen for an app because it sets up a positive user experience. Also, if you've gone to the Start screen, you've probably noticed that you have a new tile there called MyWX. You should also customize the tile as part of the app preparation process. There are other customizations that you can perform, as defined in the Package Manifest file, called package.appxmanifest, within Solution Explorer. This section examines some customizations.

Adding a splash screen, logo, and tile image

Adding a splash screen and tile is accomplished within the Package Manifest file. You open the Package Manifest file by double-clicking package.appxmanifest in Solution Explorer. Doing so opens the file in a customized editor provided by Visual Studio.

The splash screen and tile definitions are found within the Application UI tab. The images need to be of a specific size, depending on where they'll be used. For example, splash screen images must be 620 × 300 pixels, while the main logo tile needs to be 150 × 150 pixels. Other tiles have their specific sizes as well. The wide logo tile needs to be 310 × 150 pixels, and the small logo tile needs to be 30 × 30 pixels. All images need to be PNG (.png) or JPEG (.jpg or .jpeg) formatted.

The process for adding a splash screen or tile is as follows:

1. Create or access an appropriately sized and formatted image.

2. Add the image to your project, typically in the images folder, by right-clicking images and selecting Add | Add Existing Item within the Visual Studio Solution Explorer.

3. Open the Package Manifest in Visual Studio, and scroll to the Splash Screen or Tile section.

4. Choose the image from the image folder of your project.

The app's logo as it will appear in the Windows Store is defined on the Packaging tab and needs to be 50 × 50 pixels. The process for changing the app's logo is the same as for the splash screen and tile. The only difference is that it's found on the Packaging tab.

Defining capabilities

When your app will access the user's Documents library, you must declare that as part of the app's capabilities, defined in the Capabilities tab of the Package Manifest editor.

Figure 23-4 shows the Capabilities tab for the MyWX app. Notice that these capabilities were defined by default.

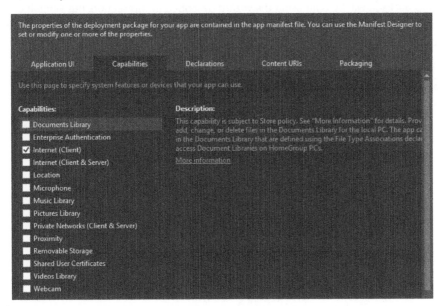

FIGURE 23-4 The Capabilities tab in the Package Manifest editor.

There is also a Declarations tab that's used to declare extensions that your app will use to work with the system.

More Info See *http://msdn.microsoft.com/en-us/library/windows/apps/hh464936.aspx* for information about capabilities, and see *http://msdn.microsoft.com/en-us/library/windows /apps/hh464906.aspx* for more information about declarations and extensions.

Testing the app

With the app's splash screen, tile, logo, and other meta information configured for the app, you can prepare it for release in the Windows Store. Part of this process is to create an app package and to test the app with the Windows App Certification Kit.

Packages are created by using the Create App Packages option found in the Store menu in Visual Studio. However, prior to creating the package, you should set the build type to Release. This is accomplished by using the drop-down menu in Visual Studio. Specifically, you can change it from Debug to Release on the toolbar, as shown in Figure 23-5.

FIGURE 23-5 Changing from Debug to Release.

Making this change enables you to run the Windows App Certification Kit. If you forget or don't do this step, the app package will be built using the wizard described in this section, but when it completes you won't be given the option to certify the application. Therefore, changing this option now means that you'll be able to run the Windows App Certification Kit later.

Begin the packaging processing by selecting Create App Packages from the Project/Store menu. When you do so, the Create App Packages Wizard begins, shown in Figure 23-6.

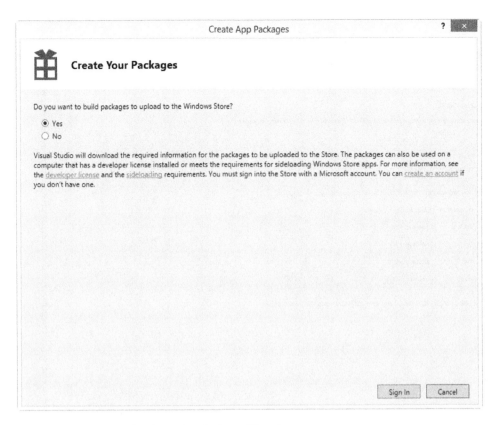

FIGURE 23-6 Beginning the Create App Packages Wizard.

If you have a developer account, leave this dialog as-is for release into the Windows Store; otherwise, select No and then click Next. This chapter discusses app packaging outside the Windows Store.

Within the Create App Packages Wizard, you can set the location for the outputted package, change the version number of the package, and also select the architectures on which it'll be available, as shown in Figure 23-7.

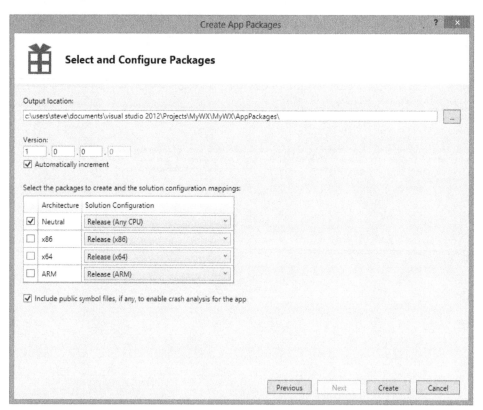

FIGURE 23-7 Selecting the architectures and version for the package.

When the package creation process is complete, you'll be shown a dialog box similar to that in Figure 23-8, noting that the next step is to launch the Windows App Certification Kit. If you don't see that option, it's likely that you still have the build type set to Debug.

FIGURE 23-8 Successful package creation.

The Windows App Certification Kit runs several tests on the app, including executing the app and closing it. The tests run by the kit are exactly the same as those run by Microsoft during the app certification process. Even though these tests aren't required for apps distributed in-house, it's a good idea to run them because doing so can reveal issues that might occur when the app is executed.

On the last screen of the Create App Packages Wizard, clicking Launch Windows App Certification Kit begins the process of testing, shown in Figure 23-9.

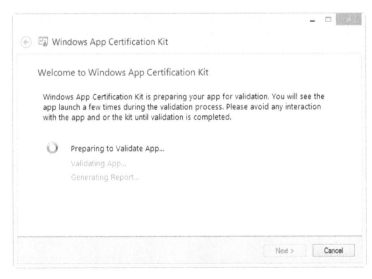

FIGURE 23-9 Running the Windows App Certification Kit.

When complete, the results will be displayed, as shown in Figure 23-10.

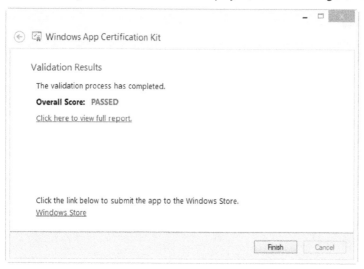

FIGURE 23-10 The results of the Windows App Certification Kit.

Now that the app has been tested, you could take the next step and submit it to the Windows Store for approval through the Upload process. See *http://msdn.microsoft.com/library/windows/apps/ jj193603.aspx* for more information about submitting your app—and good luck!

Summary

This chapter built a Windows app using Visual Studio. The app was built using the Split App template and added JavaScript to retrieve weather conditions by using XML from the U.S. National Weather Service. As part of the app build process, you saw how to use *promise* objects, which enable work to be done while data is gathered. You also saw how data from the JavaScript is displayed through the HTML pages in an app.

The chapter also showed how to change information about the app, such as its splash screen, tile, and logo. Finally, you saw a bit about the testing and certification process using tools provided in Visual Studio.

Answer key to exercises

This appendix shows the answers and explanations for the exercises that have appeared through-out the book. In many cases, there is more than one way to solve a problem. Therefore, unless the question specified a particular way to solve the problem, any working implementation is acceptable. It's also expected that your function names could differ from the ones in this appendix.

Chapter 1

1. False. Although JavaScript is indeed defined by a standards body, ECMA International, it is not supported on all web browsers. And the support that does exist varies (sometimes widely) among browsers.

2. False. There are many reasons why a visitor to your website might have JavaScript disabled. The browser they're using might not support it; they might have special software installed that doesn't support it; or they simply might have JavaScript disabled as a personal preference. You should strive to make your site work without JavaScript, or at least have it fail gracefully for those visitors who don't have JavaScript enabled.

3. A typical JavaScript definition block looks like this:

```
<script type="text/javascript">
// JavaScript code goes here
</script>
```

4. False. The version of JavaScript isn't placed within the DOCTYPE definition. In fact, it's quite uncommon to declare the version of JavaScript being used at all.

5. True. JavaScript code can appear in both the head and the body of a Hypertext Markup Language (HTML) document.

Chapter 2

1. The code of mysecondpage.htm looks similar to this, though yours may differ slightly (and of course will contain your name instead of mine!):

```
<!doctype html>
<html>
```

```
<head>
<title>My Second Page</title>
</head>
<body>
<script type="text/javascript">
alert("Steve Suehring");
</script>
<p>My Second Page</p>
</body>
</html>
```

2. Here's the new code, with the changes shown in bold type:

```
<!doctype html>
<html>
<head>
<title>My Second Page</title>
<script type="text/javascript">
function callAlert() {
    alert("Steve Suehring");
}
</script>
</head>
<body>
<script type="text/javascript">
callAlert();
</script>
<p>My Second Page</p>
</body>
</html>
```

3. I created a file called 3.htm and a file called 3.js. Here they are (the reference in 3.htm to 3.js is shown in boldface type).

3.js:

```
function callAlert() {
    alert("Steve Suehring");
}
```

3.htm:

```
<!doctype html>
<html>
<head>
<title>My Second Page</title>
<script type="text/javascript" src="3.js"> </script>
</head>
<body>
<script type="text/javascript">
callAlert();
</script>
<p>My Second Page</p>
</body>
</html>
```

Chapter 3

1. The valid statements are b, c, and d. Both a and e are invalid, because they both use reserved words.

2. False. Not all JavaScript statements require a semicolon at the end. In fact, semicolons are usually optional.

3. The orderTotal variable is changed after the visitor is alerted to how many of each item was ordered, but before the value is returned from the function. The lesson here is that you must be careful not to alter the value or contents of variables unexpectedly. The visitor is expecting to order a certain quantity, but the code clearly changes that quantity after telling the visitor how many he or she ordered!

Chapter 4

1. Variable declarations:

```
var first = 120;
var second = "5150";
var third = "Two Hundred Thirty";
```

2. Array (your values will probably be different, but the data types and syntax are the important part):

```
var newArray = new Array(10, 20, 30, "first string", "second string");
```

3. Escaped string:

```
alert("Steve's response was \"Cool!\"");
```

4. This exercise is for the reader to follow. There is no right or wrong answer.

Chapter 5

1. Alerts (your values will probably be different, but the data types and syntax are the important part):

```
var num1 = 1;
var num2 = 1;
var num3 = 19;
var fourthvar = "84";
var name1 = "Jakob";
var name2 = "Edward";
alert(num1 + num2);
alert(num3 + fourthvar);
alert(name1 + name2);
```

2. Postfix:

```
var theNum = 1;
alert(theNum);
alert(theNum++);
alert(theNum);
```

Prefix:

```
var theNum = 1;
alert(theNum);
alert(++theNum);
alert(theNum);
```

3. Code:

```
var num1 = 1;
var num2 = 1;
var num3 = 19;
var fourthvar = "84";
var name1 = "Jakob";
var name2 = "Edward";
alert(typeof num1);
alert(typeof num2);
alert(typeof num3);
alert(typeof fourthvar);
alert(typeof name1);
alert(typeof name2);
```

This should result in three alerts with the word number followed by three others with the word string.

4. False. Unary operators appear fairly often in JavaScript, especially within for loops that increment a variable using the ++ postfix operator.

5. False. Even though saving a few bytes is helpful, especially for web applications, it's almost always preferable to spend those same few bytes making the code readable and maintainable. This is largely a matter for your style and coding standards, however. In a later chapter, you are introduced to jQuery. That library's typical "minified" version is an example of taking the byte saving to an extreme.

Chapter 6

1. Replace YOUR NAME in the following code with the appropriate content:

```
var inputName = prompt("Please enter your name:");
switch(inputName) {
    case "YOUR NAME":
        alert("Welcome " + inputName);
        break;
    case "Steve":
        alert("Go Away");
```

```
        break;
    default:
        alert("Please Come Back Later " + inputName);
}
```

2. Here's the code:

```
var temp = prompt("Please enter the current temperature");
if (temp > 100) {
    alert("Please cool down");
} else if (temp < 20) {
    alert("Better warm up");
}
```

Note that it would also be a good idea to provide a default action in case the temperature is between 20 and 100!

3. This exercise is actually impossible to accomplish as specified. Because ternary operators expect a single test condition and Exercise 2 required two conditions, a ternary operator cannot be used to accomplish exactly the same task. The following code creates an alert that tells the visitor to cool down when the temperature is above 100 and to warm up when the temp is less than or equal to 100:

```
var temp = prompt("Please enter the current temperature");
temp > 100 ? alert("Please cool down") : alert("Better warm up");
```

4. Here's the code:

```
for (var i = 1; i < 101; i++) {
    if (i == 99) {
        alert("The number is " + i);
    }
}
```

Note that because the variable i began counting at 1 (as was called for in the exercise), the counter needs to go to 101 to meet the requirement of counting from 1 to 100.

5. Here's the code:

```
var i = 1;
while (i < 101) {
    if (i == 99) {
        alert("The number is " + i);
    }
    i++;
}
```

Note the placement of the postfix increment of the i variable within the loop. You could also use i=i+1, but the postfix operator is preferred.

Chapter 7

1. It's important to note that this code uses the isNaN function to check whether the input was a number. This is a best practice that may not always be obvious. Another way to accomplish the ultimate return value here is to use return theNumber++; as the final return, rather than as shown. Here's the code:

```
<head>
    <title>Chapter 7 Exercise 1</title>
    <script type="text/javascript">
     function incrementNum(theNumber) {
    if (isNaN(theNumber)) {
        alert("Sorry, " + theNumber + " isn't a number.");
        return;
    }
    return theNumber + 1;
}
</script>
</head>
<body>
    <script type="text/javascript">
     alert(incrementNum(3));
</script>
</body>
```

2. Here's the code:

```
function addNums(firstNum,secondNum) {
    if ((isNaN(firstNum)) || (isNaN(secondNum))) {
        alert("Sorry, both arguments must be numbers.");
        return;
    }
    else if (firstNum > secondNum) {
        alert(firstNum + " is greater than " + secondNum);
    }
    else {
        return firstNum + secondNum;
    }
}
```

3. This exercise is meant to show variable scoping problems. Note how the value of the result variable changes outside the function—even though the change is made only within the function. The two locations for alerts are shown in boldface in the following code:

```
function addNumbers() {
    firstNum = 4;
    secondNum = 8;
    result = firstNum + secondNum;
    return result;
}
result = 0;
alert(result);
result = addNumbers();
alert(result);
```

4. Here's the code:

```
<head>
<title>Chapter 7 Exercise 4</title>
<script type="text/javascript">
var stars = ["Polaris","Aldebaran","Deneb","Vega","Altair","Dubhe","Regulus"];
var constells = ["Ursa Minor","Taurus","Cygnus","Lyra","Aquila","Ursa Major","Leo"];

function searchStars(star) {
    var starLength = stars.length;
    for (var i = 0; i < starLength; i++) {
        if (stars[i] == star) {
            return constells[i];
        }
    }
    return star + " Not Found.";
}
</script>
</head>
<body>
<script type="text/javascript">
var inputStar = prompt("Enter star name: ");
alert(searchStars(inputStar));
</script>
<p>Stars</p>
</body>
```

Chapter 8

1. Here's the code:

```
var star = ["Polaris", "Deneb", "Vega", "Altair"];
var starLength = star.length;
for (var i = 0; i < starLength; i++) {
    alert(star[i]);
}
```

2. Here's one way:

```
function Song(artist,length,title) {
    this.artist = artist;
    this.length = length;
    this.title = title;
}

song1 = new Song("First Artist","3:30","First Song Title");
song2 = new Song("Second Artist","4:11","Second Song Title");
song3 = new Song("Third Artist","2:12","Third Song Title");
```

3. Assuming you are using the code given in the exercise, this code in the body would concatenate all the names into one long string, as follows:

```
var names = new Array;
for (var propt in star) {
```

```
        names += propt;
    }
    alert(names);
```

The code to comma-delimit the names would look like this:

```
var names = new Array;
for (var propt in star) {
    if (names != "") {
        names += "," + propt;
    } else {
        names = propt;
    }
}
alert(names);
```

Chapter 9

1. Here's the code:

```
if (screen.availHeight < 768) {
    alert("Available Height: " + screen.availHeight);
}
if (screen.availWidth < 1024) {
    alert("Available Width: " + screen.availWidth);
}
```

2. The full code is shown here, including the code from the step-by-step exercise. The additional code for this exercise is shown in boldface. Note the use of the unescape() function to remove the URL-encoded %20 (space) character from the country name. This is necessary because the country name "Great Britain" specified in this exercise must be URL-escaped for HTTP GET requests.

```
<!doctype html>
<html>
<head>
    <title>Location, Location, Location</title>

</head>
<body>
    <script type="text/javascript">
            var body = document.getElementsByTagName("body")[0];
            for (var prop in location) {
                var elem = document.createElement("p");
                var text = document.createTextNode(prop + ": " + location[prop]);
                elem.appendChild(text);
                body.appendChild(elem);
            }
            if (location.search) {
                var querystring = location.search.substring(1);
                var splits = querystring.split('&');
                for (var i = 0; i < splits.length; i++) {
```

```
                    var splitpair = splits[i].split('=');
                    var elem = document.createElement("p");
                    var text = document.createTextNode(splitpair[0] + ": " +
splitpair[1]);

                    if (splitpair[0] == "country") {
                        switch(unescape(splitpair[1])) {
                            case "Brazil":
                                alert("Obrigado");
                                break;
                            case "Great Britain":
                                alert("Thank You");
                                break;
                        }
                    }
                    elem.appendChild(text);
                    body.appendChild(elem);
                }
            }
        </script>
    </body>
</html>
```

3. This exercise doesn't have an answer in the answer key. You can install the User Agent Switcher to complete the exercise.

Chapter 10

1. Both jQuery and MooTools offer a small learning curve, though PrototypeJS is also fairly easy to learn. Dojo doesn't aim for the beginner-level JavaScript programmer, and I've encountered more than one developer confused by YUI, even though it has extensive documentation. However, everyone learns differently, so I'd recommend trying each one yourself rather than taking my word for it!

2. The Step by Step exercise in this chapter provides an example of creating your own library and including it in a page.

Chapter 11

1. Here's one way to do it:

```
<!doctype html>
<html>
<head>
<title>Adding jQuery</title>
<script type="text/javascript" src="jquery-1.7.2.min.js"></script>
</head>
<body>
<script type="text/javascript">
        $(document).ready(function() {
                $('body').html('<div>Adding an element</div>');
```

```
        });
    </script>
    </body>
    </html>
```

2. Here's an example:

```
<!doctype html>
<html>
<head>
<title>Adding jQuery</title>
<script type="text/javascript" src="jquery-1.7.2.min.js"></script>
</head>
<body>
<script type="text/javascript">
        $(document).ready(function() {
                $('body').html('<div id="myDiv">Adding an element</div>');
                $('#myDiv').css('background-color','#abacab');
        });
</script>
</body>
</html>
```

Chapter 12

1. Here's the code:

```
var newelement = document.createElement("p");
newelement.setAttribute("id","pelement");
document.body.appendChild(newelement);
newelement.appendChild(document.createTextNode("This is a paragraph, albeit a short
one."));
var anchorelem = document.createElement("a");
anchorelem.setAttribute("id","aelement");
anchorelem.setAttribute("href","http://www.braingia.org/");
document.body.appendChild(anchorelem);
anchorelem.appendChild(document.createTextNode("Go To Steve Suehring's Web Site."));
```

2. Here's the code:

```
// create the initial elements (if you use an existing HTML file, you won't need to do
this)
var newelement = document.createElement("p");
newelement.setAttribute("id","pelement");
document.body.appendChild(newelement);
newelement.appendChild(document.createTextNode("This is a paragraph, albeit a short
one."));
var anchorelem = document.createElement("a");
anchorelem.setAttribute("id","aelement");
anchorelem.setAttribute("href","http://www.braingia.org/");
document.body.appendChild(anchorelem);
anchorelem.appendChild(document.createTextNode("Click Here"));

// make the change
```

```
var existingp = document.getElementById("pelement");
existingp.firstChild.nodeValue="This is the new text.";
var newanchor = document.getElementById("aelement");
newanchor.setAttribute("href","http://www.microsoft.com/");
```

3. Here's the code:

```
<head>
<title>Chapter 10 Exercises</title>
</script>
</head>
<body>
<div id="thetable"></div>
<script type="text/javascript">
var table = document.createElement("table");
table.border = "1";
var tbody = document.createElement("tbody");

// Append the body to the table
table.appendChild(tbody);
var row = document.createElement("tr");

// Create table row
for (i = 1; i < 3; i++) {
    var row = document.createElement("tr");
    // Create the row/td elements
    for (j = 1; j < 3; j++) {
        // Insert the actual text/data from the XML document.
        var td = document.createElement("td");
        var data = document.createTextNode("Hello - I'm Row " + i + ", Column " + j);
        td.appendChild(data);
        row.appendChild(td);
    }
    tbody.appendChild(row);
}
document.getElementById("thetable").appendChild(table);
</script>
</body>
```

Chapter 13

1. Here's the code:

```
<!doctype html>
<html>
<head>
<title>Onclick</title>
<script type="text/javascript">
function handleclick() {
    alert("You Clicked Here");
    return false;
}

</script>
```

```
</head>
<body>
<p><a href="#" onclick="return handleclick();">Click Here</a></p>
</body>
</html>
```

2. Here's the code:

```
                 <!doctype html>
<html>
<head>
<title>Onclick</title>
<script type="text/javascript" src="jquery-1.7.2.min.js"></script>
<script type="text/javascript">
function handleclick() {
    alert("You Clicked Here");
    return false;
}
</script>
</head>
<body>
<p><a href="#" id="clickMe">Click Here</a></p>
<script type="text/javascript">
$(document).ready(function() {
    $("#clickMe").on("click",function() {
        return handleclick();z
    });
        });
</script>
</body>
</html>
```

3. No JavaScript is necessary for this exercise. The HTML code looks as follows:

```
<!doctype html>
<html>
<head>
<title>New Tab</title>
</head>
<body>
<p><a target="Microsoft" href="http://www.microsoft.com" id="mslink">Go To Microsoft
</a></p>
</body>
</html>
```

Chapter 14

1. See Example 14-2 in Chapter 14 for an example of this exercise.

2. See Listing 14-2 in this chapter for an example of preloading images. You would apply that same code logic to the image map that you make for this exercise.

Chapter 15

1. See the section titled "Working with Select Boxes" in Chapter 15 for an example solution for this exercise.

2. Based on the pizza.htm example, the `<head>` portion of code now looks like this, with the additions shown in boldface:

```
<head>
    <title>Pizza</title>
    <script type = "text/javascript">

    function prepza() {
        var checkboxes = document.forms["pizzaform"].toppingcheck.length;
        var crusttype = document.forms["pizzaform"].crust;
        var size = document.forms["pizzaform"].size;
        var crustlength = crusttype.length;
        var sizelength = crusttype.length;
        var newelement = document.createElement("p");
        newelement.setAttribute("id","orderheading");
        document.body.appendChild(newelement);
        newelement.appendChild(document.createTextNode("This pizza will have:"));

        for (var c = 0; c < crustlength; c++) {
            if (crusttype[c].checked) {
                var newelement = document.createElement("p");
                newelement.setAttribute("id","crustelement" + i);
                document.body.appendChild(newelement);
                newelement.appendChild(document.createTextNode(
                    crusttype[c].value + " Crust"));
            }
        }

        for (var s = 0; s < sizelength; s++) {
            if (size[s].checked) {
                var newelement = document.createElement("p");
                newelement.setAttribute("id","sizeelement" + i);
                document.body.appendChild(newelement);
                newelement.appendChild(document.createTextNode(size[s].value + "
                Size"));
            }
        }

        for (var i = 0; i < checkboxes; i++) {
            if (document.forms["pizzaform"].toppingcheck[i].checked) {
                var newelement = document.createElement("p");
                newelement.setAttribute("id","newelement" + i);
                document.body.appendChild(newelement);
                newelement.appendChild(document.createTextNode(
                    document.forms["pizzaform"].toppingcheck[i].value));
            }
        }
    }
    </script>
</head>
```

The HTML follows. This particular solution uses a three-column table, though that's not technically required for this answer to be correct; that's just one way to do it. The additions are again shown in boldface:

```
<form id="pizzaform" action="#">
<table>
<tr><td>Toppings</td><td>Crust</td><td>Size</td></tr>
<tr>
<td><input type="checkbox" id="topping1" value="Sausage" name="toppingcheck" />Sausage</
td>
<td><input type="radio" name="crust" value="Regular" checked="checked" id="radio1"
/>Regular</td>
<td><input type="radio" name="size" value="Small" checked="checked" id="radiosize1"
/>Small</td>
</tr>
<tr>
<td><input type="checkbox" id="topping2" value="Pepperoni" name="toppingcheck"
/>Pepperoni</td>
<td><input type="radio" name="crust" value="Deep Dish" id="radio2" />Deep Dish</td>
<td><input type="radio" name="size" value="Medium" id="radiosize2" />Medium</td>
</tr>
<tr>
<td><input type="checkbox" id="topping3" value="Ham" name="toppingcheck" />Ham</td>
<td><input type="radio" name="crust" value="Thin" id="radio3" />Thin</td>
<td><input type="radio" name="size" value="Large" id="radiosize3" />Large</td>
</tr>
<tr>
<td><input type="checkbox" id="topping4" value="Green Peppers" name="toppingcheck"
/>Green Peppers</td>
<td></td>
<td></td>
</tr>
<tr>
<td><input type="checkbox" id="topping5" value="Mushrooms" name="toppingcheck"
/>Mushrooms</td>
<td></td>
<td></td>
</tr>
<tr>
<td><input type="checkbox" id="topping6" value="Onions" name="toppingcheck" />Onions
</td>
<td></td>
<td></td>
</tr>
<tr>
<td><input type="checkbox" id="topping7" value="Pineapple"
name="toppingcheck">Pineapple</td>
<td></td>
<td></td>
</tr>
</table>
<p><input type="submit" id="prepBtn" name="prepBtn" value="Prep Pizza"></p>
</form>
```

3. Add the following code to the <head> portion of the pizza application from the previous exercise:

```
function flip(pizzatype) {
    if (pizzatype == "veggiespecial") {
        document.getElementById("peppers").checked = "true";
        document.getElementById("onions").checked = "true";
        document.getElementById("mushrooms").checked = "true";
    } else if (pizzatype == "meatspecial") {
        document.getElementById("sausage").checked = "true";
        document.getElementById("pepperoni").checked = "true";
        document.getElementById("ham").checked = "true";
    } else if (pizzatype == "hawaiian") {
        document.getElementById("ham").checked = "true";
        document.getElementById("pineapple").checked = "true";
    }
}
```

Use the following HTML form. (Note the addition of the three buttons and the change to each ingredient's id attribute.)

```
<form id="pizzaform" action="#">
<p>
<input type="button" id="veggiespecial" name="veggiespecial" value="Veggie Special" />
<input type="button" id="meatspecial" name="meatspecial" value="Meat Special" />
<input type="button" id="hawaiian" name="hawaiian" value="Hawaiian" />
</p>
<table>
<tr><td>Toppings</td><td>Crust</td><td>Size</td></tr>
<tr>
<td><input type="checkbox" id="sausage" value="Sausage" name="toppingcheck" />Sausage</
td>
<td><input type="radio" name="crust" value="Regular" checked="checked" id="radio1"
/>Regular</td>
<td><input type="radio" name="size" value="Small" checked="checked" id="radiosize1"
/>Small</td>
</tr>
<tr>
<td><input type="checkbox" id="pepperoni" value="Pepperoni" name="toppingcheck"
/>Pepperoni</td>
<td><input type="radio" name="crust" value="Deep Dish" id="radio2" />Deep Dish</td>
<td><input type="radio" name="size" value="Medium" id="radiosize2" />Medium</td>
</tr>
<tr>
<td><input type="checkbox" id="ham" value="Ham" name="toppingcheck" />Ham</td>
<td><input type="radio" name="crust" value="Thin" id="radio3" />Thin</td>
<td><input type="radio" name="size" value="Large" id="radiosize3" />Large</td>
</tr>
<tr>
<td><input type="checkbox" id="peppers" value="Green Peppers" name="toppingcheck" />Green
Peppers</td>
<td></td>
<td></td>
</tr>
<tr>
<td><input type="checkbox" id="mushrooms" value="Mushrooms" name="toppingcheck"
```

```
/>Mushrooms</td>
<td></td>
<td></td>
</tr>
<tr>
<td><input type="checkbox" id="onions" value="Onions" name="toppingcheck" />Onions</td>
<td></td>
<td></td>
</tr>
<tr>
<td><input type="checkbox" id="pineapple" value="Pineapple" name="toppingcheck"
/>Pineapple</td>
<td></td>
<td></td>
</tr>
</table>
<p><input type="submit" id="prepBtn" name="prepBtn" value="Prep Pizza"
onclick="prepza();" /></p>
</form>
```

Add handlers to the JavaScript section found within the <body> of the page:

```
var veggieBtn = document.getElementById("veggiespecial");
EHandler.add(veggieBtn,"click",function() { flip("veggiespecial"); });
var meatBtn = document.getElementById("meatspecial");
EHandler.add(meatBtn,"click",function() { flip("meatspecial"); });
var hawaiiBtn = document.getElementById("hawaiispecial");
EHandler.add(hawaiiBtn,"click",function() { flip("hawaiian"); });
```

Chapter 16

1. Here's an example page; there are many ways to complete this exercise correctly:

```
<!doctype html>
<html>
<head>
<title>CSS</title>
<link href="exercise1.css" rel="stylesheet" type="text/css">
</head>
<body>
<h1 id="h1element">The Title</h1>
<p id="firstelement">The first element.</p>
<p id="secondelement">The second element.</p>
</body>
</html>
```

Here is the stylesheet exercise1.css:

```
#h1element {
background-color: #abacab;
}

#firstelement {
color: red;
```

```
    }

    #secondelement {
        color: blue;
    }
```

2. This code changes the element named firstelement so that its font color is blue:

```
<script type="text/javascript">
var element1 = document.getElementById("firstelement");
element1.style.color = "#0000FF";
</script>
```

3. This code hides all the *<P>* elements using the Cascading Style Sheets (CSS) visibility property:

```
<script type="text/javascript">
var pelements = document.getElementsByTagName("p");
var pelmLength = pelements.length;
for (var i = 0; i < pelmLength; i++) {
    pelements[i].style.visibility = "hidden";
}
</script>
```

4. This code shows the visibility setting both before and after it has been set within the script. When you run the code, notice that the alert is empty before the property is set.

```
<script type="text/javascript">
var pelements = document.getElementsByTagName("p");
var pelmLength = pelements.length;
for (var i = 0; i < pelmLength; i++) {
    alert(pelements[i].style.visibility);
    pelements[i].style.visibility = "hidden";
    alert(pelements[i].style.visibility);
}
</script>
```

Chapter 17

1. This solution uses the same HTML from Listing 17-1 but another other valid HTML that solves the problem would suffice.

```
<!DOCTYPE html>
<html>
<head>
        <title>jQuery UI Datepicker</title>
        <link type="text/css" rel="stylesheet"
                href="css/ui-lightness/jquery-ui-1.8.22.custom.css" />
        <link type="text/css" rel="stylesheet"
            href="css/cal.css" />
        <script type="text/javascript"
                src="js/jquery-1.7.2.min.js">
            </script>
        <script type="text/javascript"
```

```
            src="js/jquery-ui-1.8.22.custom.min.js">
        </script>
    <script type="text/javascript"
        src="js/cal-ex1.js">
    </script>
</head>

    <body>
        <div id="mainContainer">
        <form action="#" method="POST">
        <input type="text" name="cal" id="cal">
        </form>
        </div> <!-- end mainContainer -->
    </body>
</html>
```

The JavaScript is similar to that seen in the chapter as well. Note that the only required options are the minDate and maxDate options:

```
$(document).ready(function () {
$('#cal').datepicker({
        changeMonth: true,
        changeYear: true,
        minDate: "-1M",
        maxDate: "+12M
 });

 });
```

2. Choosing any widget from the jQuery UI demo site (*http://jqueryui.com/demos/*) and implementing it with valid HTML provides the solution for this exercise.

Chapter 18

1. I used theme 'e', added as a data-theme attribute on the <div> identified with the data-role of header, as in this code (also found as themee.html in the Chapter 18 companion content):

```
<!doctype html>
<html>
<head>
    <title>Test Page for jQuery Mobile</title>
    <meta name="viewport" content="width=device-width, initial-scale=1">
    <link rel="stylesheet"
        href="jquery.mobile-1.1.1.css">
    <script type="text/javascript"
        src="jquery-1.7.2.min.js">
    </script>
    <script type="text/javascript"
        src="jquery.mobile-1.1.1.js">
    </script>
</head>
<body>
```

```
<div data-role="page">
    <div data-theme="e" data-role="header">
        <h1>Test Page</h1>
    </div>
    <div data-role="content">
        <p>This is some nice content.</p>
    </div>
    <div data-role="footer">
        <h2>Footer content</h2>
    </div>
</div>  <!-- end page div -->
</body>
</html>
```

2. Adding the two classes discussed in the chapter to one of the anchors in the footer does the trick here (also found as pers-active.html in the Chapter 18 companion content):

```
<!doctype html>
<html>
<head>
        <title>Test Page for jQuery Mobile</title>
        <meta name="viewport" content="width=device-width, initial-scale=1">
    <link rel="stylesheet"
        href="jquery.mobile-1.1.1.css">
    <script type="text/javascript"
        src="jquery-1.7.2.min.js">
    </script>
    <script type="text/javascript"
        src="jquery.mobile-1.1.1.js">
    </script>
</head>
<body>
<div data-role="page">
        <div data-role="header">
                <h1>Persistent Footer</h1>
        </div>
        <div data-role="content">
                <p>I love creating content.</p>
                <p>I love creating content.</p>
                <p>I love creating content.</p>
                <p>I love creating content.</p>
                <p>I love creating content.</p>
                <p>I love creating content.</p>
        </div>
        <div data-role="footer" data-id="persistent" data-position="fixed">
                <div data-role="navbar">
                        <ul>
                                <li><a class="ui-btn-active ui-state-persist" data-
icon="home"
                                    data-iconpos="top" href="#">Link 1</a></li>
                                <li><a data-icon="star" data-iconpos="top" href="#">Link
2</a></li>
                        </ul>
                </div>
        </div>
</div>  <!-- end page div -->
```

```
</body>
</html>
```

3. Implementing any of the examples from *http://jquerymobile.com/test/* using valid HTML meets the requirements for this exercise.

Chapter 19

There are no exercises for Chapter 19.

Chapter 20

1. This solution uses HTML that you've seen throughout the book, in various forms. Whatever valid HTML you use is fine, as long as the end result enables the user to type in an abbreviation and receive back a full name. Here's the HTML and JavaScript that I used:

```
<!doctype html>
<html>
<head>
<title>Solution 1</title>
<script type="text/javascript" src="jquery-1.7.2.min.js"></script>
</head>
<body>
<form action="#" method="POST" id="myForm">
State Abbreviation: <input type="text" name="state" id="state"><br />
<input type="submit" name="submitForm" id="submitForm">
</form>
<div id="output"></div>
<script type="text/javascript">

function successFunction(data,status) {
    $("#output").text("State: " + data);
}

$(document).ready(function() {
    $("#myForm").on("submit", function() {
        var myState = $("#state").val();
        var myData = "state=" + myState;
         $.ajax({
            type: "POST",
            url: "statefull.php",
            dataType: "json",
            success: successFunction,
            data: myData
        });
        return false;
    });
});
</script>
</body>
</html>
```

2. The PHP file used (statefull.php) looks like this:

```php
<?php


$stateAbbrev = trim($_POST['state']);

if ($stateAbbrev == "WI") {
        print json_encode("Wisconsin");
}

?>
```

Chapter 21

There are no exercises for Chapter 21.

Chapter 22

1. This task is accomplished by adding an anchor within the default.html page. I added one below the *<H1>* element, resulting in this HTML:

```html
<!DOCTYPE html>
<html>
<head>
    <meta charset="utf-8" />
    <title>BlankApp1</title>

    <!-- WinJS references -->
    <link href="//Microsoft.WinJS.1.0/css/ui-dark.css" rel="stylesheet" />
    <script src="//Microsoft.WinJS.1.0/js/base.js"></script>
    <script src="//Microsoft.WinJS.1.0/js/ui.js"></script>

    <!-- BlankApp1 references -->
    <link href="/css/default.css" rel="stylesheet" />
    <script src="/js/default.js"></script>
</head>
<body>
    <h1>Here's my app!</h1>
    <a href="http://www.microsoft.com">Microsoft</a>
</body>
</html>
```

2. The file that gets loaded is items.html found in pages\items within Solution Explorer.

Chapter 23

There are no exercises for Chapter 23.

Index

Symbols

About the Author

STEVE SUEHRING is a technology architect who specializes in finding simple solutions to complex problems and complex solutions to simple problems. When not writing technology books, Steve enjoys playing several musical instruments. You can follow Steve on Twitter, @stevesuehring.

How To Download Your eBook

Thank you for purchasing this Microsoft Press® title. Your companion PDF eBook is ready to download from O'Reilly Media, official distributor of Microsoft Press titles.

To download your eBook, go to

http://go.microsoft.com/FWLink/?Linkid=224345

and follow the instructions.

Please note: You will be asked to create a free online account and enter the access code below.

Your access code:

> ## PXMRJZN
>
> JavaScript Step by Step, Third Edition

Your PDF eBook allows you to:

- Search the full text
- Print
- Copy and paste

Best yet, you will be notified about free updates to your eBook.

If you ever lose your eBook file, you can download it again just by logging in to your account.

Need help? Please contact:
mspbooksupport@oreilly.com
or call 800-889-8969.

Now that you've read the book...

Tell us what you think!

Was it useful?
Did it teach you what you wanted to learn?
Was there room for improvement?

Let us know at http://aka.ms/tellpress

Your feedback goes directly to the staff at Microsoft Press,
and we read every one of your responses. Thanks in advance!

 Microsoft

CPSIA information can be obtained at www.ICGtesting.com
Printed in the USA
BVOW100616310513

322019BV00001B/1/P